New Progress in
Mathematics

Rose Anita McDonnell

Catherine D. LeTourneau

Anne Veronica Burrows

Francis H. Murphy

M. Winifred Kelly

with

Dr. Elinor R. Ford

Sadlier-Oxford
A Division of William H. Sadlier, Inc.

Table of Contents

Chapter 1

Facts Review

Chapter 2

Place Value

Chapter 6

Dividing by One Digit

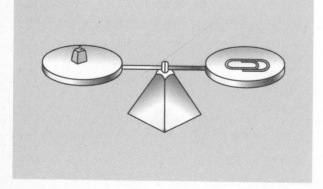

Chapter 7

Measurement

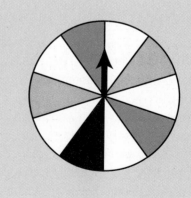

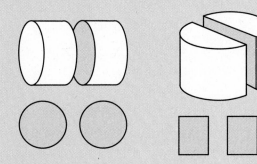

Photo Credits:
Diane J. Ali 459. Myrleen Cate 5, 85, 133, 148, 250. FPG International/ Michael Simpson 165; Ken Korsh 239; John Terence Turner 95. Rob Houston 59. The Image Bank/ Phillipe Sion 67; A.T. Willet 125; Gerard Matheiu 325; Dan Esgro 357; Alberto Incrocci 381. H. Armstrong Roberts 295. Joe Sohm/ ALLSTOCK 35. The Stock Market/ Tom Sanders 265; Clayton J. Price 441. Tony Stone Images/ Ralph Mercer 205; Neil & Mary Mishler 411. Viesti Associates/ Ken Ross 1.

Photo Research: Jim Saylor
Art Manager: Michael McNally
Cover Illustration: Batelman Illustration
Cover Design: Chattum Design
Text Design: José Urbach
Illustrators:
    Diane Ali   Bea Leute   Batelman Illustration
    Blaine Martin   Fernando Rangel   Adam Gordon
    Wendy Pierson   Sintora Vanderhorst
Home Office: 9 Pine Street, New York, NY 10005-1002
ISBN 0-8215-1704-X
 456789/987

Dear Student,

Problem solvers are super sleuths. We invite you to become a super sleuth by using these *five steps* when solving problems.

1	2	3	4	5
IMAGINE	**NAME**	**THINK**	**COMPUTE**	**CHECK**
Create a mental picture.	List the facts and the questions.	Choose and outline a plan.	Work the plan.	Test that the solution is reasonable.

Sleuths use clues to find a solution to a problem. When working together to solve a problem, you may choose to use one or more of these *strategies* as clues:

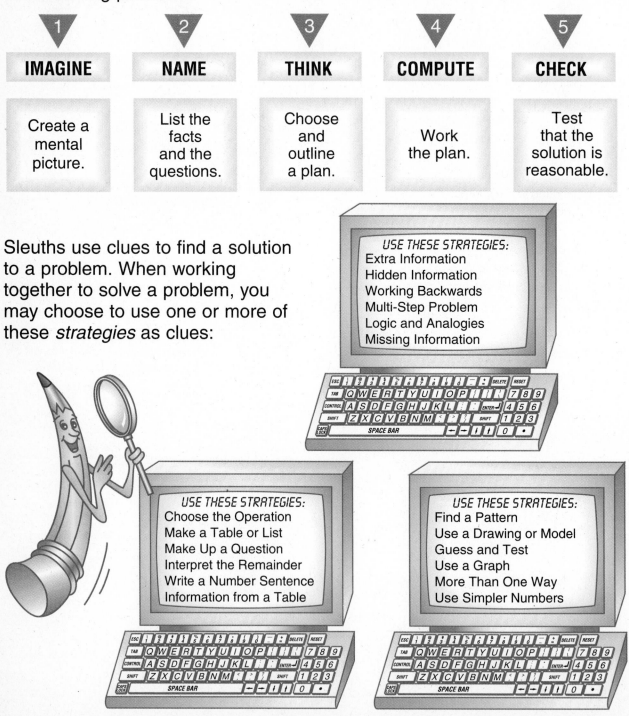

USE THESE STRATEGIES:
Extra Information
Hidden Information
Working Backwards
Multi-Step Problem
Logic and Analogies
Missing Information

USE THESE STRATEGIES:
Choose the Operation
Make a Table or List
Make Up a Question
Interpret the Remainder
Write a Number Sentence
Information from a Table

USE THESE STRATEGIES:
Find a Pattern
Use a Drawing or Model
Guess and Test
Use a Graph
More Than One Way
Use Simpler Numbers

1 IMAGINE

Create a mental picture.

As you read a problem, create a picture in your mind. Make believe you are there in the problem. This will help you think about:
- what facts you will need;
- what the problem is asking;
- how you will solve the problem.

After reading the problem, draw and label a picture of what you imagine the problem is all about.

2 NAME

List the facts and the questions.

Name or list all the facts given in the problem. Be aware of *extra* information not needed to solve the problem. Look for *hidden* information to help solve the problem. Name the question or questions the problem is asking.

3 THINK

Choose and outline a plan.

Think about how to solve the problem by:
- looking at the picture you drew;
- thinking about what you did when you solved similar problems;
- choosing a strategy or strategies for solving the problem.

4 COMPUTE

Work the plan.

Work with the listed facts and the strategy to find the solution. Sometimes a problem will require you to add, subtract, multiply, or divide. Two–step problems require more than one choice of operation or strategy. It is good to *estimate* the answer before you compute.

5 CHECK

Test that the solution is reasonable.

Ask yourself:
- "Have you answered the question?"
- "Is the answer reasonable?"

Check the answer by comparing it to the estimate. It the answer is not reasonable, check your computation. You may use a calculator.

Problem: There are some quarters in Pat's coin bank. There are 4 more dimes than quarters in the bank. Altogether there is $2.85 in the coin bank. How many quarters are in Pat's bank?

1 IMAGINE

Create a mental picture of combinations of quarters and dimes.

2 NAME

Facts: some quarters
4 more dimes than quarters
$2.85 in quarters and dimes

Question: How many quarters are in the coin bank?

3 THINK

First **guess** a number of quarters. 5 quarters

Add 4 to find the number of dimes. 9 dimes

Then **test** whether the value of the coins equals $2.85.

Make a table to record your guesses.

4 COMPUTE

		Quarter Value	Dime Value	Total Value	Test
Guesses	**1st**	5 quarters = $1.25	9 dimes = $ .90	$1.25 + $ .90 = $2.15	too low
	2nd	6 quarters = $1.50	10 dimes = $1.00	$1.50 + $1.00 = $2.50	too low
	3rd	7 quarters = $1.75	11 dimes = $1.10	$1.75 + $1.10 = $2.85	correct

5 CHECK

The third guess is correct because:

- 11 dimes is 4 coins more than 7 quarters.

- 7 quarters ($1.75) and 11 dimes ($1.10) equal $2.85.

x

Problem: Chris went to the beach. The air temperature was 90°F. The relative humidity was 70 percent. How hot did it feel to Chris?

Heat Index Table					
Percent Relative Humidity	Temperature (°F)				
	75	80	85	90	95
50	75	81	88	96	107
60	76	82	90	100	114
70	77	85	93	106	124
80	78	86	97	113	136
90	79	88	102	122	
100	80	91	108		

1 IMAGINE Place yourself in the problem.

2 NAME *Facts:* air temperature of 90°F
relative humidity of 70 percent

Question: How hot did it feel to Chris?

3 THINK The table shows a large amount of data, or information. Study the table carefully. Choose only the data needed to solve the problem.

Percent Relative Humidity—70

Temperature (°F)—90

4 COMPUTE To find how hot it feels, use the *heat index table*.

- Read *down* to 70 percent.

- Read *across* to 90°F.

The 70 percent relative humidity makes the air temperature of 90°F feel like 106°F.

5 CHECK Read across to 90°F and down to 70 percent relative humidity to find the same answer, 106°F.

Problem: A nursery donated 35 trees to the city. If the city planted 4 trees in each of all of its parks, how many parks were there? How many trees were left over?

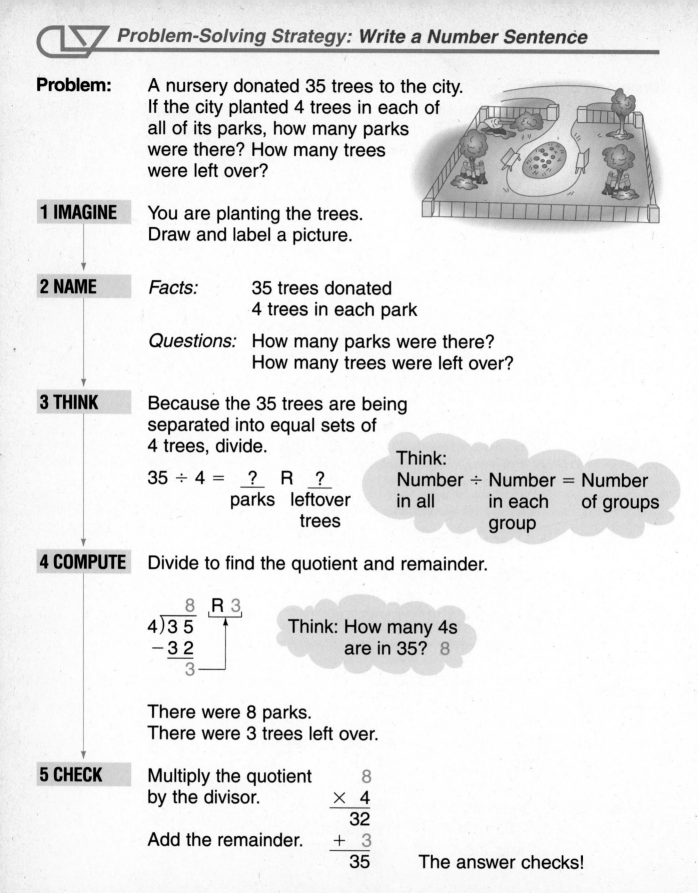

1 IMAGINE You are planting the trees. Draw and label a picture.

2 NAME *Facts:* 35 trees donated
4 trees in each park

Questions: How many parks were there?
How many trees were left over?

3 THINK Because the 35 trees are being separated into equal sets of 4 trees, divide.

$35 \div 4 = \underline{\ ?\ }$ R $\underline{\ ?\ }$
parks   leftover
trees

Think:
Number ÷ Number = Number
in all   in each   of groups
group

4 COMPUTE Divide to find the quotient and remainder.

$$\begin{array}{r} 8 \text{ R } 3 \\ 4\overline{)35} \\ -32 \\ \hline 3 \end{array}$$

Think: How many 4s
are in 35? 8

There were 8 parks.
There were 3 trees left over.

5 CHECK Multiply the quotient
by the divisor.

$$\begin{array}{r} 8 \\ \times\ 4 \\ \hline 32 \end{array}$$

Add the remainder.

$$\begin{array}{r} 32 \\ +\ 3 \\ \hline 35 \end{array}$$ The answer checks!

1 Facts Review

In this chapter you will:
Use addition, subtraction, multiplication, and division facts
Find related facts
Use technology: key sequences
Solve problems by choosing the correct operation

Do you remember?
These words are used in mathematics:
addends and sums
differences
factors and products
dividends, divisors, and quotients

Critical Thinking/Finding Together
Name all the patterns you can find in the picture.

Basic Addition Facts

On a fishing trip with her father, Linda caught 8 perch and 4 trout. How many fish did Linda catch in all?

To find how many in all, add: 8 + 4 = __?__

The addition table can help you find the sum.

+	0	1	2	3	4	5	6	7	8	9
0	0	1	2	3	4	5	6	7	8	9
1	1	2	3	4	5	6	7	8	9	10
2	2	3	4	5	6	7	8	9	10	11
3	3	4	5	6	7	8	9	10	11	12
4	4	5	6	7	8	9	10	11	12	13
5	5	6	7	8	9	10	11	12	13	14
6	6	7	8	9	10	11	12	13	14	15
7	7	8	9	10	11	12	13	14	15	16
8	8	9	10	11	12	13	14	15	16	17
9	9	10	11	12	13	14	15	16	17	18

$$\begin{array}{r} 8 \\ +4 \\ \hline 12 \end{array}$$ ← addend
← addend
← sum

$$8 + 4 = 12$$

addends sum

Remember: 8 + 4 = 12 is a number sentence for addition.

Linda caught 12 fish.

Find the sum. You may use the addition table.

1. 2 + 2   **2.** 5 + 2   **3.** 9 + 0   **4.** 7 + 8   **5.** 8 + 6

6. 7 + 7   **7.** 8 + 1   **8.** 4 + 5   **9.** 3 + 7   **10.** 6 + 6

11. 9 + 5   **12.** 3 + 2   **13.** 4 + 7   **14.** 5 + 5   **15.** 0 + 4

Add.

16. 5
    +6

17. 8
    +3

18. 3
    +5

19. 6
    +7

20. 9
    +2

21. 7
    +3

22. 6
    +4

23. 0
    +8

24. 4
    +9

25. 5
    +4

26. 5
    +5

27. 8
    +1

28. 8
    +8

29. 4
    +9

30. 6
    +4

31. 7
    +6

Find the sum. Remember the ¢ sign.

32. 8¢
    +9¢
    17¢

33. 7¢
    +4¢

34. 6¢
    +2¢

35. 4¢
    +3¢

36. 7¢
    +9¢

37. 3¢
    +8¢

38. 3¢
    +6¢

39. 8¢
    +7¢

40. 5¢
    +3¢

41. 9¢
    +1¢

42. 4¢
    +4¢

43. 5¢
    +8¢

Solve.

44. Fishermen rented 9 motorboats and 7 rowboats from the lakeside marina. How many boats did they rent in all?

45. Billy used worms as bait to catch 6 fish. He used a lure to catch 4 fish. How many fish did Billy catch altogether?

46. Lee caught 9 trout. Duong caught 8 more trout than Lee. How many trout did Duong catch?

47. Susie sells bait at the bait shop. One morning she sold 5 containers of minnows and 7 containers of worms. How many containers of bait did Susie sell?

1-2 Basic Subtraction Facts

There are 12 red swings and
9 blue swings at the playground.
How many more red swings than blue
swings are there?

To find how many more there are,
subtract: 12 − 9 = _?_

The addition table can help you
find the difference.

- Find 9 in the top row.
- Move down to 12.
- Move across to 3.

```
   12
 −  9
 ─────
    3  ← difference
```

12 − 9 = 3
    ↑
 difference

+	0	1	2	3	4	5	6	7	8	9
0	0	1	2	3	4	5	6	7	8	9
1	1	2	3	4	5	6	7	8	9	10
2	2	3	4	5	6	7	8	9	10	11
3	3	4	5	6	7	8	9	10	11	12
4	4	5	6	7	8	9	10	11	12	13
5	5	6	7	8	9	10	11	12	13	14
6	6	7	8	9	10	11	12	13	14	15
7	7	8	9	10	11	12	13	14	15	16
8	8	9	10	11	12	13	14	15	16	17
9	9	10	11	12	13	14	15	16	17	18

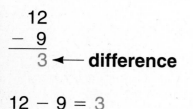

Remember: 12 − 9 = 3 is
a number sentence for
subtraction.

There are 3 more red swings.

Subtraction undoes addition.

Find the difference. You may use the table.

1. 7 − 4   **2.** 17 − 9   **3.** 12 − 7   **4.** 10 − 8   **5.** 6 − 0

6. 8 − 1   **7.** 11 − 4   **8.** 16 − 8   **9.** 15 − 9   **10.** 5 − 4

11. 5 − 2   **12.** 12 − 5   **13.** 8 − 3   **14.** 13 − 6   **15.** 9 − 7

Subtract.

16. 11 △ △ A̸ A̸ A̸ A̸
 − 9 A̸ A̸ A̸ A̸ A̸

17. 14 ▢ ▢ ▢ ▨ ▨ ▨ ▨
 − 5 ▢ ▢ ▢ ▢ ▢ ▢ ▨

18. 9
 −2

19. 11
 − 3

20. 15
 − 7

21. 6
 −3

22. 9
 −5

23. 14
 − 8

24. 13
 − 9

25. 6
 −2

26. 18
 − 9

27. 12
 − 4

28. 8
 −4

29. 13
 − 5

30. 12
 − 6

31. 7
 −7

Find the difference. Remember the ¢ sign.

32. 17¢
 − 8¢
 9¢

33. 10¢
 − 6¢

34. 9¢
 −6¢

35. 7¢
 −2¢

36. 8¢
 −7¢

37. 16¢
 − 9¢

38. 7¢
 −5¢

39. 10¢
 − 4¢

40. 4¢
 −2¢

41. 10¢
 − 7¢

42. 9¢
 −3¢

43. 8¢
 −2¢

Solve.

44. There were 10 children playing on the jungle gym. Four of the children went to play on the swings. How many children are left playing on the jungle gym?

45. Lupe took 8 turns on the slide. Delores took 13 turns. How many more turns did Delores take on the slide?

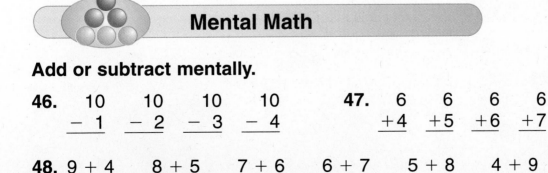

Mental Math

Add or subtract mentally.

46. 10   10   10   10
 − 1 − 2 − 3 − 4

47. 6   6   6   6
 +4 +5 +6 +7

48. 9 + 4   8 + 5   7 + 6   6 + 7   5 + 8   4 + 9

Brian rolled a 6 and a 5. He used these numbers to write four related addition and subtraction facts. What four facts did he write?

Brian wrote these four facts:

$6 + 5 = 11$ $\qquad$ $11 - 5 = 6$

$5 + 6 = 11$ $\qquad$ $11 - 6 = 5$

These four facts are **related facts.** They all use the same numbers.

Study these examples.

$12 = 4 + 8$
$12 = 8 + 4$
$8 = 12 - 4$
$4 = 12 - 8$

$3 + 3 = 6$
$6 - 3 = 3$

Write the related facts for each pair.

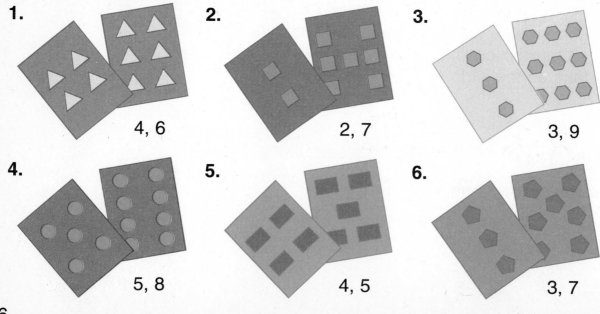

1. 4, 6

2. 2, 7

3. 3, 9

4. 5, 8

5. 4, 5

6. 3, 7

Copy and complete.

7. 3 + ? = 9
   ? + 3 = 9
   9 − ? = 3
   9 − 3 = ?

8. 6 = ? + 2
   6 = 2 + ?
   2 = 6 − ?
   ? = 6 − 2

9. 13 = 8 + ?
   13 = ? + 8
   8 = 13 − ?
   ? = 13 − 8

10. ? + 7 = 13
    7 + ? = 13
   13 − 7 = ?
   13 − ? = 7

11. ? + 9 = 17
    9 + ? = 17
   17 − ? = 9
   17 − 9 = ?

12. 15 = ? + 8
   15 = 8 + ?
   8 = 15 − ?
   ? = 15 − 8

Write the related facts for each pair.

13. 1, 5   **14.** 2, 9   **15.** 8, 2   **16.** 1, 7

17. 3, 8   **18.** 3, 4   **19.** 1, 8   **20.** 4, 9

21. 9, 5   **22.** 8, 8   **23.** 2, 5   **24.** 4, 4

25. 6, 1   **26.** 5, 7   **27.** 3, 1   **28.** 8, 6

29. 5, 3   **30.** 6, 2   **31.** 9, 6   **32.** 7, 9

Which is not a related fact? Write the letter of the correct answer.

33. 3 + 6 = 9   **a.** 6 − 3 = 3   **b.** 6 + 3 = 9   **c.** 9 − 6 = 3

34. 6 − 4 = 2   **a.** 4 − 2 = 2   **b.** 2 + 4 = 6   **c.** 4 + 2 = 6

35. 12 = 8 + 4   **a.** 12 = 4 + 8   **b.** 4 = 12 − 8   **c.** 4 = 8 − 4

Finding Together

36. Roll two number cubes.
Write all the related facts
for the number pair
you have rolled.

1-4 Multiplying by Two and Three

▶ Mirella bought 2 six-packs of spring water. How many cans of spring water did she buy in all?

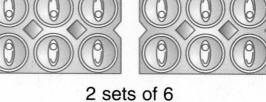

To find how many, you can add 2 sets of 6: 6 + 6 = 12

2 sets of 6
2 sixes
2 × 6

There is the *same number* in each set. You can **multiply:**

number of sets	×	number in each set	=	total number
2	×	6	=	12

or

6 ◀—— **factor**
×2 ◀—— **factor**
12 ◀—— **product**

Remember: 2 × 6 = 12 is a number sentence for multiplication.

Mirella bought 12 cans of spring water.

▶ Mirella has 3 nickels. How much are the nickels worth?

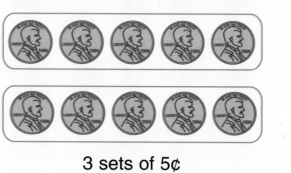

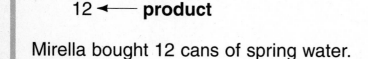
1 nickel = 5 pennies or 5¢

Add: 5¢ + 5¢ + 5¢ = 15¢

Or multiply: 3 × 5¢ = __?__

```
 5¢
×3          or      3 × 5¢ = 15¢
15¢                 ↑    ↑    ↑
                    └────┘    │
                  factors  product
```

3 sets of 5¢
3 fives
3 × 5¢

The nickels are worth 15¢.

Write an addition sentence and a multiplication sentence for each.

1.

2.

3.

Multiply.

4. Multiplying by 2

0	1	2	3	4	5	6	7	8	9
×2	×2	×2	×2	×2	×2	×2	×2	×2	×2

5. Multiplying by 3

0	1	2	3	4	5	6	7	8	9
×3	×3	×3	×3	×3	×3	×3	×3	×3	×3

Find the product.

6. 2×4 7. 3×2 8. 2×7 9. $3 \times 4¢$ 10. $2 \times 1¢$

11. 3×9 12. 2×5 13. 3×6 14. $2 \times 8¢$ 15. $3 \times 7¢$

Finding Together

16. Make a multiplication table.

   • Work together to fill in the rows for multiplying by 2 and multiplying by 3.

   • Save the table. Fill in other multiplication facts as you learn them.

Columns

Rows

×	0	1	2	3	4	5	6	7	8	9
0										
1										
2	0	2			8				16	
3			6				18			
4										
5										
6										
7										
8										
9										

Multiplying by Four and Five

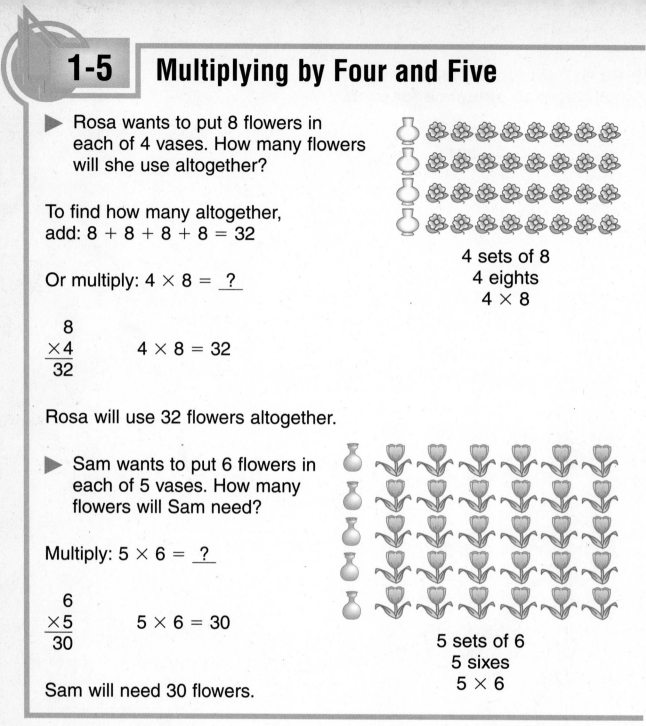

▶ Rosa wants to put 8 flowers in each of 4 vases. How many flowers will she use altogether?

To find how many altogether, add: $8 + 8 + 8 + 8 = 32$

Or multiply: $4 \times 8 = \underline{\ ?\ }$

$$\begin{array}{r} 8 \\ \times 4 \\ \hline 32 \end{array} \qquad 4 \times 8 = 32$$

4 sets of 8
4 eights
4×8

Rosa will use 32 flowers altogether.

▶ Sam wants to put 6 flowers in each of 5 vases. How many flowers will Sam need?

Multiply: $5 \times 6 = \underline{\ ?\ }$

$$\begin{array}{r} 6 \\ \times 5 \\ \hline 30 \end{array} \qquad 5 \times 6 = 30$$

5 sets of 6
5 sixes
5×6

Sam will need 30 flowers.

Add. Then multiply.

1.
$$2 + 2 + 2 + 2 = \underline{\ ?\ }$$
$$4 \times 2 = \underline{\ ?\ }$$
$$\begin{array}{r} 2 \\ \times 4 \\ \hline ? \end{array}$$

2.
$$3 + 3 + 3 + 3 + 3 = \underline{\ ?\ }$$
$$5 \times 3 = \underline{\ ?\ }$$
$$\begin{array}{r} 3 \\ \times 5 \\ \hline ? \end{array}$$

Multiply.

3.   Multiplying by 4

0	1	2	3	4	5	6	7	8	9
×4	×4	×4	×4	×4	×4	×4	×4	×4	×4

4.   Multiplying by 5

0	1	2	3	4	5	6	7	8	9
×5	×5	×5	×5	×5	×5	×5	×5	×5	×5

Find the product.

5. 3   **6.** 6   **7.** 1   **8.** 5   **9.** 2¢   **10.** 1¢   **11.** 2¢
　　×4　　　×5　　　×4　　　×5　　　×5　　　　×5　　　　×4

12. 8   **13.** 4   **14.** 6   **15.** 9   **16.** 5¢   **17.** 9¢   **18.** 7¢
　　×5　　　×5　　　×4　　　×4　　　×4　　　　×5　　　　×4

19. 4 × 8   **20.** 5 × 7   **21.** 4 × 4   **22.** 5 × 3¢   **23.** 5 × 7¢

Solve. Write the number sentence for each.

24. Ellen needs 8 daisies for each of 4 bridesmaids' bouquets. How many daisies should she order?

25. Barry uses 9 petals to make each silk rose. How many petals does he use to make 5 silk roses?

26. One factor is 4. The product is 24. What is the other factor?

27. The product is 36. One factor is 9. What is the other factor?

28. One factor is 5. The product is 20. What is the other factor?

29. One factor is 6. The product is 30. What is the other factor?

Multiplying by Six and Seven

▶ Frank the baker baked 6 cakes for a restaurant. He cut each cake into 8 slices. How many people can the cakes serve?

To find how many they can serve, multiply: $6 \times 8 = \underline{?}$

$$\begin{array}{r} 8 \\ \times 6 \\ \hline 48 \end{array}$$

$6 \times 8 = 48$

6 sets of 8
6 eights
6×8

The cakes can serve 48 people.

▶ Each of 7 fruit pies is cut into 4 pieces. How many people can the fruit pies serve?

Multiply: $7 \times 4 = \underline{?}$

$$\begin{array}{r} 4 \\ \times 7 \\ \hline 28 \end{array}$$

$7 \times 4 = 28$

7 sets of 4
7 fours
7×4

The fruit pies can serve 28 people.

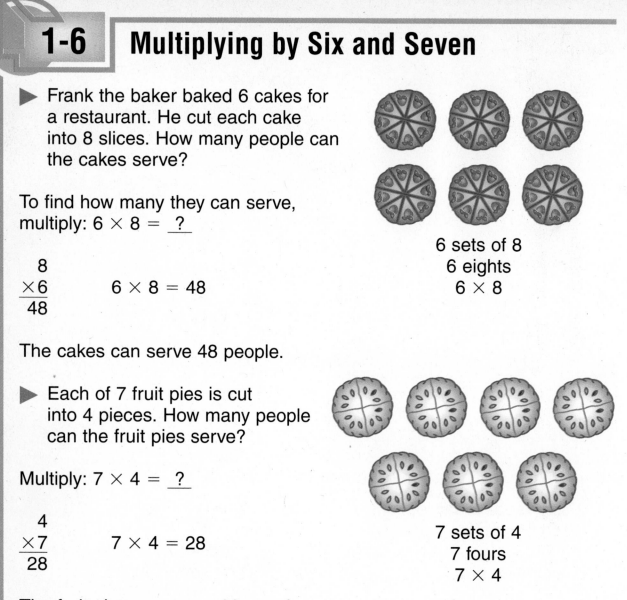

Write a multiplication sentence for each.

1.

2.

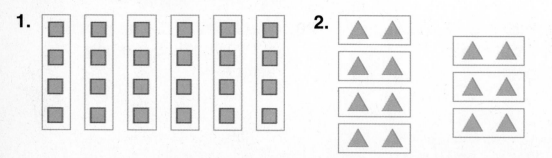

Multiply.

3.   Multiplying by 6

0	1	2	3	4	5	6	7	8	9
×6	×6	×6	×6	×6	×6	×6	×6	×6	×6

4.   Multiplying by 7

0	1	2	3	4	5	6	7	8	9
×7	×7	×7	×7	×7	×7	×7	×7	×7	×7

Find the product.

5. $\begin{array}{r} 3 \\ \times 7 \\ \hline \end{array}$
6. $\begin{array}{r} 2 \\ \times 6 \\ \hline \end{array}$
7. $\begin{array}{r} 5 \\ \times 4 \\ \hline \end{array}$
8. $\begin{array}{r} 2 \\ \times 7 \\ \hline \end{array}$
9. $\begin{array}{r} 1¢ \\ \times 6 \\ \hline \end{array}$
10. $\begin{array}{r} 3¢ \\ \times 6 \\ \hline \end{array}$

11. $\begin{array}{r} 5 \\ \times 6 \\ \hline \end{array}$
12. $\begin{array}{r} 4 \\ \times 7 \\ \hline \end{array}$
13. $\begin{array}{r} 6 \\ \times 6 \\ \hline \end{array}$
14. $\begin{array}{r} 6 \\ \times 7 \\ \hline \end{array}$
15. $\begin{array}{r} 7¢ \\ \times 7 \\ \hline \end{array}$
16. $\begin{array}{r} 4¢ \\ \times 6 \\ \hline \end{array}$

17. $\begin{array}{r} 5 \\ \times 7 \\ \hline \end{array}$
18. $\begin{array}{r} 8 \\ \times 4 \\ \hline \end{array}$
19. $\begin{array}{r} 9 \\ \times 7 \\ \hline \end{array}$
20. $\begin{array}{r} 7 \\ \times 6 \\ \hline \end{array}$
21. $\begin{array}{r} 8¢ \\ \times 7 \\ \hline \end{array}$
22. $\begin{array}{r} 9¢ \\ \times 3 \\ \hline \end{array}$

23. 7×9 **24.** 6×8 **25.** 6×9 **26.** $7 \times 8¢$ **27.** $2 \times 7¢$

28. 4×8 **29.** 7×7 **30.** 5×3 **31.** $6 \times 2¢$ **32.** $3 \times 6¢$

Solve. Write a number sentence for each.

33. The factors are 6 and 8. What is the product?

34. One factor is 7. The product is 28. What is the other factor?

35. The factors are 6 and 9. What is the product?

36. What is the product of 9 and 7?

37. Frank can bake 4 dozen rolls on each baking sheet. His oven holds 6 baking sheets. How many dozens of rolls can he bake at a time?

38. Sharonda sold 7 boxes of muffins. Each box holds 8 muffins. How many muffins did Sharonda sell?

Multiplying by Eight and Nine

▶ Ms. Black helped her class make a tile design. The design had 4 tiles in each of 8 rows. How many tiles did the class use for the design?

8 sets of 4
8 fours
8 × 4

To find how many they used,
multiply: 8 × 4 = _?_

$$\begin{array}{r} 4 \\ \times 8 \\ \hline 32 \end{array}$$ 8 × 4 = 32

The class used 32 tiles for the design.

▶ Ms. Black ordered 9 boxes of paintbrushes. Each box contained 3 brushes. How many paintbrushes did she order?

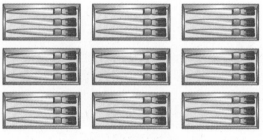

9 sets of 3
9 threes
9 × 3

Multiply: 9 × 3 = _?_

$$\begin{array}{r} 3 \\ \times 9 \\ \hline 27 \end{array}$$ 9 × 3 = 27

She ordered 27 paintbrushes.

Write a multiplication sentence for each.

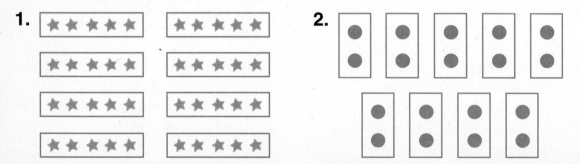

1.

2.

Multiply.

3. Multiplying by 8

0	1	2	3	4	5	6	7	8	9
×8	×8	×8	×8	×8	×8	×8	×8	×8	×8

4. Multiplying by 9

0	1	2	3	4	5	6	7	8	9
×9	×9	×9	×9	×9	×9	×9	×9	×9	×9

Find the product.

5. 2 ×8

6. 1 ×9

7. 3 ×8

8. 3 ×9

9. 1¢ ×8

10. 4¢ ×9

11. 6 ×9

12. 4 ×8

13. 5 ×9

14. 6 ×8

15. 8¢ ×9

16. 9¢ ×9

17. 8 ×8

18. 9 ×7

19. 7 ×8

20. 0 ×9

21. 2¢ ×9

22. 9¢ ×8

23. 8 × 4 **24.** 4 × 8 **25.** 9 × 6 **26.** 6 × 9¢ **27.** 8 × 2¢

28. 9 × 5 **29.** 5 × 9 **30.** 8 × 7 **31.** 7 × 8¢ **32.** 7 × 9¢

Solve.

33. Ms. Black made 7 triangles for each of 8 mobiles. How many triangles did Ms. Black make in all?

34. On each of 9 collages were 7 bottle caps and 5 stickers. How many bottle caps were there? how many stickers?

 **Challenge**

Find the product.

35. 2 × 3 × 6 **36.** 4 × 1 × 4 **37.** 3 × 3 × 3 **38.** 1 × 2 × 3

1-8 Understanding Division

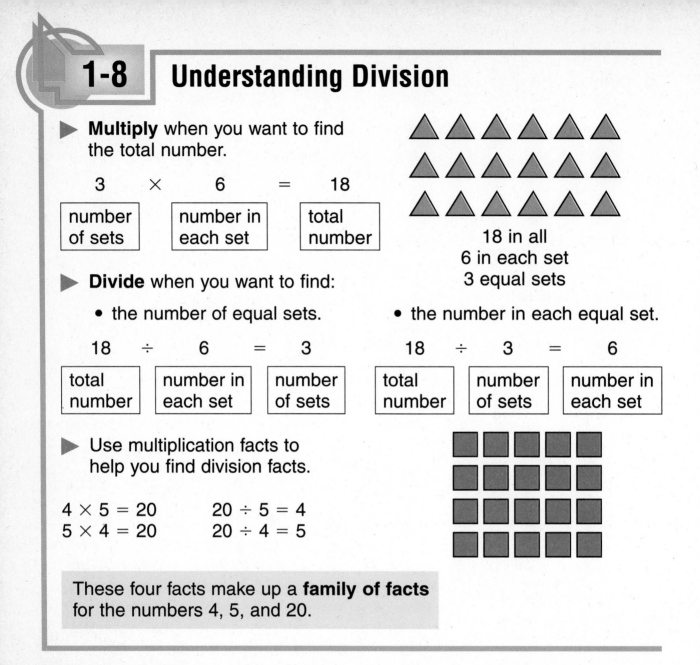

▶ **Multiply** when you want to find the total number.

3   ×   6   =   18

number of sets	number in each set	total number

18 in all
6 in each set
3 equal sets

▶ **Divide** when you want to find:

• the number of equal sets.

18   ÷   6   =   3

total number	number in each set	number of sets

• the number in each equal set.

18   ÷   3   =   6

total number	number of sets	number in each set

▶ Use multiplication facts to help you find division facts.

$4 \times 5 = 20$ $20 \div 5 = 4$
$5 \times 4 = 20$ $20 \div 4 = 5$

These four facts make up a **family of facts** for the numbers 4, 5, and 20.

Write two division facts for each.

1.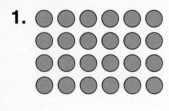

2. ★★★★★★ (array of stars)

3. (array of hexagons)

16

Copy and complete each family of facts.

4. $6 \times 5 = 30$
$\underline{?} \times 6 = 30$
$30 \div 5 = \underline{?}$
$30 \div 6 = \underline{?}$

5. $9 \times 7 = 63$
$\underline{?} \times 9 = 63$
$63 \div 7 = \underline{?}$
$63 \div 9 = \underline{?}$

6. $4 \times 4 = 16$
$16 \div 4 = \underline{?}$

7. $5 \times \underline{?} = 15$
$\underline{?} \times 5 = 15$
$15 \div \underline{?} = 5$
$15 \div 5 = \underline{?}$

8. $\underline{?} \times 7 = 28$
$7 \times \underline{?} = 28$
$28 \div 7 = \underline{?}$
$28 \div \underline{?} = 7$

9. $\underline{?} \times 6 = 54$
$6 \times \underline{?} = 54$
$54 \div 6 = \underline{?}$
$54 \div \underline{?} = 6$

Write a family of facts for each set of numbers.

10. 2, 4, 8

11. 3, 7, 21

12. 4, 3, 12

13. 5, 7, 35

14. 7, 6, 42

15. 9, 1, 9

16. 8, 3, 24

17. 3, 2, 6

18. 8, 7, 56

19. 9, 5, 45

20. 5, 8, 40

21. 6, 6, 36

Solve. Write a number sentence for each.

22. There are 14 people riding tandem bicycles. Two people are sitting on each bicycle. How many bicycles are there?

23. Each car in the miniature train at the zoo can fit 6 passengers. The train is carrying 48 passengers. How many cars are in the train?

24. Each swan boat at the park holds 3 people. There are 9 full swan boats on the lake. How many people are using the swan boats?

25. The balloon pilot is giving rides in his balloon. He takes 4 passengers at a time. There are 36 people waiting in line. How many trips will the balloon pilot make?

17

1-9　Dividing by Two and Three

▶ Belinda has 8 rabbits. She keeps 2 rabbits in each hutch. How many rabbit hutches does Belinda have?

To find the number of rabbit hutches, divide: $8 \div 2 = \underline{\ ?\ }$

8 in all
2 in each set

Think: $\underline{\ ?\ } \times 2 = 8$
$\quad\quad\ \ 4 \times 2 = 8$

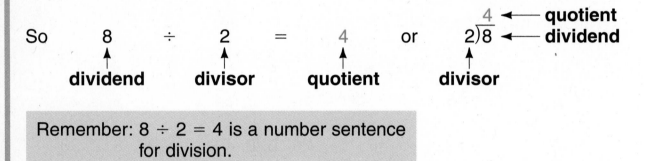

So　8　÷　2　=　4　or　$2\overline{)8}$

dividend　divisor　quotient　divisor

quotient
dividend

> Remember: $8 \div 2 = 4$ is a number sentence for division.

Belinda has 4 rabbit hutches.

▶ Belinda can buy 3 rabbit stickers for 27¢. How much does each sticker cost?

To find the cost of each sticker, divide: $27¢ \div 3 = \underline{\ ?\ }$

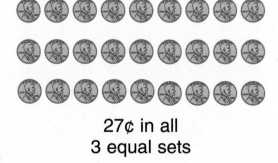

Think: $3 \times \underline{\ ?\ } = 27¢$
$\quad\quad\ \ 3 \times 9¢ = 27¢$

27¢ in all
3 equal sets

So $27¢ \div 3 = 9¢$　or　$3\overline{)27¢}$ with $9¢$

Each sticker costs 9¢.

> Division undoes multiplication.

Find the quotient.

1. Dividing by 2

$2\overline{)0}$ (0) $2\overline{)2}$ $2\overline{)4}$ $2\overline{)6}$ $2\overline{)8}$ $2\overline{)10}$ $2\overline{)12}$ $2\overline{)14}$ $2\overline{)16}$ $2\overline{)18}$

2. Dividing by 3

$3\overline{)0}$ $3\overline{)3}$ $3\overline{)6}$ $3\overline{)9}$ $3\overline{)12}$ $3\overline{)15}$ $3\overline{)18}$ $3\overline{)21}$ $3\overline{)24}$ $3\overline{)27}$

3. $12 \div 2$ **4.** $21 \div 3$ **5.** $2 \div 2$ **6.** $15 \div 3$ **7.** $6 \div 2$

8. $18 \div 3$ **9.** $4 \div 2$ **10.** $24 \div 3$ **11.** $18 \div 2$ **12.** $3 \div 3$

Divide. Write the ¢ sign in the quotient.

13. $3\overline{)6¢}$ **14.** $2\overline{)14¢}$ **15.** $3\overline{)9¢}$ **16.** $2\overline{)16¢}$ **17.** $3\overline{)27¢}$

18. $8¢ \div 2$ **19.** $15¢ \div 3$ **20.** $12¢ \div 3$ **21.** $4¢ \div 2$

Solve. Write a number sentence for each.

22. The quotient is 8. The divisor is 2. What is the dividend?

23. The dividend is 21. The divisor is 3. What is the quotient?

Finding Together

Use a multiplication table to find quotients.

24. To find $8 \div 2$:

- Find the divisor 2 in the first column.
- Move right ⟶ to 8.
- Move up ↑ to the top of the column.
  - $8 \div 2 = 4$

×	0	1	2	3	4	5	6
0	0	0	0	0	0	0	0
1	0	1	2	3	4	5	6
2	0	2	4	6	8	10	12
3	0	3	6	9	12	15	18
4	0	4	8	12	16	20	24
5	0	5	10	15	20	25	30
6	0	6	12	18	24	30	36

1-10 Dividing by Four and Five

▶ Miguel took 32 photos. He placed the same number of photos on each of 4 pages in his scrapbook. How many photos were on each page?

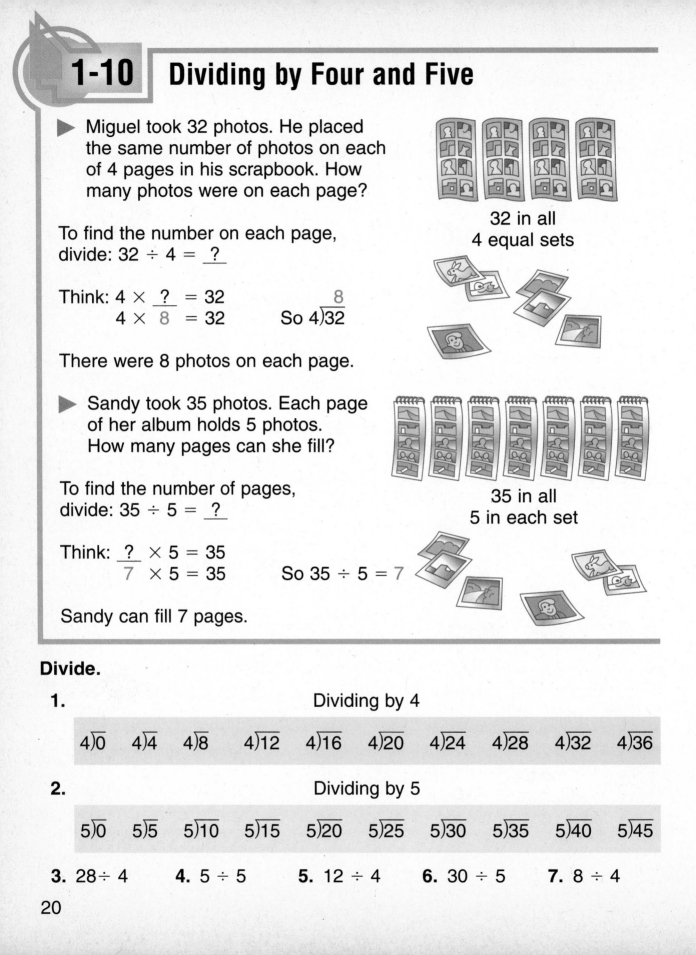

32 in all
4 equal sets

To find the number on each page, divide: $32 \div 4 = \underline{\quad?\quad}$

Think: $4 \times \underline{\quad?\quad} = 32$
$\qquad 4 \times \underline{8} = 32$ So $4\overline{)32}^{\,8}$

There were 8 photos on each page.

▶ Sandy took 35 photos. Each page of her album holds 5 photos. How many pages can she fill?

35 in all
5 in each set

To find the number of pages, divide: $35 \div 5 = \underline{\quad?\quad}$

Think: $\underline{\quad?\quad} \times 5 = 35$
$\qquad \underline{7} \times 5 = 35$ So $35 \div 5 = 7$

Sandy can fill 7 pages.

Divide.

1.   Dividing by 4

$4\overline{)0}$ $4\overline{)4}$ $4\overline{)8}$ $4\overline{)12}$ $4\overline{)16}$ $4\overline{)20}$ $4\overline{)24}$ $4\overline{)28}$ $4\overline{)32}$ $4\overline{)36}$

2.   Dividing by 5

$5\overline{)0}$ $5\overline{)5}$ $5\overline{)10}$ $5\overline{)15}$ $5\overline{)20}$ $5\overline{)25}$ $5\overline{)30}$ $5\overline{)35}$ $5\overline{)40}$ $5\overline{)45}$

3. $28 \div 4$ **4.** $5 \div 5$ **5.** $12 \div 4$ **6.** $30 \div 5$ **7.** $8 \div 4$

Use a calculator to compute. Watch for +, −, ×, and ÷.

1. 5 × $24.50

2. 88 ÷ 11

3. $4.60 + $1.05

4. 968 − 55

5. 41 × 9

6. $112.50 ÷ 15

7.   415
      514
  + 145

8. $909.00
  −   99.99

9. 9)$164.25

10. 74 × 5

11. 62.75 ÷ 5

12. 14)182

13. $5.00
  −   .51

14. $175.05
     48.12
  +   .36

15.   509
  ×   6

Solve. Use a calculator.

16. Use 5, 6, 7, and 8 to complete **a.** and **b.** What is the greatest possible product? What is the least possible product?

a. □□□ × □

b. □□ × □□

17. Use 2, 3, 4, 5 or 6 to complete **a.** and **b.** Which number will give the greatest possible quotient? Which number will give the least possible quotient?

  a. 720 ÷ _?_   **b.** 180 ÷ _?_

18. Find the greatest whole number that you can multiply by 3 to get a product less than 4000.

19. To multiply 6 × 6 × 6, press [6] [×] [6] [=] [=]. How many times do you have to press the [=] key to get a product of 7776?

20. To divide 7776 ÷ 6 ÷ 6, press [7] [7] [7] [6] [÷] [6] [=] [=]. How many times do you have to press the [=] key to get a quotient of 6?

27

1-14 Problem Solving: Choose the Operation

Number Sentence	Definition
□ + □ = □	Join equal or unequal sets, or quantities.
□ – □ = □	Separate, or take away, from a set. Compare two sets, or quantities. Find part of a set. Find how many more are needed.
□ × □ = □	Join only equal sets, or quantities.
□ ÷ □ = □	Separate a set into equal groups. Share a set equally.

Problem: Meg collects comic books. She puts 7 comic books into each envelope. How many envelopes does she need for 42 comic books?

1 IMAGINE Picture yourself in the problem.

2 NAME *Facts:* 7 comic books in each envelope
42 comic books

Question: How many envelopes does she need?

3 THINK You are separating a set into equal groups.
Divide: $42 \div 7 = \underline{\ ?\ }$

Think: $\underline{\ ?\ } \times 7 = 42$

4 COMPUTE $42 \div 7 = 6$
Meg needs 6 envelopes.

5 CHECK Use a calculator and multiply to check division:
$6 \times 7 = 42$ The answer is reasonable.

28

Choose the operation. Then solve.

1. Meg also saves newspaper cartoons. She cuts out 5 cartoons every day. How many cartoons does she save in a week?

IMAGINE　　Create a mental picture.

NAME　　*Facts:*　　5 cartoons each day
　　　　　　　　　　　7 days in a week

　　　　　　Question:　How many cartoons does she save in a week?

THINK　　You are joining many equal sets.
　　　　　　Multiply: $5 \times 7 = $ _?_

　　　　　　▸ **COMPUTE** ⟶ **CHECK**

2. Last week Meg had 42 comic books. Now she has 51. How many comic books did she get this week?

3. Mika collected 8 pounds of newspaper each day for 6 days. How many pounds of newspaper did Mika collect?

4. Cora collected cans for recycling. On the first day, she collected 18 cans. On the second day, she gathered 22 cans and on the third day, 17 more. How many cans did Cora collect in all?

5. Trina, Jake, and Sue won a total of $18 in a talent show. They decided to share the prize equally. How much money did each receive?

Make Up Your Own

6. Choose an operation. Write a problem, then solve it.

Choose the operation. Then solve.

1. Olivia works at a zoo gift shop.
   She sold 6 small, 8 medium, and 4 large
   T-shirts. How many T-shirts did she sell?

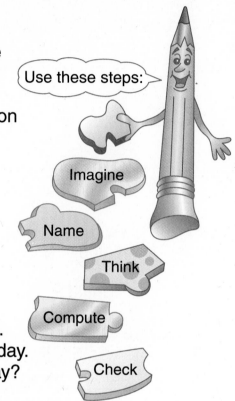

Use these steps:

Imagine

Name

Think

Compute

Check

2. Sharon sold 16 posters. Penguins were on
   7 of the posters, while pandas were on
   the rest. How many panda posters
   did she sell?

3. In the packing room, polished rocks
   are put into boxes. Stu puts 6 rocks
   in each box. How many boxes does
   he need for 54 rocks?

4. On Monday 6 birdcall whistles were sold.
   Three times as many were sold on Tuesday.
   How many whistles were sold on Tuesday?

5. The shop sells 8 different animal jigsaw puzzles.
   Each puzzle costs $4. How much would
   a complete set of puzzles cost?

6. Olivia sold 58 postcards. Sharon sold
   36 postcards. How many more postcards
   did Olivia sell?

7. Ms. Ogden bought 4 wildlife drinking mugs for $36.
   If each mug cost the same amount, how much did
   one mug cost?

8. Lin makes necklaces to sell at the shop.
   Each necklace has exactly 7 animal beads.
   How many necklaces can he make with 49 animal beads?

Solve.

9. The zoo shop is open 6 hours a day. It is open every day except Monday. How many hours a week is the shop open?

10. Mr. Wilson bought 5 packs of zoo postcards. He got 30 postcards. How many postcards are in each pack?

11. Mrs. Wilson bought a stuffed leopard for $15 and a stuffed armadillo for $9. How much did she pay for both items?

12. Zoo T-shirts cost $8. Long-sleeved sweatshirts cost $15. How much more expensive are the sweatshirts?

13. The shop sells guides in English, Spanish, French, German, and Chinese. Guides cost $5 each. How much would it cost to buy one in each language?

14. Ryan bought 20 zoo buttons for his 5 cousins. He sent the same number of buttons to each cousin. How many buttons did each cousin receive?

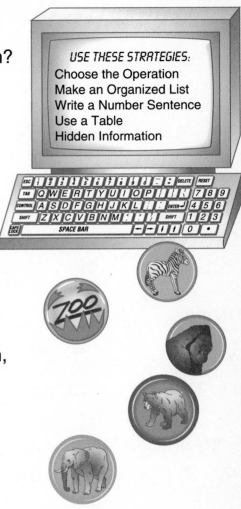

USE THESE STRATEGIES:
Choose the Operation
Make an Organized List
Write a Number Sentence
Use a Table
Hidden Information

Use the table for problems 15–17.

15. How much would it cost to buy one of each item on sale?

16. Which item is on sale for half price?

17. Name 3 possible sale items that can be bought with $15.

Sale at the Zoo Shop

Item	Regular Price	Sale Price
Polar Bear Key Chain	$ 3	$ 2
Toucan Shirt	$12	$10
Fish Cards	$ 8	$ 4

More Practice

Add.

1.	2.	3.	4.	5.	6.
8 +5	6 +7	4 +3	7 +9	8¢ +2¢	5¢ +7¢

Subtract.

7.	8.	9.	10.	11.	12.
9 −3	8 −2	10 − 8	15 − 7	13¢ − 4¢	16¢ − 8¢

Multiply.

13.	14.	15.	16.	17.	18.
7 ×0	1 ×9	8 ×3	6 ×5	2¢ ×4	9¢ ×6

Divide.

19. $3\overline{)15}$ 20. $7\overline{)28}$ 21. $2\overline{)18¢}$ 22. $8\overline{)48¢}$

23. $72 \div 9$ 24. $64 \div 8$ 25. $42¢ \div 7$ 26. $21¢ \div 3$

Copy and complete.

27. $6 + 9 = \underline{?}$
$9 + 6 = \underline{?}$
$\underline{?} - 9 = 6$
$\underline{?} - 6 = 9$

28. $8 + \underline{?} = 12$
$\underline{?} + 8 = 12$
$12 - 8 = \underline{?}$
$12 - \underline{?} = 8$

29. $7 \times 9 = \underline{?}$
$9 \times 7 = \underline{?}$
$\underline{?} \div 9 = 7$
$\underline{?} \div 7 = 9$

Solve.

30. Ed bought a package of stickers for 49¢.
There are 7 stickers in the package.
How much does each sticker cost?

31. Minh has 8 pages of stamps. There
are 6 stamps on each page. How
many stamps does she have in all?

(See *Still More Practice*, p. 461.)

FACTOR TREES

A **composite number** has more than two factors.

$$6 = 1 \times 6$$
$$= 2 \times 3$$

A **prime number** has exactly two factors, itself and 1.

$$5 = 1 \times 5$$

A **prime factor** is a prime number that is a factor of a composite number.

You can use a **factor tree** to help you find all the prime factors of a composite number.

Look at these factor trees for 12.

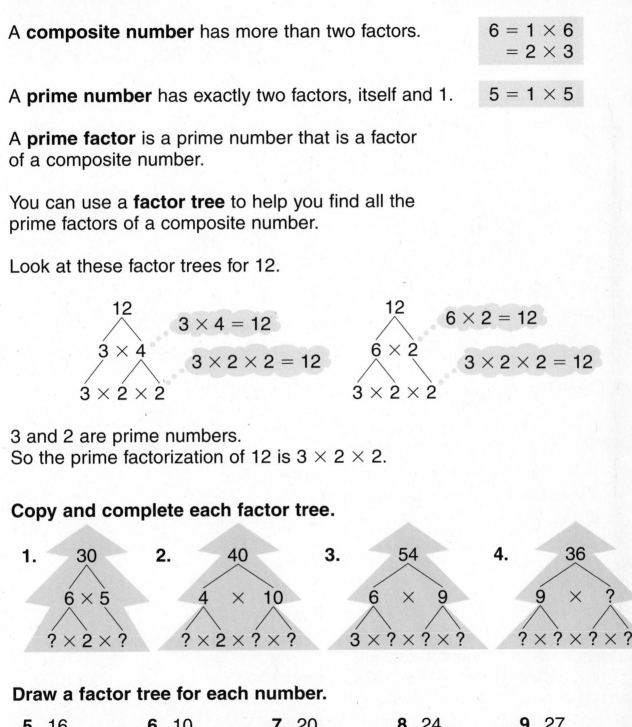

3 and 2 are prime numbers.
So the prime factorization of 12 is $3 \times 2 \times 2$.

Copy and complete each factor tree.

1. 30
6×5
$? \times 2 \times ?$

2. 40
4×10
$? \times 2 \times ? \times ?$

3. 54
6×9
$3 \times ? \times ? \times ?$

4. 36
$9 \times ?$
$? \times ? \times ? \times ?$

Draw a factor tree for each number.

5. 16   6. 10   7. 20   8. 24   9. 27

10. 32   11. 48   12. 35   13. 56   14. 72

Check Your Mastery

Find the sum.

See pp. 2–3

1.	2.	3.	4.	5.	6.
9 +8	6 +6	8 +7	0 +6	5 +9	7¢ +3¢

Find the difference.

See pp. 4–5

7.	8.	9.	10.	11.	12.
5 −0	15 − 6	12 − 7	17 − 8	13 − 5	11¢ − 3¢

Find the product.

See pp. 8–15

13.	14.	15.	16.	17.	18.
9 ×9	5 ×4	8 ×6	3 ×7	0 ×2	9¢ ×4

Find the quotient.

See pp. 16–17, 18–25

19. $5\overline{)30}$ 20. $9\overline{)27}$ 21. $4\overline{)32}$ 22. $7\overline{)56¢}$

23. $24 \div 8$ 24. $18 \div 3$ 25. $36 \div 6$ 26. $54¢ \div 9$

Solve.

See pp. 6–7, 30–31

27. There are 4 people in each table-tennis group. If there are 8 groups, how many people are playing?

28. One factor is 6. The product is 30. What is the other factor?

29. Jennifer found 17 seashells. Mark found 9 fewer shells than Jennifer. Steve found 5 more shells than Mark. How many shells did Steve find?

30. Write the related addition and subtraction facts for 8 and 5.

34

2 Place Value

In this chapter you will:

Read and write numbers
  through millions
Compare and order numbers
  and money amounts
Round numbers and money
Count money and make
  change by counting on
Solve problems by making
  a table or list

Do you remember?

A number is a quantity.
Use symbols to compare numbers.

$$3 < 5$$
$$7 = 7$$
$$9 > 6$$

Critical Thinking/Finding Together

How would you estimate how many
balloons are in the picture?

2-1 Hundreds

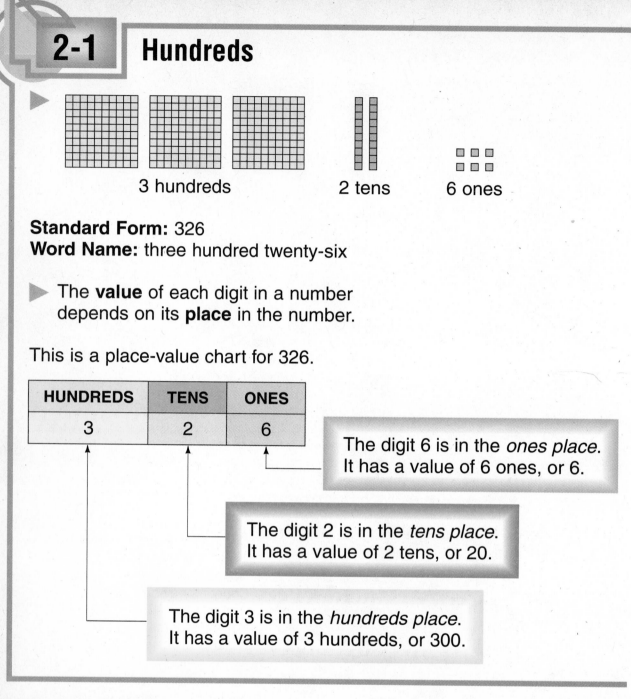

3 hundreds   2 tens   6 ones

Standard Form: 326
Word Name: three hundred twenty-six

▶ The **value** of each digit in a number depends on its **place** in the number.

This is a place-value chart for 326.

HUNDREDS	TENS	ONES
3	2	6

The digit 6 is in the *ones place*.
It has a value of 6 ones, or 6.

The digit 2 is in the *tens place*.
It has a value of 2 tens, or 20.

The digit 3 is in the *hundreds place*.
It has a value of 3 hundreds, or 300.

Write the number in standard form.

1.

2.

HUNDREDS	TENS	ONES
6	0	7

3. 1 hundred 8 tens 3 ones

4. five hundred sixty-two

36

Write the place of the red digit.
Then write its value.   607 183 562

5. 482   **6.** 369   **7.** 141   **8.** 965   **9.** 174   **10.** 218

11. 522   **12.** 697   **13.** 742   **14.** 831   **15.** 420   **16.** 505

Write each number in words.

17. 934   **18.** 158   **19.** 827   **20.** 245   **21.** 712   **22.** 306

Roman Numerals

The ancient Romans used letters to write numbers.

1 = I	4 = IV	7 = VII	10 = X	40 = XL	70 = LXX
2 = II	5 = V	8 = VIII	20 = XX	50 = L	80 = LXXX
3 = III	6 = VI	9 = IX	30 = XXX	60 = LX	90 = XC
			100 = C		

When smaller numerals come
after a larger numeral, *add*.
VIII → 5 + 1 + 1 + 1 = 8

When a smaller numeral comes
before a larger one, *subtract*.
XC → 100 − 10 = 90

CXLVII = __?__

C   XL   VII
↓   ↓   ↓
100 + 40 + 7 = 147

Write the Roman numeral in standard form.

23. LXIV   **24.** XXXIX   **25.** LXIX   **26.** CXXVI   **27.** CCVII

Write each as a Roman numeral.

28. 17   **29.** 48   **30.** 300   **31.** 89   **32.** 56   **33.** 234

37

A **place-value chart** makes understanding large numbers easier.

In 206,493 the value of:
  2 is 2 hundred thousands or 200,000.
  0 is 0 ten thousands or 0.
  6 is 6 thousands or 6000.
  4 is 4 hundreds or 400.
  9 is 9 tens or 90.
  3 is 3 ones or 3.

In numbers larger than 9999, use a comma to separate the periods.

Standard Form: 206,493

Word Name: two hundred six thousand, four hundred ninety-three

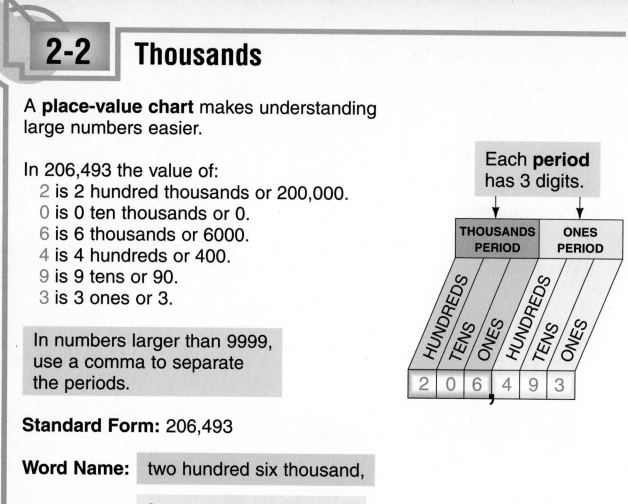

Each **period** has 3 digits.

THOUSANDS PERIOD			ONES PERIOD		
HUNDREDS	TENS	ONES	HUNDREDS	TENS	ONES
2	0	6	4	9	3

Write the place of the red digit.
Then write its value.

1. 6541

2. 7843

3. 3962

4. 5034

5. 27,142

6. 46,359

7. 65,186

8. 92,170

9. 156,143

10. 983,567

11. 495,638

12. 374,826

13. 632,018

14. 275,941

15. 321,235

16. 176,404

17. 205,866

18. 652,048

19. 520,124

20. 804,397

Write the number in standard form.

21. nine hundred four

22. twelve thousand

23. six hundred thousand

24. eight thousand

25. five hundred twenty-one thousand, one hundred twelve

26. sixty-four thousand, seven hundred thirty-five

27. two hundred forty thousand, three hundred ninety-two

28. ninety thousand, four hundred eight

29. one hundred fifteen thousand, five hundred sixty

30. three hundred thousand, two

31. four hundred one thousand, eighteen

Write the word name for each number.

32. 762   **33.** 431   **34.** 605   **35.** 911

36. 4918   **37.** 1265   **38.** 7016   **39.** 3402

40. 25,461   **41.** 51,824   **42.** 90,160   **43.** 80,007

44. 169,818   **45.** 748,295   **46.** 300,040   **47.** 809,006

Critical Thinking

48. How many different four-digit numbers can you make using all the digits in each set only once?
a. 1, 2, 3, 4   **b.** 0, 1, 2, 3   **c.** 0, 0, 1, 2

2-3 Millions

Recently, the population of Brazil was 158,202,019.

In the millions period of 158,202,019, the value of:
- 1 is 1 hundred million, or 100,000,000.
- 5 is 5 ten millions, or 50,000,000.
- 8 is 8 millions, or 8,000,000.

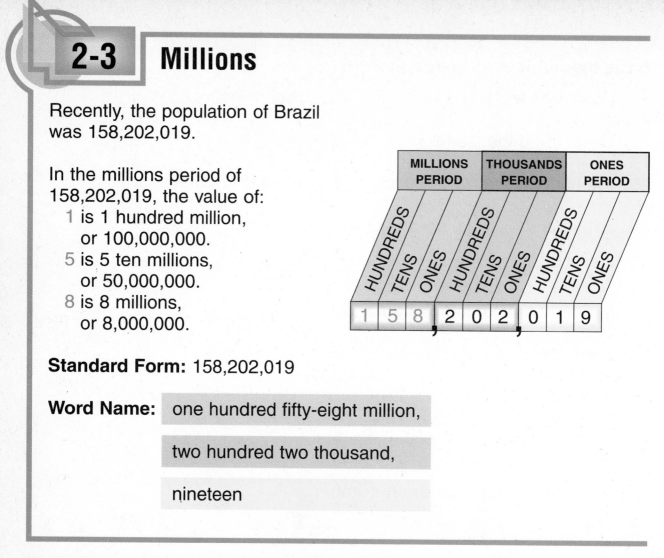

Standard Form: 158,202,019

Word Name: one hundred fifty-eight million,

two hundred two thousand,

nineteen

Write the period of the underlined digits.

1. 45,678

2. 59,650

3. 26,545

4. 456,789

5. 567,890

6. 148,337

7. 9,456,789

8. 567,890,000

9. 617,148,337

Write in standard form.

10. thirty-one million

11. three million

12. six hundred million

13. eighty million

**Write the place of the red digit.
Then write its value.**

14. 482,165,016   **15.** 904,628,153   **16.** 617,465,089

17. 38,296,145   **18.** 10,692,534   **19.** 4,797,123

20. 412,076,531   **21.** 217,945,310   **22.** 842,005,301

23. 5,287,012   **24.** 15,624,300   **25.** 76,000,000

26. 920,354,876   **27.** 105,643,129   **28.** 732,530,481

Write the word name for each number.

29. 5,460,000   **30.** 920,015,300   **31.** 10,300,000

32. 475,000   **33.** 1,006,005   **34.** 20,000,012

Solve.

35. The land area of Brazil is three million,
two hundred eighty-six thousand,
four hundred seventy square miles. How would
you write this number in standard form?

Brazil

36. In Brazil, the Amazon River flows
for 2093 miles. How would you write
this number in words?

37. In Brazil there are two million,
one hundred thirty-five thousand,
six hundred thirty-seven square miles
of forest. Write this number in standard form.

38. In 1985 the Brazilian city of Rio de Janeiro had
an estimated population of 5,615,149. Write
this number in words.

2-4 Place Value

▶ Understanding the place of each digit in a number can help you write the number in **expanded form**.

Standard Form	Expanded Form
178	$100 + 70 + 8$
25,613	$20,000 + 5,000 + 600 + 10 + 3$
4,381,256	$4,000,000 + 300,000 + 80,000 + 1000 + 200 + 50 + 6$
60,070,005	$60,000,000 + 70,000 + 5$
800,500,020	$800,000,000 + 500,000 + 20$

▶ Understanding the place of each digit in a number can help you count on and count back by 10, 100, or 1000.

Count on by 10.	Count on by 100.	Count back by 1000.
25,613	25,613	25,613
25,623	25,713	24,613
25,633	25,813	23,613
25,643	25,913	22,613

Write each number in expanded form.

1. 65

2. 38

3. 246

4. 975

5. 352

6. 810

7. 6143

8. 7924

9. 5491

10. 4035

11. 13,827

12. 62,473

13. 90,303

14. 184,001

15. 705,060

16. 350,900

17. 6,320,079

18. 19,430,600

19. 75,260,080

20. 507,104,908

21. 800,002,100

22. 300,400,050

Write each number in standard form.

23. 40 + 3　　　　　**24.** 200 + 50 + 6　　　**25.** 500 + 7

26. 2000 + 400 + 90 + 6　　　　**27.** 7000 + 100 + 80

28. 30,000 + 5000 + 800 + 20 + 9

29. 60,000 + 400 + 30 + 1

30. 800,000 + 90,000 + 4000 + 600 + 50 + 2

31. 500,000 + 6000 + 900 + 80

32. 7,000,000 + 300,000 + 50,000 + 2000 + 90 + 4

33. 1,000,000 + 20,000 + 900 + 40

34. 50,000,000 + 800,000 + 2000 + 70

35. 20,000,000 + 70,000 + 5000 + 8

36. 900,000,000 + 5,000,000 + 800,000 + 300

37. 700,000,000 + 300,000 + 4000 + 5

**Write the number that is 10 more. Then write the number
that is 10 less.**

38. 475　　　　**39.** 6095　　　　**40.** 256,183　　　**41.** 46,172,304

**Write the numbers that are 100 more and 1000 more.
Then write the numbers that are 100 less and 1000 less.**

42. 7825　　　　**43.** 92,614　　　　**44.** 365,829　　　**45.** 482,565

46. 7,342,675　　　**47.** 32,489,267　　　**48.** 107,361,072

2-5 Comparing Whole Numbers

Which stadium seats
more people?

To find which seats more,
compare 64,538 and 64,593.

Seating Capacity	
Veteran's Stadium	64,538
Anaheim Stadium	64,593

> means "is greater than"   < means "is less than"
= means "is equal to"

To compare numbers:
- Align the digits
  by place value.

  64,538
  64,593

- Start at the left. Compare
  the digits in the greatest place.

  64,538
  64,593   6 = 6

- If these are the same,
  compare the next digits.

  64,538
  64,593   4 = 4

- Keep comparing digits until
  you find two digits that
  are *not* the same.

  64,538   5 = 5
  64,593   9 > 3

So 64,593 > 64,538.

You could also say
64,538 < 64,593.

Anaheim Stadium seats more people.

Study this example.

423 _?_ 2423

423
2423

Think: There are no thousands
in 423.

0 < 2

So 423 < 2423   **or**   2423 > 423

Compare. Write <, =, or >.

1. 57 = 57

2. 65 _?_ 62

3. 48 _?_ 56

4. 82 _?_ 28

5. 325 _?_ 523

6. 649 _?_ 841

7. 127 _?_ 134

8. 525 _?_ 522

9. 6241 _?_ 9246

10. 7983 _?_ 7983

11. 9015 _?_ 9012

12. 2704 _?_ 2714

13. 8619 _?_ 8617

14. 1844 _?_ 1846

15. 33,015 _?_ 27,019

16. 10,384 _?_ 11,162

17. 25,995 _?_ 25,995

18. 51,305 _?_ 51,316

19. 48,924 _?_ 48,925

20. 67,183 _?_ 67,180

21. 285 _?_ 28

22. 3950 _?_ 39,502

23. 110 _?_ 1010

24. 8459 _?_ 84

25. 75,165 _?_ 758

26. 2022 _?_ 22,022

Solve.

27. Is four hundred sixty-two greater or less than four hundred sixty?

28. Is two thousand, three hundred twenty-five greater or less than 2329?

29. The Kingdome in Seattle seats 59,438 people. Oakland Coliseum seats 50,219 people. Which ballpark seats fewer people?

30. Fenway Park in Boston seats 33,465 people. Wrigley Field in Chicago seats 37,272 people. Which ballpark seats more people?

Challenge

Compare. Write <, =, or >.

31. 76,324,685 _?_ 272,324,685

32. 402,004,020 _?_ 402,002,040

2-6 Ordering Whole Numbers

▶ Order the skyscraper heights from least to greatest.

Use the value of the digits in each number to order the numbers.

Building	Height in feet
AMOCO, Chicago	1136
Chrysler, New York	1046
John Hancock Center, Chicago	1127
Texas, Houston	1002

Compare thousands.	Compare hundreds. Rearrange.	Compare tens. Rearrange.
1136	1046	1002
1046	1002	1046
1127	1136	1127
1002	1127	1136
1000 = 1000	0 < 100	0 < 40
		20 < 30
	So 1046 and 1002 are less than 1136 and 1127.	So 1002 < 1046 and 1127 < 1136.

The order from least to greatest: 1002; 1046; 1127; 1136

The order from greatest to least: 1136; 1127; 1046; 1002

▶ Order from greatest to least: 26,750; 38,475; 3847.

Compare ten thousands.

38,475   30,000 > 20,000
26,750
 3 847 ◄ No ten thousands. 3847 is least.

The order from greatest to least:
38,475; 26,750; 3847

Write in order from least to greatest.

1. 23; 29; 25; 21

2. 426; 505; 431; 424

3. 671; 680; 707; 679; 702

4. 843; 839; 87; 841; 836

5. 4515; 3204; 7661; 1139; 4500

6. 6714; 6783; 6756; 679; 6744

7. 24,316; 34,316; 24,416; 34,416; 24,404

8. 57,554; 58,641; 5784; 57,590; 579

Write in order from greatest to least.

9. 86; 89; 84; 82

10. 343; 349; 434; 352

11. 526; 642; 589; 538; 658

12. 295; 32; 289; 27; 281

13. 8451; 8468; 8450; 8464; 8445

14. 3605; 3679; 369; 3610; 3600

15. 46,824; 46,785; 46,804; 46,815; 46,790

16. 94,747; 9547; 95,754; 959; 94,763

Challenge

Solve.

17. List the countries in order from greatest area to least area.

18. List the countries with areas greater than two hundred thousand square miles.

Country	Area in Square Miles
France	210,039
Germany	137,746
Ireland	27,136
Italy	116,304
Japan	142,727
Kenya	224,960
Mexico	761,604

Recognizing and Counting Money

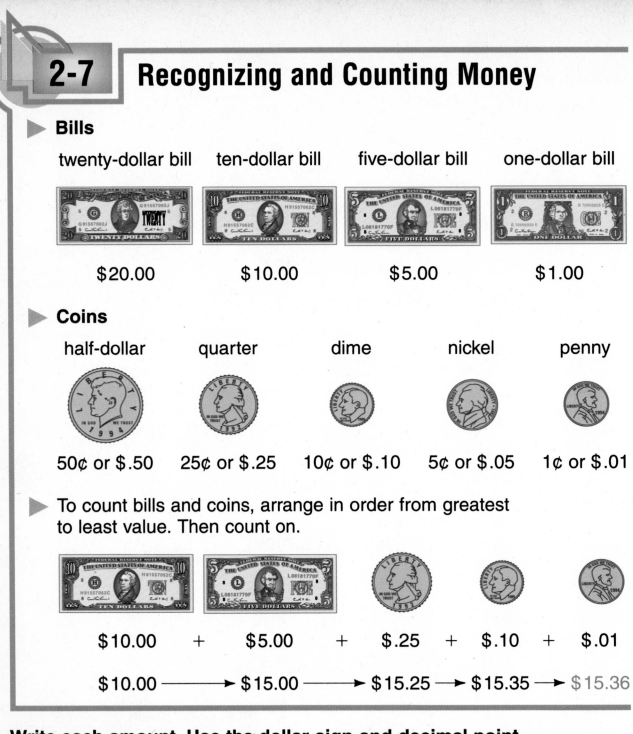

▶ **Bills**

twenty-dollar bill	ten-dollar bill	five-dollar bill	one-dollar bill
$20.00	$10.00	$5.00	$1.00

▶ **Coins**

half-dollar	quarter	dime	nickel	penny
50¢ or $.50	25¢ or $.25	10¢ or $.10	5¢ or $.05	1¢ or $.01

▶ To count bills and coins, arrange in order from greatest to least value. Then count on.

$10.00 + $5.00 + $.25 + $.10 + $.01

$10.00 ⟶ $15.00 ⟶ $15.25 → $15.35 → $15.36

Write each amount. Use the dollar sign and decimal point.

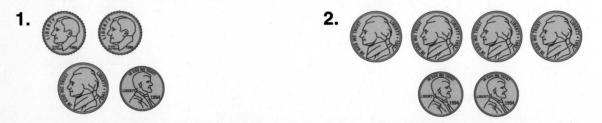

1.

2.

Write each amount. Use the dollar sign and decimal point.

3.

4.

5.

6.

7.

8.

9. 1 dollar, 1 half-dollar, 3 dimes, 1 nickel

10. 2 quarters, 6 dimes, 4 nickels, 8 pennies

11. 1 five-dollar bill, 3 quarters, 1 dime, 3 nickels, 2 pennies

12. 4 dollars, 1 quarter, 2 nickels

Copy and complete the table.

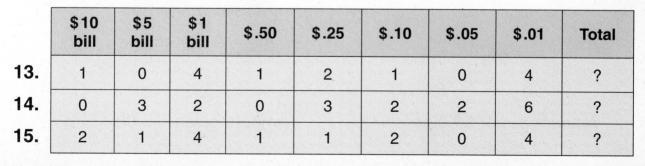

	$10 bill	$5 bill	$1 bill	$.50	$.25	$.10	$.05	$.01	Total
13.	1	0	4	1	2	1	0	4	?
14.	0	3	2	0	3	2	2	6	?
15.	2	1	4	1	1	2	0	4	?

Making Change

Sabtir buys a notebook for $3.68. She gives the clerk a ten-dollar bill. What coins and bills might she receive as change? What is the value of her change?

To make change:
- Count up from the cost to the amount given.
- Start with the coins that have the least value.
- Use the fewest possible coins and bills.

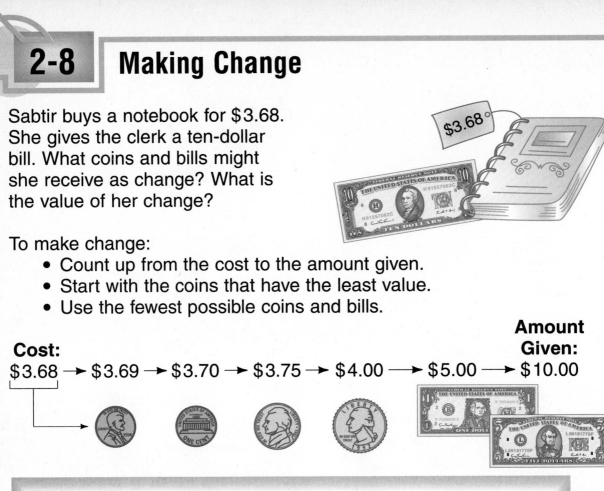

Cost:

$3.68 → $3.69 → $3.70 → $3.75 → $4.00 → $5.00 → **Amount Given:** $10.00

Count: $5.00 + $1.00 + $.25 + $.05 + $.01 + $.01

$5.00 → $6.00 → $6.25 → $6.30 → $6.31 → $6.32

Sabtir receives 2 pennies, 1 nickel, 1 quarter, 1 one-dollar bill, and 1 five-dollar bill as change. The value of her change is $6.32.

Write the fewest coins and bills you would receive as change. Then write the value of the change.

1.

Amount given: $1.00

2.

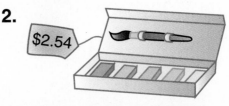

Amount given: $3.00

Write the fewest coins and bills you would receive as change. Then write the value of the change.

3.  $2.75

Amount given: $5.00

4.  $4.51

Amount given: $5.00

5. Cost: $3.16
Amount given: $10.00

6. Cost: $4.22
Amount given: $10.00

7. Cost: $12.99
Amount given: $15.00

8. Cost: $13.08
Amount given: $14.00

9. Cost: $13.70
Amount given: $20.00

10. Cost: $14.10
Amount given: $20.00

11. Cost: $15.46
Amount given: $20.00

12. Cost: $19.55
Amount given: $20.00

13. Cost: $10.60
Amount given: $20.00

14. Cost: $2.67
Amount given: $20.00

 **Finding Together**

Use nickels, dimes, and quarters. List all the ways you can make each amount. You may use play money.

$ .20	
nickels	dimes
4	0
2	1
0	2

15. $.15

16. $.30

17. $.25

18. $.35

19. $.50

20. $.40

21. $.60

22. $.75

2-9 Comparing and Ordering Money

Chuck earned $25.35.
Evan earned $24.50.
Who earned more?

To find who earned more,
compare $25.35 and $24.50.

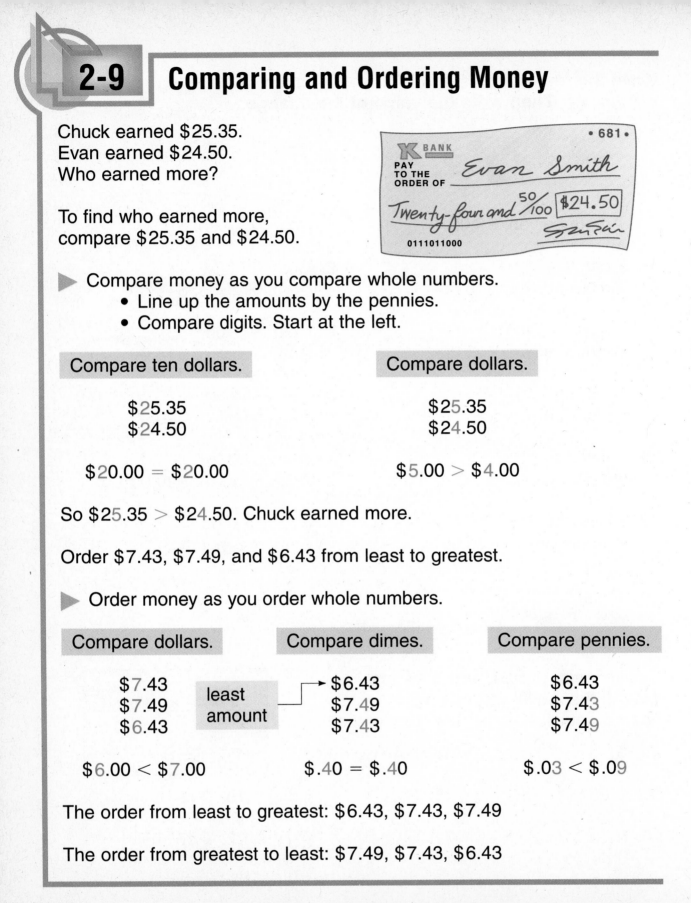

▶ Compare money as you compare whole numbers.
- Line up the amounts by the pennies.
- Compare digits. Start at the left.

Compare ten dollars.	Compare dollars.
$25.35 $24.50	$25.35 $24.50
$20.00 = $20.00	$5.00 > $4.00

So $25.35 > $24.50. Chuck earned more.

Order $7.43, $7.49, and $6.43 from least to greatest.

▶ Order money as you order whole numbers.

Compare dollars.	Compare dimes.	Compare pennies.
$7.43 $7.49 $6.43	least amount → $6.43 $7.49 $7.43	$6.43 $7.43 $7.49
$6.00 < $7.00	$.40 = $.40	$.03 < $.09

The order from least to greatest: $6.43, $7.43, $7.49

The order from greatest to least: $7.49, $7.43, $6.43

Compare. Write <, =, or >.

1. $.07 _?_ $.09   2. $.76 _?_ $.73   3. $.52 _?_ $.52   4. $.38 _?_ $.37

5. $3.49 _?_ $4.69   6. $8.03 _?_ $8.50   7. $2.81 _?_ $2.80

8. $5.38 _?_ $5.36   9. $9.75 _?_ $9.75   10. $7.63 _?_ $7.66

11. $10.30 _?_ $10.70   12. $42.25 _?_ $25.42   13. $87.95 _?_ $87.75

14. $36.99 _?_ $36.98   15. $77.07 _?_ $77.70   16. $61.18 _?_ $61.18

17. $1.95 _?_ $.19   18. $2.67 _?_ $26.07   19. $74.50 _?_ $7.85

Write in order from least to greatest.

20. $.76, $.35, $.57, $.83   21. $.18, $.15, $.19, $.12, $.17

22. $4.65, $4.62, $4.26, $5.24, $5.42

23. $75.39, $78.36, $7.48, $74.48, $75.93

Write in order from greatest to least.

24. $1.11, $1.10, $1.01, $1.17, $1.71

25. $24.42, $24.48, $24.24, $2.48, $2.84

26. $9.91, $9.19, $91.19, $91.91, $99.11

27. $68.50, $65.80, $68.05, $6.85, $65.08

Solve.

28. Adam has saved $85.25. Can he buy a jacket that costs $58.82?

29. Jill saved $32.40. Ed saved $34.20. Lynn saved $34.40. Who saved the most money? Who saved the least money?

2-10 | Rounding

Round numbers and money amounts to tell **about** how much or **about** how many.

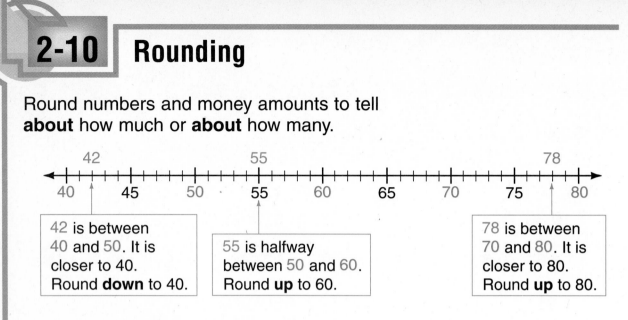

42 is between 40 and 50. It is closer to 40. Round **down** to 40.

55 is halfway between 50 and 60. Round **up** to 60.

78 is between 70 and 80. It is closer to 80. Round **up** to 80.

To round numbers:
- find the place you are rounding to.
- look at the digit to its right.

Round 65 to the nearest ten.

65
↓
70

5 = 5
Round **up** to 70.

Round $2.53 to the nearest ten cents.

$2.53
↓
$2.50

3 < 5
Round **down** to $2.50.

Round $5.86 to the nearest dollar.

$5.86
↓
$6.00

8 > 5
Round **up** to $6.00.

Round 2174 to the nearest hundred.

2174
↓
2200

7 > 5
Round **up** to 2200.

Round 8214 to the nearest thousand.

8214
↓
8000

2 < 5
Round **down** to 8000.

Round $625.95 to the nearest ten dollars.

$625.95
↓
$630.00

5 = 5
Round **up** to $630.00.

Round to the nearest ten or ten cents.

1. 16   **2.** 49   **3.** 94   **4.** 315   **5.** 871

6. $.55   **7.** $.83   **8.** $1.24   **9.** $8.39   **10.** $5.66

Round to the nearest hundred or dollar.

11. 285   **12.** 674   **13.** 503   **14.** 857   **15.** 449

16. 9173   **17.** 3426   **18.** 1250   **19.** 7314   **20.** 2693

21. $1.44   **22.** $6.70   **23.** $3.95   **24.** $7.56   **25.** $8.39

26. $55.20   **27.** $38.98   **28.** $27.49   **29.** $18.88   **30.** $71.53

Round to the nearest thousand or ten dollars.

31. 9437   **32.** 1878   **33.** 8564   **34.** 2946

35. 74,806   **36.** 32,521   **37.** 60,719   **38.** 45,133

39. $53.68   **40.** $15.89   **41.** $94.87   **42.** $27.95

43. $836.42   **44.** $351.25   **45.** $708.50   **46.** $484.62

Challenge

Round to the nearest ten thousand or hundred dollars.

47. 36,455   **48.** 52,630   **49.** $654.70   **50.** $895.99

Round to the nearest hundred thousand.

51. 743,299   **52.** 250,343   **53.** 571,320

54. 462,135   **55.** 325,523   **56.** 2,704,810

Number Sense: Using a Number Line

Halfway points can help you to find numbers
on a number line.

▶ About where on each number line is 75?

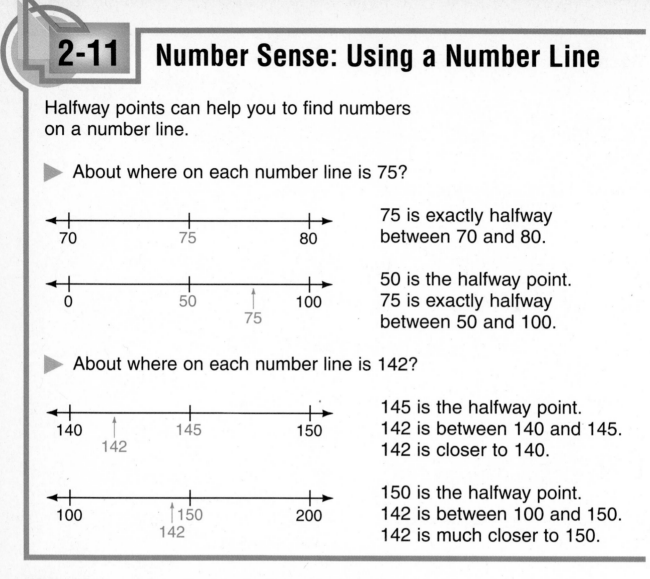

75 is exactly halfway
between 70 and 80.

50 is the halfway point.
75 is exactly halfway
between 50 and 100.

▶ About where on each number line is 142?

145 is the halfway point.
142 is between 140 and 145.
142 is closer to 140.

150 is the halfway point.
142 is between 100 and 150.
142 is much closer to 150.

**Write the number that is halfway between
the two numbers.**

1. 20; 30   **2.** 0; 50   **3.** 600; 700   **4.** 0; 200

5. 0; 500   **6.** 0; 80   **7.** 10; 70   **8.** 150; 200

**Draw a number line to show the halfway point
between the two numbers.**

9. 0; 10   **10.** 40; 50   **11.** 0; 60   **12.** 800; 900

13. 0; 1000   **14.** 510; 520   **15.** 1000; 2000   **16.** 0; 2000

About what number is each arrow pointing toward?

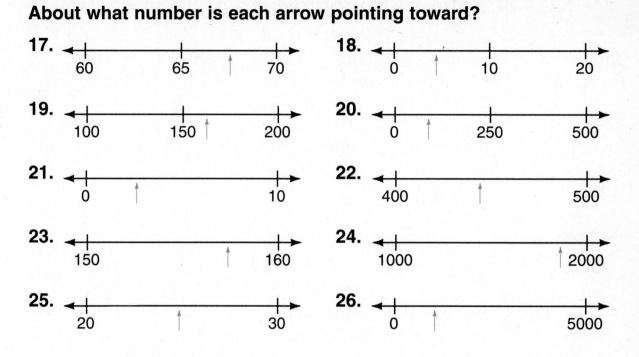

17. 60 65 ↑ 70

18. 0 ↑ 10 20

19. 100 150 ↑ 200

20. 0 ↑ 250 500

21. 0 ↑ 10

22. 400 ↑ 500

23. 150 ↑ 160

24. 1000 ↑ 2000

25. 20 ↑ 30

26. 0 ↑ 5000

Draw each number line.

27. Draw a number line from 50 to 60. Show the halfway point. Draw an arrow that points toward 53.

28. Draw a number line from 0 to 100. Show the halfway point. Draw an arrow that points toward 40.

29. Draw a number line from 0 to 500. Draw an arrow that points toward 300.

Skills to Remember

Add or subtract. Watch the signs.

30.	31.	32.	33.	34.	35.
7 +2	0 +4	8 −6	9 −9	6 +7	13 − 8

36.	37.	38.	39.	40.	41.
5 −0	3 +5	10 − 7	8 +8	15 − 9	5 +6

2-12 Problem Solving: Make a Table or List

Problem: Steve has 24 marbles. Each marble is green or red. For every green marble, Steve has 3 red marbles. How many red marbles does Steve have?

Color	Number of Marbles			
green	1	2	?	?
red	3	?	?	?
total	4	?	?	?

1 IMAGINE Make a table.

2 NAME *Facts:* Steve has 24 marbles. For 1 green marble, there are 3 red marbles.

Question: How many red marbles does Steve have?

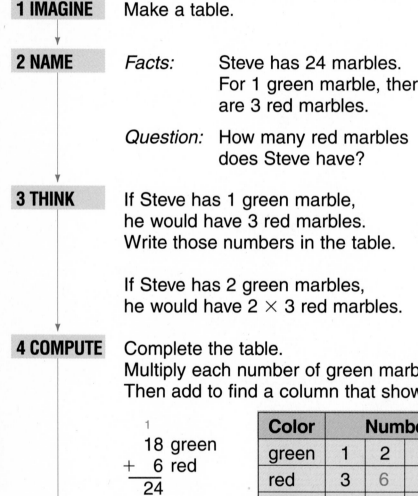

3 THINK If Steve has 1 green marble, he would have 3 red marbles. Write those numbers in the table.

If Steve has 2 green marbles, he would have 2 × 3 red marbles.

4 COMPUTE Complete the table. Multiply each number of green marbles by 3. Then add to find a column that shows 24 marbles.

$$\begin{array}{r} \overset{1}{}18 \text{ green} \\ + 6 \text{ red} \\ \hline 24 \end{array}$$

Color	Number of Marbles					
green	1	2	3	4	5	6
red	3	6	9	12	15	18
total	4	8	12	16	20	24

Steve has 18 red marbles.

5 CHECK Use a calculator to check your computation, or act out the problem.

Solve.

1. Mr. Hoody bought 3 shirts and 4 ties. The shirts are blue, gray, and white. The ties are red, brown, green, and yellow. How many ways can he wear the shirts and ties together?

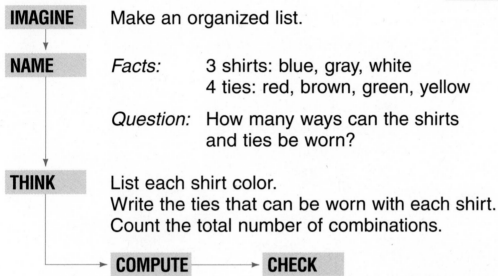

Tie Colors	Blue Shirt	Gray Shirt	White Shirt
red			
brown			
green			
yellow			

IMAGINE   Make an organized list.

NAME   *Facts:*   3 shirts: blue, gray, white
                          4 ties: red, brown, green, yellow

             Question: How many ways can the shirts and ties be worn?

THINK   List each shirt color.
             Write the ties that can be worn with each shirt.
             Count the total number of combinations.

COMPUTE ⟶ **CHECK**

2. Apple juice costs 50¢. The juice machine accepts quarters, dimes, and nickels. Make a list of coin combinations that can be used to buy juice.

3. Adam and Ashlee use three 1-6 number cubes. They look for different ways to roll the sum of 12. How many ways will they find?

4. Calvin has 90 stamps. For every Mexican stamp, Calvin has 8 U.S. stamps. How many Mexican stamps does Calvin have?

Make Up Your Own

5. Write a problem that uses a table or list. Ask a classmate to solve the problem.

2-13 Problem-Solving Applications

Solve.

1. The school book fair wanted to raise $1500. It raised $2500. What is the difference in the amounts?

Use these steps:

2. Abigail bought a science fiction novel for $17.89. How much change did she receive from a twenty-dollar bill? What coins and bills could she have received as change?

3. Abigail's science fiction novel describes life one hundred thousand years from now. What will the date be one hundred thousand years from today?

4. Paperbacks sold for 50¢ each. Hardcover books sold for $1.25 each. Was it more expensive to buy 3 paperbacks or 1 hardcover book?

5. Ray sold handmade bookmarks for 75¢ each. What five coins could be used to pay for 1 bookmark?

6. One book at the sale was printed 100 years ago. In what year was that book printed?

7. The book fair sold 437 books this year. Last year it sold 327 books. In which year were more books sold and by how many?

8. Zena brought 10 dollars to the book fair. She bought 2 books about mountain climbing for $4.20 each. How much change did she get?

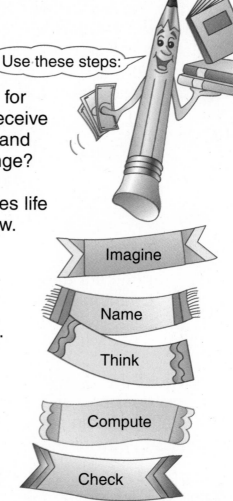

Imagine

Name

Think

Compute

Check

Solve.

9. There were 428 people at the book fair. Three hundred eighteen of them bought books. How many people did not buy a book?

10. Stella made a triangular book display. She put 9 books in the first row, 8 books in the second row, 7 books in the third row, and so on. How many books did Stella use in her display?

11. Hank wrote 14 poems. He illustrated 6 of them. How many poems were not illustrated?

12. Ray's bookmarks were made of red or blue plastic with purple, white, or yellow fringe. How many different bookmarks could Ray make?

13. Sue reads adventure books. There are 11 books on her desk. She has read 7 books. How many books does Sue have left to read?

14. The book fair charged 30¢ admission. How many different ways could people give the exact amount if no pennies were allowed?

USE THESE STRATEGIES:
Make a Table or List
Use a Graph
Choose the Operation
Guess and Test
Missing Information
Write a Number Sentence

Use the graph for problems 15–16.

15. Which encyclopedia has more than ten thousand pages?

16. About how many pages does the New American Encyclopedia have?

Encyclopedia Pages

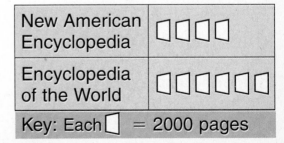

New American Encyclopedia	
Encyclopedia of the World	
Key: Each ▯ = 2000 pages	

More Practice

Write the number in standard form.

1. eighty-four thousand, two hundred, six   **2.** six hundred thousand, five

Write the place of the red digit.

3. 56,651,020   **4.** 205,640,311   **5.** 67,451

Compare. Write <, =, or >.

6. 74 _?_ 47   **7.** 450 _?_ 450   **8.** 61,905 _?_ 61,950

Write in order from greatest to least.

9. 27; 30; 56; 21   **10.** 625; 217; 451; 332

11. 3542; 3320; 4310; 5403   **12.** 46,532; 46,503; 46,330

Write each amount. Use the dollar sign and decimal point.

13. 6 quarters   **14.** 5 nickels   **15.** 4 quarters
      2 dimes   4 pennies   15 dimes
      1 nickel   6 nickels

About what number is each arrow pointing toward?

16.

```
  ←—+——+——+——↓——+——+——+——→
    5   10  15  20  25  30
```

17.

```
  ←—+——+——+——↓——+——+——→
    70  80  90  100 110 120
```

Round each number.

To the nearest 100:   **18.** 4486   **19.** 6824

To the nearest 1000:   **20.** 76,534   **21.** 153,462

To the nearest dollar: **22.** $12.75   **23.** $57.45

(See *Still More Practice,* pp. 461–462.)

WORDS FOR LARGER NUMBERS

Raymond wondered how many grains of sand
there were on the beach. He knew
there were too many grains for him
to count, so he asked his grandfather.

This is what Raymond's grandfather said:
"You could say a hundred trillion,
or you could say a zillion. But
I think there are **googol** grains
of sand on the beach."

10000000000000000000000000000000000000000000000
0
0
0
0   *A GOOGOL is the number 1*
0   *followed by a hundred zeros.*
0
0
0
0000000000000000000000000000000000000000000000000

10000000000000000000000000000000000000000000000
0
0
0   *A GOOGOLPLEX is the number*
0   *1 followed by a googol of zeros.*
0
0
0
0000000000000000000000000000000000000000000000000

Solve.

1. Write a googol.

2. How many commas did you need?

3. How many digits are there in a googol?

4. Name some things that might be counted
   using a googol.

Check Your Mastery

Write in standard form. See pp. 36–41

1. five hundred eight   **2.** LVII   **3.** two hundred four thousand

4. fourteen million, fifteen   **5.** 700 thousands + 60 tens + 8 ones

Write in expanded form. See pp. 42–43

6. 420,635,010   **7.** 56,431   **8.** 7,532,060

Write in order from least to greatest. See pp. 44–47, 52–53

9. $56.20; $50.62; $52.60   **10.** 72,310; 72,130; 73,303

Write each amount. See pp. 48–51
Use the dollar sign and decimal point.

11. 8 quarters   **12.** 16 dimes   **13.** 3 dollars
  5 dimes   5 nickels   42 pennies

Round each number. See pp. 54–55

To the nearest 10:   **14.** 1471   To the nearest 100:   **15.** 732

To the nearest dollar: **16.** $24.31   **17.** $162.58

Write the change you would receive. See pp. 50–51

18.   Cost $4.21   **19.**   Cost $14.95
  Amount given $5.00   Amount given $20.00

Solve. Then round the answer to the nearest dollar. See pp. 60–61

20. The cost of a jacket is $17.95. Ramon gave
the clerk one $10 bill and two $5 bills. About
how much change will he get back?

Choose the best answer.

1.   9
    +6
- **a.** 14
- **b.** 16
- **c.** 15
- **d.** not given

2.   11
    − 5
- **a.** 8
- **b.** 7
- **c.** 14
- **d.** not given

3.   5¢
    +9¢
- **a.** 13¢
- **b.** 14¢
- **c.** 16¢
- **d.** not given

4.   17
    − 8
- **a.** 11
- **b.** 9
- **c.** 7
- **d.** not given

5. 3 + 9
- **a.** 12
- **b.** 14
- **c.** 13
- **d.** not given

6. 16¢ − 8¢
- **a.** 12¢
- **b.** 6¢
- **c.** 7¢
- **d.** not given

7. What is the value of 8 in 826?
- **a.**   800
- **b.**   8
- **c.** 8000
- **d.**   100

8. What is the Roman numeral for 27?
- **a.** XVII
- **b.** XXVII
- **c.** VII
- **d.** XVII

9. What is the standard form of: seven hundred eighteen?
- **a.** 708
- **b.** 780
- **c.** 718
- **d.** 728

10. What is the standard form of: ninety-one thousand, four hundred sixty?
- **a.** 19,460
- **b.** 9,146
- **c.** 91,460
- **d.** 9,460

11.   7
    ×3
- **a.** 18
- **b.** 21
- **c.** 24
- **d.** not given

12.   2
    ×9
- **a.** 18
- **b.** 27
- **c.** 11
- **d.** not given

13.   9¢
    ×5
- **a.** 40¢
- **b.** 45¢
- **c.** 35¢
- **d.** not given

14. 6)24
- **a.** 3
- **b.** 6
- **c.** 5
- **d.** not given

15. 7)56
- **a.** 6
- **b.** 9
- **c.** 8
- **d.** not given

16. 9)36¢
- **a.** 5¢
- **b.** 3¢
- **c.** 4¢
- **d.** not given

17. 4 × 6
- **a.** 10
- **b.** 24
- **c.** 28
- **d.** not given

18. 16 ÷ 2
- **a.** 9
- **b.** 14
- **c.** 7
- **d.** not given

19. 42¢ ÷ 7
- **a.** 8¢
- **b.** 9¢
- **c.** 6¢
- **d.** not given

20. Compare.

585 _?_ 282
- **a.** <
- **b.** =
- **c.** >

21. Compare.

84,429 _?_ 84,529
- **a.** <
- **b.** =
- **c.** >

22. Compare.

$6.54 _?_ $6.49
- **a.** <
- **b.** =
- **c.** >

Choose the best answer.

23. What is the standard form of:

90,000 + 500 + 1

    a. 95,100
    b. 95,001
    c. 90,501
    d. 90,051

24. Which fact is *not* in the family of facts for 3, 7, 21?

    a. $3 \times 7 = 21$
    b. $21 \div 7 = 3$
    c. $21 \div 3 = 7$
    d. $7 + 3 = 10$

25. What is the period of the underlined digits?

56,722,086

    a. billions
    b. hundreds
    c. thousands
    d. millions

26. What is the amount?

1 twenty-dollar bill, 1 five-dollar bill, 2 dimes, 3 nickels, and 4 pennies

    a. $25.39
    b. $25.35
    c. $25.34
    d. $25.29

27. Round $37.59 to the nearest dollar.

    a. $37.00
    b. $39.00
    c. $38.00
    d. $40.00

28. Round 5638 to the nearest thousand.

    a. 6000
    b. 5600
    c. 5000
    d. 5700

29. What is the value of the change?

Cost: $14.52
Amount given: $20.00

    a. $5.48
    b. $6.58
    c. $6.48
    d. $6.52

30. About what number is the arrow pointing toward?

    a. 225
    b. 252
    c. 255
    d. 270

250   260

31. Thirteen boys and 8 girls are present. How many more boys than girls is that?

    a. 21   **b.** 5   **c.** 6   **d.** 4

32. Carla bought 8 cartons of juice. There are 2 cans in each carton. How many cans of juice did Carla buy?

    a. 4   **b.** 32   **c.** 16   **d.** 24

33. Fifty-six cents is shared by 7 friends. How much money does each receive?

    a. 7¢   **b.** 8¢   **c.** 9¢   **d.** not given

34. Paul bought 6 pens and 9 notebooks. How many school supplies did he purchase?

    a. 12   **b.** 13   **c.** 14   **d.** not given

In this chapter you will:

Add and subtract mentally
using addition and subtraction
strategies and concepts
Estimate sums and differences
Add and subtract numbers and
money without regrouping
Use technology:
read/data commands
Solve problems by logical
reasoning

Do you remember?

$$8 + 9 = 17$$
$$9 + 8 = 17$$
$$17 - 8 = 9$$
$$17 - 9 = 8$$

Critical Thinking/Finding Together
Round all of the money in this picture
to the nearest dollar.

3-1 Addition Properties

The properties of addition can help you to add quickly and correctly.

- Changing the *order* of addends does not change the sum.

Think: "order."

$$5 + 6 = 11 \qquad \begin{array}{r} 5 \\ +6 \\ \hline 11 \end{array} \qquad \begin{array}{r} 6 \\ +5 \\ \hline 11 \end{array}$$
$$6 + 5 = 11$$

- The sum of *zero* and a number is the same as that number.

Think: "same number."

$$7 + 0 = 7 \qquad \begin{array}{r} 7 \\ +0 \\ \hline 7 \end{array} \qquad \begin{array}{r} 0 \\ +7 \\ \hline 7 \end{array}$$
$$0 + 7 = 7$$

- Changing the *grouping* of the addends does not change the sum.

Think: "grouping."

Always do the computation in parentheses first.

$$(4 + 5) + 2 = 4 + (5 + 2)$$
$$9 \quad + 2 = 4 + \quad 7$$
$$11 = 11$$

Use the properties to make adding a list of numbers easier.

Change the order.

Add down.   Add up.

$$\begin{array}{r} 4 \\ 5 \\ 1 \\ +3 \\ \hline 13 \end{array} \begin{array}{l} 9 \\ 10 \\ 13 \end{array} \qquad \begin{array}{r} 4 \\ 5 \\ 1 \\ +3 \\ \hline 13 \end{array} \begin{array}{l} 13 \\ 9 \\ 4 \end{array}$$

Change the order and the grouping.

$$10 \begin{cases} 2 \\ 3 \\ 0 \\ 7 \end{cases} \quad \begin{array}{r} (3 + 7) + 2 + 0 + 5 = 17 \\ 10 \quad + 2 + 0 + 5 = 17 \end{array}$$
$$\begin{array}{r} +5 \\ \hline 17 \end{array}$$

Add. Use the addition properties.

1. 3
   +0

2. 6
   +3

3. 3
   +6

4. 8
   +7

5. 7
   +8

6. 8
   +0

7. 0
   +5

8. 5
   +4

9. 0
   +6

10. 9
    +7

11. 7
    +9

12. 4
    +8

13. 9
    +0

14. 8
    +4

15. 7
    9
    0
    +3

16. 2
    6
    1
    +4

17. 5
    4
    2
    +5

18. 1
    2
    8
    +0

19. 2
    1
    3
    +9

20. 1
    9
    7
    +0

21. 3
    4
    3
    +6

22. 1
    2
    7
    +8

Add the number in the center to each number around it.

23.   24.   25.

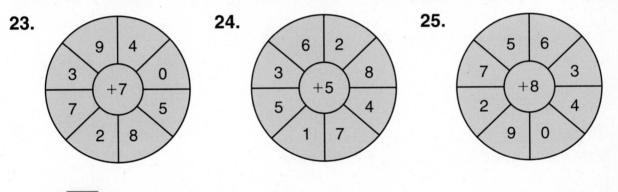

Critical Thinking

Use the scoreboard to answer the questions.

Inning	1	2	3	4	5	6	7	8	9
Bluebirds	5	1	0	0	4	0	1	3	0
Robins	0	2	1	3	0	0	3	3	4

26. Who won the game?

27. What was the final score?

28. After which inning was the score 11 to 9?

29. After which inning was there a tie score?

30. What was the score after 2 innings? 6 innings? 8 innings?

31. How many runs did the Bluebirds and Robins score in the 5th inning?

69

3-2 Addition Strategies

Tyrone and Maria use doubles to find 6 + 7.

doubles

Tyrone thinks: 6 + 6 = 12
6 + 7 = 13

Maria thinks: 7 + 7 = 14
6 + 7 = 13

1 more than 6 + 6

1 less than 7 + 7

James uses 10 to find 9 + 4.

James thinks: 10 + 4 = 14
So, 9 + 4 = 13

1 more than 9 + 4

Tania looks for sums of 10 and doubles
when she adds more than two numbers.

$$
\begin{array}{r}
2 \\
5 \\
+\ 8 \\
\hline
15
\end{array}
$$
10

10 + 5 = 15

$$
\begin{array}{r}
6 \\
3 \\
6 \\
+\ 2 \\
\hline
17
\end{array}
$$
12

12 + 3 + 2 = 17

Find the sum.

1. $\begin{array}{r} 3 \\ +4 \\ \hline \end{array}$
2. $\begin{array}{r} 5 \\ +6 \\ \hline \end{array}$
3. $\begin{array}{r} 8 \\ +7 \\ \hline \end{array}$
4. $\begin{array}{r} 6 \\ +7 \\ \hline \end{array}$
5. $\begin{array}{r} 5 \\ +4 \\ \hline \end{array}$
6. $\begin{array}{r} 8 \\ +8 \\ \hline \end{array}$

7. $\begin{array}{r} 9 \\ +5 \\ \hline \end{array}$
8. $\begin{array}{r} 7 \\ +9 \\ \hline \end{array}$
9. $\begin{array}{r} 4 \\ +9 \\ \hline \end{array}$
10. $\begin{array}{r} 9 \\ +9 \\ \hline \end{array}$
11. $\begin{array}{r} 3 \\ +9 \\ \hline \end{array}$
12. $\begin{array}{r} 9 \\ +2 \\ \hline \end{array}$

13. 3 + 2
14. 4 + 4
15. 8 + 9
16. 9 + 6

Add mentally.

17. 1   **18.** 3   **19.** 2   **20.** 4   **21.** 3   **22.** 5
     2   3   7   5   7   6
  +9   +8   +8   +4   +7   +5

23. 1   **24.** 4   **25.** 5   **26.** 3   **27.** 6   **28.** 1
     4   2   7   3   2   8
     8   3   0   3   4   1
  +2   +2   +3   +3   +2   +7

29. 10 + 5   **30.** 9 + 5   **31.** 6 + 5   **32.** 6 + 7

33. 8 + 10   **34.** 8 + 9   **35.** 9 + 9   **36.** 8 + 8

37. 3 + 10   **38.** 3 + 4   **39.** 9 + 3   **40.** 4 + 9

Solve.

41. Tara needs to mail 6 letters and 5 postcards. How many stamps does she need?

42. Kim has 4 Canadian stamps, 5 English stamps, and 6 French stamps in his collection. How many stamps does he have altogether?

 **Calculator Activity**

Find the first sum. Predict the second sum.

43. 42 + 42   **44.** 16 + 16   **45.** 35 + 35   **46.** 48 + 48

    42 + 41   17 + 16   45 + 35   48 + 38

47. 50 + 50   **48.** 20 + 20   **49.** 26 + 26   **50.** 21 + 21

    50 + 65   20 + 25   27 + 27   25 + 25

3-3 Subtraction Concepts

Subtraction has four different meanings.

▶ Take Away

Mr. Wu displayed 12 Planet Search videogames. He sold 9 of the games. How many Planet Search games does he have left?

$12 - 9 = 3$

He has 3 Planet Search games left.

▶ Compare

Jenny had 4 baby dolls. Inez had 8 baby dolls. How many more baby dolls did Inez have than Jenny?

$8 - 4 = 4$

Inez had 4 more baby dolls.

▶ Part of a Whole

Lisa packed 15 cartons of model trucks. She shipped 8 of the cartons to Ohio. How many cartons were *not* shipped to Ohio?

$15 - 8 = 7$

Seven cartons were not shipped to Ohio.

▶ How Many More Are Needed

Manny had 6 bull's-eyes in a board game. He needed 10 bull's-eyes to win. How many more bull's-eyes did Manny need?

$10 - 6 = 4$

Manny needed 4 more bull's-eyes.

Solve.

1. Bobby had 10 action figures. He gave 2 of them away. How many action figures does Bobby have left?

2. Mr. Wu put 5 puppets on a shelf that can hold 14 puppets. How many more puppets can fit on the shelf?

3. Cara had 12 dolls. Three of them were from Russia. How many were from other countries?

4. Mr. Wu sold 8 soft bears and 14 soft rabbits. How many more rabbits did he sell?

Rules for Subtraction

Use these rules to help you subtract quickly and correctly.

When zero is subtracted from a number, the difference is that same number.

$$\begin{array}{r} 4 \\ -0 \\ \hline 4 \end{array} \qquad 4 - 0 = 4$$

When a number is subtracted from itself, the difference is zero.

$$\begin{array}{r} 9 \\ -9 \\ \hline 0 \end{array} \qquad 9 - 9 = 0$$

Subtract.

5. $\begin{array}{r} 7 \\ -0 \\ \hline \end{array}$
6. $\begin{array}{r} 5 \\ -5 \\ \hline \end{array}$
7. $\begin{array}{r} 9 \\ -0 \\ \hline \end{array}$
8. $\begin{array}{r} 6 \\ -6 \\ \hline \end{array}$
9. $\begin{array}{r} 4 \\ -4 \\ \hline \end{array}$
10. $\begin{array}{r} 1 \\ -1 \\ \hline \end{array}$
11. $\begin{array}{r} 3 \\ -0 \\ \hline \end{array}$

12. $\begin{array}{r} 13¢ \\ -6¢ \\ \hline \end{array}$
13. $\begin{array}{r} 8¢ \\ -8¢ \\ \hline \end{array}$
14. $\begin{array}{r} 3¢ \\ -3¢ \\ \hline \end{array}$
15. $\begin{array}{r} 9¢ \\ -9¢ \\ \hline \end{array}$
16. $\begin{array}{r} 10¢ \\ -5¢ \\ \hline \end{array}$
17. $\begin{array}{r} 12¢ \\ -3¢ \\ \hline \end{array}$
18. $\begin{array}{r} 16¢ \\ -9¢ \\ \hline \end{array}$

Make Up Your Own

19. Use 15 and 8 and use 13 and 5. Make up two different kinds of subtraction problems for your friends to solve.

3-4 Addition and Subtraction Sentences

Nicki is making a 12-square red and blue quilt. She has cut 7 red squares. How many blue squares does she need?

To find how many blue squares, find the missing addend: $7 + \underline{\ ?\ } = 12$

To find a missing number in a number sentence, think of a related fact.

Think: $12 - 7 = 5$
   So $7 + 5 = 12$

> Remember: You can write $7 + 5 = 12$ as $12 = 7 + 5$.

Nicki needs 5 blue squares.

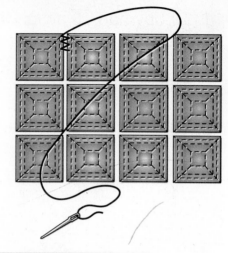

Minuend
− Subtrahend
Difference

Study these examples.

Find the missing minuend:

$$8 = \underline{\ ?\ } - 3$$
Think: $8 + 3 = 11$
   So $8 = 11 - 3$

Find the missing subtrahend:

$$15 - \underline{\ ?\ } = 9$$
Think: $15 - 9 = 6$
   So $15 - 6 = 9$

Find the missing addend.

1. $5 + \underline{\ ?\ } = 11$

2. $9 + \underline{\ ?\ } = 16$

3. $8 + \underline{\ ?\ } = 15$

4. $\underline{\ ?\ } + 4 = 10$

5. $\underline{\ ?\ } + 5 = 13$

6. $\underline{\ ?\ } + 2 = 6$

7. $8 = 5 + \underline{\ ?\ }$

8. $12 = 3 + \underline{\ ?\ }$

9. $4 = 1 + \underline{\ ?\ }$

10. $14 = \underline{\ ?\ } + 6$

11. $7 = \underline{\ ?\ } + 4$

12. $5 = \underline{\ ?\ } + 0$

Find the missing minuend or subtrahend.

13. $\underline{?} - 8 = 2$ 14. $\underline{?} - 6 = 6$ 15. $\underline{?} - 7 = 4$

16. $12 - \underline{?} = 5$ 17. $14 - \underline{?} = 8$ 18. $18 - \underline{?} = 9$

19. $\underline{?} - 3 = 9$ 20. $\underline{?} - 8 = 5$ 21. $\underline{?} - 9 = 4$

22. $13 - \underline{?} = 6$ 23. $5 - \underline{?} = 0$ 24. $15 - \underline{?} = 8$

25. $2 = 9 - \underline{?}$ 26. $7 = \underline{?} - 6$ 27. $3 = \underline{?} - 8$

28. $7 = \underline{?} - 8$ 29. $1 = \underline{?} - 9$ 30. $3 = 11 - \underline{?}$

Find the missing number.

31.
$$\begin{array}{r} ? \\ +3 \\ \hline 6 \end{array}$$

32.
$$\begin{array}{r} 4 \\ +\ ? \\ \hline 12 \end{array}$$

33.
$$\begin{array}{r} ? \\ -6 \\ \hline 4 \end{array}$$

34.
$$\begin{array}{r} 13 \\ -\ ? \\ \hline 5 \end{array}$$

35.
$$\begin{array}{r} 8 \\ +\ ? \\ \hline 16 \end{array}$$

36.
$$\begin{array}{r} ? \\ -7 \\ \hline 6 \end{array}$$

37.
$$\begin{array}{r} ? \\ +7 \\ \hline 15 \end{array}$$

38.
$$\begin{array}{r} ? \\ -9 \\ \hline 5 \end{array}$$

39.
$$\begin{array}{r} 4 \\ +\ ? \\ \hline 13 \end{array}$$

40.
$$\begin{array}{r} 12 \\ -\ ? \\ \hline 3 \end{array}$$

41.
$$\begin{array}{r} ? \\ +\ 5 \\ \hline 12 \end{array}$$

42.
$$\begin{array}{r} ? \\ -8 \\ \hline 9 \end{array}$$

Skills to Remember

Round to the nearest ten or ten cents.

43. 35   44. 452   45. 928   46. $.83   47. $3.95

Round to the nearest hundred or dollar.

48. 734   49. 3946   50. $4.75   51. $7.28   52. $54.62

Round to the nearest thousand or ten dollars.

53. 6789   54. 5412   55. $62.43   56. $17.29   57. $25.20

Estimating Sums and Differences

You can use rounding to estimate sums and differences.

- Round each number to the greatest place of the smaller number.

- Add or subtract the rounded numbers.

Estimate: 4360 + 254 + 1207

Round to hundreds.

$$
\begin{array}{rcl}
4360 & \longrightarrow & 4400 \\
254 & \longrightarrow & 300 \\
+\,1207 & \longrightarrow & +\,1200 \\
& \text{about} & 5900
\end{array}
$$

Estimate: 6924 − 3123

Round to thousands.

$$
\begin{array}{rcl}
6924 & \longrightarrow & 7000 \\
-\,3123 & \longrightarrow & -\,3000 \\
& \text{about} & 4000
\end{array}
$$

Study these examples.

Round to dollars.

$$
\begin{array}{rcl}
\$56.39 & \longrightarrow & \$56.00 \\
-\quad 4.25 & \longrightarrow & -\quad 4.00 \\
& \text{about} & \$52.00
\end{array}
$$

Round to ten cents.

$$
\begin{array}{rcl}
\$.27 & \longrightarrow & \$.30 \\
.12 & \longrightarrow & .10 \\
+\ .39 & \longrightarrow & +\ .40 \\
& \text{about} & \$.80
\end{array}
$$

Estimate the sum.

1. 53
    + 76

2. $.25
    + .14

3. 632
    + 149

4. $5.25
    + 2.30

5. $37.47
    + 42.58

6. 1432
     4290
    + 134

7. 625
      38
    + 707

8. $1.52
      .18
    + .13

9. $21.07
     14.95
    + 42.78

10. $61.35
      2.75
    + 14.38

11. 42 + 25 + 22

12. 243 + 627 + 139

13. 2163 + 155 + 547

Estimate the difference.

14.	54 − 23	**15.**	$.38 − .16	**16.**	932 − 629	**17.**	$8.57 − 5.08	**18.**	$42.34 − 15.75

19.	6152 − 2830	**20.**	4819 − 592	**21.**	$7.29 − .11	**22.**	$84.88 − 16.27	**23.**	$29.13 − 6.58

Using Estimation to Check

Use estimation to check addition or subtraction
to see if your answer is reasonable.

Estimated Sum		**Estimated Difference**	
3 5 6 ⟶ + 4 3 ⟶ 3 9 9	3 6 0 + 4 0 4 0 0	6 7 8 ⟶ − 4 5 1 ⟶ 2 2 7	7 0 0 − 5 0 0 2 0 0

399 is close to 400.
The answer is reasonable.

227 is close to 200.
The answer is reasonable.

Is the answer reasonable? Estimate to check.
Then write "yes" or "no."

24. $34 + 15 = 49$ **25.** $61 + 30 = 201$ **26.** $56 - 22 = 34$

27. $43 - 21 = 22$ **28.** $121 + 405 = 426$ **29.** $2.61 + $3.28 = 5.89

30. $302 + 517 + 160 = 979$ **31.** $49.95 - $36.20 = 13.75

32. $9428 - 207 = 9221$ **33.** $.17 + $.20 + $3.55 = 7.92

34. $859 - 33 = 526$ **35.** $2462 + 1301 + 5234 = 8997$

36. $88.89 - $6.27 = 82.62 **37.** $21.46 + $3.98 + $32.54 = 87.98

3-6 Mental Math

Here are some methods to help you add and subtract mentally.

Think of tens or hundreds.

Add: 120 + 30 = __?__

Think: 120 = 12 tens

$$\begin{array}{r} 12 \text{ tens} \\ + \ 3 \text{ tens} \\ \hline 15 \text{ tens} = 150 \end{array}$$

Subtract: 6500 − 400 = __?__

Think: 6500 = 65 hundreds

$$\begin{array}{r} 65 \text{ hundreds} \\ - \ 4 \text{ hundreds} \\ \hline 61 \text{ hundreds} = 6100 \end{array}$$

Look for patterns.

$$\begin{array}{r} 375 \\ - \ 10 \\ \hline 365 \end{array} \qquad \begin{array}{r} 375 \\ - \ 20 \\ \hline 355 \end{array} \qquad \begin{array}{r} 375 \\ - \ 30 \\ \hline 345 \end{array}$$

$$\begin{array}{r} 500 \\ + \ 26 \\ \hline 526 \end{array} \qquad \begin{array}{r} 500 \\ + \ 36 \\ \hline 536 \end{array} \qquad \begin{array}{r} 500 \\ + \ 46 \\ \hline 546 \end{array}$$

Look for pairs of numbers that add to 10 or 100.

Add: 5 + 7 + 5 = __?__

$$\begin{array}{r} 5 \\ 7 \\ + \ 5 \\ \hline 17 \end{array}$$

10

10 + 7 = 17

Add: 26 + 70 + 30 = __?__

$$\begin{array}{r} 26 \\ 70 \\ + \ 30 \\ \hline 126 \end{array}$$

100

100 + 26 = 126

Add mentally.

1. 40 + 50

2. 60 + 60

3. 30 + 20

4. 50 + 70

5. 500 + 100

6. 300 + 800

7. 400 + 700

8. 600 + 900

9. 250 + 20

10. 160 + 30

11. 2200 + 600

12. 7400 + 500

Subtract mentally.

13. 90 − 80   **14.** 60 − 10   **15.** 70 − 40   **16.** 80 − 80

17. 600 − 400   **18.** 500 − 300   **19.** 400 − 100   **20.** 900 − 700

21. 470 − 30   **22.** 690 − 80   **23.** 180 − 40   **24.** 320 − 20

25. 2600 − 500   **26.** 9400 − 300   **27.** 5700 − 200   **28.** 3900 − 700

Add or subtract mentally.

29.
$$\begin{array}{r} 267 \\ -\ 10 \\ \hline \end{array} \quad \begin{array}{r} 267 \\ -\ 20 \\ \hline \end{array} \quad \begin{array}{r} 267 \\ -\ 30 \\ \hline \end{array} \quad \begin{array}{r} 267 \\ -\ 40 \\ \hline \end{array} \quad \begin{array}{r} 267 \\ -\ 50 \\ \hline \end{array} \quad \begin{array}{r} 267 \\ -\ 60 \\ \hline \end{array}$$

30.
$$\begin{array}{r} 915 \\ +\ 20 \\ \hline \end{array} \quad \begin{array}{r} 915 \\ +\ 30 \\ \hline \end{array} \quad \begin{array}{r} 915 \\ +\ 40 \\ \hline \end{array} \quad \begin{array}{r} 915 \\ +\ 50 \\ \hline \end{array} \quad \begin{array}{r} 915 \\ +\ 60 \\ \hline \end{array} \quad \begin{array}{r} 915 \\ +\ 70 \\ \hline \end{array}$$

31.
$$\begin{array}{r} 300 \\ +\ 32 \\ \hline \end{array} \quad \begin{array}{r} 300 \\ +\ 42 \\ \hline \end{array} \quad \begin{array}{r} 300 \\ +\ 52 \\ \hline \end{array} \quad \begin{array}{r} 400 \\ +\ 62 \\ \hline \end{array} \quad \begin{array}{r} 400 \\ +\ 72 \\ \hline \end{array} \quad \begin{array}{r} 400 \\ +\ 82 \\ \hline \end{array}$$

Add mentally.

32.
$$\begin{array}{r} 4 \\ 6 \\ +8 \\ \hline \end{array}$$
33.
$$\begin{array}{r} 3 \\ 4 \\ +7 \\ \hline \end{array}$$
34.
$$\begin{array}{r} 5 \\ 2 \\ +8 \\ \hline \end{array}$$
35.
$$\begin{array}{r} 5 \\ 5 \\ +3 \\ \hline \end{array}$$
36.
$$\begin{array}{r} 9 \\ 6 \\ +1 \\ \hline \end{array}$$
37.
$$\begin{array}{r} 6 \\ 6 \\ +4 \\ \hline \end{array}$$

38.
$$\begin{array}{r} 50 \\ 87 \\ +50 \\ \hline \end{array}$$
39.
$$\begin{array}{r} 76 \\ 40 \\ +60 \\ \hline \end{array}$$
40.
$$\begin{array}{r} 20 \\ 53 \\ +80 \\ \hline \end{array}$$
41.
$$\begin{array}{r} 70 \\ 30 \\ +62 \\ \hline \end{array}$$
42.
$$\begin{array}{r} 20 \\ 80 \\ +28 \\ \hline \end{array}$$
43.
$$\begin{array}{r} 10 \\ 97 \\ +90 \\ \hline \end{array}$$

Challenge

Add and subtract mentally. Compute from left to right.

44. 12 − 4 + 2 − 6 + 0 − 4 + 7   **45.** 6 + 3 − 5 + 5 + 6 − 8 − 2

46. 2 + 7 + 8 − 6 − 2 + 1 − 5 + 3   **47.** 11 − 8 − 3 + 5 + 9 − 8 + 6

Adding Numbers without Regrouping

The Artists' Guild held a three-day craft fair. What was the total paid attendance at the fair?

	Paid Attendance
Friday	2110
Saturday	3022
Sunday	1657

First estimate: 2110 + 3022 + 1657

$$
\begin{array}{rcl}
2110 & \longrightarrow & 2000 \\
3022 & \longrightarrow & 3000 \\
+\ 1657 & \longrightarrow & +\ 2000 \\
& \text{about} & 7000
\end{array}
$$

To find the total, add:
2110 + 3022 + 1657 = __?__

Align. Add. Start with the ones.

Add ones.	Add tens.	Add hundreds.	Add thousands.
2110	2110	2110	2110
3022	3022	3022	3022
+ 1657	+ 1657	+ 1657	+ 1657
9	89	789	6789

The total paid attendance was 6789.

6789 is close to 7000. The answer is reasonable.

Study these examples.

$$
\begin{array}{r}
1421 \\
32 \\
+\ 534 \\
\hline
1987
\end{array}
\qquad
\begin{array}{r}
251 \\
+\ 437 \\
\hline
688
\end{array}
\qquad
12 + 40 + 30 + 13 = 95
$$

Estimate. Then find the sum.

1. 42 + 33	**2.** 32 + 25	**3.** 15 + 62	**4.** 53 + 42	**5.** 72 + 26
6. 140 + 57	**7.** 658 + 220	**8.** 128 + 820	**9.** 321 + 66	**10.** 173 + 13
11. 8317 + 1222	**12.** 4375 + 5014	**13.** 6416 + 2103	**14.** 1624 + 255	**15.** 8117 + 782
16. 12 13 + 51	**17.** 124 331 + 533	**18.** 212 260 + 132	**19.** 1141 4013 + 1224	**20.** 2145 4202 + 3031

21. 15 + 22 + 50 + 11

22. 23 + 11 + 34 + 21

23. 464 + 203 + 122

24. 300 + 240 + 159

25. 310 + 146 + 222

26. 104 + 531 + 263

27. 2007 + 1031 + 6640

28. 4116 + 1722 + 2051

29. 5104 + 2681 + 1232

30. 3033 + 2512 + 3251

Solve.

31. Keith used 425 red tiles, 210 blue tiles, and 153 yellow tiles to make a mosaic for the fair. How many tiles did he use in all?

Challenge

Align and add.

32. 316 + 200 + 51 + 1002

33. 3321 + 307 + 20 + 4111

34. 103 + 3101 + 321 + 5040

35. 1012 + 24 + 2000 + 312

36. 7010 + 453 + 12 + 2100

37. 41 + 230 + 2611 + 5014

Subtracting Numbers without Regrouping

Ronda and Maurice are playing
Cosmic Raiders. How many more points
has Ronda scored than Maurice?

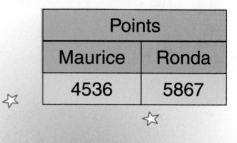

Points	
Maurice	Ronda
4536	5867

First estimate: 5867 − 4536

$$
\begin{array}{r}
5867 \longrightarrow 6000 \\
-\,4536 \longrightarrow -\,5000 \\
\hline
\text{about} \quad 1000
\end{array}
$$

To find how many more points,
subtract: 5867 − 4536 = ?

Align. Subtract. Start with the ones.

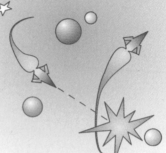

Subtract ones.	Subtract tens.	Subtract hundreds.	Subtract thousands.
$\begin{array}{r} 5867 \\ -4536 \\ \hline 1 \end{array}$	$\begin{array}{r} 5867 \\ -4536 \\ \hline 31 \end{array}$	$\begin{array}{r} 5867 \\ -4536 \\ \hline 331 \end{array}$	$\begin{array}{r} 5867 \\ -4536 \\ \hline 1331 \end{array}$

Check by adding.

$$
\begin{array}{r}
5867 \\
-4536 \\
\hline
1331
\end{array}
\qquad
\begin{array}{r}
1331 \\
+4536 \\
\hline
5867
\end{array}
$$

1331 is close to 1000.
The answer is reasonable.

Ronda has scored 1331 more points than Maurice.

Study these examples.

$$
\begin{array}{r} 94 \\ -54 \\ \hline 40 \end{array}
\qquad
\begin{array}{r} 347 \\ -210 \\ \hline 137 \end{array}
\qquad
\begin{array}{r} 689 \\ -632 \\ \hline 57 \end{array}
\qquad
\begin{array}{r} 2475 \\ -321 \\ \hline 2154 \end{array}
$$

Estimate. Then find the difference.

1. 53 − 21	**2.** 85 − 23	**3.** 26 − 12	**4.** 74 − 11	**5.** 46 − 25
6. 279 − 151	**7.** 657 − 242	**8.** 878 − 843	**9.** 793 − 243	**10.** 886 − 475
11. 5986 − 5082	**12.** 9929 − 7806	**13.** 6495 − 3122	**14.** 4819 − 2107	**15.** 8576 − 1423
16. 167 − 35	**17.** 581 − 21	**18.** 724 − 12	**19.** 398 − 75	**20.** 465 − 23
21. 6837 − 434	**22.** 7389 − 176	**23.** 5677 − 307	**24.** 4985 − 562	**25.** 9688 − 647

Subtract.

26. 67 − 5   **27.** 175 − 25   **28.** 438 − 16

29. 655 − 33   **30.** 4766 − 541   **31.** 9584 − 283

32. 8675 − 613   **33.** 3987 − 26   **34.** 4796 − 96

Solve.

35. Nina has 675 points. Tran has 989 points. By how many points is Nina behind Tran?

36. Yoki scored 3788 points in two games. She scored 2174 points in the 2nd game. How many points did she score in the 1st game?

 **Finding Together**

Find the difference.

37. 46,875 − 22,831   **38.** 198,747 − 4506

3-9 Adding and Subtracting Money

Suppose you bought a racquet and a pair of tennis shoes. How much money would you spend in all? How much more would you pay for the racquet than the shoes?

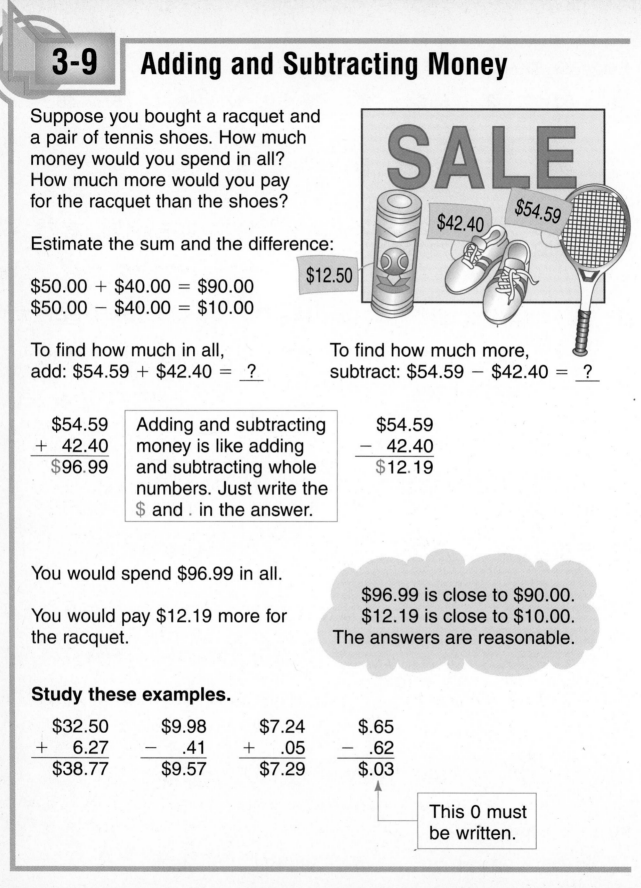

Estimate the sum and the difference:

$50.00 + $40.00 = $90.00
$50.00 − $40.00 = $10.00

To find how much in all, add: $54.59 + $42.40 = ?

To find how much more, subtract: $54.59 − $42.40 = ?

$54.59
+ 42.40
$96.99

Adding and subtracting money is like adding and subtracting whole numbers. Just write the $ and . in the answer.

$54.59
− 42.40
$12.19

You would spend $96.99 in all.

You would pay $12.19 more for the racquet.

$96.99 is close to $90.00.
$12.19 is close to $10.00.
The answers are reasonable.

Study these examples.

$32.50
+ 6.27
$38.77

$9.98
− .41
$9.57

$7.24
+ .05
$7.29

$.65
− .62
$.03

This 0 must be written.

Estimate. Then add.

1. $.18
  + .20

2. $.24
  + .34

3. $.50
  + .38

4. $.51
  + .25

5. $7.23
  + 2.55

6. $4.21
  + 1.75

7. $2.22
  + 6.37

8. $17.26
  + 12.73

9. $50.62
  + 24.15

10. $71.40
  + 26.48

11. $9.13
  + .82

12. $8.52
  + .35

13. $43.77
  + 6.02

14. $50.33
  + 8.24

15. $67.91
  + .08

16. $32.13 + $4.75

17. $5.23 + $.06

18. $24.08 + $1.91

Estimate. Then subtract.

19. $.84
  − .62

20. $.66
  − .44

21. $.39
  − .19

22. $8.95
  − 4.51

23. $7.55
  − 2.10

24. $4.67
  − 2.64

25. $3.95
  − 1.85

26. $78.89
  − 74.13

27. $56.39
  − 15.25

28. $99.98
  − 67.50

29. $6.26
  − .24

30. $9.58
  − .46

31. $29.99
  − 8.75

32. $75.83
  − 4.40

33. $86.37
  − .05

34. $49.86 − $7.21

35. $2.86 − $.05

36. $57.92 − $.32

Solve.

37. Lauren had $15.95. She bought a pedometer for $4.75. How much money did she have left?

38. Ana bought a bike helmet for $32.25 and elbow pads for $15.60. How much did she spend in all?

READ/DATA Commands

A **computer program** is a set of commands written in a computer language that tells the computer what to do. Line numbers are used in programs to tell the computer the order in which to process the commands.

▶ The program below shows different ways the PRINT command can be used.

PROGRAM	OUTPUT
10 PRINT "10 + 10 = "	10 + 10 =
20 PRINT 10 + 10	20
30 PRINT "10 + 10 = " 10 + 10	10 + 10 = 20
40 END	

> Remember: Use a PRINT command *with* quotation marks to display exact information.
> Use a PRINT command *without* quotation marks to display an answer.

▶ The program below introduces the REM, READ, and DATA commands.

A remark statement. It explains what the program does. This statement is not processed.

10 REM This program finds the sum of three numbers.

20 READ A, B, C ◀—— Reads information stored in a DATA statement and assigns it to a letter.

30 PRINT A+B+C

40 GOTO 20

50 DATA 123, 45, 210, 90, 108, 310 ◀—— Stores information used by the program.

60 END

Output: 378
        508
        Out of DATA in 20

The program will run until all the information in the DATA statement is used.

Write the output for each program.

1. 10 READ A,B
   20 PRINT "A+B= " A+B
   30 GOTO 10
   40 DATA 453, 187
   50 END

2. 10 READ A,B
   20 PRINT "A−B= " A−B
   30 GOTO 10
   40 DATA 605, 232
   50 END

3. 10 READ A,B,C
   20 PRINT "A+B+C= " A+B+C
   30 GOTO 10
   40 DATA 48, 25, 100, 32, 51, 49
   50 END

4. 10 READ A,B
   20 PRINT "A−B= " A−B
   30 GOTO 10
   40 DATA 99, 20, 185, 49
   50 END

Solve.

5. Complete the program below so that it will find the sum of 327 and 194 and of 809 and 36. What will be the output?

   50 DATA _?_ , _?_ , _?_ , _?_
   30 PRINT _?_ + _?_
   10 _?_ This program finds the sum of two numbers.
   60 END
   20 _?_ A,B
   40 GOTO 20

6. Write a program to find the distance around the rectangle at the right. Include REM, READ, and DATA commands. What is the distance?

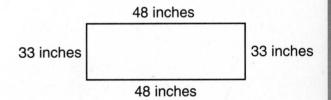

48 inches

33 inches   33 inches

48 inches

7. Write a program that will find the sum of all the even numbers from 0 to 10. Include REM, READ, and DATA commands. What is the sum?

8. Write a program that will find the sum, difference, product, and quotient of 256 and 8. Include REM, READ, and DATA commands. What is the output?

3-11 | Problem Solving: Logical Reasoning

Problem: Lee, Hoshi, and Yori have their hats and scarves mixed up. Each boy puts on another boy's cap and a different boy's scarf. Hoshi wears Yori's cap. Whose cap and scarf does each boy wear?

1 IMAGINE   Create a mental picture.

2 NAME   *Facts:*   Hoshi wears Yori's cap.
Each wears another boy's cap and a different boy's scarf.

Question: Whose cap and scarf is each boy wearing?

3 THINK   Draw and label a table.
Fill in the facts you know.
Consider the possible answers.

	Lee	Hoshi	Yori
cap	Hoshi's	Yori's	Lee's
scarf	Yori's	Lee's	Hoshi's

4 COMPUTE   Hoshi wears Yori's cap, so he must wear Lee's scarf.

Lee didn't wear his own cap, so he must wear Hoshi's cap and Yori's scarf.

That means that Yori wears Lee's cap and Hoshi's scarf.

5 CHECK   Are the answers reasonable?
Is each boy wearing another boy's cap and a different boy's scarf?   Yes.

Solve.

1. Mimi, Pedro, and Martin live in three houses in a row on Mountain Lane. Mimi does not live next to Pedro. Pedro lives on a corner. Who lives in the middle house?

Mountain Lane

IMAGINE	Create a mental picture.
NAME	*Facts:* Mimi, Pedro, and Martin live on Mountain Lane. Mimi does not live next to Pedro. Pedro lives on a corner.
	Question: Who lives in the middle house?
THINK	Pedro cannot live in the middle house.

COMPUTE ⟶ CHECK

2. What number would you move from one box to another to make the sums in each box equal?

1	2	3

4	5	6

7	8	9

3. Van has six coins that are worth 57¢ in all. Only one coin is a quarter. What are the other coins?

4. Rudy was born in the month whose name has the most letters. The date is an even 2-digit number. The sum of the digits is 5. What is Rudy's birthday?

5. Mary, Anne, and Rose spent $43.51, $47.46, and $50.44. Rose spent the least and did not buy a blazer. Anne's skirt did not cost the most. How much money did each girl spend? Who bought a sweater?

Make Up Your Own

6. Write a problem modeled on problem 3 above. Have a classmate solve it.

Solve.

1. Deirdre needs 14 yards of white fabric to make costumes for the play. She has 3 yards. How many yards does she have to buy?

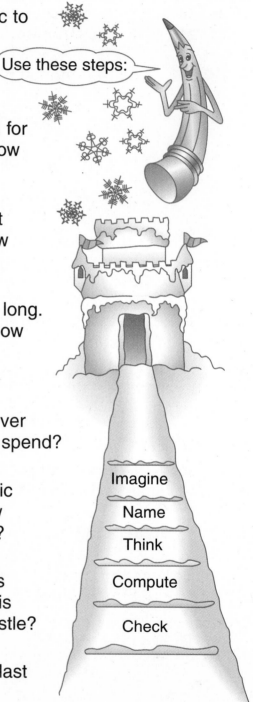

Use these steps:

2. Glenn brought home 50 tickets to sell for the school play. He sold 20 tickets. How many does he have left to sell?

3. The theater has 100 seats on the first level and 55 seats in the balcony. How many seats does the theater have?

4. The first act of the play is 69 minutes long. The second act is 54 minutes long. How much longer is the first act?

5. Gini plays the ice queen. She buys a plastic crown for $ 5.80 and a jar of silver glitter for $ 1.10. How much does she spend?

6. The director bought 12 boxes of plastic snowflakes and has 7 boxes left. How many boxes have been used already?

Imagine

Name

Think

7. Bill paints the ice castle door, which is 72 inches high. The top of the castle is 84 inches taller. How tall is the ice castle?

Compute

Check

8. There are 58 penguin puppets in the last scene of the play. Ida has finished making 42 of them. How many does she still have to make?

Solve.

9. The two-act play is 84 pages long. The first act is 43 pages long. How long is the second act?

10. The play was performed on Thursday, Friday, and Saturday. Ben, Sue, and Dana went on different nights. Sue went after Dana. Ben missed the first night, so he went the next night. When did Sue and Dana see the play?

11. The cast received 3 curtain calls Thursday and double that on Friday. Saturday had 2 more than Thursday. What is the total number of curtain calls the cast received?

12. There were 142 people in the audience on Thursday night. Forty of them were adults. How many were children?

13. There are 3 bears and 2 penguins in the animal dance line. In how many different ways can the animals be arranged?

14. Jake, Kyle, and Lou play the jester, the king, and the leopard. No one plays a part that begins with the same letter as his name. Kyle decided not to play the jester. Who plays the king?

Use the sign for problems 15 and 16.

15. Mr. Mendez bought tickets for 2 adults and 2 children. How much more than ten dollars did he spend?

16. Ms. Shapiro spent $14.50 on tickets. What tickets did she buy?

USE THESE STRATEGIES:
Logical Reasoning
Choose the Operation
Make a Table or List
Guess and Test

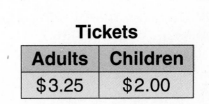

Tickets

Adults	Children
$3.25	$2.00

More Practice

Find the sum.

1. 7 2 +4	**2.** 6 5 +4	**3.** 9 0 +7	**4.** 8 6 +2	**5.** 9 4 +4	**6.** 7 9 +3

7. 10 37 +52	**8.** 153 412 +323	**9.** 205 381 +413	**10.** 3050 1738 + 211	**11.** $23.74 1.12 + .13

Find the difference.

12. 8 −0	**13.** 56 −16	**14.** 549 −427	**15.** 798 − 55	**16.** $94.36 − 40.13

Estimate.

17. 42 +38	**18.** $5.49 + .23	**19.** 85 −23	**20.** 568 −399	**21.** $8.39 − .21

Find the missing number.

22. $3 + \underline{} = 11$ **23.** $\underline{} + 7 = 15$ **24.** $7 = \underline{} + 0$

25. $12 - \underline{} = 7$ **26.** $\underline{} - 9 = 8$ **27.** $9 - \underline{} = 0$

Solve.

28. The Madison Arts and Crafts Fair had 33 art exhibits and 49 craft exhibits. About how many exhibits were at the Arts and Crafts Fair?

29. Does $5 + (7 + 9) + 8$ equal $(8 + 9) + (7 + 5)$?

92

(See *Still More Practice*, p. 462.)

THE ABACUS

The ancient Greeks and Romans used an **abacus** to make computations. The abacus is still used today in Asian cultures.

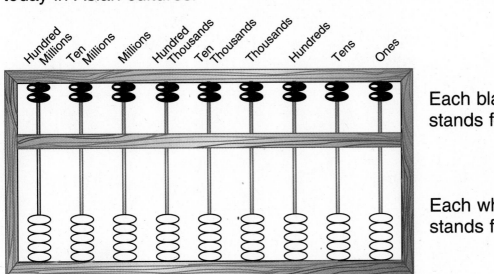

Each black bead stands for 5 units.

Each white bead stands for 1 unit.

A number is shown by moving the appropriate beads to the crossbar.

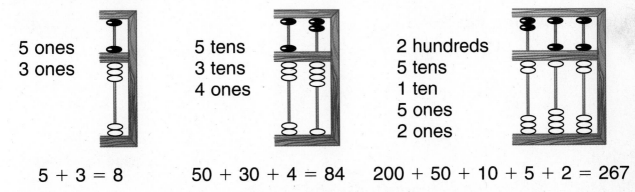

5 ones
3 ones

5 tens
3 tens
4 ones

2 hundreds
5 tens
1 ten
5 ones
2 ones

$5 + 3 = 8$ $50 + 30 + 4 = 84$ $200 + 50 + 10 + 5 + 2 = 267$

Make your own abacus. Use buttons, beads, or counters.

Show each number on your abacus.

1. 39   **2.** 326   **3.** 26   **4.** 681   **5.** 78   **6.** 589

Check Your Mastery

Add.

See pp. 68–71, 78–81, 84–85

1.
```
  8
  5
+ 9
```

2.
```
  7
  2
+ 3
```

3.
```
  4
  0
+ 8
```

4.
```
  5
  6
+ 3
```

5.
```
  5
  8
+ 5
```

6.
```
  7
  6
+ 1
```

7.
```
  15
  20
+ 44
```

8.
```
  172
  205
+  22
```

9.
```
  1583
   112
+  204
```

10.
```
  $42.63
    5.12
+    .14
```

Subtract.

See pp. 72–73, 82–85

11.
```
  98
- 38
```

12.
```
  846
- 230
```

13.
```
  497
-  43
```

14.
```
  $24.98
-    3.05
```

Estimate.

See pp. 76–77

15.
```
  275
+  13
```

16.
```
  $5.02
+  3.69
```

17.
```
  473
- 109
```

18.
```
  $6.89
-    .49
```

Find the missing number.

See pp. 74–75

19. $5 + \underline{\ ?\ } = 13$

20. $\underline{\ ?\ } + 3 = 12$

21. $8 = \underline{\ ?\ } + 8$

22. $7 - \underline{\ ?\ } = 0$

23. $\underline{\ ?\ } - 4 = 6$

24. $6 = 15 - \underline{\ ?\ }$

Solve.

See pp. 90–91

25. Maria went to the grocery store. She bought items that cost $3.59, $1.39, $.30, and $4.15. Did Maria pay more than $10 for the items? Estimate to find the answer.

26. Joseph picked 264 apples and 613 pears. How many pieces of fruit did he pick in all?

In this chapter you will:
  Estimate and then add or subtract
  up to 5-digit numbers with regrouping
  Add three or more addends
  Solve problems by eliminating
  extra information

Do you remember?

687	Minuend
− 342	Subtrahend
345	Difference

Critical Thinking/Finding Together
Suppose there were double the number
of white cars. Would this be more
or less than triple the number of
black cars?

Front-End Estimation

Students in the Hilldale elementary schools held a Read-a-Thon in October. About how many books did they read altogether?

To find about how many, estimate: 2534 + 2496 + 3875

School	Books Read
Central	2534
North	2496
South	3875

▶ **Add the front digits.**

```
  2534
  2496
+ 3875
─────
     7
```

Write 0s for the other digits.

```
  2534
  2496
+ 3875
─────
about 7000
```

Rough estimate: 7000

▶ To get a closer estimate, make groups of about 1000 from the other digits.

2<u>534</u> + 2<u>496</u> + 3<u>875</u>

about 1000   about 1000

Think: 7000 + 1000 + 1000 = 9000

Adjusted estimate: 9000

Altogether, the students read about 9000 books.

Study these examples.

```
$5.26
 1.52 ⟩ about $1
 3.78 ⟩ about $1
+2.45
about $11.00
```

$11 + $1 + $1 = $13
Rough estimate: $11
Adjusted estimate: $13

```
 738
 223 ⟩ about 100
+569
about 1400
```

1400 + 100 = 1500
Rough estimate: 1400
Adjusted estimate: 1500

Make a rough estimate. Then adjust.

1. 212 672 + 827	**2.** 358 143 + 796	**3.** 588 419 + 622	**4.** $3.47 1.30 + 9.65	**5.** $6.98 4.25 + 6.10

6. 3235   **7.** 9139   **8.** 5405   **9.** $67.99   **10.** $78.65
    5871   2584   1679   73.46   18.98
   + 1886   + 4475   + 2961   + 36.49   + 21.49

11. 635 + 198 + 474 + 360   **12.** $5.32 + $7.12 + $3.69 + $1.95

13. 283 + 722 + 542 + 156   **14.** $6.58 + $1.40 + $2.56 + $4.61

Solve. Use the table on page 96.

15. Hilldale Middle School students read 4073 books. About how many books did all the students read?

Estimating Differences

To estimate differences using front-end estimation:

- Subtract the front digits.
- Write 0s for the other digits.

| $73.45
 − 26.50 <br> about $50.00 | 5736
 − 1775 <br> about 4000 | $8.21
 − 7.35 <br> about $1.00 | 963
 − 315 <br> about 600 |

Estimate the difference. Use front-end estimation.

16. 646 − 519	**17.** 441 − 193	**18.** 938 − 256	**19.** $8.98 − 3.50	**20.** $2.56 − 1.48

21. 7149 − 3861	**22.** 5460 − 1509	**23.** 8432 − 5954	**24.** $49.90 − 24.95	**25.** $37.21 − 18.88

Adding with Regrouping

What was the total membership of the
U.S. House of Representatives in 1987?

To find the total,
add: 258 + 177 = __?__

1987 U.S. House of Representatives	
Democrats	Republicans
258	177

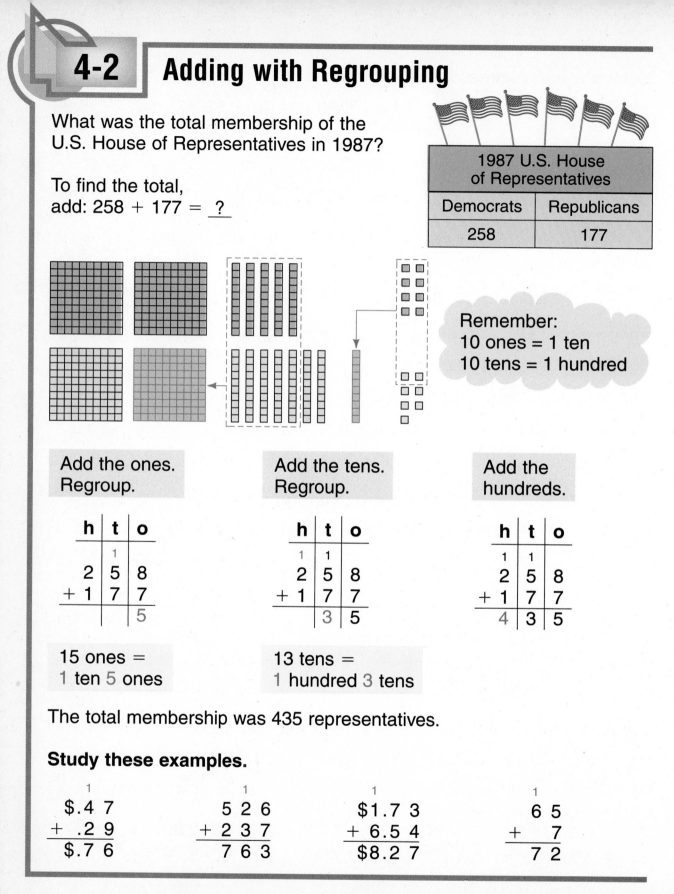

Remember:
10 ones = 1 ten
10 tens = 1 hundred

Add the ones. Regroup.	Add the tens. Regroup.	Add the hundreds.

h	t	o
	1	
2	5	8
+ 1	7	7
		5

h	t	o
1	1	
2	5	8
+ 1	7	7
	3	5

h	t	o
1	1	
2	5	8
+ 1	7	7
4	3	5

15 ones =
1 ten 5 ones

13 tens =
1 hundred 3 tens

The total membership was 435 representatives.

Study these examples.

```
    1              1                1                 1
  $.4 7          5 2 6           $1.7 3             6 5
+  .2 9        + 2 3 7          + 6.5 4           +   7
  $.7 6          7 6 3           $8.2 7             7 2
```

Estimate. Then add.

1. 48
+ 46

2. 37
+ 16

3. 58
+ 22

4. 85
+ 8

5. 73
+ 9

6. 329
+ 543

7. 480
+ 253

8. 675
+ 162

9. 781
+ 47

10. 909
+ 64

11. 168
+ 743

12. 643
+ 259

13. 345
+ 469

14. 877
+ 95

15. 768
+ 99

16. $.78
+ .06

17. $.46
+ .28

18. $1.75
+ 3.61

19. $5.28
+ 2.49

20. $4.65
+ 4.99

21. 75 + 18

22. 389 + 276

23. 581 + 229

24. $.19 + $.66

25. $6.19 + $2.32

26. $3.97 + $4.33

Solve.

27. There were 156 Democrats and 137 Republicans in the U.S. House of Representatives in 1878. How many members of the House were there?

28. In 1925 the U.S. Congress was made up of 435 Representatives and 96 Senators. How many members of Congress were there in 1925?

Challenge

29. Find two 3-digit addends with the same digits in each number whose sum is 404.

30. What are the largest and the smallest possible addends of two 3-digit numbers whose sum is 555? 999?

4-3 Four-Digit Addition

How many votes were cast in the School Board election?

To find how many votes, add: 1279 + 2355 = ?

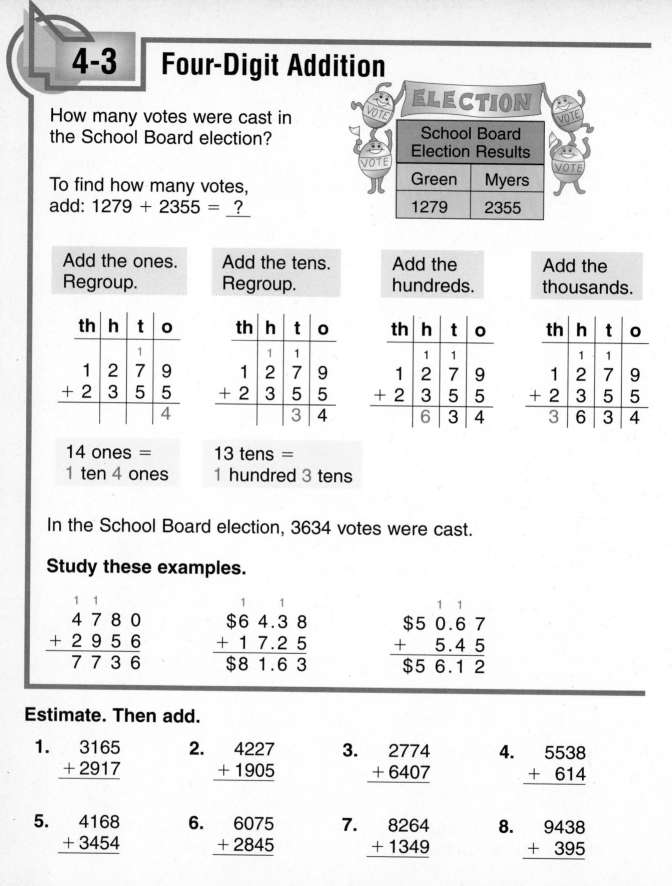

ELECTION

School Board Election Results	
Green	Myers
1279	2355

Add the ones. Regroup.	Add the tens. Regroup.	Add the hundreds.	Add the thousands.

Add the ones. Regroup.

th	h	t	o
		1	
1	2	7	9
+ 2	3	5	5
			4

14 ones =
1 ten 4 ones

Add the tens. Regroup.

th	h	t	o
	1	1	
1	2	7	9
+ 2	3	5	5
		3	4

13 tens =
1 hundred 3 tens

Add the hundreds.

th	h	t	o
	1	1	
1	2	7	9
+ 2	3	5	5
	6	3	4

Add the thousands.

th	h	t	o
	1	1	
1	2	7	9
+ 2	3	5	5
3	6	3	4

In the School Board election, 3634 votes were cast.

Study these examples.

```
   1 1
   4 7 8 0
 + 2 9 5 6
   7 7 3 6
```

```
   1     1
 $6 4.3 8
 + 1 7.2 5
 $8 1.6 3
```

```
      1 1
 $5 0.6 7
 +    5.4 5
 $5 6.1 2
```

Estimate. Then add.

1. 3165
   + 2917

2. 4227
   + 1905

3. 2774
   + 6407

4. 5538
   + 614

5. 4168
   + 3454

6. 6075
   + 2845

7. 8264
   + 1349

8. 9438
   + 395

Find the sum.

9.	3670 + 3458	**10.**	5891 + 2768	**11.**	6655 + 1563	**12.**	8492 + 945
13.	5329 + 1398	**14.**	4921 + 3486	**15.**	6482 + 1843	**16.**	7560 + 488
17.	$34.27 + 46.17	**18.**	$65.05 + 13.98	**19.**	$87.98 + 10.75	**20.**	$51.75 + 9.15

Align and add.

21. 6414 + 979   **22.** 495 + 1272   **23.** 8067 + 86

24. $28.95 + $56.60   **25.** $69.75 + $8.94

26. $4.35 + $24.89   **27.** $6.08 + $44.56

Solve.

28. Ms. Davis and Mr. Brown ran for mayor of Newton. Ms. Davis received 2365 votes and Mr. Brown received 4915 votes. How many people voted in the election?

29. A campaign worker spent $23.96 on phone calls and $57.32 for posters. How much did she spend?

30. Three people ran for town manager. Mr. Miller received 4286 votes. Mr. Rush received 3907 votes. Ms. Adams received 7454 votes. Did Mr. Miller and Mr. Rush together receive more or fewer votes than Ms. Adams?

31. Mr. Jones received 2487 votes for sheriff. Mr. Long received double that number. How many votes did Mr. Long receive?

Three- and Four-Digit Addition

The Botanical Gardens held a two-day open house. What was the total attendance at the open house?

Attendance	
Saturday	7465
Sunday	6592

To find the total, add: 7465 + 6592 = __?__

Add the ones.

```
  7 4 6 5
+ 6 5 9 2
        7
```

**Add the tens.
Regroup.**

```
    1
  7 4 6 5
+ 6 5 9 2
      5 7
```

15 tens =
1 hundred 5 tens

**Add the hundreds.
Regroup.**

```
  1 1
  7 4 6 5
+ 6 5 9 2
    0 5 7
```

10 hundreds =
1 thousand 0 hundreds

Add the thousands.

```
      1 1
    7 4 6 5
+   6 5 9 2
  1 4,0 5 7
```

The total attendance was 14,057.

Add.

1.
```
    1 1
  $  8.79
+    4.46
  $13.25
```

2.
```
  $6.39
+ 6.21
```

3.
```
  $41.75
+ 54.50
```

4.
```
  $65.49
+ 82.90
```

Estimate. Then find the sum.

5. 951
  + 735

6. 694
  + 508

7. 873
  + 456

8. 298
  + 769

9. 3742
  + 8616

10. 5390
  + 6475

11. 2615
  + 9218

12. 1979
  + 8360

13. $6.75
  + 4.37

14. $5.92
  + 7.35

15. $2.36
  + 8.84

16. $9.06
  + 4.85

17. $47.29
  + 72.36

18. $20.82
  + 91.33

19. $38.91
  + 64.07

20. $57.35
  + 52.72

Align and add.

21. 742 + 381

22. 397 + 721

23. 876 + 950

24. 6344 + 5812

25. 1423 + 9182

26. 7227 + 5090

27. $2.89 + $7.56

28. $8.25 + $6.96

29. $98.99 + $9.62

Solve.

30. Visitors to the Botanical Gardens bought 8429 flowering plants and 4872 vegetable plants. How many plants did they buy?

Skills to Remember

Add.

31. 4
  6
  7
  + 2

32. 3
  9
  3
  + 4

33. 8
  2
  4
  + 4

34. 9
  0
  1
  + 6

35. 5
  4
  3
  + 4

36. 9
  7
  4
  + 8

Three or More Addends

Ms. Pei drove from Chicago to Kansas City. Then she drove to Indianapolis and Pittsburgh before returning to Chicago. How many miles did she travel?

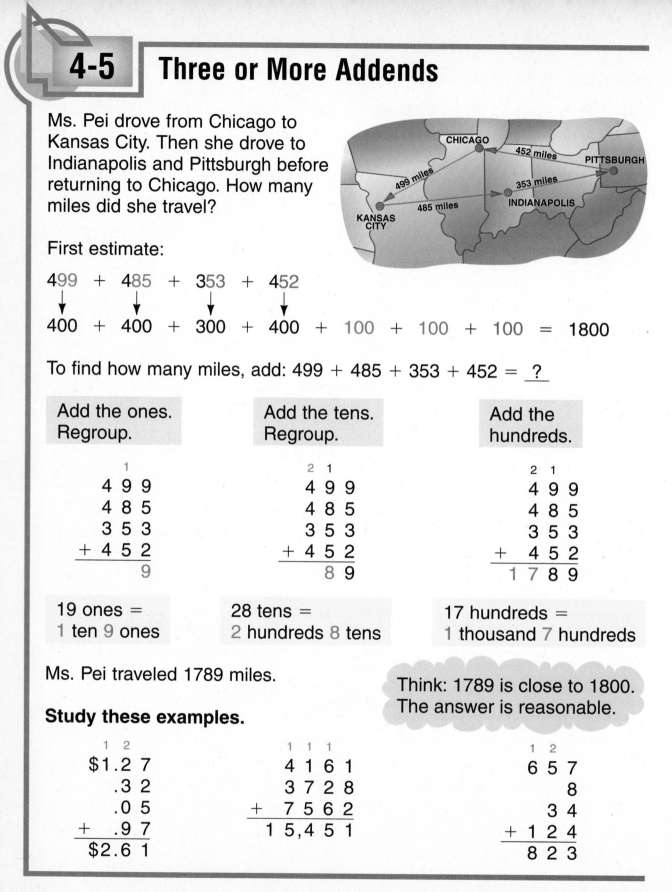

First estimate:

499 + 485 + 353 + 452

↓   ↓   ↓   ↓

400 + 400 + 300 + 400 + 100 + 100 + 100 = 1800

To find how many miles, add: 499 + 485 + 353 + 452 = __?__

Add the ones. Regroup.	Add the tens. Regroup.	Add the hundreds.
¹ 4 9 9 4 8 5 3 5 3 + 4 5 2 —— 9	² ¹ 4 9 9 4 8 5 3 5 3 + 4 5 2 —— 8 9	² ¹ 4 9 9 4 8 5 3 5 3 + 4 5 2 —— 1 7 8 9
19 ones = 1 ten 9 ones	28 tens = 2 hundreds 8 tens	17 hundreds = 1 thousand 7 hundreds

Ms. Pei traveled 1789 miles.

Think: 1789 is close to 1800. The answer is reasonable.

Study these examples.

```
  1 2
$1.2 7
  .3 2
  .0 5
+ .9 7
———————
$2.6 1
```

```
  1 1 1
  4 1 6 1
  3 7 2 8
+ 7 5 6 2
—————————
1 5,4 5 1
```

```
   1 2
   6 5 7
       8
      3 4
+  1 2 4
—————————
   8 2 3
```

Estimate. Then find the sum.

1.	2.	3.	4.	5.
27	15	93	$.33	$.84
34	70	9	.12	.07
61	46	56	.68	.55
+ 58	+ 22	+ 82	+ .71	+ .06

6.	7.	8.	9.	10.
247	539	316	$7.32	$5.51
191	293	875	5.17	.99
322	612	26	1.97	6.37
+ 423	+ 109	+ 6	+ 3.28	+ .03

11.	12.	13.	14.
3219	9002	5806	$41.55
8604	2756	275	97.60
+ 6154	+ 4321	+ 1888	+ 3.28

Align and add.

15. 63 + 147 + 735 + 8

16. 2905 + 324 + 55

17. $.51 + $2.76 + $4.29 + $.77

18. $4.26 + $22.79 + $56.07

Solve.

19. One week, Mr. Mills made several business trips of 16 miles, 29 miles, 9 miles, and 42 miles. How many miles did he travel?

20. Ms. Sims spent $13.48, $19.76, and $9.88 on gasoline last month. How much money did she spend on gasoline?

Critical Thinking

Three of the four addends have a sum of 1000.
Write the addend that does *not* belong.

21. 421, 391, 198, 381

22. 510, 237, 253, 233

23. 173, 125, 225, 602

24. 345, 352, 303, 355

Subtracting with Regrouping

How much taller is the
Allied Bank Plaza than
One Houston Center?

First estimate:
$900 - 600 = 300$

To find how much taller,
subtract: $992 - 678 = $?

Height of Tall Buildings in Houston, Texas	
Texas Commerce Tower	1002 feet
Allied Bank Plaza	992 feet
InterFirst Plaza	744 feet
One Houston Center	678 feet

See if there are
enough ones
to subtract.

```
  h | t | o
  9 | 9 | 2
- 6 | 7 | 8
```

More ones are needed.
Regroup the tens to
get more ones.

92 = 9 tens 2 ones
   = 8 tens 12 ones

Subtract the ones.

```
  h |  t  |  o
    |  8  | 12
  9 |  9̸  |  2̸
- 6 |  7  |  8
    |     |  4
```

Subtract the tens.

```
  h |  t  |  o
    |  8  | 12
  9 |  9̸  |  2̸
- 6 |  7  |  8
    |  1  |  4
```

Subtract the hundreds.

```
  h |  t  |  o
    |  8  | 12
  9 |  9̸  |  2̸
- 6 |  7  |  8
  3 |  1  |  4
```

Check by adding.

```
      1
    3 1 4
  + 6 7 8
    9 9 2
```

The Allied Bank Plaza is 314 feet taller.

Think: 314 is close to 300.
The answer is reasonable.

Study these examples.

```
  6 14
  7̸ 4̸
- 4 6
  2 8
```

```
  7 13
 $8.3̸ 8
- 7.9 5
 $ .4 3
```

```
  5 11
  6̸ 1̸ 2
-    9 1
  5 2 1
```

Estimate. Then find the difference.

1.	2.	3.	4.	5.
82 − 17	60 − 34	72 − 25	$.94 − .58	$.43 − .29

6.	7.	8.	9.	10.
572 − 143	720 − 418	886 − 249	$3.61 − 2.25	$6.84 − 4.19

11.	12.	13.	14.	15.
927 − 692	435 − 172	228 − 147	$5.43 − 2.83	$9.69 − 5.90

16.	17.	18.	19.	20.
23 − 9	132 − 28	429 − 75	$.52 − .06	$2.75 − .08

Align and subtract.

21. 75 − 9   **22.** 32 − 8   **23.** 480 − 36

24. $6.21 − $.16   **25.** $8.19 − $.54   **26.** $5.33 − $.07

Solve. Use the table on page 106.

27. How much shorter is the InterFirst Plaza than the Allied Bank Plaza?

28. How much taller is the InterFirst Plaza than One Houston Center?

29. The Texas Commerce Tower has 75 stories. One Houston Center has 47 stories. How many more stories does the Texas Commerce Tower have?

30. The Wells Fargo Tower in Los Angeles is 750 feet tall. Is it taller or shorter than the InterFirst Plaza? How much taller or shorter?

4-7 Subtraction: Regrouping Twice

How many more home runs did Babe Ruth hit than Frank Robinson?

To find how many more, subtract:
714 − 586 = ?

All-Time Home Run Leaders			
H. Aaron	755	H. Killebrew	573
B. Ruth	714	R. Jackson	563
W. Mays	660	M. Schmidt	548
F. Robinson	586	M. Mantle	536

More ones are needed. Regroup. Subtract ones.	More tens are needed. Regroup. Subtract tens.	Subtract hundreds.
$$\begin{array}{r} {}^{0}\;{}^{14} \\ 7\,\cancel{1}\,\cancel{4} \\ -\;5\,8\,6 \\ \hline 8 \end{array}$$	$$\begin{array}{r} {}^{10} \\ 6\;\cancel{0}\;{}^{14} \\ \cancel{7}\,\cancel{1}\,\cancel{4} \\ -\;5\,8\,6 \\ \hline 2\,8 \end{array}$$	$$\begin{array}{r} {}^{10} \\ 6\;\cancel{0}\;{}^{14} \\ \cancel{7}\,\cancel{1}\,\cancel{4} \\ -\;5\,8\,6 \\ \hline 1\,2\,8 \end{array}$$
1 ten 4 ones = 0 tens 14 ones	7 hundreds 0 tens = 6 hundreds 10 tens	Check.

Babe Ruth hit 128 more home runs than Frank Robinson.

$$\begin{array}{r} {}^{1}\;{}^{1} \\ 1\,2\,8 \\ +\;5\,8\,6 \\ \hline 7\,1\,4 \end{array}$$

Study these examples.

$$\begin{array}{r} {}^{12} \\ 7\;\cancel{2}\;{}^{11} \\ \$8.3\,\cancel{1} \\ -\;7.8\,4 \\ \hline \$\;.4\,7 \end{array}$$

$$\begin{array}{r} {}^{11} \\ 3\;\cancel{1}\;{}^{16} \\ \cancel{4}\,\cancel{2}\,\cancel{6} \\ -\;\;\;8\,9 \\ \hline 3\,3\,7 \end{array}$$

Estimate. Then subtract.

1. 624 − 137

2. 930 − 452

3. 846 − 669

4. 561 − 265

5. 734 − 587

Find the difference.

6.	452 − 378	**7.**	360 − 185	**8.**	922 − 734	**9.**	712 − 499	**10.**	653 − 578
11.	835 − 79	**12.**	561 − 94	**13.**	454 − 65	**14.**	946 − 58	**15.**	137 − 48
16.	$3.25 − 1.58	**17.**	$5.37 − 2.49	**18.**	$8.64 − 4.87	**19.**	$9.52 − .99

Align and subtract.

20. 456 − 179   **21.** 837 − 488   **22.** 671 − 95

23. $9.36 − $7.59   **24.** $2.91 − $1.97   **25.** $5.42 − $.67

Solve. Use the table on page 108.

26. How many more home runs did Henry Aaron hit than Frank Robinson?

27. How many fewer home runs did Harmon Killebrew hit than Willie Mays?

28. Did Babe Ruth and Reggie Jackson combined hit more or fewer home runs than Henry Aaron and Mickey Mantle combined? How many more or fewer?

29. Which is the greater difference: between the number of home runs hit by Willie Mays and Mike Schmidt or between the number of home runs hit by Henry Aaron and Willie Mays?

30. Babe Ruth, Mickey Mantle, and Reggie Jackson all played for the New York Yankees. What was their combined home run total?

Three- and Four-Digit Subtraction

The Mississippi is the longest river in the United States. How much longer than the Colorado River is it?

U.S. Rivers Length in Miles			
Colorado	862	Mississippi	2348
Porcupine	569	Missouri	2315
Rio Grande	1760	Tennessee	652

To find how much longer, subtract: 2348 − 862

Subtract the ones.	More tens are needed. Regroup. Subtract.	More hundreds are needed. Regroup. Subtract.

$$
\begin{array}{r} 2\ 3\ 4\ 8 \\ -\ \ \ 8\ 6\ 2 \\ \hline 6 \end{array}
$$

$$
\begin{array}{r} {}^{2\ 14} \\ 2\ \cancel{3}\ \cancel{4}\ 8 \\ -\ \ \ 8\ 6\ 2 \\ \hline 8\ 6 \end{array}
$$

$$
\begin{array}{r} {}^{12} \\ {}^{1\ \cancel{2}\ 14} \\ \cancel{2}\ \cancel{3}\ \cancel{4}\ 8 \\ -\ \ \ 8\ 6\ 2 \\ \hline 4\ 8\ 6 \end{array}
$$

	3 hundreds 4 tens = 2 hundreds 14 tens	2 thousands 2 hundreds = 1 thousand 12 hundreds

Subtract the thousands.	Check.

$$
\begin{array}{r} {}^{12} \\ {}^{1\ \cancel{2}\ 14} \\ \cancel{2}\ \cancel{3}\ \cancel{4}\ 8 \\ -\ \ \ 8\ 6\ 2 \\ \hline 1\ 4\ 8\ 6 \end{array}
$$

$$
\begin{array}{r} {}^{1\ \ 1} \\ 1\ 4\ 8\ 6 \\ +\ \ \ 8\ 6\ 2 \\ \hline 2\ 3\ 4\ 8 \end{array}
$$

The Mississippi is 1486 miles longer than the Colorado River.

Study these examples.

$$
\begin{array}{r} {}^{13} \\ {}^{5\ \cancel{6}\ 10} \\ 7\ \cancel{6}\ \cancel{4}\ \cancel{0} \\ -\ 4\ 1\ 9\ 5 \\ \hline 3\ 4\ 4\ 5 \end{array}
$$

$$
\begin{array}{r} {}^{14} \\ {}^{5\ \cancel{4}\ 11} \\ \cancel{6}\ \cancel{5}\ \cancel{1} \\ -\ 3\ 7\ 5 \\ \hline 2\ 7\ 6 \end{array}
$$

$$
\begin{array}{r} {}^{12} \\ {}^{0\ \cancel{2}\ 15} \\ \$\cancel{1}.3\ \cancel{5} \\ -\ \ \ .8\ 9 \\ \hline \$\ \ .4\ 6 \end{array}
$$

$$
\begin{array}{r} {}^{5\ 12\ 8\ 13} \\ \$\cancel{6}\ \cancel{2}.\cancel{9}\ \cancel{3} \\ -\ 3\ 9.0\ 5 \\ \hline \$2\ 3.8\ 8 \end{array}
$$

Estimate. Then find the difference.

1. $\begin{array}{r} 521 \\ -\ 347 \end{array}$
2. $\begin{array}{r} 825 \\ -\ 169 \end{array}$
3. $\begin{array}{r} 612 \\ -\ 248 \end{array}$
4. $\begin{array}{r} \$2.79 \\ -\ 1.89 \end{array}$
5. $\begin{array}{r} \$9.91 \\ -\ 1.97 \end{array}$

6. $\begin{array}{r} 6218 \\ -\ 5354 \end{array}$
7. $\begin{array}{r} 9743 \\ -\ 4467 \end{array}$
8. $\begin{array}{r} \$74.36 \\ -\ 46.72 \end{array}$
9. $\begin{array}{r} \$84.23 \\ -\ 23.47 \end{array}$

10. $\begin{array}{r} 634 \\ -\ 58 \end{array}$
11. $\begin{array}{r} 1274 \\ -\ 990 \end{array}$
12. $\begin{array}{r} \$4.22 \\ -\ 3.48 \end{array}$
13. $\begin{array}{r} \$63.35 \\ -\ 8.16 \end{array}$

Align and subtract.

14. $142 - 69$
15. $360 - 74$
16. $\$4.21 - \$1.38$

17. $7218 - 533$
18. $6182 - 2804$
19. $\$55.47 - \$8.95$

Solve. Use the table on page 110.

20. How much longer is the Rio Grande River than the Porcupine River?

21. How much shorter is the Tennessee River than the Missouri River?

22. Is the difference in length of the Missouri and Rio Grande Rivers greater or less than the length of the Porcupine River?

Challenge

Find the missing digits.

23. $\begin{array}{r} 923 \\ -\ 14\square \\ \hline 776 \end{array}$
24. $\begin{array}{r} 629 \\ -\ \square 8\square \\ \hline 441 \end{array}$
25. $\begin{array}{r} 231 \\ -\ \square\square\square \\ \hline 85 \end{array}$
26. $\begin{array}{r} 856 \\ -\ 4\square 8 \\ \hline \square 6\square \end{array}$

4-9 Zeros in Subtraction

Shawn has 300 baseball cards in his collection. Sasha has 158 baseball cards. How many more baseball cards does Shawn have than Sasha?

To find how many more, subtract: $300 - 158 = \underline{\ ?\ }$

Remember:
300 = 3 hundreds =
2 hundreds 10 tens

2 hundreds 10 tens =
2 hundreds 9 tens 10 ones

When there are zeros in the minuend, you may need to regroup more than once *before* you start to subtract.

Regroup to get more tens.	Regroup to get more ones.	Subtract.	Check.
$\begin{array}{r} {}^{2}\ {}^{10}\\ \cancel{3}\,\cancel{0}\ 0\\ -\ 1\ 5\ 8\\ \hline \end{array}$	$\begin{array}{r} {}^{9}\\ {}^{2}\ \cancel{10}\ {}^{10}\\ \cancel{3}\,\cancel{0}\ 0\\ -\ 1\ 5\ 8\\ \hline \end{array}$	$\begin{array}{r} {}^{9}\\ {}^{2}\ \cancel{10}\ {}^{10}\\ \cancel{3}\,\cancel{0}\ 0\\ -\ 1\ 5\ 8\\ \hline 1\ 4\ 2 \end{array}$	$\begin{array}{r} {}^{1}\ {}^{1}\\ 1\ 4\ 2\\ +\ 1\ 5\ 8\\ \hline 3\ 0\ 0 \end{array}$
3 hundreds 0 tens = 2 hundreds 10 tens	10 tens 0 ones = 9 tens 10 ones		

Shawn has 142 more baseball cards than Sasha.

Study these examples.

$\begin{array}{r} {}^{9}\\ 4\ \cancel{10}\ {}^{17}\\ \$\cancel{5}.\cancel{0}\ \cancel{7}\\ -\ 3.2\ 9\\ \hline \$1.7\ 8 \end{array}$
$\begin{array}{r} {}^{9}\ {}^{9}\\ 7\ \cancel{10}\ \cancel{10}\ {}^{10}\\ \$\cancel{8}\,0.0\ 0\\ -\ \ \ \ 9.6\ 4\\ \hline \$7\,0.3\ 6 \end{array}$
$\begin{array}{r} {}^{9}\ {}^{9}\\ 5\ \cancel{10}\ \cancel{10}\ {}^{15}\\ \cancel{6}\,0\,0\ \cancel{5}\\ -\ 2\,4\,6\ 8\\ \hline 3\,5\,3\ 7 \end{array}$
$\begin{array}{r} {}^{9}\\ 8\ \cancel{10}\ {}^{14}\ {}^{13}\\ 9\,\cancel{0}\,\cancel{5}\ \cancel{3}\\ -\ 3\,7\,6\ 4\\ \hline 5\,2\,8\ 9 \end{array}$

Regroup. Then find the difference.

1. $\begin{array}{r} 500 \\ -329 \\ \hline \end{array}$
2. $\begin{array}{r} 600 \\ -277 \\ \hline \end{array}$
3. $\begin{array}{r} 800 \\ -672 \\ \hline \end{array}$
4. $\begin{array}{r} \$9.00 \\ -\ 5.41 \\ \hline \end{array}$
5. $\begin{array}{r} \$4.00 \\ -\ 1.16 \\ \hline \end{array}$

6. $\begin{array}{r} 407 \\ -239 \\ \hline \end{array}$
7. $\begin{array}{r} 806 \\ -447 \\ \hline \end{array}$
8. $\begin{array}{r} 205 \\ -127 \\ \hline \end{array}$
9. $\begin{array}{r} \$7.01 \\ -\ 3.65 \\ \hline \end{array}$
10. $\begin{array}{r} \$1.05 \\ -\ .88 \\ \hline \end{array}$

11. $\begin{array}{r} 6000 \\ -4531 \\ \hline \end{array}$
12. $\begin{array}{r} 5000 \\ -\ 718 \\ \hline \end{array}$
13. $\begin{array}{r} \$70.00 \\ -\ 59.88 \\ \hline \end{array}$
14. $\begin{array}{r} \$40.00 \\ -\ 16.95 \\ \hline \end{array}$

15. $\begin{array}{r} 8006 \\ -1938 \\ \hline \end{array}$
16. $\begin{array}{r} 9002 \\ -7865 \\ \hline \end{array}$
17. $\begin{array}{r} \$30.04 \\ -\ 21.35 \\ \hline \end{array}$
18. $\begin{array}{r} \$52.01 \\ -\ 8.98 \\ \hline \end{array}$

Align and subtract.

19. 800 − 639
20. 700 − 83
21. $3.01 − $.77

22. 406 − 98
23. 505 − 16
24. $2.02 − $.49

25. 3000 − 1231
26. 9000 − 825
27. $10.00 − $6.41

28. 8007 − 639
29. 7002 − 564
30. $50.05 − $4.29

Solve.

31. Greg has 200 baseball cards. He has 96 cards for National League players. How many cards does he have for American League players?

32. Abby has collected 235 baseball cards. She wants to have 400 cards by the end of the year. How many more cards will Abby need?

33. Zach earned $50.00. He wants to buy a set of new baseball cards for $39.35. How much money would Zach receive in change?

34. Find two 3-digit numbers you can subtract that have a difference of 99.

Larger Sums and Differences

To add or subtract larger numbers:

- Start by adding or subtracting at the right.
- Regroup as necessary.

Add: $567.86 + $341.95 = _?_

Subtract: 87,731 − 65,954 = _?_

```
   1    1 1
 $5 6 7.8 6
+ 3 4 1.9 5
 $9 0 9.8 1
```

```
         16 12
     6  ⁶ ² 11
  8 7,7 3 1
− 6 5,9 5 4
  2 1,7 7 7
```

Add: 36,428 + 83,985 + 759 = _?_

Subtract: $490.00 − $478.81 = _?_

```
   1 2 1  2
   3 6,4 2 8
   8 3,9 8 5
 +       7 5 9
 1 2 1,1 7 2
```

```
             9  9
         8 10 10 10
 $4 9 0.0 0
 − 4 7 8.8 1
 $   1 1.1 9
```

Add or subtract. Watch for + or − .

1. 42,937 + 11,426	**2.** 32,864 + 94,828	**3.** 85,963 + 28,279	**4.** $562.43 + 680.79
5. 94,361 − 22,087	**6.** 75,937 − 12,649	**7.** 82,616 − 51,499	**8.** $262.71 − 140.99
9. 62,734 + 45,926	**10.** 39,513 − 9,975	**11.** 42,511 + 8,979	**12.** $624.37 − 97.58
13. 37,268 + 51,929	**14.** 79,755 − 46,325	**15.** 88,214 + 94,297	**16.** $726.38 + 99.72

Find the sum or the difference.

17.
```
  13,584
  41,592
+ 26,437
```

18.
```
  64,205
  39,811
+ 52,406
```

19.
```
  82,099
   4,157
+ 79,862
```

20.
```
$902.67
  51.81
+ 235.27
```

21.
```
  53,007
- 21,979
```

22.
```
  70,064
- 19,155
```

23.
```
  80,102
-  9,516
```

24.
```
$600.08
-  59.99
```

25.
```
  98,694
     287
+  5,148
```

26.
```
     675
  44,526
+     67
```

27.
```
  75,628
   8,073
+     48
```

28.
```
$   4.97
  826.13
+  65.39
```

29.
```
  81,000
- 19,625
```

30.
```
  94,000
- 67,887
```

31.
```
  70,000
- 36,678
```

32.
```
$600.00
-  47.89
```

Align and add or subtract.

33. 21,863 + 2,684 + 1,326

34. 82,010 + 395 + 13,692

35. 65,600 − 1,592

36. $200.00 − $126.74

37. 90,506 − 3,729

38. $645.16 + $8.88 + $.56

Calculator Activity

Find the missing addends.

EXAMPLE: 60,800 + _?_ = 92,350

$$\boxed{9}\boxed{2}\boxed{3}\boxed{5}\boxed{0} \boxed{-} \boxed{6}\boxed{0}\boxed{8}\boxed{0}\boxed{0} \boxed{=} \boxed{31550.}$$

39. _?_ + 72,001 = 602,301

40. 71,020 + _?_ = 82,602

41. 4545 + _?_ = 99,999

42. _?_ + 4567 = 98,732

43. 30,303 = _?_ + 21,210

44. 505,980 = 50,098 + _?_

4-11 | Problem Solving: Extra Information

Problem: The Keep Fit Shop ordered 487 pairs of high-tops. The factory has 1000 pairs in stock. The prices range from $30 to $85. How many pairs of high-tops will the factory have after they fill the order?

1 IMAGINE Create a mental picture.

2 NAME *Facts:* 487 pairs ordered
1000 pairs in stock at the factory
Pairs cost $30 to $85.

Question: How many pairs will be left after the order is filled?

3 THINK What information do you need?

- the number of pairs ordered
- the number of pairs in stock

What information is unnecessary?

- the price range

4 COMPUTE Estimate the difference.
$1000 - 500 = 500$
Then subtract.

```
  0 9 9 10
  1 0 0 0
-   4 8 7
  5 1 3
```

The factory will have 513 pairs of high-tops left.

5 CHECK The answer is close to the estimate.
It is reasonable.

Add to check subtraction. $513 + 487 = 1000$

Solve.

1. Rock climbing shoes cost $82.55.
   Running shoes are on sale for $62.79.
   The regular price is $8.55 more.
   What is the regular price for the running shoes?

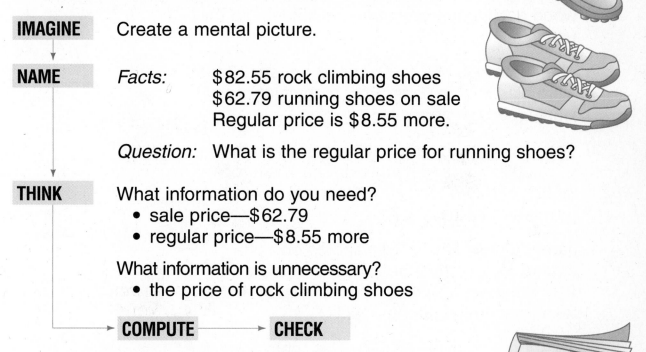

IMAGINE Create a mental picture.

NAME *Facts:* $82.55 rock climbing shoes
                        $62.79 running shoes on sale
                        Regular price is $8.55 more.

       Question: What is the regular price for running shoes?

THINK What information do you need?
   • sale price—$62.79
   • regular price—$8.55 more

What information is unnecessary?
   • the price of rock climbing shoes

COMPUTE ⟶ **CHECK**

2. The Keep Fit Catalog sells 376 clothing items,
   29 books, and 107 trail maps. There are
   6 order clerks and 2 managers. How many
   different items does the catalog sell?

3. Shipping costs $3 for orders under $10 and
   $5.50 for orders over $10. Delivery takes 6 to 9
   days. What is the total cost of a $14.98 order?

4. The company sent 4850 catalogs in April and 5782 catalogs
   in May. They received 853 orders in April and 118 more than that
   in May. How many orders did they receive in May?

5. The Keep Fit Shop has sponsored a charity bike race for
   15 years. The race is 35 miles long and there are rest stops
   every 5 miles. How many rest stops are there?

Solve.

Use these steps:

Imagine
Name
Think
Compute
Check

1. Jan and Kelly built a giant domino chain. They used 1378 plastic dominoes and 2267 wood dominoes. How many dominoes did they use in all?

2. The chain was 300 feet long. The first 127 feet were plastic dominoes. How many feet of chain were wood dominoes?

3. They set up the chain in the school gym that is 10,000 square feet in area. The chain took up 6341 square feet. How much of the gym floor was not covered?

4. Jan and Kelly spent 192 minutes on Friday setting up the dominoes. They worked for 218 minutes on Saturday. How long did it take them to set up the chain?

5. Their project raised $1070. They paid $318 for the dominoes. They gave the rest to charity. How much money did Jan and Kelly donate?

6. The audience included 175 children, 275 adults and 75 teenagers. How many people were there in all?

7. The plastic dominoes fell in 109 seconds. Then the wood dominoes fell in 189 seconds. How long did it take the entire chain to fall down?

8. Jan and Kelly are planning next year's chain. It will use 2567 plastic dominoes and 3271 wood dominoes. How many dominoes will it use?

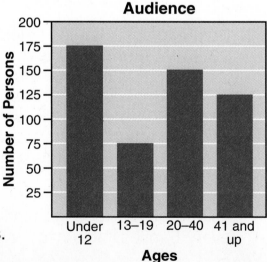

Audience

Number of Persons

200
175
150
125
100
75
50
25

Under 12 | 13–19 | 20–40 | 41 and up

Ages

Solve.

9. A class held a jump rope contest for charity. The winner jumped 9278 times without missing. The second prize went to someone who jumped 8765 times. How many more times did the winner jump?

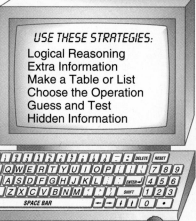

USE THESE STRATEGIES:
Logical Reasoning
Extra Information
Make a Table or List
Choose the Operation
Guess and Test
Hidden Information

10. Asa, Max, and Jemma came in first, second, and third in the jump rope contest. Max did not win, but he jumped more times than Asa. Who came in first, second, and third?

11. There were 108 people in the contest. They each paid $2 to enter. The winner won $25. Only 27 jumpers made it to the second round. How many jumpers were eliminated after round one?

12. Marcia jumped for 47 minutes. How many minutes less than an hour did Marcia jump?

13. Paul, Maria, Gail, and Leroy entered the Double Dutch contest. Two people hold ropes and two jump. How many different ways could the four friends play?

14. Paula hopped on her right foot 876 times, then on her left foot 954 times. Then she switched back to her right foot and hopped 212 times before tripping. How many times did she hop in all?

15. Al counted each time he jumped. He counted forward to 999 and then counted back to zero. How many times did he jump?

Make Up Your Own

16. Write a problem modeled on problem 12. Have someone solve it.

More Practice

Estimate. Use front-end estimation.

1. $\begin{array}{r} 382 \\ +216 \end{array}$	**2.** $\begin{array}{r} 648 \\ +175 \end{array}$	**3.** $\begin{array}{r} 7060 \\ -2955 \end{array}$	**4.** $\begin{array}{r} \$63.49 \\ -\ 19.79 \end{array}$

Add.

5. 392 + 26   **6.** 276 + 477   **7.** 4234 + 477

8. $\begin{array}{r} 258 \\ 314 \\ +126 \end{array}$	**9.** $\begin{array}{r} 527 \\ 198 \\ +\ 56 \end{array}$	**10.** $\begin{array}{r} \$32.38 \\ 4.43 \\ +\ 20.37 \end{array}$	**11.** $\begin{array}{r} 12,476 \\ 9,830 \\ +31,579 \end{array}$

Subtract.

12. 982 − 54   **13.** 2816 − 129   **14.** 17,150 − 3594

15. $\begin{array}{r} 6000 \\ -1406 \end{array}$	**16.** $\begin{array}{r} 2603 \\ -\ 186 \end{array}$	**17.** $\begin{array}{r} \$54.93 \\ -\ 16.17 \end{array}$	**18.** $\begin{array}{r} 15,168 \\ -\ 7,619 \end{array}$

Solve.

19. Memorial School has 630 students. If 437 students are girls, how many are boys?

20. The new stadium has 60,000 seats. The old stadium had 45,500 seats. How many more seats does the new stadium have?

21. There are 127 roses, 416 daisies, and 216 lilies in the flower shop. How many flowers are in the shop?

(See *Still More Practice*, p. 463.)

VARIABLES

▶ You can let symbols stand for numbers. Then you can decide whether a number sentence is true or false.

Let ■ = 25.

true or false? 5 + ■ = 30

> Think: 5 + 25 = 30?
> **Yes**.

So 5 + ■ = 30 is true
when ■ = 25.

Let ● = 16.

true or false? 20 − ● = 10

> Think: 20 − 16 = 10?
> **No**. 20 − 16 = 4

So 20 − ● = 10 is false
when ● = 16.

▶ You can let letters stand for numbers.

Decide whether each number sentence is true or false.

Let n = 21.

true or false? n − 8 = 15

> Think: 21 − 8 = 15?
> **No**. 21 − 8 = 13

So n − 8 = 15 is false
when n = 21.

Let a = 10.

true or false? a + 85 = 95

> Think: 10 + 85 = 95?
> **Yes**.

So a + 85 = 95 is true
when a = 10.

Write *true* or *false* for each number sentence.

1. Let ■ = 9.
   a. 6 + ■ = 18
   b. 15 − ■ = 6
   c. 93 − ■ = 85
   d. ■ + 63 = 72

2. Let ● = 36.
   a. ● − 29 = 7
   b. 74 − ● = 34
   c. 59 + ● = 85
   d. ● + 99 = 135

3. Let x = 78.
   a. 328 − x = 250
   b. x + 99 = 177
   c. x − 19 = 59
   d. 145 + x = 225

4. Let n = 208.
   a. 395 + n = 603
   b. n − 179 = 29
   c. 812 − n = 404
   d. n + n = 808

Check Your Mastery

Estimate. Use front-end estimation.   See pp. 96–97

1.	2.	3.	4.
532 + 350	480 + 310	3451 − 2157	$57.25 − 31.75

Find the sum.   See pp. 98–105, 114–115

5. 509 + 45   **6.** 283 + 179   **7.** 8059 + 397

8.	9.	10.	11.
176 205 + 387	374 162 + 51	$78.50 .99 + 5.38	23,154 96 + 4,129

Find the difference.   See pp. 106–115

12. 750 − 29   **13.** 5123 − 99   **14.** 56,150 − 3777

15.	16.	17.	18.
5430 − 298	3000 − 2951	$29.39 − 18.42	29,126 − 8,437

Solve.   See pp. 118–119

19. Cindy's car cost $15,935. She paid $8,599.
How much more does she owe?

20. The Harveys must travel 128 miles to the shore.
They have traveled 76 miles. How many more miles
must they travel?

21. Mrs. Grant bought gifts for her 4 children. The gifts
cost $29.99, $17.59, $35.79, and $49.99. How much
did Mrs. Grant pay for the gifts? If she gave the cashier
$135.00, how much change did she receive?

Cumulative Review II

Choose the best answer.

1.
$$\begin{array}{r} 9 \\ +7 \\ \hline \end{array}$$
a. 11
b. 16
c. 14
d. not given

2.
$$\begin{array}{r} 8 \\ +0 \\ \hline \end{array}$$
a. 8
b. 0
c. 80
d. not given

3.
$$\begin{array}{r} 6¢ \\ 7¢ \\ +4¢ \\ \hline \end{array}$$
a. 13¢
b. 17¢
c. 20¢
d. not given

4.
$$\begin{array}{r} 7 \\ 4 \\ +7 \\ \hline \end{array}$$
a. 19
b. 11
c. 18
d. not given

5. 10 + 9
a. 20
b. 90
c. 19
d. not given

6. 7 − 0
a. 0
b. 4
c. 6
d. not given

7.
$$\begin{array}{r} 9 \\ -9 \\ \hline \end{array}$$
a. 18
b. 0
c. 17
d. not given

8.
$$\begin{array}{r} 13¢ \\ -5¢ \\ \hline \end{array}$$
a. 12¢
b. 7¢
c. 8¢
d. not given

9.
$$\begin{array}{r} 5 \\ 4 \\ 2 \\ +5 \\ \hline \end{array}$$
a. 11
b. 17
c. 14
d. not given

10. Find the missing addend.

12 = _?_ + 4
a. 16
b. 5
c. 8
d. 12

11. Find the missing subtrahend.

17 − _?_ = 9
a. 8
b. 7
c. 6
d. 9

12. Find the missing number.
$$\begin{array}{r} ? \\ +\ 3 \\ \hline 12 \end{array}$$
a. 9
b. 15
c. 6
d. 8

13. Find the missing number.
$$\begin{array}{r} ? \\ -9 \\ \hline 6 \end{array}$$
a. 3
b. 15
c. 13
d. 14

14. Make a front-end estimate.
143 + 527 + 249
a. 600
b. 500
c. 650
d. 900

15. Estimate by rounding.
$$\begin{array}{r} 4956 \\ -3684 \\ \hline \end{array}$$
a. 9000
b. 3000
c. 1000
d. 4000

16. Estimate by rounding.
$$\begin{array}{r} \$50.24 \\ 3.69 \\ +\ 12.28 \\ \hline \end{array}$$
a. $54.00
b. $66.00
c. $70.00
d. $55.00

17. 8500 − 200
a. 6500
b. 8700
c. 7700
d. 8300

Choose the best answer.

18. 340 + 20 + 10

    a. 450
    b. 400
    c. 370
    d. not given

19. 5877 − 452

    a. 5429
    b. 5225
    c. 1357
    d. not given

20.
$$\begin{array}{r} \$4.21 \\ 1.33 \\ +\ 3.35 \\ \hline \end{array}$$

    a. $6.45
    b. $7.89
    c. $8.89
    d. not given

21.
$$\begin{array}{r} \$.87 \\ -\ .43 \\ \hline \end{array}$$

    a. $ .44
    b. $ .24
    c. $1.30
    d. not given

22.
$$\begin{array}{r} 7275 \\ +4607 \\ \hline \end{array}$$

    a. 12,882
    b. 11,872
    c. 11,472
    d. not given

23.
$$\begin{array}{r} \$70.04 \\ -\ 29.85 \\ \hline \end{array}$$

    a. $99.89
    b. $59.81
    c. $40.19
    d. not given

24. 4638 + 7458 + 4008

    a. 26,401
    b. 20,806
    c. 16,104
    d. not given

25. $10.00 − $7.52

    a. $3.52
    b. $3.48
    c. $3.58
    d. not given

26.
$$\begin{array}{r} 48,166 \\ +57,369 \\ \hline \end{array}$$

    a. 105,535
    b. 95,348
    c. 90,797
    d. not given

27.
$$\begin{array}{r} 80,000 \\ -47,789 \\ \hline \end{array}$$

    a. 47,789
    b. 32,211
    c. 42,211
    d. not given

28. Dan's Deli sold 134 tuna sandwiches, 246 cheese and 371 ham sandwiches. How many sandwiches is that altogether?

    a. 984 **b.** 751 **c.** 1260 **d.** 741

29. Adela bought a quart of yogurt for $3.89. How much change did she receive from $5.00?

    a. $.64 **b.** $.89 **c.** $2.89 **d.** $1.11

30. Daly's Dairy produces 4865 gallons of milk on Monday and 4215 gallons on Tuesday. About how many gallons is produced on both days?

    a. 8000 **b.** 7000 **c.** 6000 **d.** 9000

31. Fisherman Fred caught 224 crabs. He sold 195 crabs to a local fish store. How many crabs did he keep?

    a. 29 **b.** 46 **c.** 72 **d.** 129

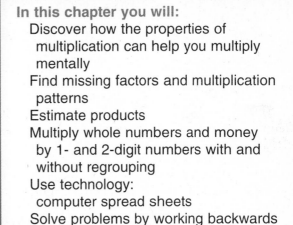

In this chapter you will:
  Discover how the properties of
    multiplication can help you multiply
    mentally
  Find missing factors and multiplication
    patterns
  Estimate products
  Multiply whole numbers and money
    by 1- and 2-digit numbers with and
    without regrouping
  Use technology:
    computer spread sheets
  Solve problems by working backwards

Do you remember?
  $42 = 40 + 2$
  $368 = 300 + 60 + 8$

Critical Thinking/Finding Together
Estimate how many pounds the compacted
trash weighs if each bundle weighs
25 pounds.

5-1 Multiplication Properties

The properties of multiplication can help you to multiply quickly and correctly.

- Changing the *order* of the factors does not change the product.

$$4 \times 5 = 20 \qquad 5 \qquad 4$$
$$5 \times 4 = 20 \qquad \underline{\times 4} \qquad \underline{\times 5}$$
$$ \quad 20 \qquad 20$$

Think: "order"

- Changing the *grouping* of the factors does not change the product.

$$(2 \times 4) \times 1 = 2 \times (4 \times 1)$$

$$8 \qquad \times 1 = 2 \times \qquad 4$$
$$8 = 8$$

Think: "grouping"

- The product of *one* and a number is the same as that number.

$$1 \times 6 = 6 \qquad 6 \qquad 1$$
$$6 \times 1 = 6 \qquad \underline{\times 1} \qquad \underline{\times 6}$$
$$ \quad 6 \qquad 6$$

Think: "same number"

- The product of *zero* and a number is 0.

$$0 \times 3 = 0 \qquad 3 \qquad 0$$
$$3 \times 0 = 0 \qquad \underline{\times 0} \qquad \underline{\times 3}$$
$$ \quad 0 \qquad 0$$

Think: "zero"

Find the product.

1. $\begin{array}{r} 5 \\ \times 2 \\ \hline \end{array}$ $\begin{array}{r} 2 \\ \times 5 \\ \hline \end{array}$

2. $\begin{array}{r} 6 \\ \times 3 \\ \hline \end{array}$ $\begin{array}{r} 3 \\ \times 6 \\ \hline \end{array}$

3. $\begin{array}{r} 7 \\ \times 9 \\ \hline \end{array}$ $\begin{array}{r} 9 \\ \times 7 \\ \hline \end{array}$

4. $\begin{array}{r} 4 \\ \times 0 \\ \hline \end{array}$ $\begin{array}{r} 0 \\ \times 4 \\ \hline \end{array}$

5. $\begin{array}{r} 1 \\ \times 8 \\ \hline \end{array}$ $\begin{array}{r} 8 \\ \times 1 \\ \hline \end{array}$

6. $\begin{array}{r} 9 \\ \times 4 \\ \hline \end{array}$ $\begin{array}{r} 4 \\ \times 9 \\ \hline \end{array}$

7. $\begin{array}{r} 2 \\ \times 6 \\ \hline \end{array}$ $\begin{array}{r} 6 \\ \times 2 \\ \hline \end{array}$

8. $\begin{array}{r} 7 \\ \times 5 \\ \hline \end{array}$ $\begin{array}{r} 5 \\ \times 7 \\ \hline \end{array}$

9. 4×8

10. 7×3

11. 5×9

12. 1×0

13. 6×7

14. 8×5

15. 6×0

16. 9×1

Copy and complete.

17. $2 \times (3 \times 1) = (2 \times 3) \times 1$
$2 \times \underline{\ ?\ } = \underline{\ ?\ } \times 1$
$\underline{\ ?\ } = \underline{\ ?\ }$

18. $(3 \times 2) \times 2 = 3 \times (2 \times 2)$
$\underline{\ ?\ } \times \underline{\ ?\ } = \underline{\ ?\ } \times \underline{\ ?\ }$
$\underline{\ ?\ } = \underline{\ ?\ }$

19. $2 \times (5 \times 0) = (2 \times \underline{\ ?\ }) \times \underline{\ ?\ }$
$\underline{\ ?\ } \times \underline{\ ?\ } = \underline{\ ?\ } \times \underline{\ ?\ }$
$\underline{\ ?\ } = \underline{\ ?\ }$

20. $(1 \times 6) \times 2 = \underline{\ ?\ } \times (\underline{\ ?\ } \times \underline{\ ?\ })$
$\underline{\ ?\ } \times \underline{\ ?\ } = \underline{\ ?\ } \times \underline{\ ?\ }$
$\underline{\ ?\ } = \underline{\ ?\ }$

Solve.

21. The product is 8. One factor is 8. What is the other factor?

22. The product is 9. One factor is 1. What is the other factor?

23. If $8 \times 12 = 96$, what is the product of 12×8?

24. Write two multiplication facts using 5 and 0.

Multiplying Sums

The product of a number and the sum of two addends is the same as the sum of the two products.

$5 \times (2 + 1) = (5 \times 2) + (5 \times 1)$
$5 \times \quad 3 \quad = \quad 10 \quad + \quad 5$
$15 \quad = \quad 15$

Think: "sum"

Copy and complete.

25. $2 \times (3 + 2) = (2 \times 3) + (2 \times 2)$
$2 \times \underline{\ ?\ } = \underline{\ ?\ } + \underline{\ ?\ }$
$\underline{\ ?\ } = \underline{\ ?\ }$

26. $3 \times (5 + 4) = (3 \times \underline{\ ?\ }) + (3 \times \underline{\ ?\ })$
$3 \times \underline{\ ?\ } = \underline{\ ?\ } + \underline{\ ?\ }$
$\underline{\ ?\ } = \underline{\ ?\ }$

27. $5 \times (6 + 3) = (\underline{\ ?\ } \times \underline{\ ?\ }) + (\underline{\ ?\ } \times \underline{\ ?\ })$
$\underline{\ ?\ } \times \underline{\ ?\ } = \underline{\ ?\ } + \underline{\ ?\ }$
$\underline{\ ?\ } = \underline{\ ?\ }$

5-2 Missing Factors

Jill designed 24 greeting cards. She wants to box them in sets of 6 cards each. How many sets of cards can she make?

To find how many sets, think:
$\underline{\ ?\ }$ sets of 6 cards = 24 cards
$\underline{\ ?\ }$ sixes = 24
$\underline{\ ?\ } \times 6 = 24$

To find the **missing factor**, think: What number times 6 is 24?

$2 \times 6 = 12$ too small
$3 \times 6 = 18$ too small
$4 \times 6 = 24$ just right!

She can make 4 sets of cards.

Study these examples.

$3 \times \underline{\ ?\ } = 21$
$3 \times \ 5\ = 15$ too small
$3 \times \ 6\ = 18$ too small
$3 \times \ 7\ = 21$ just right!

$\underline{\ ?\ } \times 7 = 42$
$8 \ \times 7 = 56$ too large
$7 \ \times 7 = 49$ too large
$6 \ \times 7 = 42$ just right!

Find the missing factor.

1. $\underline{\ ?\ } \times 3 = 6$

2. $\underline{\ ?\ } \times 5 = 15$

3. $\underline{\ ?\ } \times 4 = 20$

4. $\underline{\ ?\ } \times 6 = 36$

5. $\underline{\ ?\ } \times 7 = 56$

6. $\underline{\ ?\ } \times 8 = 72$

7. $\underline{\ ?\ } \times 2 = 2$

8. $\underline{\ ?\ } \times 9 = 36$

9. $\underline{\ ?\ } \times 3 = 9$

10. $\underline{\ ?\ } \times 1 = 8$

11. $\underline{\ ?\ } \times 4 = 28$

12. $\underline{\ ?\ } \times 6 = 42$

Copy and complete.

13. $9 \times \underline{\ ?\ } = 18$ **14.** $4 \times \underline{\ ?\ } = 16$ **15.** $7 \times \underline{\ ?\ } = 21$

16. $2 \times \underline{\ ?\ } = 16$ **17.** $8 \times \underline{\ ?\ } = 40$ **18.** $5 \times \underline{\ ?\ } = 25$

19. $54 = 9 \times \underline{\ ?\ }$ **20.** $24 = 3 \times \underline{\ ?\ }$ **21.** $49 = 7 \times \underline{\ ?\ }$

22. $63 = \underline{\ ?\ } \times 9$ **23.** $64 = \underline{\ ?\ } \times 8$ **24.** $48 = \underline{\ ?\ } \times 6$

25.
$$\begin{array}{r} ? \\ \times\ 5 \\ \hline 30 \end{array}$$
26.
$$\begin{array}{r} ? \\ \times\ 2 \\ \hline 12 \end{array}$$
27.
$$\begin{array}{r} ? \\ \times\ 6 \\ \hline 0 \end{array}$$
28.
$$\begin{array}{r} ? \\ \times\ 3 \\ \hline 27 \end{array}$$
29.
$$\begin{array}{r} ? \\ \times\ 7 \\ \hline 35 \end{array}$$
30.
$$\begin{array}{r} ? \\ \times\ 4 \\ \hline 32 \end{array}$$

31.
$$\begin{array}{r} 1 \\ \times\ ? \\ \hline 9 \end{array}$$
32.
$$\begin{array}{r} 5 \\ \times\ ? \\ \hline 10 \end{array}$$
33.
$$\begin{array}{r} 4 \\ \times\ ? \\ \hline 12 \end{array}$$
34.
$$\begin{array}{r} 9 \\ \times\ ? \\ \hline 45 \end{array}$$
35.
$$\begin{array}{r} 3 \\ \times\ ? \\ \hline 18 \end{array}$$
36.
$$\begin{array}{r} 6 \\ \times\ ? \\ \hline 24 \end{array}$$

Solve.

37. The product of 8 and another factor is 72. What is the other factor?

38. How many threes are equal to 18? How many nines are equal to 18?

39. What number times 7 is 35?

40. The product is 81. One factor is 9. What is the other factor?

Critical Thinking

Complete the pattern.

41.
$$\begin{array}{r} 11 \\ \times\ 2 \\ \hline 22 \end{array} \quad \begin{array}{r} 11 \\ \times\ 3 \\ \hline 33 \end{array} \quad \begin{array}{r} 11 \\ \times\ 4 \\ \hline 44 \end{array} \quad \begin{array}{r} 11 \\ \times\ 5 \\ \hline \end{array} \quad \begin{array}{r} 11 \\ \times\ 6 \\ \hline \end{array} \quad \begin{array}{r} 11 \\ \times\ 7 \\ \hline \end{array} \quad \begin{array}{r} 11 \\ \times\ 8 \\ \hline \end{array} \quad \begin{array}{r} 11 \\ \times\ 9 \\ \hline \end{array}$$

42.
$$\begin{array}{r} 11 \\ \times\ 10 \\ \hline 110 \end{array} \quad \begin{array}{r} 11 \\ \times\ 11 \\ \hline 121 \end{array} \quad \begin{array}{r} 11 \\ \times\ 12 \\ \hline 132 \end{array} \quad \begin{array}{r} 11 \\ \times 13 \\ \hline \end{array} \quad \begin{array}{r} 11 \\ \times 14 \\ \hline \end{array} \quad \begin{array}{r} 11 \\ \times 15 \\ \hline \end{array} \quad \begin{array}{r} 11 \\ \times 16 \\ \hline \end{array} \quad \begin{array}{r} 11 \\ \times 17 \\ \hline \end{array}$$

▶ Sharon uses 16 paper clips to make a necklace. How many paper clips will she need to make 2 necklaces?

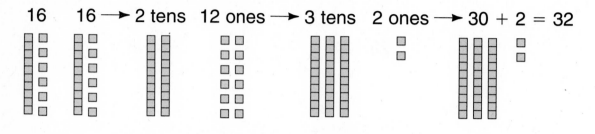

16   16 → 2 tens 12 ones → 3 tens 2 ones → 30 + 2 = 32

$2 \times 16 = 32$ Sharon needs 32 paper clips.

▶ Holly makes a bracelet with 3 rows of beads. Each row has 15 beads. How many beads are in the bracelet?

15 + 15 + 15 = 45

$3 \times 15 = 45$ There are 45 beads in the bracelet.

▶ Ito wants to make 4 headbands. Each headband uses 34 rubber bands. How many rubber bands does he need?

4×3 tens = 12 tens = 120 4×4 ones = 16 ones = 16

120 + 16 = 136

$4 \times 34 = 136$ Ito needs 136 rubber bands.

Write a multiplication sentence for each model.

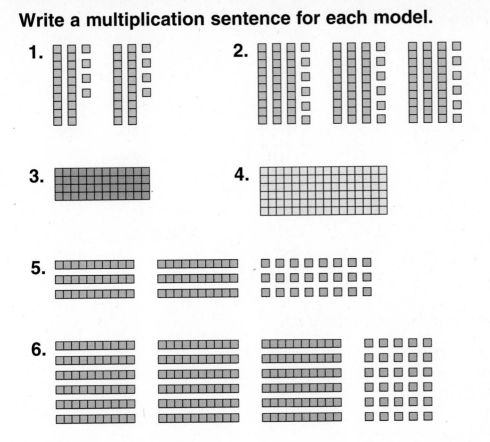

1.

2.

3.

4.

5.

6.

Solve.

7. Raul has 3 paper-clip chains. Each one is 55 paper clips long. He connects them. How long is the new chain?

8. Monica paints T-shirts. She paints 17 dots on each T-shirt. How many dots does she paint on 9 T-shirts?

9. Marva makes stained-glass designs. One design has 5 rows of squares. There are 10 squares in each row. How many squares does Marva use?

10. Paul builds model boats. He uses 25 craft sticks to build a rowboat. How many craft sticks does he need to build 4 rowboats?

11. Peter uses 52 toothpicks to build a model house. How many toothpicks does he need for 6 model houses?

5-4 Special Factors

Look for a pattern when you multiply tens.

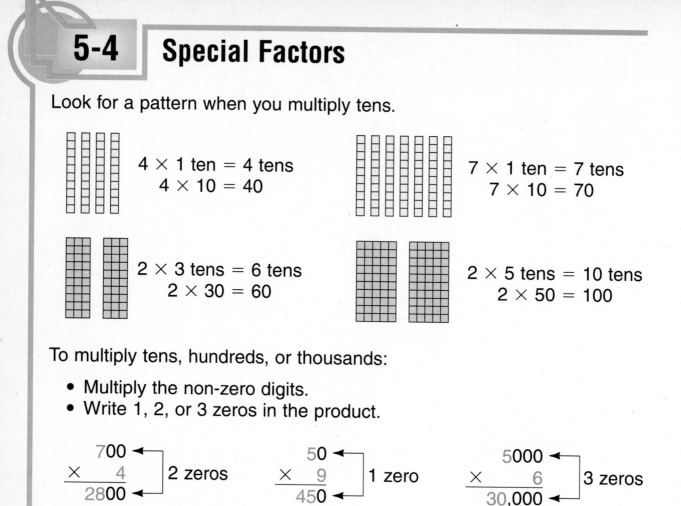

4×1 ten $= 4$ tens
$4 \times 10 = 40$

7×1 ten $= 7$ tens
$7 \times 10 = 70$

2×3 tens $= 6$ tens
$2 \times 30 = 60$

2×5 tens $= 10$ tens
$2 \times 50 = 100$

To multiply tens, hundreds, or thousands:

- Multiply the non-zero digits.
- Write 1, 2, or 3 zeros in the product.

$$\begin{array}{r} 700 \\ \times \quad 4 \\ \hline 2800 \end{array}$$ 2 zeros

$$\begin{array}{r} 50 \\ \times \quad 9 \\ \hline 450 \end{array}$$ 1 zero

$$\begin{array}{r} 5000 \\ \times \quad 6 \\ \hline 30{,}000 \end{array}$$ 3 zeros

Write a number sentence for each.

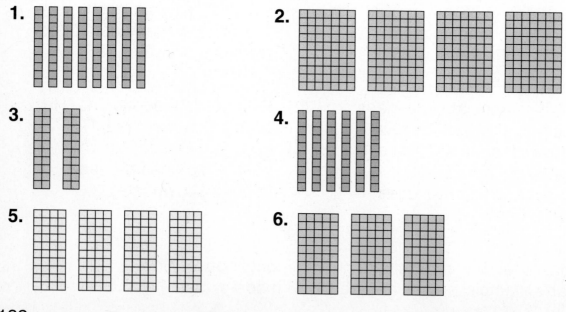

1.

2.

3.

4.

5.

6.

Copy and complete.

7. 6 × 3 tens = 6 × 30 = 180   **8.** 5 × 4 tens = 5 × 40 = _?_

9. 9 × 1 hundred = 9 × 100 = _?_   **10.** 2 × 4 hundreds = 2 × _?_ = _?_

11. 4 × 1 thousand = 4 × 1000 = _?_

12. 7 × 3 thousands = _?_ × _?_ = _?_

Find the product.

13. 4 × 1 ten   **14.** 7 × 3 tens   **15.** 8 × 1 hundred

16. 9 × 6 tens   **17.** 2 × 5 hundreds   **18.** 4 × 7 hundreds

19. 7 × 1 thousand   **20.** 6 × 3 thousands   **21.** 5 × 8 thousands

Multiply.

22. 90   **23.** 70   **24.** 80   **25.** 50
      × 3   × 2   × 4   × 5

26. 500   **27.** 900   **28.** 400   **29.** 300
      × 3   × 9   × 5   × 8

30. 1000   **31.** 6000   **32.** 5000   **33.** 9000
      × 6   × 4   × 7   × 6

Solve.

34. There are 5000 seats at Carver Stadium. Baseball games are played there 4 nights a week. How many tickets can the stadium sell each week?

35. Glen runs the 50-yard dash 8 times. How many yards does he run in all?

36. Ms. Spero swims 8 laps every day. How many laps does she swim in September?

133

Multiplying by One-Digit Numbers

There are 24 tropical fish in each of 2 fish tanks at Fish World. How many tropical fish are there at Fish World?

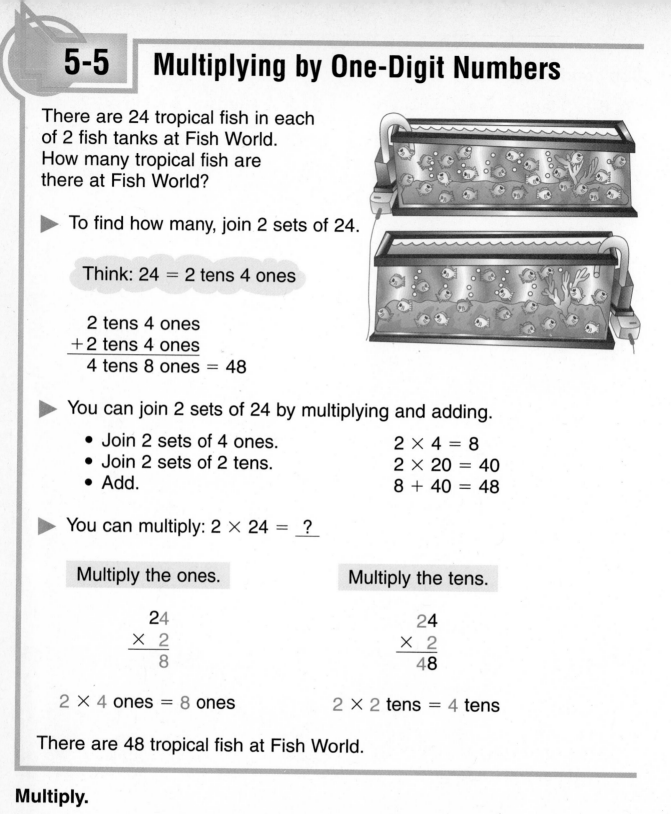

▶ To find how many, join 2 sets of 24.

Think: 24 = 2 tens 4 ones

    2 tens 4 ones
  + 2 tens 4 ones
    4 tens 8 ones = 48

▶ You can join 2 sets of 24 by multiplying and adding.

- Join 2 sets of 4 ones. $2 \times 4 = 8$
- Join 2 sets of 2 tens. $2 \times 20 = 40$
- Add. $8 + 40 = 48$

▶ You can multiply: $2 \times 24 = \underline{\ ?\ }$

Multiply the ones.	Multiply the tens.
$\begin{array}{r} 24 \\ \times\ 2 \\ \hline 8 \end{array}$	$\begin{array}{r} 24 \\ \times\ 2 \\ \hline 48 \end{array}$
2×4 ones $= 8$ ones	2×2 tens $= 4$ tens

There are 48 tropical fish at Fish World.

Multiply.

1.	2.	3.	4.	5.	6.
$\begin{array}{r} 12 \\ \times\ 2 \\ \hline \end{array}$	$\begin{array}{r} 22 \\ \times\ 3 \\ \hline \end{array}$	$\begin{array}{r} 13 \\ \times\ 3 \\ \hline \end{array}$	$\begin{array}{r} 11 \\ \times\ 5 \\ \hline \end{array}$	$\begin{array}{r} 14 \\ \times\ 2 \\ \hline \end{array}$	$\begin{array}{r} 12 \\ \times\ 4 \\ \hline \end{array}$

Find the product.

7. 11
  × 9

8. 34
  × 2

9. 22
  × 4

10. 44
  × 2

11. 12
  × 3

12. 33
  × 3

13. 32
  × 3

14. 13
  × 2

15. 43
  × 2

16. 31
  × 3

17. 26
  × 1

18. 41
  × 2

19. 2 × 23

20. 4 × 22

21. 2 × 33

22. 3 × 31

23. 2 × 42

24. 3 × 21

25. 4 × 21

26. 8 × 11

27. 2 × 14

28. 2 × 31

29. 7 × 11

30. 2 × 32

Solve.

31. Fish World received 3 cartons of fish food. There were 12 boxes of food in each carton. How many boxes of fish food did Fish World receive?

32. Niqui displayed 22 fish care booklets on each of 4 shelves. How many fish care booklets did Niqui display on the shelves?

33. Greg filled each of 2 fish tanks with 14 gallons of water. How much water did Greg use to fill the tanks?

34. There were 2 shipments of 42 goldfish each to Fish World. How many goldfish were there in both shipments?

Challenge

Find the next three numbers.

35. 10, 15, 25, 30, 40, _?_ , _?_ , _?_

36. 1, 3, 2, 4, 3, 5, _?_ , _?_ , _?_

37. 24, 30, 28, 34, 32, _?_ , _?_ , _?_

38. 1, 3, 2, 6, 5, 15, _?_ , _?_ , _?_

39. 1, 2, 3, 6, 7, 14, _?_ , _?_ , _?_

40. 2, 4, 6, 12, 14, _?_ , _?_ ,_?_

5-6 Products: Front-End Estimation

Will 5 games cost more or less than $100?

To find if the games will cost more or less than $100, estimate.

Video game cartridges now only $25.95 each

| Multiply the front digit of the greater factor. | | Write 0s for the other digits. |

$$\begin{array}{r} \$25.95 \\ \times\ \ \ \ \ 5 \\ \hline 10 \end{array}$$

Write $ and . in the product.

$$\begin{array}{r} \$25.95 \\ \times\ \ \ \ \ 5 \\ \hline \text{about } \$100.00 \end{array}$$

Think: $20.00
$$\begin{array}{r} \$20.00 \\ \times\ \ \ \ \ 5 \\ \hline \$100.00 \end{array}$$

Since $25.95 is greater than $20, the actual cost is close to but greater than $100.

The 5 games will cost more than $100.

Study these examples.

$$\begin{array}{r} 62 \\ \times\ \ 6 \\ \hline \text{about } 360 \end{array}$$

$$\begin{array}{r} \$5.28 \\ \times\ \ \ \ \ \ 7 \\ \hline \text{about } \$35.00 \end{array}$$

$$\begin{array}{r} 8406 \\ \times\ \ \ \ \ \ 8 \\ \hline \text{about } 64,000 \end{array}$$

Estimate the product.

1. $$\begin{array}{r} 82 \\ \times\ 6 \\ \hline \end{array}$$

2. $$\begin{array}{r} 98 \\ \times\ 7 \\ \hline \end{array}$$

3. $$\begin{array}{r} 46 \\ \times\ 5 \\ \hline \end{array}$$

4. $$\begin{array}{r} \$.73 \\ \times\ \ \ 3 \\ \hline \end{array}$$

5. $$\begin{array}{r} \$.57 \\ \times\ \ \ 2 \\ \hline \end{array}$$

6. $$\begin{array}{r} 473 \\ \times\ \ 8 \\ \hline \end{array}$$

7. $$\begin{array}{r} \$9.01 \\ \times\ \ \ \ \ 4 \\ \hline \end{array}$$

8. $$\begin{array}{r} 5125 \\ \times\ \ \ \ \ 9 \\ \hline \end{array}$$

9. $$\begin{array}{r} 1070 \\ \times\ \ \ \ \ 6 \\ \hline \end{array}$$

10. $$\begin{array}{r} \$32.95 \\ \times\ \ \ \ \ \ \ 7 \\ \hline \end{array}$$

11. $$\begin{array}{r} 849 \\ \times\ \ 4 \\ \hline \end{array}$$

12. $$\begin{array}{r} \$6.53 \\ \times\ \ \ \ \ 3 \\ \hline \end{array}$$

13. $$\begin{array}{r} \$46.73 \\ \times\ \ \ \ \ \ \ 8 \\ \hline \end{array}$$

14. $$\begin{array}{r} 7211 \\ \times\ \ \ \ \ 5 \\ \hline \end{array}$$

15. $$\begin{array}{r} \$32.24 \\ \times\ \ \ \ \ \ \ 9 \\ \hline \end{array}$$

Estimate.

16. 55
    × 2

17. 49
    × 9

18. 31
    × 7

19. 64
    × 6

20. 78
    × 3

21. 437
    × 9

22. 622
    × 5

23. 145
    × 4

24. 744
    × 7

25. 609
    × 8

26. 7832
    × 6

27. 8209
    × 5

28. 9848
    × 4

29. 4633
    × 2

30. $.65
    × 9

31. $8.33
    × 7

32. $34.72
    × 5

33. $21.24
    × 6

34. 4 × $7.10

35. 2 × $9.67

36. 9 × $37.55

Use estimation to solve.

37. Will 3 joysticks cost more or less than $60?

38. About how much would a set of 2 speakers cost?

39. Will 7 joysticks cost more than 2 game systems?

40. Jenique wants to buy 1 game system, 2 speakers, and 3 joysticks. About how much will she spend?

Home Video Games
Systems $144 each
Speakers $ 54.95 each
Joysticks $ 13.95 each

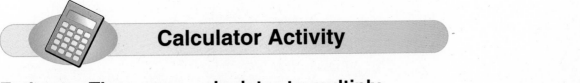

Calculator Activity

Estimate. Then use a calculator to multiply.

41. 788
    × 8

42. 9237
    × 4

43. $6.97
    × 7

44. $89.09
    × 9

Multiplying with Regrouping

How many miles does Mr. Ames drive in 5 work days?

First estimate.

$$\begin{array}{r} 35 \\ \times\ 5 \\ \hline \text{about } 150 \end{array}$$

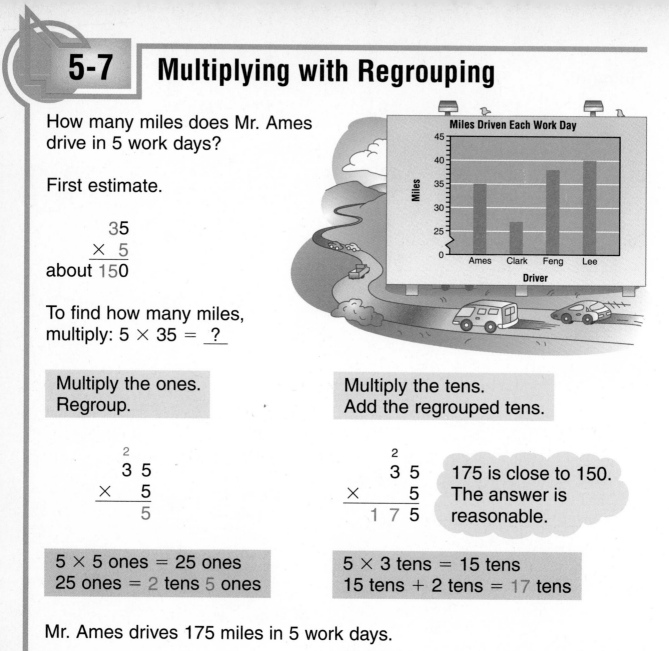

Miles Driven Each Work Day

To find how many miles,
multiply: $5 \times 35 =$ __?__

Multiply the ones. Regroup.	Multiply the tens. Add the regrouped tens.

$$\begin{array}{r} \overset{2}{3}\ 5 \\ \times\quad 5 \\ \hline 5 \end{array}$$

$$\begin{array}{r} \overset{2}{3}\ 5 \\ \times\quad 5 \\ \hline 1\ 7\ 5 \end{array}$$

175 is close to 150. The answer is reasonable.

5×5 ones $= 25$ ones 25 ones $= 2$ tens 5 ones	5×3 tens $= 15$ tens 15 tens $+ 2$ tens $= 17$ tens

Mr. Ames drives 175 miles in 5 work days.

Study this example.

$$\begin{array}{r} \overset{1}{4}\ 8 \\ \times\quad 2 \\ \hline 6 \end{array}$$

$$\begin{array}{r} \overset{1}{4}\ 8 \\ \times\quad 2 \\ \hline 9\ 6 \end{array}$$

2×8 ones $= 16$ ones 16 ones $= 1$ ten 6 ones	2×4 tens $= 8$ tens 8 tens $+ 1$ ten $= 9$ tens

Multiply.

1.	18 × 3	2.	16 × 5	3.	38 × 2	4.	24 × 3	5.	16 × 4	6.	25 × 2
7.	28 × 2	8.	17 × 3	9.	24 × 4	10.	19 × 3	11.	17 × 5	12.	19 × 4
13.	24 × 6	14.	46 × 4	15.	68 × 5	16.	78 × 2	17.	36 × 3	18.	86 × 9
19.	74 × 8	20.	64 × 9	21.	37 × 6	22.	52 × 7	23.	82 × 8	24.	96 × 5

Find the product.

25. 5×15 26. 6×15 27. 4×23 28. 2×49

29. 3×27 30. 4×63 31. 5×84 32. 6×77

33. 9×58 34. 7×45 35. 8×67 36. 9×99

Solve. Use the bar graph on page 138.

37. How many miles does Ms. Feng drive in 5 work days? in 7 work days? in 9 work days?

38. Does Mr. Lee drive more or fewer miles in 5 work days than Ms. Clark drives in 7?

Calculator Activity

Use a calculator to solve.

39. Find a 1-digit factor and a 2-digit factor whose product is 396.

40. Find a 1-digit factor and a 2-digit factor whose product is 220.

41. Find the missing factors in this number sentence:
    $\underline{?} \times \underline{?} \times 61 = 488$

42. Find the missing factors in this number sentence:
    $\underline{?} \times \underline{?} \times 99 = 891$

5-8 Multiplying Three-Digit Numbers

Each of the 8 families on Pine Road receives a newspaper delivery each day of the year. How many newspapers are delivered on Pine Road each year?

To find how many, multiply: 8 × 365 = __?__

Multiply the ones. Regroup.

$$
\begin{array}{r}
{}^{4} \\
3\ 6\ 5 \\
\times \qquad 8 \\
\hline
0
\end{array}
$$

8 × 5 ones = 40 ones
40 ones = 4 tens 0 ones

Multiply the tens. Add the regrouped tens. Regroup.

$$
\begin{array}{r}
{}^{5}\ {}^{4} \\
3\ 6\ 5 \\
\times \qquad 8 \\
\hline
2\ 0
\end{array}
$$

8 × 6 tens = 48 tens
48 tens + 4 tens = 52 tens
52 tens = 5 hundreds 2 tens

Multiply the hundreds. Add the regrouped hundreds.

$$
\begin{array}{r}
{}^{5}\ {}^{4} \\
3\ 6\ 5 \\
\times \qquad 8 \\
\hline
2\ 9\ 2\ 0
\end{array}
$$

8 × 3 hundreds = 24 hundreds
24 hundreds + 5 hundreds = 29 hundreds
29 hundreds = 2 thousands 9 hundreds

Each year, 2920 newspapers are delivered on Pine Road.

Study these examples.

$$
\begin{array}{r}
{}^{1} \\
504 \\
\times \quad 4 \\
\hline
2016
\end{array}
\qquad
\begin{array}{r}
321 \\
\times \quad 2 \\
\hline
642
\end{array}
\qquad
\begin{array}{r}
{}^{1} \\
621 \\
\times \quad 6 \\
\hline
3726
\end{array}
$$

Estimate. Then multiply.

1. 214
   × 2
   _128_

2. 101
   × 3
   _303_

3. 210
   × 4
   _940_

4. 323
   × 2
   _646_

5. 223
   × 3
   _469_

6. 308
   × 5
   _540_

7. 410
   × 8

8. 271
   × 7

9. 505
   × 9

10. 192
    × 4

11. 634
    × 6

12. 279
    × 9

13. 844
    × 7

14. 575
    × 8

15. 397
    × 5

Find the product.

16. 2 × 304

17. 3 × 131

18. 2 × 642

19. 5 × 160

20. 6 × 702

21. 4 × 261

22. 8 × 625

23. 7 × 444

24. 9 × 368

Solve.

25. The Ecology Club brought 6 bundles of junk mail to the recycling center. Each bundle weighed 275 pounds. How many pounds of junk mail did the Ecology Club recycle?

26. Troop 42 collected 8 bins of newspaper for recycling. Four of the bins held 325 pounds of newspaper each. The other 4 bins held 450 pounds of newspaper each. How many pounds of newspaper did Troop 42 collect?

27. Six of the families on Pine Road each recycled at least 8 aluminum cans each week last year. There are 52 weeks in a year. Altogether, did these families recycle more or less than 2000 aluminum cans last year?

Multiplying Money

Cesar buys 8 notebooks for the Detective Club. Each notebook costs $3.39. What is the total cost of the notebooks?

Walkie-Talkies	$11.59 each
Periscopes	$14.58 each
Magnifying Glasses	$7.50 each
Decoder Rings	$.99 each
Invisible Ink Markers	$1.56 each
Notebooks	$3.39 each

First estimate:

$$\begin{array}{r} \$3.39 \\ \times \quad 8 \\ \hline \text{about } \$24.00 \end{array}$$

To find the total cost, multiply: 8 × $3.39 = __?__

To multiply money:

- Multiply the same way you multiply whole numbers.

- Write a decimal point in the product two places from the right.

- Write the dollar sign.

The total cost is $27.12.

$$\begin{array}{r} {\scriptstyle 3 \quad 7} \\ \$3.3\,9 \\ \times \quad\quad 8 \\ \hline \$2\,7.1\,2 \end{array}$$

$27.12 is close to $24.00. The answer is reasonable.

Study this example.

$$\begin{array}{r} {\scriptstyle 1} \\ \$.6\,4 \\ \times \quad\quad 3 \\ \hline \$1.9\,2 \end{array}$$

Estimate. Then multiply.

| 1. $.46 × 6 | 2. $.38 × 8 | 3. $.52 × 7 | 4. $.74 × 9 | 5. $.25 × 3 |

| 6. $1.05 × 2 | 7. $5.73 × 5 | 8. $6.26 × 4 | 9. $8.30 × 7 | 10. $4.52 × 9 |

Estimate. Then find the product.

11. $\begin{array}{r} \$.42 \\ \times\ \ \ 8 \\ \hline \end{array}$	**12.** $\begin{array}{r} \$.95 \\ \times\ \ \ 2 \\ \hline \end{array}$	**13.** $\begin{array}{r} \$.79 \\ \times\ \ \ 3 \\ \hline \end{array}$	**14.** $\begin{array}{r} \$.12 \\ \times\ \ \ 5 \\ \hline \end{array}$
15. $\begin{array}{r} \$8.31 \\ \times\ \ \ 4 \\ \hline \end{array}$	**16.** $\begin{array}{r} \$7.95 \\ \times\ \ \ 9 \\ \hline \end{array}$	**17.** $\begin{array}{r} \$4.36 \\ \times\ \ \ 2 \\ \hline \end{array}$	**18.** $\begin{array}{r} \$8.95 \\ \times\ \ \ 6 \\ \hline \end{array}$
19. $\begin{array}{r} \$7.50 \\ \times\ \ \ 8 \\ \hline \end{array}$	**20.** $\begin{array}{r} \$4.31 \\ \times\ \ \ 7 \\ \hline \end{array}$	**21.** $\begin{array}{r} \$6.08 \\ \times\ \ \ 5 \\ \hline \end{array}$	**22.** $\begin{array}{r} \$9.49 \\ \times\ \ \ 3 \\ \hline \end{array}$

23. $4 \times \$.53$

24. $6 \times \$.87$

25. $8 \times \$.19$

26. $7 \times \$4.03$

27. $9 \times \$1.71$

28. $3 \times \$7.47$

29. $2 \times \$9.76$

30. $5 \times \$5.98$

31. $4 \times \$6.61$

Solve. Use the sign on page 142.

32. How much would you spend for 8 magnifying glasses?

33. What is the cost of 7 decoder rings?

34. How much would 5 periscopes cost? 2 walkie talkies?

35. What is the cost of 4 walkie talkies and 6 invisible ink markers?

36. How much would 2 periscopes and 3 pairs of walkie talkies cost?

Challenge

37. The Detective Club sells children's T-shirts for $4.50 each and adults' T-shirts for $5.75 each. One family spent $25 on T-shirts. How many T-shirts did the family buy?

Multiplying Four-Digit Numbers

Mr. Carter built houses on 6 neighboring plots of land. Each plot is 6875 square feet. On how many square feet of land did he build the houses?

First estimate:

$$\begin{array}{r} 6875 \\ \times \quad 6 \\ \hline \text{about } 36{,}000 \end{array}$$

6875 > 6000 So the answer is close to, but greater than, 36,000.

To find how many square feet, multiply: 6 × 6875 = _?_

$$\begin{array}{r} {\scriptstyle 5\ 4\ 3} \\ 6\ 8\ 7\ 5 \\ \times \quad\quad 6 \\ \hline 4\ 1{,}2\ 5\ 0 \end{array}$$

41,250 is close to and greater than 36,000. The answer is reasonable.

He built the houses on 41,250 square feet of land.

Study these examples.

$$\begin{array}{r} {\scriptstyle 1\quad\ 2} \\ 1\ 4\ 0\ 6 \\ \times \quad\quad 4 \\ \hline 5\ 6\ 2\ 4 \end{array} \qquad \begin{array}{r} {\scriptstyle 3\ 1} \\ \$2\ 5.2\ 0 \\ \times \quad\quad 7 \\ \hline \$1\ 7\ 6.4\ 0 \end{array}$$

Estimate. Then multiply.

1.	2221 × 3	**2.**	1022 × 4	**3.**	2432 × 2	**4.**	3123 × 3
5.	1035 × 7	**6.**	2164 × 4	**7.**	1146 × 6	**8.**	3257 × 3

Estimate. Then find the product.

9.	1415 $\times\quad 9$	**10.**	6423 $\times\quad 7$	**11.**	7536 $\times\quad 5$	**12.**	3341 $\times\quad 8$
13.	4372 $\times\quad 6$	**14.**	5279 $\times\quad 4$	**15.**	2523 $\times\quad 9$	**16.**	8119 $\times\quad 9$
17.	$34.68 $\times\qquad 7$	**18.**	$94.12 $\times\qquad 5$	**19.**	$21.77 $\times\qquad 6$	**20.**	$74.41 $\times\qquad 3$

21. 2 × 9455   **22.** 5 × 3408   **23.** 4 × 6472

24. 6 × $36.75   **25.** 8 × $42.56   **26.** 7 × $22.95

27. 3 × $54.66   **28.** 9 × $19.87   **29.** 8 × $69.57

Solve.

30. Each ranch house in Shady Acres has 1256 square feet of floor space. How many square feet of flooring were used for the 8 ranch houses in Shady Acres?

31. There are 4 miles of roads through Shady Acres. One mile is equal to 5280 feet. How many feet long are all the roads through Shady Acres?

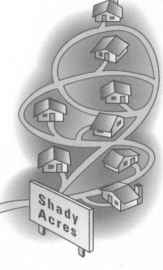

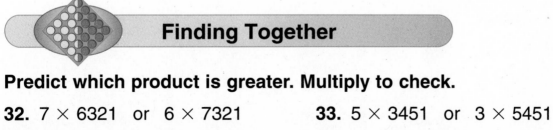

Finding Together

Predict which product is greater. Multiply to check.

32. 7 × 6321 or 6 × 7321   **33.** 5 × 3451 or 3 × 5451

34. 8 × 9310 or 9 × 8310   **35.** 4 × 9999 or 9 × 4999

Patterns in Multiplication

▶ Look for patterns to help you multiply by 10.

$1 \times 35 = 35$	$1 \times 50 = 50$	$1 \times 457 = 457$
$10 \times 35 = 350$	$10 \times 50 = 500$	$10 \times 457 = 4570$
$10 \times 350 = 3500$	$10 \times 500 = 5000$	

To multiply a number by 10:

- Write the number in the product.
- Place a 0 to its right.

$$\begin{array}{r} 35 \\ \times\ 10 \\ \hline 350 \end{array} \qquad \begin{array}{r} 500 \\ \times\ 10 \\ \hline 5000 \end{array} \qquad \begin{array}{r} 457 \\ \times\ 10 \\ \hline 4570 \end{array}$$

▶ Look for patterns to help you multiply by tens.

$9 \times 31 = 279$	$8 \times 40 = 320$
$90 \times 31 = 2790$	$80 \times 40 = 3200$
$90 \times 310 = 27,900$	$80 \times 400 = 32,000$

To multiply a number by tens:

- Multiply the number by the tens digit.
- Write 0 in the ones place in the product.

$$\begin{array}{r} 31 \\ \times\ 90 \\ \hline 2790 \end{array} \qquad \begin{array}{r} 310 \\ \times\ 90 \\ \hline 27,900 \end{array} \qquad \begin{array}{r} 40 \\ \times\ 80 \\ \hline 3200 \end{array} \qquad \begin{array}{r} 400 \\ \times\ 80 \\ \hline 32,000 \end{array}$$

Multiply mentally.

1. $\begin{array}{r}18\\ \times 10\\ \hline\end{array}$	2. $\begin{array}{r}24\\ \times 10\\ \hline\end{array}$	3. $\begin{array}{r}57\\ \times 10\\ \hline\end{array}$	4. $\begin{array}{r}61\\ \times 10\\ \hline\end{array}$	5. $\begin{array}{r}50\\ \times 10\\ \hline\end{array}$
6. $\begin{array}{r}345\\ \times\ 10\\ \hline\end{array}$	7. $\begin{array}{r}638\\ \times\ 10\\ \hline\end{array}$	8. $\begin{array}{r}999\\ \times\ 10\\ \hline\end{array}$	9. $\begin{array}{r}450\\ \times\ 10\\ \hline\end{array}$	10. $\begin{array}{r}690\\ \times\ 10\\ \hline\end{array}$

Find the product.

11.	23 $\times 20$	12.	42 $\times 60$	13.	61 $\times 30$	14.	70 $\times 40$	15.	60 $\times 50$

16.	230 $\times\ 20$	17.	420 $\times\ 60$	18.	610 $\times\ 30$	19.	700 $\times\ 40$	20.	600 $\times\ 50$

21.	52 $\times 80$	22.	25 $\times 90$	23.	19 $\times 70$	24.	80 $\times 80$	25.	40 $\times 90$

26.	520 $\times\ 80$	27.	250 $\times\ 90$	28.	190 $\times\ 70$	29.	800 $\times\ 80$	30.	400 $\times\ 90$

Copy and complete each pattern.

31.
$1 \times 78 = \underline{?}$
$10 \times 78 = \underline{?}$
$10 \times 780 = \underline{?}$

32.
$9 \times 60 = \underline{?}$
$90 \times 60 = \underline{?}$
$90 \times 600 = \underline{?}$

33.
$2 \times 78 = \underline{?}$
$20 \times 78 = \underline{?}$
$20 \times 780 = \underline{?}$

34.
$7 \times 60 = \underline{?}$
$70 \times 60 = \underline{?}$
$70 \times 600 = \underline{?}$

35.
$8 \times 50 = \underline{?}$
$80 \times 50 = \underline{?}$
$80 \times 500 = \underline{?}$

36.
$6 \times 35 = \underline{?}$
$60 \times 35 = \underline{?}$
$60 \times 350 = \underline{?}$

Solve. Compute mentally.

37. How many zeros are in the product when you multiply 10×670?

38. How many zeros are in the product when you multiply 40×500?

Mental Math

Complete each pattern mentally.

39.
$1 \times 56 = \underline{?}$
$10 \times 56 = \underline{?}$
$100 \times 56 = \underline{?}$
$100 \times 560 = \underline{?}$
$100 \times 5600 = \underline{?}$

40.
$7 \times 41 = 287$
$70 \times 41 = \underline{?}$
$700 \times 41 = \underline{?}$
$700 \times 410 = \underline{?}$
$700 \times 4100 = \underline{?}$

147

Estimating Products

Nahn works in his parents' hardware store 28 hours each month. He earns $4.25 an hour. About how much does he earn each month?

To find about how much he earns, estimate: 28 × $4.25

To estimate products:

- Round each factor to its greatest place.
- Multiply.

$$\begin{array}{r} \$4.25 \longrightarrow \$4.00 \\ \times\ \ \ 28 \longrightarrow \times\ \ \ \ 30 \\ \hline \text{about } \$120.00 \end{array}$$

You can write $120.00 as $120.

Nahn earns about $120 each month.

Study these examples.

$$\begin{array}{r} 43 \longrightarrow 40 \\ \times 62 \longrightarrow \times 60 \\ \hline \text{about } 2400 \end{array}$$

$$\begin{array}{r} 586 \longrightarrow 600 \\ \times\ \ 55 \longrightarrow \times\ \ 60 \\ \hline \text{about } 36{,}000 \end{array}$$

$$\begin{array}{r} \$.48 \longrightarrow \$.50 \\ \times\ \ 32 \longrightarrow \times\ \ 30 \\ \hline \text{about } \$15.00 \end{array}$$

Estimate the product.

1. 52
    × 75

2. 68
    × 41

3. 91
    × 22

4. 86
    × 57

5. 47
    × 33

6. 19
    × 62

7. 53
    × 78

8. 29
    × 58

9. 34
    × 92

10. 85
    × 38

11. $.17
    × 27

12. $.36
    × 81

13. $.42
    × 74

14. $.66
    × 65

15. $.26
    × 57

Estimate.

16. 348 × 23	**17.** 551 × 66	**18.** 619 × 72	**19.** 809 × 94	**20.** 748 × 88
21. 315 × 38	**22.** 754 × 24	**23.** 449 × 57	**24.** 938 × 46	**25.** 656 × 53
26. $4.59 × 34	**27.** $6.53 × 76	**28.** $7.24 × 83	**29.** $5.39 × 24	**30.** $8.57 × 79

31. 27 × 426   **32.** 14 × 643   **33.** 36 × 338

34. 27 × $2.04   **35.** 54 × $7.15   **36.** 68 × $7.46

Solve.

37. There were 24 gallons of white paint in each of 17 cartons in the storeroom. About how many gallons of white paint were in the storeroom?

38. Each sheet of wall paneling covers 48 square feet. Mr. Troc sold 22 sheets of the paneling. About how many square feet of paneling did he sell?

39. Each sheet of rosewood paneling sells for $152. Were the total sales of the 22 sheets of paneling between $2000 and $3000, between $3000 and $4000, or between $4000 and $5000?

Skills to Remember

Align and add.

40. 94 + 360   **41.** 78 + 645   **42.** 65 + 940   **43.** 26 + 392

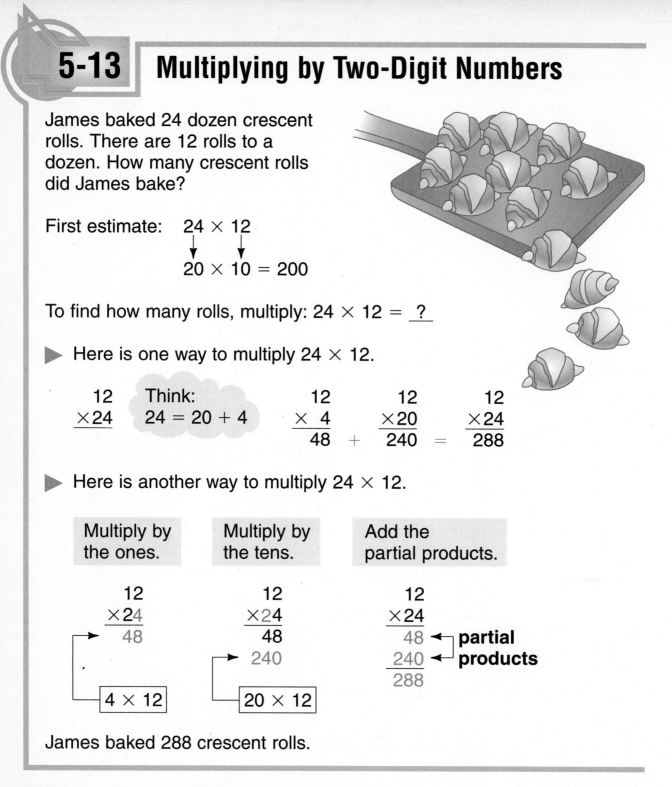

James baked 24 dozen crescent rolls. There are 12 rolls to a dozen. How many crescent rolls did James bake?

First estimate: 24 × 12

20 × 10 = 200

To find how many rolls, multiply: 24 × 12 = ?

▶ Here is one way to multiply 24 × 12.

12	Think:	12	12	12
× 24	24 = 20 + 4	× 4	×20	×24
		48 + 240 = 288

▶ Here is another way to multiply 24 × 12.

Multiply by the ones.	Multiply by the tens.	Add the partial products.
12	12	12
×24	×24	×24
48	48	48 ◀ partial
	240	240 ◀ products
		288
4 × 12	20 × 12	

James baked 288 crescent rolls.

Estimate. Then multiply.

1. 33	2. 23	3. 42	4. 24	5. 32
× 22	× 11	× 12	× 21	× 13

Find the product.

6. 12 × 44	**7.** 56 × 11	**8.** 32 × 32	**9.** 14 × 12	**10.** 22 × 21
11. 13 × 31	**12.** 21 × 21	**13.** 74 × 11	**14.** 11 × 11	**15.** 33 × 33
16. 12 × 21	**17.** 42 × 24	**18.** 23 × 32	**19.** 12 × 12	**20.** 13 × 13

Multiplying Money

To multiply money by a 2-digit number:

- Multiply the same way you multiply whole numbers.
- Write a decimal point in the product two places from the right.
- Write the dollar sign in the product.

$$\begin{array}{r} \$\ .23 \\ \times\ \ 13 \\ \hline 69 \\ 230 \\ \hline \$2.99 \end{array}$$

$$\begin{array}{r} \$.64 \\ \times\ \ 10 \\ \hline \$6.40 \end{array} \qquad \begin{array}{r} \$8.00 \\ \times\ \ \ 40 \\ \hline \$320.00 \end{array}$$

Multiply.

21. $.52 × 10	**22.** $6.00 × 50	**23.** $.23 × 23	**24.** $.41 × 21
25. $.43 × 20	**26.** $4.00 × 30	**27.** $.11 × 85	**28.** $.12 × 14
29. $.71 × 40	**30.** $7.00 × 20	**31.** $.23 × 21	**32.** $.43 × 12

5-14 More Multiplying by Two-Digit Numbers

Kara packed 24 pieces of fruit into each of 58 fruit baskets. How many pieces of fruit did Kara pack into the baskets?

First estimate:

$$24 \longrightarrow 20$$
$$\times 58 \longrightarrow \times 60$$
$$\text{about } 1200$$

To find how many, multiply: $58 \times 24 = \underline{\ ?\ }$

Think:

$$\begin{array}{r} 2\ 4 \\ \times\ 5\ 8 \\ \hline \end{array}$$

$58 = 50 + 8$

$$\overset{3}{\begin{array}{r} 2\ 4 \\ \times\quad\ 8 \\ \hline 1\ 9\ 2 \end{array}}$$
$+$
$$\overset{2}{\begin{array}{r} 2\ 4 \\ \times\ 5\ 0 \\ \hline 1\ 2\ 0\ 0 \end{array}}$$
$=$
$$\begin{array}{r} 2\ 5 \\ \times\ 5\ 8 \\ \hline 1\ 3\ 9\ 2 \end{array}$$

Multiply by the ones.	Multiply by the tens.	Add the partial products.

$$\overset{3}{\begin{array}{r} 2\ 4 \\ \times\ 5\ 8 \\ \hline 1\ 9\ 2 \end{array}}$$

8×24

$$\overset{2}{\begin{array}{r} 2\ 4 \\ \times\ 5\ 8 \\ \hline 1\ 9\ 2 \\ 1\ 2\ 0\ 0 \end{array}}$$

50×24

$$\overset{2}{\begin{array}{r} 2\ 4 \\ \times\ 5\ 8 \\ \hline 1\ 9\ 2 \\ 1\ 2\ 0\ 0 \\ \hline 1\ 3\ 9\ 2 \end{array}}$$

1392 is close to 1200. The answer is reasonable.

Study these examples.

$$\overset{1}{\begin{array}{r} 2\ 2 \\ \times\ 4\ 6 \\ \hline 1\ 3\ 2 \\ 8\ 8\ 0 \\ \hline 1\ 0\ 1\ 2 \end{array}}$$

$6 \times 22 \longrightarrow$

$40 \times 22 \longrightarrow$

This zero does not have to be written.

$$\overset{3}{\begin{array}{r} \$.3\ 5 \\ \times\ 6\ 7 \\ \hline 2\ 4\ 5 \\ 2\ 1\ 0\ 0 \\ \hline \$2\ 3.4\ 5 \end{array}}$$

7×35

60×35

Estimate. Then multiply.

1. $\begin{array}{r} 21 \\ \times\,46 \\ \hline \end{array}$
2. $\begin{array}{r} 36 \\ \times\,18 \\ \hline \end{array}$
3. $\begin{array}{r} 42 \\ \times\,62 \\ \hline \end{array}$
4. $\begin{array}{r} 57 \\ \times\,19 \\ \hline \end{array}$
5. $\begin{array}{r} 73 \\ \times\,31 \\ \hline \end{array}$

6. $\begin{array}{r} 64 \\ \times\,39 \\ \hline \end{array}$
7. $\begin{array}{r} 83 \\ \times\,44 \\ \hline \end{array}$
8. $\begin{array}{r} 56 \\ \times\,92 \\ \hline \end{array}$
9. $\begin{array}{r} 29 \\ \times\,75 \\ \hline \end{array}$
10. $\begin{array}{r} 48 \\ \times\,99 \\ \hline \end{array}$

11. $\begin{array}{r} 76 \\ \times\,95 \\ \hline \end{array}$
12. $\begin{array}{r} 55 \\ \times\,39 \\ \hline \end{array}$
13. $\begin{array}{r} 63 \\ \times\,47 \\ \hline \end{array}$
14. $\begin{array}{r} 84 \\ \times\,56 \\ \hline \end{array}$
15. $\begin{array}{r} 92 \\ \times\,25 \\ \hline \end{array}$

16. $\begin{array}{r} \$.49 \\ \times\,\ \ 32 \\ \hline \end{array}$
17. $\begin{array}{r} \$.67 \\ \times\,\ \ 58 \\ \hline \end{array}$
18. $\begin{array}{r} \$.99 \\ \times\,\ \ 64 \\ \hline \end{array}$
19. $\begin{array}{r} \$.53 \\ \times\,\ \ 28 \\ \hline \end{array}$
20. $\begin{array}{r} \$.35 \\ \times\,\ \ 76 \\ \hline \end{array}$

Find the product.

21. 16×52
22. 28×82
23. 34×93
24. 71×37

25. $15 \times \$.94$
26. $34 \times \$.92$
27. $85 \times \$.55$
28. $26 \times \$.78$

Solve.

29. Tyrone put together 62 boxes of canned food. There were 45 cans in each box. How many cans of food were there?

30. Mill Farms donated 85 turkeys to soup kitchens in the city. Each turkey weighed 25 pounds. How many pounds of turkey did Mill Farms donate?

Calculator Activity

Use a calculator to multiply. Then write the products from least to greatest.

31. 24×223
32. 28×214
33. 17×406
34. 42×121

35. 16×387
36. 22×436
37. 33×613
38. 48×295

Multiplying with Three-Digit Numbers

Letisha, Marc, Robin, and Tim all made beaded wall hangings. How many beads did Robin use?

First estimate: 64 × 225

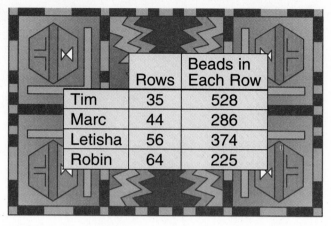

	Rows	Beads in Each Row
Tim	35	528
Marc	44	286
Letisha	56	374
Robin	64	225

$$\begin{array}{r} 225 \longrightarrow 200 \\ \times\ 64 \longrightarrow \times\ 60 \\ \hline \text{about } 12{,}000 \end{array}$$

To find how many, multiply: 64 × 225 = ?

Multiply by the ones.	Multiply by the tens.	Add the partial products.

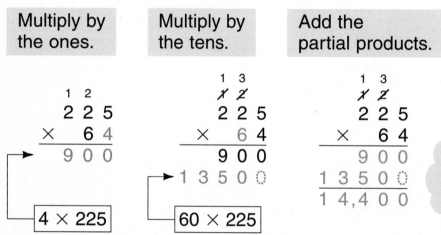

14,400 is close to 12,000. The answer is reasonable.

Robin used 14,400 beads.

Study these examples.

$$\begin{array}{r} \overset{6}{\cancel{4}} \\ 309 \\ \times\ 75 \\ \hline 1545 \\ 21630 \\ \hline 23{,}175 \end{array} \qquad \begin{array}{r} 132 \\ \times\ 31 \\ \hline 132 \\ 3960 \\ \hline 4092 \end{array} \qquad \begin{array}{r} \overset{4}{\cancel{2}} \\ \$6.51 \\ \times\ 84 \\ \hline 2604 \\ 52080 \\ \hline \$546.84 \end{array}$$

Estimate. Then find the product.

1. 201
$\times$ 44

2. 132
$\times$ 23

3. 312
$\times$ 11

4. 402
$\times$ 31

5. 611
$\times$ 43

6. 242
$\times$ 33

7. 404
$\times$ 32

8. 723
$\times$ 24

9. 312
$\times$ 42

10. 841
$\times$ 56

11. 492
$\times$ 67

12. 387
$\times$ 75

13. 525
$\times$ 98

14. 906
$\times$ 86

15. 759
$\times$ 52

16. $2.37
$\times$ 45

17. $4.99
$\times$ 68

18. $8.17
$\times$ 39

19. $6.30
$\times$ 53

20. $7.88
$\times$ 47

Multiply.

21. 84 $\times$ 634

22. 52 $\times$ 928

23. 79 $\times$ 837

24. 24 $\times$ $5.09

25. 59 $\times$ $3.25

26. 46 $\times$ $9.72

Solve. Use the table on page 154.

27. How many beads did Tim use?

28. How many beads did Marc use?

29. Did Letisha use more or fewer beads than Tim? How many more or fewer?

30. Estimate. Suppose Marc and Robin had the same number of rows. Who would use more beads?

31. Molly had the same number of rows as Tim. She used the same number of beads in each row as Marc. How many beads did Molly use?

32. Miguel used 656 beads in each of 28 rows. How many beads did Miguel use?

TECHNOLOGY

Computer Spreadsheets

A **spreadsheet** organizes information into *columns* and *rows*. The columns of a spreadsheet are labeled with letters. The rows are labeled with numbers. Each section of a spreadsheet is called a *cell*.

The spreadsheet below shows how information can be organized.

column B

	A	B	C	D
1	Item	Price	Number Sold	Total Price
2	table	$69.95	1	$ 69.95
3	chair	$29.95	4	$119.80
4	lamp	$45.99	2	$ 91.98
5		cell	Total Spent	$281.73

row 3 → 3

A cell is identified by its column and row.

In which cell is the price for 1 chair?

▶ To find the cell, first locate the column labeled *Price*. The label *Price* is in column B.

Then locate the row labeled *chair*. The label *chair* is in row 3.

So the price for one chair is in cell B3.

What information is in cell C4?

▶ To find the information, locate the cell C4. Cell C4 is in column C, row 4. The number of lamps sold is in cell C4.

156

Solve.

1. Freddy's car needs 4 new tires, a muffler, and brakes. He called 4 garages to get prices for the work. Complete the spreadsheet below by using the list Freddy made.

Thelma's Garage
Tires : $199.80
Muffler : $28.00
Brakes : $180.00

Park Hill
Tires : $222.00
Muffler : $48.85
Brakes : $157.59

Louie's
Tires : $197.50
Muffler : $36.40
Brakes : $200.00

Brown's
Tires : $208.00
Muffler : $36.40
Brakes : $200.00

	A	B	C	D	E
1	Garage	Tires	Muffler	Brakes	Total Cost
2		$208.00			
3	Louie's				
4				$157.59	
5			$28.00		

2. Which columns contain money amounts?

3. Which row contains labels?

4. In which cell is the cost for a muffler at Louie's?

5. What information is in cell A4?

6. Which garage has the best buy on tires?

7. How would you find the amount in cell E2?

8. Find the total cost for the work at each garage. Enter the amounts in the spreadsheet.

9. Which garage has the best buy for all the work Freddy needs done?

10. Create a spreadsheet using the information below.

	Week 1	Week 2	Week 3	Total Miles
Marty	15 mi	9 mi	8 mi	?
Sarah	10 mi	12 mi	14 mi	?
Josh	20 mi	18 mi	11 mi	?

5-17 | Problem Solving: Working Backwards

Problem: Karl bought some guppies in March. He had four times as many guppies by the end of May. He had 46 fish by the end of June, which was 10 more than at the end of May. How many guppies did he buy in March?

1 IMAGINE   Create a mental picture.

2 NAME   *Facts:*   Karl bought fish in March.
4 times as many in May
10 more than that in June
46 fish in June

Question: How many fish did Karl buy in March?

3 THINK   Work backwards. Use the opposite operation.
- First find the number of guppies at the end of May:
Subtract 10 from the number of guppies he had in June.

$$46 - 10 = \underline{\ ?\ } \text{ number in May}$$

- Then to find the number of guppies he had in March:
Divide the number of guppies in May by 4.
number in May $\div$ 4 = number in March

4 COMPUTE $46 - 10 = 36$ number in May
$36 \div 4 = 9$ number in March
Karl bought 9 guppies in March.

5 CHECK   Start with 9. Use the opposite operation.
9 guppies in March
$9 \times 4 = 36$ in May
$36 + 10 = 46$ in June   The answer checks.

Solve.

1. The Torres family came home from
   the matinee at 5:00 P.M. The trip
   to and from the cinema was 15 minutes
   each way. They spent 1 hour and 45 minutes
   at the cinema. What time did they leave home?

IMAGINE   Draw a clock.

NAME   *Facts:*   5:00 P.M. arrived home
                         15 minutes travel time each way
                         1 hour 45 minutes at the cinema

            Question: What time did they leave home?

THINK   Count back each time that was added.
             5:00 − 15 minutes − 15 minutes − 1 hour 45 minutes = _?_
                      time to   *time from*   *at the cinema*

             COMPUTE ⟶ **CHECK**

2. Kari had $4.25 left after shopping. She spent
   $11.80 for party favors and $22.55 for a giant
   party pizza. How much money did Kari have
   when she began shopping?

3. Bev, Ruth, and Lisa are sisters. Bev is 8 years
   older than Ruth. Ruth is 5 years older than Lisa,
   who is 16 years old. How old is Bev?

4. Don bought a bookcase for $36 and a lamp for $28. He
   received $6 change. How much money did he give the cashier?

5. After lunch there were 2 pizzas left over. Grades 1, 2, and 3
   finished 6 pizzas. Grades 4 and 5 each finished 7 pizzas.
   If the teachers finished 2 pizzas, how many pizzas had
   been ordered?

5-18 | Problem-Solving Applications

Solve.

1. Oscar's Orchard has 128 Macintosh apple trees. A tree produces about 115 pounds of fruit each year. About how many pounds of Macintosh apples grow each year?

Use these steps:

Imagine
Name
Think
Compute
Check

2. The orchard has 17 rows of peach trees. There are 16 trees in each row. Does the orchard have more than 300 peach trees?

3. Sonal works for 5 hours every day during harvest. How many hours does she work in thirty days?

4. A fence around the orchard is 894 feet long. Every foot of fencing has three posts. How many posts are in the fence?

5. Customers can pick raspberries for $1.75 per quart. How much would 12 quarts of berries cost?

6. The pick-your-own price at Oscar's Orchard is $3.25 per bushel of apples. Mr. Ennis picked 8 bushels. How much did he spend?

7. Mr. Ennis uses 3 pounds of apples to make 1 pint of apple butter. How many apples does he need to make 14 pints of apple butter?

8. Each pot of strawberry plants produces about 8 dozen berries. There are 58 pots of plants. About how many strawberries do 58 pots of plants produce?

Solve.

9. Emily picked 34 apples. Half of the apples were golden delicious. How many were not golden delicious?

10. Tia gave 5 apples to Ms. Lu and half of what she had left to her grandmother. She used the remaining 6 apples in a pie. How many apples had she brought home?

USE THESE STRATEGIES:
Working Backwards
Choose the Operation
Extra Information
Logical Reasoning
Guess and Test

11. Mia, Nate, and Rob each picked either apples, pears, or grapes. Mia did not pick pears, and Rob did not pick grapes. Nate shared his apples. Which fruit did Rob pick?

12. Liam picked 124 apples and Cleo picked 152. The pick-your-own apples cost about 4 cents each. Did Cleo spend more than $5?

13. Chad stopped picking fruit at 2:30 P.M. He had picked pears for 1 hour and apples for 45 minutes. When did he start picking?

14. One apple has about 25 seeds. There are about 160 apples in a bushel. About how many seeds are in a bushel of apples?

Use the graph for problems 15 and 16.

15. How many more peach than plum trees were planted in Oscar's Orchard?

16. What kind of trees are double the number of pear trees?

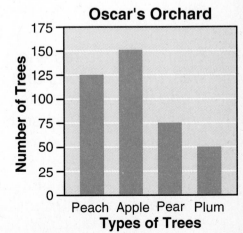

Oscar's Orchard

Number of Trees vs. Types of Trees (Peach, Apple, Pear, Plum)

More Practice

Find the product.

1. 2 × 34   **2.** 6 × 30   **3.** 5 × 68   **4.** 4 × 77

5. 3 × 323   **6.** 3 × 450   **7.** 9 × $5.37   **8.** 8 × 6124

9. 10 × 43   **10.** 50 × 30   **11.** 60 × 94   **12.** 10 × 364

13.   53   **14.**   74   **15.**   84   **16.**   30
       × 55   × 38   × 46   × 27

17.   524   **18.**   608   **19.**   735   **20.**   450
       ×   5   × 54   × 46   × 76

21. $6.30   **22.** $4.50   **23.** $9.40   **24.** $5.09
       ×   26   ×   34   ×   17   ×   46

Estimate the product.

25. 8 × 35   **26.** 6 × 736   **27.** 5 × 612   **28.** 9 × $27.50

29. 61 × 54   **30.** 86 × 91   **31.** 32 × $.17   **32.** 16 × 307

Solve.

33. The product is zero. One factor is 8.
    What is the other factor?

34. Sharon drew a rectangle. The rectangle
    was 14 inches long and 5 inches wide.
    If she divided the rectangle into 1 inch
    squares, how many squares would
    she have?

35. Jamal bicycles 18 kilometers each day.
    How far does he bicycle in 12 days?

(See *Still More Practice,* p. 464.)

CLUSTERING

Tommy kept a record of his
family's daily mileage on
a car trip to Mexico.
About how many miles long
was the trip?

Day	Miles
Sunday	432
Monday	396
Tuesday	394
Wednesday	402

On each of the 4 days of the trip,
Tommy's family traveled about 400 miles.
So you can use 400 to estimate
by **clustering**.

$$\begin{array}{r} 400 \\ \times \quad 4 \\ \hline 1600 \end{array}$$

The trip was about 1600 miles long.

Estimate the total by clustering.

1. 37 + 41 + 43 + 35

2. 85 + 98 + 87 + 88

3. 105 + 98 + 96

4. 510 + 483 + 503

5. 326 + 289 + 301 + 313

6. 740 + 675 + 690 + 727

7. 2943 + 3201 + 3065

8. 5624 + 4875 + 5133

Solve.

9. In Elmsford's schools, East
has 489 students, Central
has 535 students, and West
has 492 students. About how
many students are in Elmsford?

10. VideoLand rented out 199
movies on Friday, 248
movies on Saturday, and 218
movies on Sunday. About how
many movies was this?

Check Your Mastery

Find the product.

See pp. 130–135, 138–147, 150–155

1. 3 × 21

2. 7 × 20

3. 4 × 59

4. 8 × 47

5. 6 × 101

6. 5 × 360

7. 3 × $2.29

8. 9 × 5473

9. 10 × 77

10. 90 × 80

11. 50 × 26

12. 10 × 133

13.
$$\begin{array}{r} 16 \\ \times\, 39 \\ \hline \end{array}$$

14.
$$\begin{array}{r} 54 \\ \times\, 97 \\ \hline \end{array}$$

15.
$$\begin{array}{r} 43 \\ \times\, 21 \\ \hline \end{array}$$

16.
$$\begin{array}{r} 60 \\ \times\, 39 \\ \hline \end{array}$$

17.
$$\begin{array}{r} 858 \\ \times\, 4 \\ \hline \end{array}$$

18.
$$\begin{array}{r} 307 \\ \times\, 85 \\ \hline \end{array}$$

19.
$$\begin{array}{r} 442 \\ \times\, 36 \\ \hline \end{array}$$

20.
$$\begin{array}{r} 590 \\ \times\, 73 \\ \hline \end{array}$$

21.
$$\begin{array}{r} \$5.50 \\ \times\, 18 \\ \hline \end{array}$$

22.
$$\begin{array}{r} \$3.25 \\ \times\, 37 \\ \hline \end{array}$$

23.
$$\begin{array}{r} \$1.52 \\ \times\, 20 \\ \hline \end{array}$$

24.
$$\begin{array}{r} \$3.07 \\ \times\, 45 \\ \hline \end{array}$$

Estimate.

See pp. 136–137, 148–149

25. 7 × 29

26. 3 × 326

27. 4 × 550

28. 6 × $12.75

29. 25 × 82

30. 43 × 56

31. 15 × $.32

32. 68 × 421

Solve.

See pp. 126–129, 160–161

33. The product is 6. One factor is 6. What is the other factor?

34. Cassettes are $9.95 each. How much will Jean pay for 10 cassettes?

35. Mr. Adams creates designs on T-shirts. His new design requires 125 beads for each shirt. How many beads does he need to design 25 T-shirts?

36. What is the product of 0 and any number?

In this chapter you will:
  Understand the rules
  for division
  Find missing numbers
  in division and in
  patterns
  Estimate quotients
  Divide whole numbers
  and money by 1-digit
  and check by multiplying
  Use divisibility and
  order of operations
  Find averages
  Solve problems by
  interpreting the
  remainder

Do you remember?
  $5 \times 3 = 15$
  $3 \times 5 = 15$
  $15 \div ? = 3$
  $15 \div ? = 5$

**Critical Thinking/
Finding Together**
How many more flags are
needed to complete the array?
Write the family of facts for the
completed array.

6-1 Division Concepts

▶ You **divide** when you want to:

- separate a set into equal parts.

  Cal has 12 pears. He puts 4 pears into each bag. How many bags does he use?

  $$12 \div 4 = 3$$

  He uses 3 bags.

- share a set equally.

  Jo, Meg, and Cara share 12 pears equally. How many pears does each girl get?

  $$12 \div 3 = 4$$

  Each girl gets 4 pears.

▶ Here are some rules that can help you to divide quickly and correctly.

- When you divide a number by one, the quotient is the same as the dividend.

$$1\overline{)8} = 8$$
$$8 \div 1 = 8$$

- When you divide a number other than zero by itself, the quotient is 1.

$$5\overline{)5} = 1$$
$$5 \div 5 = 1$$

- When you divide zero by any other number, the quotient is 0.

$$6\overline{)0} = 0$$
$$0 \div 6 = 0$$

- It is *impossible* to divide a number by 0.

Divide.

1. $6\overline{)6}$ 2. $5\overline{)0}$ 3. $1\overline{)7}$ 4. $3\overline{)3}$ 5. $2\overline{)0}$ 6. $9\overline{)9}$

7. $4\overline{)0}$ 8. $1\overline{)5}$ 9. $1\overline{)0}$ 10. $4\overline{)4}$ 11. $1\overline{)2}$ 12. $1\overline{)6}$

Find the quotient.

13. $2 \div 2$ **14.** $9 \div 1$ **15.** $0 \div 7$ **16.** $8 \div 8$ **17.** $3 \div 1$

18. $0 \div 8$ **19.** $7 \div 7$ **20.** $4 \div 1$ **21.** $0 \div 9$ **22.** $1 \div 1$

23. $5 \div 5$ **24.** $8 \div 1$ **25.** $0 \div 3$ **26.** $0 \div 6$ **27.** $9 \div 9$

Solve.

28. The dividend is 7.
The quotient is 1.
What is the divisor?

29. The divisor is 4.
The quotient is 1.
What is the dividend?

30. The divisor is 5.
The quotient is 5.
What is the dividend?

31. The quotient is 2.
The dividend is 2.
What is the divisor?

32. The dividend is 1.
The quotient is 1.
What is the divisor?

33. The quotient is 0.
What is the dividend?

34. How should 4 friends share 24 apples equally?

35. Dal and 4 friends share 15 oranges. What is a fair share for each child?

36. Sara has 64 plums. She packs them 8 to a basket. How many baskets does she use?

37. Ty packs 8 baskets with 5 peaches to a basket. How many peaches are there?

Mental Math

Use the rules to divide mentally.

38. $0 \div 15$ **39.** $26 \div 26$ **40.** $49 \div 1$ **41.** $0 \div 99$ **42.** $75 \div 1$

43. $429 \div 429$ **44.** $867 \div 1$ **45.** $0 \div 539$ **46.** $938 \div 938$

Missing Numbers in Division

You can use multiplication facts
to find missing numbers in division.

▶ Find the missing divisor:
$63 \div \underline{\ ?\ } = 9$

Think: $9 \times \underline{\ ?\ } = 63$
$9 \times \underline{\ 7\ } = 63$

So $\quad 63 \div 7 = 9$

Remember:
dividend ÷ divisor = quotient
or
$\dfrac{\text{quotient}}{\text{divisor)dividend}}$

▶ Find the missing dividend: $7\overline{)?}^{\,6}$

Think: $6 \times 7 = \underline{\ ?\ }$
$6 \times 7 = \underline{\ 42\ }$

So $7\overline{)42}^{\,6}$

Study these examples.

$?\overline{)36}^{\,9}$

Think: $9 \times \underline{\ ?\ } = 36$
$9 \times \underline{\ 4\ } = 36$

So $4\overline{)36}^{\,9}$

$\underline{\ ?\ } \div 6 = 1$

Think: $1 \times \underline{\ ?\ } = 6$
$1 \times \underline{\ 6\ } = 6$
So $\quad 6 \div 6 = 1$

Find the missing divisor.

1. $?\overline{)12}^{\,6}$

2. $?\overline{)30}^{\,5}$

3. $?\overline{)32}^{\,8}$

4. $?\overline{)54}^{\,6}$

5. $?\overline{)49}^{\,7}$

6. $?\overline{)36}^{\,4}$

7. $?\overline{)56}^{\,7}$

8. $?\overline{)14}^{\,2}$

9. $?\overline{)15}^{\,3}$

10. $?\overline{)48}^{\,6}$

Find the missing dividend.

11. $9\overline{)?}$ with quotient 5

12. $4\overline{)?}$ with quotient 6

13. $5\overline{)?}$ with quotient 8

14. $9\overline{)?}$ with quotient 3

15. $8\overline{)?}$ with quotient 4

16. $6\overline{)?}$ with quotient 9

17. $2\overline{)?}$ with quotient 0

18. $8\overline{)?}$ with quotient 2

19. $5\overline{)?}$ with quotient 4

20. $3\overline{)?}$ with quotient 1

21. $7\overline{)?}$ with quotient 6

22. $5\overline{)?}$ with quotient 9

23. $6\overline{)?}$ with quotient 5

24. $9\overline{)?}$ with quotient 2

25. $4\overline{)?}$ with quotient 4

Find the missing number.

26. $35 \div \underline{?} = 5$

27. $42 \div \underline{?} = 6$

28. $72 \div \underline{?} = 9$

29. $\underline{?} \div 3 = 4$

30. $\underline{?} \div 7 = 8$

31. $\underline{?} \div 2 = 5$

32. $64 \div \underline{?} = 8$

33. $18 \div \underline{?} = 3$

34. $9 \div \underline{?} = 1$

35. $\underline{?} \div 9 = 3$

36. $\underline{?} \div 8 = 5$

37. $\underline{?} \div 7 = 4$

38. $24 \div \underline{?} = 3$

39. $48 \div \underline{?} = 6$

40. $25 \div \underline{?} = 5$

Skills to Remember

Write the digit in the tens place.

41. 432

42. 7604

43. 28

44. 35,196

45. 8172

Write the digit in the hundreds place.

46. 3584

47. 67,312

48. 192

49. 2837

50. 495

Write the place of the red digit.

51. 7183

52. 14,697

53. 13,452

54. 8306

55. 9563

Number Patterns

▶ What is the next number in this pattern?

16, 8, 4, 2, ?

- First find the rule.

Think: 16, 8, 4, 2
$\div 2 \div 2 \div 2$

Rule: Divide by 2.

- Then complete the pattern.

16, 8, 4, 2, ?

16, 8, 4, 2, 1

Think: $2 \div 2 = 1$

The next number in the pattern is 1.

▶ Here is another pattern. What is the next number?

2, 7, 6, 11, 10, ?

Think: 2, 7, 6, 11, 10
$+5 \ -1 \ +5 \ -1$

Rule: Add 5. Subtract 1.

2, 7, 6, 11, 10, ?

2, 7, 6, 11, 10, 15

Think: $10 + 5 = 15$

The next number is 15.

Write the rule for each pattern. Then write the next number.

1. 10, 12, 14, 16, ?

2. 20, 40, 50, ?

3. 25, 30, 35, ?

4. 10, 13, 16, 19, ?

Write the rule. Complete the pattern.

5. 27, 9, 3, _?_

6. 33, 31, 29, _?_

7. 42, 38, 34, _?_

8. 4, 8, 16, 32, _?_

9. 16, 20, 18, 22, 20, _?_

10. 54, 51, 52, 49, 50, _?_

11. 4, 12, 10, 30, 28, _?_

12. 5, 10, 13, 26, 29, _?_

13. 1, 4, 4, 7, 7, 10, _?_

14. 10, 12, 6, 8, 4, 6, _?_

Write a pattern of eight numbers for each rule.

15. Rule: Add 6.

16. Rule: Subtract 3.

17. Rule: Multiply by 2.

18. Rule: Add 50.

19. Rule: Add 3. Add 1.

20. Rule: Add 10. Subtract 1.

21. Rule: Add 5.
Multiply by 2.

22. Rule: Multiply by 3.
Subtract 4.

Finding Together

Even numbers have either 0, 2, 4, 6, or 8
as their ones digits.

Odd numbers are all the whole numbers that
are not even.

Is the sum or product odd or even? Write *O* or *E*.

23. Even + Even

24. Even × Even

25. Odd + Odd

26. Odd × Odd

27. Even + Odd

28. Odd × Even

171

6-4 Estimating in Division

You can estimate quotients before you divide.

Estimate: 2672 ÷ 8

- Find where the quotient begins.

  Try dividing thousands.

  8)2672   8 > 2   **Not enough thousands**

  Try dividing hundreds.

  8)2672   8 < 26   **Enough hundreds**

  So the quotient begins in the hundreds place.

  $$\overset{X}{8)\overline{2672}}$$

- Find the first digit of the quotient.

  Think: About how many 8s in 26?

  2 × 8 = 16   too small

  3 × 8 = 24 ◄───── | 26 is between

  4 × 8 = 32   too large | 16 and 32. Try 3. |

  $$\overset{3}{8)\overline{2672}}$$

- Write zeros for the other digits.

  $$\overset{\text{about } 300}{8)\overline{2672}}$$

Study these examples.

$$\overset{\text{about } 200}{2)\overline{523}} \qquad \overset{\text{about } 70}{6)\overline{425}} \qquad \overset{\text{about \$ 6.00}}{5)\overline{\$32.75}}$$

Write in what place the quotient begins.

1. $\overset{X}{4)\overline{76}}$ **2.** 6)48   **3.** 2)451   **4.** 7)927   **5.** 8)745

6. 3)127   **7.** 5)370   **8.** 2)1468   **9.** 7)4303

172

Estimate the quotient.

10. $9\overline{)95}$ **11.** $6\overline{)43}$ **12.** $2\overline{)87}$ **13.** $5\overline{)38}$ **14.** $4\overline{)92}$

15. $4\overline{)591}$ **16.** $7\overline{)862}$ **17.** $3\overline{)947}$ **18.** $2\overline{)815}$

19. $6\overline{)275}$ **20.** $9\overline{)467}$ **21.** $8\overline{)744}$ **22.** $5\overline{)342}$

23. $7\overline{)2439}$ **24.** $4\overline{)3622}$ **25.** $3\overline{)1729}$ **26.** $9\overline{)5649}$

27. $2\overline{)\$4.94}$ **28.** $3\overline{)\$6.42}$ **29.** $5\overline{)\$17.50}$ **30.** $4\overline{)\$28.58}$

Estimating with Compatible Numbers

Estimate: $53 \div 6$

Think: What number times 6 has a product close to 53?

$9 \times 6 = 54$

So $53 \div 6$ is about 9.

Estimate: $223 \div 7$

Think: How many tens times 7 has a product close to 22 tens?

3 tens $\times$ 7 = 21 tens

So $223 \div 7$ is about 3 tens, or 30.

Write the dividend you would use to estimate the quotient.

31. $55 \div 8$ **32.** $46 \div 6$ **33.** $362 \div 5$ **34.** $178 \div 3$

Estimate the quotient. Use compatible numbers.

35. $4\overline{)29}$ **36.** $5\overline{)33}$ **37.** $8\overline{)26}$ **38.** $3\overline{)11}$ **39.** $7\overline{)40}$

40. $3\overline{)61}$ **41.** $4\overline{)84}$ **42.** $2\overline{)63}$ **43.** $5\overline{)56}$ **44.** $3\overline{)91}$

45. $7\overline{)285}$ **46.** $5\overline{)161}$ **47.** $6\overline{)524}$ **48.** $9\overline{)472}$ **49.** $7\overline{)551}$

One-Digit Quotients

Jaime gave the same number of pens to each of 5 friends. He had 22 pens. How many pens did each friend receive? How many pens were left over?

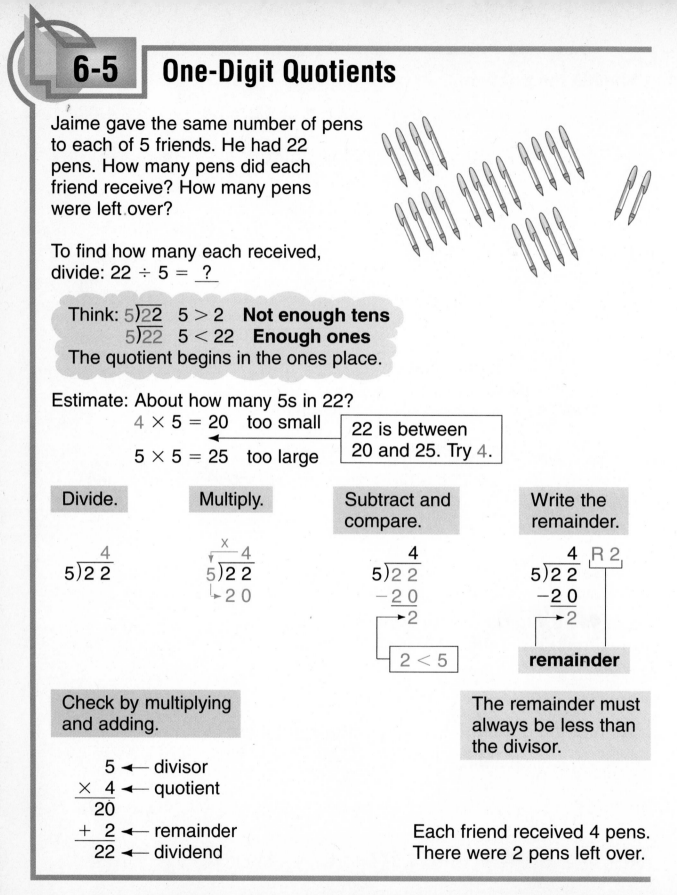

To find how many each received, divide: 22 ÷ 5 = _?_

Think: 5)22   5 > 2   **Not enough tens**
5)22   5 < 22   **Enough ones**
The quotient begins in the ones place.

Estimate: About how many 5s in 22?

4 × 5 = 20   too small

5 × 5 = 25   too large

22 is between 20 and 25. Try 4.

Divide.	Multiply.	Subtract and compare.	Write the remainder.
4 5)2 2	× 4 5)2 2 20	4 5)2 2 −2 0 2	4 R 2 5)2 2 −2 0 2 **remainder**

2 < 5

Check by multiplying and adding.

5 ← divisor
× 4 ← quotient
20
+ 2 ← remainder
22 ← dividend

The remainder must always be less than the divisor.

Each friend received 4 pens. There were 2 pens left over.

Copy and complete.

1. $\begin{array}{r} 6 \\ 4\overline{)24} \\ -24 \\ \hline 0 \end{array}$ ← There is no remainder.

2. $\begin{array}{r} 6 \text{ R } ? \\ 3\overline{)20} \\ -18 \\ \hline 2 \end{array}$

3. $\begin{array}{r} 9 \text{ R } ? \\ 5\overline{)48} \\ -45 \\ \hline ? \end{array}$

4. $\begin{array}{r} ? \text{ R } ? \\ 2\overline{)13} \\ -?? \\ \hline ? \end{array}$

Divide.

5. $2\overline{)15}$ 6. $4\overline{)35}$ 7. $3\overline{)23}$ 8. $5\overline{)17}$ 9. $6\overline{)27}$

10. $6\overline{)14}$ 11. $4\overline{)26}$ 12. $5\overline{)37}$ 13. $7\overline{)50}$ 14. $4\overline{)33}$

15. $6\overline{)55}$ 16. $5\overline{)38}$ 17. $8\overline{)68}$ 18. $2\overline{)19}$ 19. $7\overline{)45}$

20. $8\overline{)23}$ 21. $3\overline{)26}$ 22. $7\overline{)35}$ 23. $7\overline{)29}$ 24. $8\overline{)38}$

25. $9\overline{)64}$ 26. $8\overline{)52}$ 27. $6\overline{)45}$ 28. $9\overline{)71}$ 29. $9\overline{)82}$

Find the quotient and the remainder.

30. $25 \div 3$ 31. $23 \div 7$ 32. $84 \div 9$

33. $50 \div 8$ 34. $38 \div 4$ 35. $57 \div 6$

Solve.

36. Caryn put away 36 crayons in boxes. Each box holds 8 crayons. How many boxes could be filled? How many crayons would be left over?

37. Mika put 37 drawings in folders. She put 4 drawings in each folder. How many folders were there? How many extra drawings were there?

38. Bill placed the same number of pencils at each of 6 tables. He began with 44 pencils. At most, how many pencils could he place at each table? How many pencils would be left over?

6-6 Divisibility

A number is **divisible** by another number when the remainder is zero.

List the whole numbers from 1 to 50.

▶ Skip count to 50 by 2. Circle the numbers you counted. Look at the digits in the *ones* place. What pattern do you see?

> Even numbers end in 0, 2, 4, 6, or 8. **All even numbers are divisible by 2.**

▶ Skip count to 50 by 5. Draw a box around the numbers you counted. Look at the digits in the ones place. What pattern do you see?

> **All numbers ending in 0 or 5 are divisible by 5.**

▶ Skip count to 50 by 10. Mark an "X" on these numbers. What pattern do you see?

> **All numbers ending in 0 are divisible by 10.**

Is the number divisible by 2? Write *yes* or *no*.

1. 28	**2.** 75	**3.** 700	**4.** 144	**5.** 807
6. 516	**7.** 343	**8.** 2931	**9.** 1462	**10.** 7749
11. 6847	**12.** 2900	**13.** 75,192	**14.** 27,346	**15.** 92,983

Is the number divisible by 5? Write *yes* or *no*.

16. 64	**17.** 85	**18.** 900	**19.** 245	**20.** 819
21. 703	**22.** 456	**23.** 1820	**24.** 4795	**25.** 9240
26. 8675	**27.** 3299	**28.** 10,000	**29.** 42,685	**30.** 74,007

Is the number divisible by 10? Write *yes* or *no*.

31. 70
32. 35
33. 102
34. 680
35. 462

36. 930
37. 749
38. 6820
39. 5000
40. 8304

41. 1006
42. 4673
43. 52,651
44. 66,830
45. 90,060

Copy and complete the table.

46.

Divisible by	60	88	75	600	494	750	2313	1026	8750
2	yes	?	?	?	?	?	no	?	?
5	yes	?	yes	?	?	?	?	?	?
10	?	?	?	yes	?	?	?	?	?

Divisibility by 3

If the sum of the digits of a number is divisible by 3, that number is divisible by 3.

$27 \longrightarrow 2 + 7 = 9 \longrightarrow 9 \div 3 = 3$
27 is divisible by 3.

$435 \longrightarrow 4 + 3 + 5 = 12 \longrightarrow 12 \div 3 = 4$
435 is divisible by 3.

Is the number divisible by 3? Write *yes* or *no*.

47. 72
48. 54
49. 253
50. 534
51. 312

52. 932
53. 210
54. 842
55. 1065
56. 4906

Critical Thinking

Solve.

57. For each divisor, what number is the greatest possible remainder?

Divisors			
2	3	4	5
6	7	8	9

6-7 Two-Digit Quotients

Ian cut a 72-inch length of cloth into 2 equal strips. What was the length of each strip?

To find the length of each strip, divide: $72 \div 2 = \underline{\ ?\ }$

Think: $2\overline{)72}$ $2 < 7$ **Enough tens**

Estimate: About how many 2s in 7?

$2 \times 3 = 6$ — 7 is between
$2 \times 4 = 8$ — 6 and 8. Try 3.

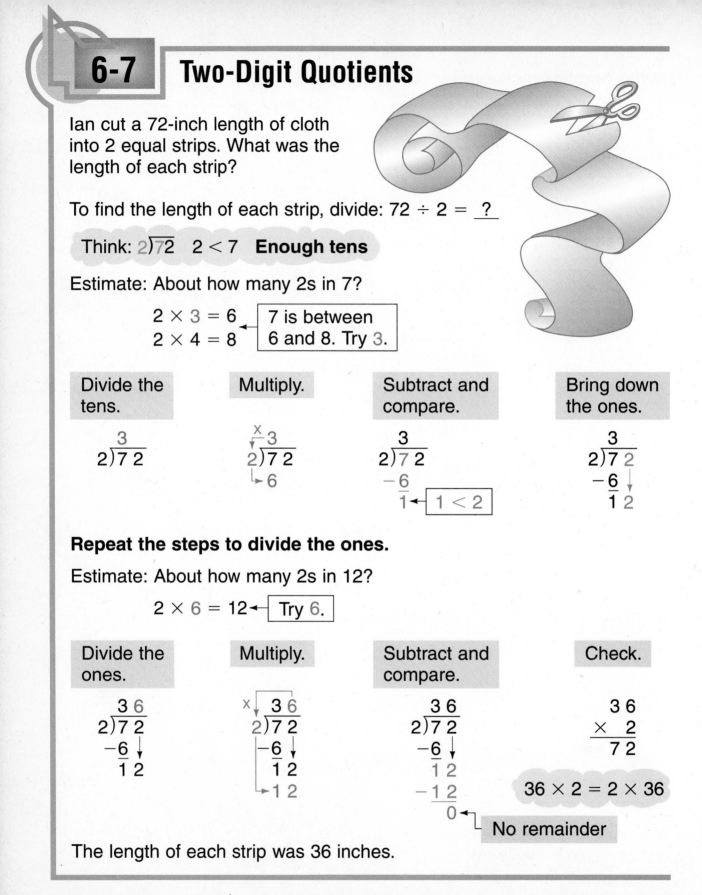

Divide the tens.	Multiply.	Subtract and compare.	Bring down the ones.
$\dfrac{3}{2\overline{)72}}$	$\begin{array}{r} \times\ 3 \\ 2\overline{)72} \\ {}_{\llcorner}6 \end{array}$	$\begin{array}{r} 3 \\ 2\overline{)72} \\ -6 \\ \hline 1 \leftarrow \boxed{1 < 2} \end{array}$	$\begin{array}{r} 3 \\ 2\overline{)72} \\ -6\ \downarrow \\ \hline 1\,2 \end{array}$

Repeat the steps to divide the ones.

Estimate: About how many 2s in 12?

$2 \times 6 = 12$ ← Try 6.

Divide the ones.	Multiply.	Subtract and compare.	Check.
$\begin{array}{r} 3\,6 \\ 2\overline{)72} \\ -6\ \downarrow \\ \hline 1\,2 \end{array}$	$\begin{array}{r} \times\ 3\,6 \\ 2\overline{)72} \\ -6\ \downarrow \\ \hline 1\,2 \\ {}_{\llcorner}1\,2 \end{array}$	$\begin{array}{r} 3\,6 \\ 2\overline{)72} \\ -6\ \downarrow \\ \hline 1\,2 \\ -1\,2 \\ \hline 0 \end{array}$	$\begin{array}{r} 3\,6 \\ \times\ \ 2 \\ \hline 7\,2 \end{array}$

$36 \times 2 = 2 \times 36$

No remainder

The length of each strip was 36 inches.

178

Copy and complete.

$$
\begin{array}{r}
1\ 0 \\
1.\ 4\overline{)4\ 0} \\
-4\downarrow \\
\hline
0\ 0 \\
-\ ? \\
\hline
?
\end{array}
\qquad
\begin{array}{r}
2\ ? \\
2.\ 4\overline{)8\ 4} \\
-8\downarrow \\
\hline
0\ 4 \\
-\ ? \\
\hline
?
\end{array}
\qquad
\begin{array}{r}
1\ ? \\
3.\ 6\overline{)7\ 8} \\
-?\downarrow \\
\hline
?\ ? \\
-?\ ? \\
\hline
?
\end{array}
\qquad
\begin{array}{r}
?\ ? \\
4.\ 2\overline{)3\ 4} \\
-?\downarrow \\
\hline
?\ ? \\
-?\ ? \\
\hline
?
\end{array}
$$

Estimate. Then divide.

5. $2\overline{)76}$ 6. $5\overline{)85}$ 7. $3\overline{)78}$ 8. $7\overline{)98}$ 9. $4\overline{)68}$

10. $4\overline{)92}$ 11. $3\overline{)57}$ 12. $5\overline{)65}$ 13. $2\overline{)46}$ 14. $5\overline{)95}$

15. $3\overline{)42}$ 16. $4\overline{)48}$ 17. $2\overline{)50}$ 18. $3\overline{)75}$ 19. $2\overline{)60}$

20. $5\overline{)60}$ 21. $6\overline{)84}$ 22. $4\overline{)64}$ 23. $7\overline{)91}$ 24. $3\overline{)69}$

25. $8\overline{)96}$ 26. $4\overline{)92}$ 27. $6\overline{)96}$ 28. $3\overline{)48}$ 29. $9\overline{)99}$

Find the quotient.

30. $84 \div 3$ 31. $80 \div 5$ 32. $56 \div 4$

33. $45 \div 3$ 34. $90 \div 2$ 35. $88 \div 2$

36. $70 \div 2$ 37. $66 \div 6$ 38. $90 \div 3$

Solve.

39. Renny made 80 pompons for clown costumes. Each costume had 5 pompons. How many clown costumes were there?

40. Kate cut an 84-inch long ribbon into 3 equal parts. How many inches long was each part?

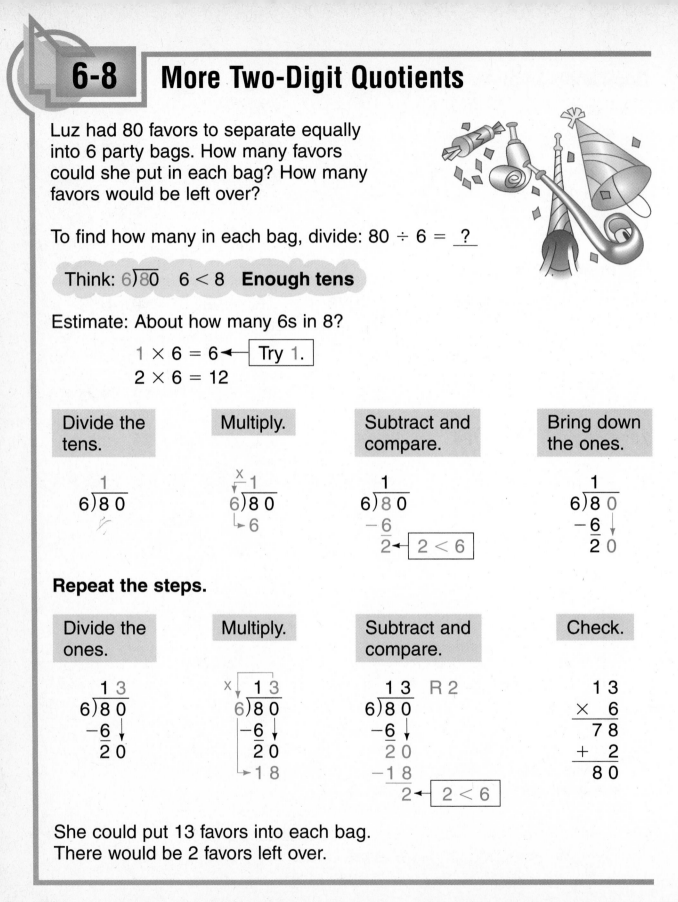

6-8 More Two-Digit Quotients

Luz had 80 favors to separate equally into 6 party bags. How many favors could she put in each bag? How many favors would be left over?

To find how many in each bag, divide: 80 ÷ 6 = __?__

Think: 6)80   6 < 8   **Enough tens**

Estimate: About how many 6s in 8?

$1 \times 6 = 6$ ← Try 1.
$2 \times 6 = 12$

Divide the tens.	Multiply.	Subtract and compare.	Bring down the ones.
$\begin{array}{r} 1 \\ 6\overline{)8\,0} \end{array}$	$\begin{array}{r} ^{\times}1 \\ 6\overline{)8\,0} \\ 6 \end{array}$	$\begin{array}{r} 1 \\ 6\overline{)8\,0} \\ -6 \\ \hline 2 \end{array}$ 2 < 6	$\begin{array}{r} 1 \\ 6\overline{)8\,0} \\ -6\downarrow \\ \hline 2\,0 \end{array}$

Repeat the steps.

Divide the ones.	Multiply.	Subtract and compare.	Check.
$\begin{array}{r} 1\,3 \\ 6\overline{)8\,0} \\ -6\downarrow \\ \hline 2\,0 \end{array}$	$\begin{array}{r} ^{\times}1\,3 \\ 6\overline{)8\,0} \\ -6\downarrow \\ \hline 2\,0 \\ 1\,8 \end{array}$	$\begin{array}{r} 1\,3 \;\; \text{R 2} \\ 6\overline{)8\,0} \\ -6\downarrow \\ \hline 2\,0 \\ -1\,8 \\ \hline 2 \end{array}$ 2 < 6	$\begin{array}{r} 1\,3 \\ \times\;\;6 \\ \hline 7\,8 \\ +\;\;2 \\ \hline 8\,0 \end{array}$

She could put 13 favors into each bag.
There would be 2 favors left over.

Copy and complete.

```
      1 0  R ?            2 ?  R ?            1 ?  R ?            ? ?  R 3
1. 5)5 4              2. 3)7 4            3. 8)9 8            4. 4)9 9
   −5 ↓                  −6 ↓               −? ↓               −8 ↓
     4                     1 4               ? ?                1 ?
   −  ?                  −? ?               −? ?               −? ?
   ────                  ────               ────               ────
      ?                      ?                  ?                  3
```

Estimate. Then divide.

5. 4)49   6. 2)81   7. 5)92   8. 6)83   9. 3)92

10. 8)91   11. 7)87   12. 3)58   13. 4)89   14. 2)74

15. 3)37   16. 5)63   17. 7)94   18. 6)67   19. 8)89

20. 5)86   21. 2)93   22. 4)51   23. 2)47   24. 7)79

25. 6)97   26. 4)86   27. 6)99   28. 5)87   29. 9)98

30. 61 ÷ 2   31. 47 ÷ 3   32. 71 ÷ 4   33. 76 ÷ 5

34. 92 ÷ 9   35. 84 ÷ 8   36. 96 ÷ 7   37. 85 ÷ 6

Solve.

38. There were 65 balloons at Willy's party. He tied 6 balloons to each tree in his yard and the extra balloons to his mailbox. What is the greatest number of trees that could have been in Willy's yard? How many balloons would he have tied to his mailbox?

39. Val hid 96 eggs in the yard. Each of 7 children found the same number of eggs. What is the greatest number of eggs each child could have found? How many eggs would still have remained hidden?

Divide: $745 \div 2 = \underline{\ ?\ }$

Use the division steps to find three-digit quotients.

- Divide the hundreds.

  Estimate: $\underline{\ ?\ } \times 2 = 7$
  $3 \times 2 = 6$
  $4 \times 2 = 8$
  Try 3.

  $$\begin{array}{r} 3 \\ 2\overline{)7\,4\,5} \\ -6\downarrow \\ \hline 1\,4 \end{array}$$

- Divide the tens.

  Estimate: $\underline{\ ?\ } \times 2 = 14$
  $7 \times 2 = 14$
  Try 7.

  $$\begin{array}{r} 3\,7 \\ 2\overline{)7\,4\,5} \\ -6\downarrow \\ \hline 1\,4 \\ -1\,4\downarrow \\ \hline 0\,5 \end{array}$$

- Divide the ones.

  Estimate: $\underline{\ ?\ } \times 2 = 5$
  $2 \times 2 = 4$
  $3 \times 2 = 6$
  Try 2.

  $$\begin{array}{r} 3\,7\,2 \quad R\ 1 \\ 2\overline{)7\,4\,5} \\ -6\downarrow \\ \hline 1\,4 \\ -1\,4\downarrow \\ \hline 0\,5 \\ -\ 4 \\ \hline 1 \end{array}$$

  This 0 need not be written.

- Check.

  $$\begin{array}{r} 3\,7\,2 \\ \times2 \\ \hline 7\,4\,4 \\ +1 \\ \hline 7\,4\,5 \end{array}$$

Division Steps

- Estimate.
- Divide.
- Multiply.
- Subtract.
- Compare.
- Bring down.
- Repeat the steps as necessary.
- Check.

Remember:
Write the remainder in the quotient.

Copy and complete.

1.
```
        1 2 5  R 3
   5) 6 2 8
     - 5 ↓
       1 2
     - ? ? ↓
         2 8
       - ? ?
           3
```

Check.
```
      1 2 5
   ×      5
      6 2 5
   +      ?
      6 2 8
```

2.
```
        2 4 3  R 2
   3) 7 3 1
     - 6 ↓
       1 3
     - 1 2 ↓
         1 1
       -   ?
           2
```

Check.
```
      2 4 3
   ×      3
      7 2 9
   +      ?
      7 3 1
```

3.
```
        2 6 ?
   3) 8 0 7
     - ? ↓
       2 0
     - ? ? ↓
         2 7
       - ? ?
           0
```

Check.
```
      2 6 ?
   ×      3
      ? ? ?
```

4.
```
        ? 2 ?  R ?
   2) 6 5 1
     - 6 ↓
       0 5
       - ? ↓
         1 1
       - 1 0
           ?
```

Check.
```
      ? 2 ?
   ×      2
      ? ? ?
   +      ?
      6 5 1
```

Estimate. Then divide.

5. 2)632 **6.** 4)976 **7.** 3)733 **8.** 4)762 **9.** 7)931

10. 5)568 **11.** 7)868 **12.** 4)907 **13.** 6)918 **14.** 4)872

15. 8)936 **16.** 5)860 **17.** 2)524 **18.** 7)802 **19.** 2)922

20. 3)988 **21.** 3)537 **22.** 6)714 **23.** 5)815 **24.** 3)884

Solve.

25. At the supermarket 950 apples were placed in 3 piles. Each pile contained the same number of apples. How many apples were there in each pile? How many apples were left over?

6-10 More Difficult Quotients

Handcraft Toys had 274 trains to ship to 8 stores.
The same number of trains were shipped to each
store. How many trains did each store receive?
How many trains were left over?

To find how many each received, divide: 274 ÷ 8 = _?_

Think: 8)274   8 > 2   **Not enough hundreds**
8)274   8 < 27   **Enough tens**

Estimate: 3 × 8 = 24 ◄─ Try 3.
4 × 8 = 32

Divide the tens.	Divide the ones.	Check.

```
      3                34  R 2              34
 8)2 7 4          8)2 7 4               ×     8
 −2 4 ↓           −2 4 ↓                 2 7 2
   3 4              3 4                +     2
                   −3 2                  2 7 4
                     2
```

Each store received 34 trains.
There were 2 trains left over.

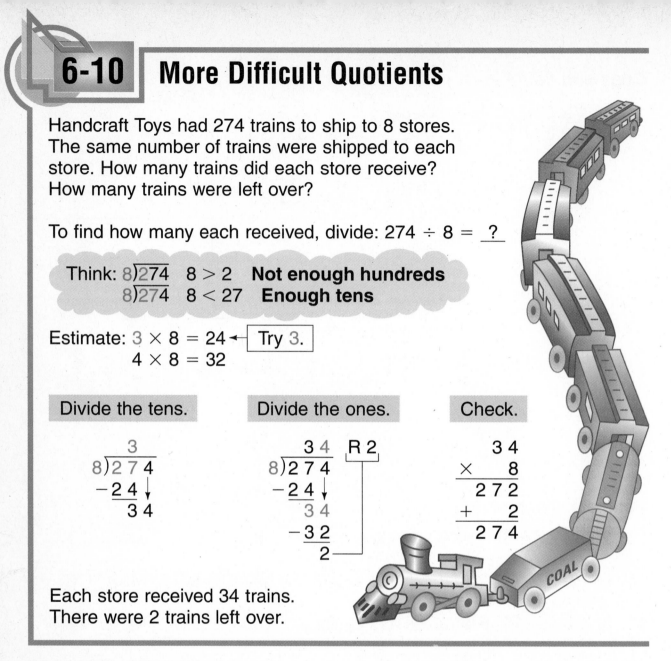

Copy and complete.

```
        7 ?              8 ?  R _?_              ? ?  R 4              ? ?  R _?_
1.  8)6 0 8      2.  5)4 3 3            3.  6)3 5 8            4.  9)4 7 2
    −5 6 ↓            −? ? ↓                −3 0 ↓                −4 ? ↓
      ? 8              3 ?                    ? 8                    ? 2
    −? ?              −? ?                  −? ?                  −? ?
       ?                3                      4                      ?
```

184

Estimate. Then find the quotient.

5. 3)105   **6.** 4)232   **7.** 6)258   **8.** 3)186   **9.** 5)130

10. 6)436   **11.** 7)201   **12.** 5)359   **13.** 4)354   **14.** 7)182

15. 9)756   **16.** 3)202   **17.** 9)337   **18.** 6)576   **19.** 8)197

20. 6)220   **21.** 4)228   **22.** 7)195   **23.** 5)295   **24.** 6)335

25. 7)308   **26.** 9)823   **27.** 8)692   **28.** 7)666   **29.** 9)717

Divide.

30. 657 ÷ 9   **31.** 267 ÷ 8   **32.** 396 ÷ 4

33. 462 ÷ 5   **34.** 498 ÷ 6   **35.** 591 ÷ 7

Solve.

36. The dividend is 272.
The quotient is 34.
What is the divisor?

37. The dividend is 359.
The divisor is 7.
What is the remainder?

38. Peg packs 594 wooden
animals into 6 boxes of the
same size. How many wooden
animals does she pack into
each box?

39. Brendan carves 193 figurines of
people for dollhouses. There
are 4 people in each dollhouse
family. How many families
does he carve? How many
figurines are left over?

40. There are 147 tops at the
factory store. If the same
number of tops are sold on
each of 5 days, what is the
greatest number of tops that
could be sold each day? How
many tops would not be sold?

Divide: 928 ÷ 9 = ?

Think: 9)928   9 = 9   **Enough hundreds**

Estimate: ? × 9 = 9
           1 × 9 = 9 ← Try 1.

Divide the hundreds.	Divide the tens.	Divide the ones.

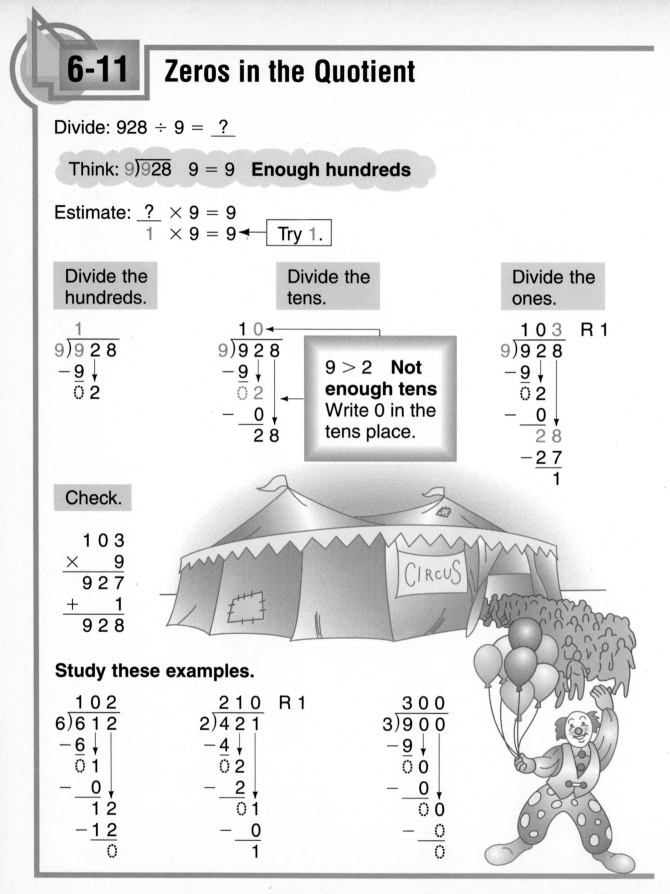

Divide the hundreds.

```
    1
9)9 2 8
 -9↓
  0 2
```

Divide the tens.

```
   1 0 ←
9)9 2 8
 -9↓
  0 2
 -  0↓
    2 8
```

9 > 2   **Not enough tens** Write 0 in the tens place.

Divide the ones.

```
   1 0 3   R 1
9)9 2 8
 -9↓
  0 2
 -  0↓
    2 8
   -2 7
       1
```

Check.

```
    1 0 3
  ×     9
    9 2 7
  +     1
    9 2 8
```

Study these examples.

```
    1 0 2
6)6 1 2
 -6↓
  0 1
 -  0↓
    1 2
   -1 2
       0
```

```
    2 1 0   R 1
2)4 2 1
 -4↓
  0 2
 -  2↓
    0 1
   -  0
       1
```

```
    3 0 0
3)9 0 0
 -9↓
  0 0
 -  0↓
    0 0
   -  0
       0
```

Copy and complete.

```
        3 0 4              2 0 ? R ?            1 ? 0              ? 0 ?
1.  3)9 1 2          2.  4)8 3 8           3.  3)4 2 0        4.  5)5 0 0
    -9↓                  -8↓                   -3↓                -5↓
     0̲ 1↓                 0̲ 3↓                  1 2↓               0̲ 0↓
     -0↓                  -0↓                   -1 2↓              -0↓
      1 2                  3 8                    0̲ 0               0̲ ?
     -? ?                 -? ?                   -0                -?
                            ?
```

Divide.

5. 4)800   6. 2)600   7. 3)390   8. 4)840   9. 5)550

10. 3)918   11. 4)824   12. 8)832   13. 9)954   14. 6)642

15. 6)609   16. 2)817   17. 4)842   18. 7)745   19. 5)508

20. 5)851   21. 9)985   22. 2)615   23. 3)902   24. 8)847

Solve.

25. At the circus 7 clowns gave away 763 balloons to small children. Each clown gave away the same number of balloons. At most, how many balloons did each clown give away?

26. There were 407 teddy bears to be used as prizes at 4 booths. Each booth gave out the same number of teddy bears. How many teddy bears did each booth give out? How many teddy bears were left over?

27. Five vendors sold 545 buckets of popcorn. Each vendor sold the same number of buckets. How many buckets of popcorn did each vendor sell?

Larger Numbers in Division

Divide: 4925 ÷ 7 = _?_

Think: $7\overline{)4925}$ 7 > 4 **Not enough thousands**
    $7\overline{)4925}$ 7 < 49 **Enough hundreds**

- Divide the hundreds.
  Estimate: _?_ × 7 = 49
      7 × 7 = 49
      Try 7.

$$
\begin{array}{r}
7 \\
7\overline{)4\,9\,2\,5} \\
-4\,9\downarrow \\
\hline
0\,2
\end{array}
$$

- Divide the tens.
  Estimate: 7 > 2
      Not enough tens
      Write 0 in the
      tens place.

$$
\begin{array}{r}
7\,0 \\
7\overline{)4\,9\,2\,5} \\
-4\,9\downarrow \\
\hline
0\,2\downarrow \\
-\;\;0 \\
\hline
2\,5
\end{array}
$$

- Divide the ones.
  Estimate: _?_ × 7 = 25
      3 × 7 = 21
      4 × 7 = 28
      Try 3.

$$
\begin{array}{r}
7\,0\,3 \quad \text{R 4} \\
7\overline{)4\,9\,2\,5} \\
-4\,9\downarrow \\
\hline
0\,2 \\
-\;\;0 \\
\hline
2\,5 \\
-2\,1 \\
\hline
4
\end{array}
$$

- Check.

$$
\begin{array}{r}
7\,0\,3 \\
\times7 \\
\hline
4\,9\,2\,1 \\
+4 \\
\hline
4\,9\,2\,5
\end{array}
$$

Copy and complete.

1.
```
     2 3 ? ?
  4)9 5 6 0
  −?↓
   ? 5
  −??↓
    ? 6
   −??↓
     ? 0
```

2.
```
       5 ? ?  R  ?
    4)2 2 4 2
    −??↓
      2 4
     −??↓
       0 2
      −?
       ?
```

3.
```
       3 ? ?  R  ?
    7)2 5 0 1
    −??↓
      4 0
     −3 5↓
       5 1
      −4 9
        ?
```

Estimate. Then divide.

4. 4)7576   5. 6)1344   6. 3)8217   7. 7)2982   8. 5)7870

9. 8)4336   10. 2)5566   11. 9)1962   12. 3)4545   13. 7)4361

14. 6)2418   15. 8)7249   16. 9)4567   17. 7)5320   18. 8)3600

19. 4)6204   20. 6)5043   21. 5)9990   22. 3)8181   23. 3)1311

24. 9)2884   25. 7)3225   26. 9)2772   27. 8)2884   28. 9)3675

Find the quotient and any remainder.

29. 1332 ÷ 6   30. 2562 ÷ 4   31. 2454 ÷ 5

32. 1753 ÷ 7   33. 4638 ÷ 6   34. 6834 ÷ 7

Solve.

35. Felipe has 2943 stamps. He keeps an equal number of stamps in each of 3 stamp albums. How many stamps does Felipe keep in each stamp album?

36. In 9 months Jill collected 941 stamps and Joe collected 931 stamps. The total number of stamps collected each month was the same. How many stamps did they collect each month together?

6-13 Dividing Money

Meghan bought 4 identical garden spades for $95.92. What did each spade cost?

To find the cost of each, divide: $95.92 ÷ 4 = __?__

Write the dollar sign and decimal point in the quotient above the dollar sign and decimal point in the dividend.

Divide as usual.

$$\begin{array}{r} \$\quad\ .\ \\ 4\overline{)\$9\ 5.9\ 2} \end{array}$$

$$\begin{array}{r} \$2\ 3.9\ 8\ \\ 4\overline{)\$9\ 5.9\ 2}\ \\ -8\ \\ \overline{1\ 5}\ \\ -1\ 2\ \\ \overline{3\ 9}\ \\ -3\ 6\ \\ \overline{3\ 2}\ \\ -3\ 2\ \end{array}$$

Check.

$$\begin{array}{r} \$2\ 3.9\ 8 \\ \times\qquad 4 \\ \hline \$9\ 5.9\ 2 \end{array}$$

Each spade cost $23.98.

Study these examples.

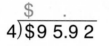

$$\begin{array}{r} \$.0\ 7 \\ 7\overline{)\$.4\ 9} \\ -4\ 9 \\ \hline \end{array}$$

Check.
$$\begin{array}{r} \$.0\ 7 \\ \times\quad 7 \\ \hline \$.4\ 9 \end{array}$$

$$\begin{array}{r} \$\ .9\ 0 \\ 5\overline{)\$4.5\ 0} \\ -4\ 5 \\ \hline 0\ 0 \end{array}$$

Check.
$$\begin{array}{r} \$\ .9\ 0 \\ \times\quad 5 \\ \hline \$4.5\ 0 \end{array}$$

There are no dimes in the quotient. Write a zero.

Copy and complete.

1.
```
      $2.0 1
   4)$8.0 4
    -8 ↓
       0 ↓
     -? ↓
       ?
     -?
```

2.
```
      $  5.? ?
   9)$4 9.9 5
    -? ? ↓
       4 9 ↓
     -4 5 ↓
         ? ?
       -? ?
```

3.
```
      $.1 ?
   7)$.8 4
    -? ↓
     1 4
    -? ?
```

4.
```
      $  .0 ?
   8)$0.5 6
       -5 6
```

Estimate. Then find the quotient.

5. 5)$1.35 6. 2)$4.94 7. 4)$2.44 8. 7)$2.31 9. 2)$8.58

10. 4)$20.84 11. 8)$24.16 12. 7)$14.28 13. 3)$24.72 14. 5)$18.10

15. 9)$49.77 16. 6)$14.82 17. 7)$27.93 18. 8)$20.88 19. 5)$26.00

20. 7)$21.63 21. 7)$17.01 22. 4)$63.00 23. 9)$73.53 24. 6)$22.20

Solve.

25. Help Meghan copy and complete the order form.

Amount	Description	Cost per Item	Total Cost
2 pairs	Gardening Gloves	?	$18.74
3	Lawn Chairs	?	$29.97
6	Tulip Bulbs	$3.79	?
8	Daylily Plants	?	$98.80
5	Flower Pots	?	$12.95
24	Gladiola Bulbs	$.98	?
4	Trowels	?	$17.40
2	Grass Rakes	$18.09	?
	Total		?

Order of Operations

Tim and Tom were given this problem to solve.

$$6 + 54 \div 2 - 4 \times 5 = \underline{\ ?\ }$$

Tim did this:

$$6 + 54 = 60$$
$$60 \div 2 = 30$$
$$30 - 4 = 26$$
$$26 \times 5 = 130$$

Tom did this:

$$54 \div 2 = 27$$
$$4 \times 5 = 20$$
$$6 + 27 = 33$$
$$33 - 20 = 13$$

Whose answer was correct?

Tom's answer was correct.
He used special mathematical rules
called the **order of operations.**

These are the rules for the
order of operations:

• *First* multiply or divide.
  Work in order from left to right.

• *Then* add or subtract.
  Work in order from left to right.

Solve
us
first.

Solve
us next.

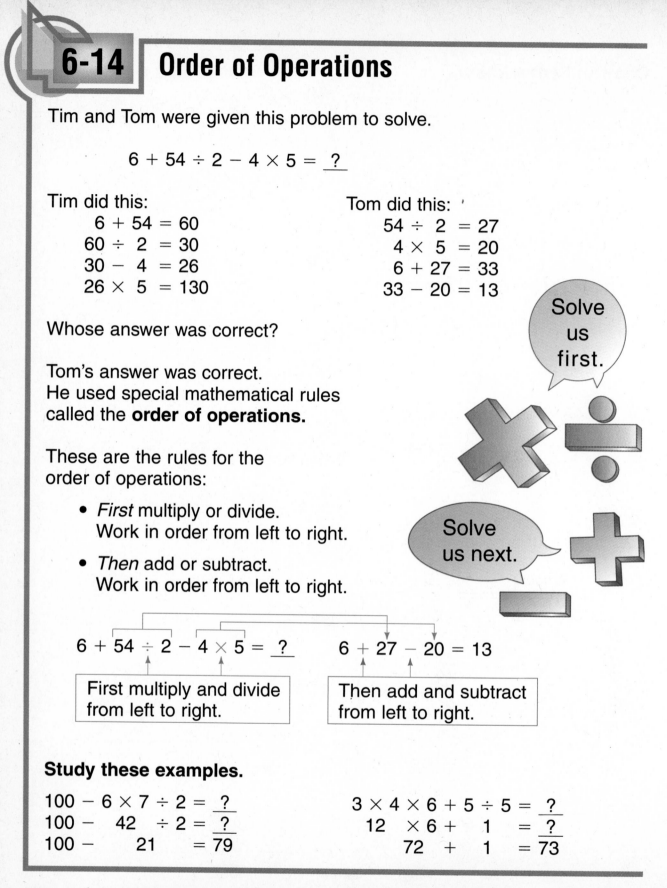

$$6 + 54 \div 2 - 4 \times 5 = \underline{\ ?\ } \qquad 6 + 27 - 20 = 13$$

First multiply and divide
from left to right.

Then add and subtract
from left to right.

Study these examples.

$$100 - 6 \times 7 \div 2 = \underline{\ ?\ }$$
$$100 - \quad 42 \quad \div 2 = \underline{\ ?\ }$$
$$100 - \qquad 21 \qquad = 79$$

$$3 \times 4 \times 6 + 5 \div 5 = \underline{\ ?\ }$$
$$12 \quad \times 6 + \quad 1 \quad = \underline{\ ?\ }$$
$$72 \quad + \quad 1 \quad = 73$$

Use the order of operations to solve.

1. $18 - 5 + 6$
2. $9 + 6 - 7$
3. $8 \times 6 \div 4$
4. $54 \div 6 \times 3$
5. $5 \times 7 - 4$
6. $25 + 10 \div 5$
7. $20 + 20 - 16$
8. $85 - 15 \times 2$
9. $9 \times 3 \div 3$
10. $21 + 6 \div 3 - 5$
11. $10 \div 5 + 5 \times 3$
12. $8 - 4 \div 4 + 4$
13. $7 \times 5 + 20 \div 5$
14. $5 \times 3 + 9 \div 3$
15. $24 + 4 \div 4 - 5$
16. $35 - 5 + 10 \div 2$
17. $100 \div 2 - 25$
18. $50 - 10 + 20 \div 2$
19. $6 \times 6 + 10 \div 5 - 1$
20. $64 \div 8 \times 10 - 40 - 5$
21. $30 \div 6 \times 9 + 9 - 1$
22. $25 \times 3 - 50 \div 2 + 25$
23. $18 + 6 \div 2 - 11 + 5$
24. $20 \div 4 + 54 \div 6 + 4$
25. $7 \times 30 - 10 + 150 \div 3$
26. $45 \div 5 - 1 + 3 \times 7$
27. $44 \div 2 \times 3 - 12 + 4$
28. $20 \times 5 - 50 \times 2 + 0$
29. $30 + 20 - 25 \div 5 \times 5$
30. $200 \div 4 \times 3 - 50 + 1$

Challenge

Compute.

31. $46 \times 8 + 10 - 50 \div 2 + 75 \div 3 - 100$

32. $500 - 10 \times 6 + 22 \div 2 - 48 \div 6 - 125$

6-15 Finding Averages

Amanda scored 75, 85, 90, 80, and 90 on math tests last term. What was her average test score?

To find an average:

| Add the numbers. | Divide the sum by the number of addends. |

```
   75
   85
   90
   80
 + 90
  420
```

Think:
5 addends

```
        84 ◄── average
     5)420
      -40↓
       20
      -20
```

Amanda's average test score was 84.

Study this example.

Find the average: $2.44, $3.68, $4.20, $1.64

```
 $  2.44
    3.68
    4.20
 +  1.64
  $11.96
```

Think:
4 addends

```
        $  2.99 ◄── average
     4)$11.96
       - 8↓
         3 9
        -3 6↓
          36
         -36
```

Find the average.

1. 36, 42, 72

2. 256, 498

3. 93, 126, 117

4. 500, 250

5. 49, 93, 86

6. 88, 0, 78, 90

194

Find the average.

7. 23, 37, 41, 19

8. 56, 18, 42, 64

9. 633, 495, 711

10. 420, 504, 297

11. $4.32, $.88, $4.00, $.76

12. 488, 128, 952, 720

13. 72, 216, 96, 108

14. $1.84, $2.76, $4.08, $2.32

15. 58, 77, 95, 49, 81

16. 93, 102, 115, 83, 42

17. 517, 423, 648, 212, 555

18. $4.25, $6.71, $3.24, $5.06, $4.94

19. $8.44, $.31, $2.97, $3.13, $.80

Solve. Use the information in the grade book.

20. What was Bob's average test score?

21. What was Eric's average test score?

22. What was Carly's average test score? Was her average greater or less than Dawn's?

Students' Names	Test Scores				
	A	B	C	D	E
Bob	75	63	77	80	90
Carly	82	73	68	72	85
Dawn	75	76	83	87	94
Eric	82	68	85	85	80
Gary	86	85	92	82	70

23. How many points greater or less was Carly's average than Eric's average?

24. Did the five students have a higher average score on Test A or Test B?

25. Did the five students have the lowest average score on Test A, Test B, or Test C?

26. List the students in order from the highest average to the lowest average.

6-16 | Problem Solving: Interpret the Remainder

Problem: A diner has 98 mugs. They should be stored in stacks of 8. How many more mugs are needed to make the last stack complete?

1 IMAGINE   You are storing mugs in stacks of 8.

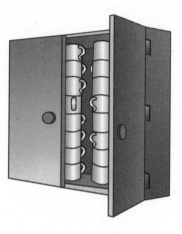

2 NAME   *Facts:*   98 mugs in all
8 mugs in each stack

Question: How many more mugs are needed?

3 THINK   Divide because a whole is being separated into equal sets of 8. Find the remainder.

That will tell how many mugs are in the *incomplete* stack.

number of mugs   mugs in stack
98   ÷   8   = ? R ?

4 COMPUTE

$$
\begin{array}{r}
12 \ \ \text{R } 2 \\
8\overline{)98} \\
-8 \downarrow \\
\hline
18 \\
-16 \\
\hline
2
\end{array}
$$

Think: What number plus the remainder will make a stack of 8?

? + 2 = 8
6 + 2 = 8

The diner needs 6 more mugs to make complete stacks.

5 CHECK   Multiply and add to check division.

12 × 8 = 96   and   96 + 2 = 98

Your answer checks.

Solve.

1. Jason uses 9-inch strips of plastic. He can buy a 75-inch roll of plastic or a 125-inch roll of plastic. Which roll will have less wasted material?

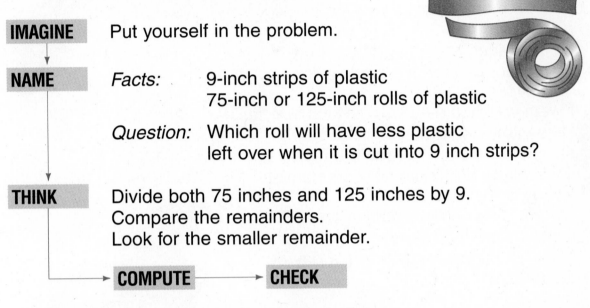

IMAGINE	Put yourself in the problem.
NAME	*Facts:* 9-inch strips of plastic 75-inch or 125-inch rolls of plastic *Question:* Which roll will have less plastic left over when it is cut into 9 inch strips?
THINK	Divide both 75 inches and 125 inches by 9. Compare the remainders. Look for the smaller remainder.

COMPUTE → **CHECK**

2. Each CD bin at Sound City holds 8 disks. How many bins are needed to hold 195 disks?

3. Each treasure hunt team will have 5 people. So far 42 people have signed up. How many more people are needed to make every team equal? How many teams will there be?

4. Cans of juice are sold in packs of 6. The Day Center needs 103 cans of juice. How many packs should the center buy?

5. A soccer card club has 7 members. The club has 1305 cards. How many more cards do they need to share the cards equally?

Make Up Your Own

6. Write a problem that uses a remainder. Have a classmate solve it.

6-17 Problem-Solving Applications

Solve.

1. Nora buys a 32-minute cartoon video. The cartoons are 4 minutes each.
   a. How many cartoons are on the video?

   b. The video costs $6. About how much did Nora spend for each cartoon?

2. Kwam watches a 1-hour cartoon special. How many 5-minute cartoons can be shown if there are no commercials? What if there are 15 minutes of commercials?

3. The cartoon channel shows only 192 cartoons each day. They show 8 cartoons each hour. How many hours a day does the channel broadcast?

4. There are 28 characters in a film. Half of them are animals. How many are not animals?

5. A movie is 84 minutes long. A hopping frog appears every third minute. How many times does the frog appear?

6. There are 128 different animal T-shirts displayed about equally on 8 shelves. About how many are on each shelf?

Use the pictograph for problem 7.

7. Fourth grade students used animation to illustrate their stories. How many more students used space creatures than animals?

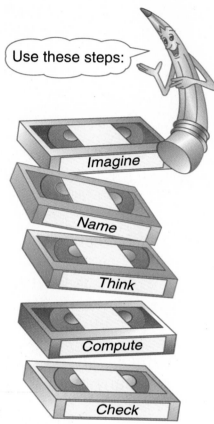

Use these steps:

Imagine

Name

Think

Compute

Check

Fourth Grade Students

People	☺ ☺ ☺ ☺ ◖
Animals	☺ ☺ ☺ ◖
Space Creatures	☺ ☺ ☺ ☺ ☺ ☺

Key ☺ = 6 students
◖ = 3 students

Solve.

8. Mae makes 24 drawings to make 1 second of an animated cartoon. How many drawings does she make for a 1-minute cartoon?

9. A cartoon is 4 minutes long. The filmmaker created 5760 drawings to make the film. How many drawings were used for each minute of film?

USE THESE STRATEGIES:
Interpret the Remainder
Choose the Operation
Logical Reasoning
Missing Information
Write a Number Sentence
Extra Information

10. Chris watches a 30-minute cartoon show. If it shows as many 8-minute cartoons as possible, will there be enough time left to show a 7-minute cartoon?

11. A videotape includes 4 cartoons. They are 5 minutes, 6 minutes, 8 minutes, and 9 minutes long. What is the average length?

12. Another cartoon tape is 60 minutes long and costs $8.95. How much will 3 tapes cost?

13. Three cartoon characters are a chicken, a dog, and an octopus. Flick has more legs than Click, but fewer legs than Glick. Name each animal.

14. A video store orders 60 cartoon videotapes. Each shipping box holds 8 tapes. How many boxes will the store receive?

Make Up Your Own

15. Write a problem modeled on problem 13. Have a classmate solve it.

More Practice

Divide.

1. $4\overline{)32}$ **2.** $5\overline{)45}$ **3.** $3\overline{)27}$ **4.** $5\overline{)65}$ **5.** $6\overline{)72}$

6. $2\overline{)53}$ **7.** $6\overline{)93}$ **8.** $4\overline{)75}$ **9.** $6\overline{)86}$ **10.** $8\overline{)808}$

11. $3\overline{)723}$ **12.** $5\overline{)621}$ **13.** $8\overline{)337}$ **14.** $7\overline{)256}$ **15.** $4\overline{)160}$

16. $6\overline{)\$36.36}$ **17.** $8\overline{)\$72.64}$ **18.** $5\overline{)\$17.55}$ **19.** $4\overline{)\$16.48}$ **20.** $3\overline{)\$15.00}$

Write the rule. Complete the pattern.

21. 4, 7, 10, 13, ___, ___.

22. 2, 6, 18, 54, ___, ___.

23. 8, 15, 13, 20, 18, ___, ___.

24. 69, 64, 58, 51, ___, ___.

Answer *yes* or *no*.

25. Is 45 divisible by 2? ___   by 3? ___   by 5? ___   by 10? ___

26. Is 300 divisible by 2? ___   by 3? ___   by 5? ___   by 10? ___

Estimate the quotient.

27. $8\overline{)464}$ **28.** $7\overline{)5397}$ **29.** $9\overline{)7686}$

Solve.

30. Crayons were put on each of 8 tables. There were 84 crayons. How many crayons were put on each table? How many were left over?

31. What was Billy's average score for basketball if he scored the following points: 24, 30, 18, 15, 28?

32. There are 278 students in the Oak School. About how many are in each of the nine classrooms?

33. A bag of apples costs $1.62. There are 6 apples in the bag. How much does each apple cost?

(See *Still More Practice,* p. 465.)

SQUARE NUMBERS

You can arrange 4 dots in a square.

• •

• •   Think: 2 rows
          2 dots in each row
          2 × 2 = 4   4 is a square number.

You can arrange 9 dots in a square.

• • •

• • •   Think: 3 rows
          3 dots in each row
• • •   3 × 3 = 9   9 is a square number.

You *cannot* arrange 3 dots or 5 dots in a square.

• •   • • •

•   • •   3 and 5 are *not* square numbers.

When you multiply a number by itself,
the product is a **square number**.

Solve. You may arrange dots in squares.

1. Are there any square numbers between 10
   and 30? If so, which numbers are
   square numbers?

2. What is the next square number
   after 25?

3. Write *square* or *not square* for each number.

   a. 81   **b.** 50   **c.** 36
   d. 48   **e.** 64   **f.** 100

201

Check Your Mastery

Write the missing number.

See pp. 166–169

1. $7\overline{)?}$ quotient 6

2. $8\overline{)?}$ quotient 2

3. $9\overline{)?}$ quotient 2

4. $6\overline{)?}$ quotient 0

5. $7\overline{)?}$ quotient 1

6. $?\overline{)40}$ quotient 5

7. $?\overline{)28}$ quotient 7

8. $?\overline{)9}$ quotient 9

9. $4\overline{)?}$ quotient 3

10. $5\overline{)?}$ quotient 5

Estimate. Then divide.

See pp. 172–175, 178–187

11. $4\overline{)24}$

12. $5\overline{)35}$

13. $6\overline{)42}$

14. $6\overline{)50}$

15. $8\overline{)63}$

16. $6\overline{)45}$

17. $5\overline{)880}$

18. $8\overline{)268}$

19. $7\overline{)\$8.26}$

20. $6\overline{)660}$

21. $2\overline{)408}$

22. $6\overline{)804}$

23. $5\overline{)610}$

24. $7\overline{)700}$

25. $3\overline{)406}$

26. $4\overline{)\$24.16}$

27. $3\overline{)\$13.23}$

28. $7\overline{)\$7.84}$

29. $8\overline{)\$12.48}$

30. $9\overline{)\$11.70}$

Write the rule. Complete the pattern.

See pp. 170–171

31. 3, 7, 11, 15, ___, ___.

32. 57, 54, 51, 48, ___, ___.

33. 1, 2, 4, 8, ___, ___.

34. 3, 8, 7, 12, 11, ___, ___.

Find the average.

See pp. 194–195

35. 98, 81, 76, 33

36. 621, 243, 426

Solve.

See pp. 176–177, 198–199

37. Find the cost of one eraser if Carlos paid $.54 for 6 erasers. Is the quotient divisible by 2?

38. Thuy put 45 papers in packets. She put 5 papers in each packet. How many packets did she have?

39. Aunt Marie has 1467 stamps. She gives the same number to each of her 4 nephews. How many does each boy receive? How many are left over?

40. On four days Jan read 156 pages, 274 pages, 856 pages, and 306 pages. What was the average per day read by Jan?

Choose the best answer.

1. 6
  ×3
- **a.** 12
- **b.** 15
- **c.** 18
- **d.** not given

2. 7)0
- **a.** 7
- **b.** 6
- **c.** 0
- **d.** not given

3. 6 × 8
- **a.** 14
- **b.** 48
- **c.** 42
- **d.** not given

4. 3 × 3 × 5
- **a.** 30
- **b.** 14
- **c.** 35
- **d.** not given

5. ? × 8 = 72
- **a.** 9
- **b.** 10
- **c.** 7
- **d.** not given

6. 5
  6)?
- **a.** 20
- **b.** 11
- **c.** 30
- **d.** not given

7.   90
  × 6
- **a.** 150
- **b.** 540
- **c.** 480
- **d.** not given

8.   23
  × 3
- **a.** 59
- **b.** 69
- **c.** 66
- **d.** not given

9. 50 ÷ 7
- **a.** 6
- **b.** 7 R1
- **c.** 8 R3
- **d.** not given

10. 4 × 36
- **a.** 124
- **b.** 144
- **c.** 130
- **d.** not given

11.   244
  ×   6
- **a.** 1464
- **b.** 1062
- **c.** 1444
- **d.** not given

12.   708
  ×   5
- **a.** 4035
- **b.** 3540
- **c.** 3045
- **d.** not given

13. $9.27
  ×   7
- **a.** $64.49
- **b.** $63.89
- **c.** $64.89
- **d.** not given

14.   2357
  ×   8
- **a.** 18,856
- **b.** 22,568
- **c.** 24,685
- **d.** not given

15. 9 × $.25
- **a.** $2.20
- **b.** $1.85
- **c.** $2.05
- **d.** not given

16.   47
  ×13
- **a.** 141
- **b.** 611
- **c.** 591
- **d.** not given

17. 5)50
- **a.** 45
- **b.** 12
- **c.** 250
- **d.** not given

18. $5.27
  ×   46
- **a.** $168.28
- **b.** $242.42
- **c.** $224.86
- **d.** not given

19. 3)48
- **a.** 18
- **b.** 16
- **c.** 24
- **d.** not given

20. 6)97
- **a.** 16 R1
- **b.** 11 R6
- **c.** 12 R3
- **d.** not given

21. 8)968
- **a.** 121
- **b.** 131
- **c.** 101
- **d.** not given

22. Estimate by rounding.

  483
  × 21
- **a.** 10,000
- **b.** 12,000
- **c.** 14,000
- **d.** 8,000

23. Estimate.

  9)97
- **a.** 6
- **b.** 10
- **c.** 12
- **d.** 11

Choose the best answer.

24. What multiplication sentence is shown?

    a. $2 \times 12 = 24$
    b. $3 \times 12 = 36$
    c. $3 \times 11 = 33$
    d. $3 \times 10 = 30$

25. What is the next number in the pattern?

3, 9, 7, 21, __?__

    a. 19
    b. 63
    c. 24
    d. 18

26. Make a front-end estimate.

8737
$\times$ 4

    a. 12,000
    b. 40,000
    c. 32,000
    d. 24,000

27. 60×530

    a. 12,800
    b. 30,900
    c. 3180
    d. not given

28. 465 is divisible by which number?

    a. 2 **b.** 10 **c.** 4 **d.** 5

29. Find the average:
498, 636, 714

    a. 612 **b.** 507 **c.** 616 **d.** 1848

30. Compute.

$8 + 6 \div 3 - 2$

    a. 2
    b. 14
    c. 9
    d. 8

31. Peter feeds his dog twice a day. How many times does he feed his dog in 15 days?

    a. 30 **b.** 45 **c.** 40 **d.** 17

32. Alana pays $11.96 for 4 identical plants. How much does each plant cost?

    a. $1.56
    b. $2.99
    c. $2.49
    d. $1.99

33. The dividend is 832. The quotient is 104. What is the divisor?

    a. 4 **b.** 80 **c.** 8 **d.** 6

34. Joe has 46 rare coins. Nel has about 8 times that number. About how many rare coins does Nel have?

    a. 400 **b.** 300 **c.** 500 **d.** not given

35. What is the cost of 32 theater tickets at $9.79 each?

    a. $48.95
    b. $302.28
    c. $358.38
    d. not given

In this chapter you will:

Use customary and metric units for length, capacity, and mass

Compute customary units and rename customary and metric units

Estimate, compare, and choose reasonable customary and metric units

Read a thermometer in degrees Fahrenheit and Celsius

Tell time to the minute and compute elapsed time

Use technology: memory keys

Solve two-step problems

Do you remember?
1 gal = 4 qt = 8 pt = 16 c

Critical Thinking/Finding Together
How many half inches are there from the 9 to the 4F on the tape measure?

205

Inch

The **inch (in.)** is a customary unit of length.

▶ A quarter is about 1 inch wide.
You can use a quarter as a benchmark
for 1 inch.

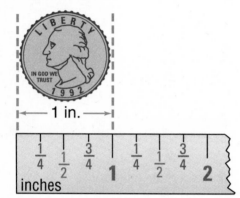

A **benchmark** is an object
of known measure that
can be used to estimate
the measure of other objects.

▶ You can use a ruler to measure an object
to the **nearest inch**, **nearest half inch**,
and **nearest quarter inch**.

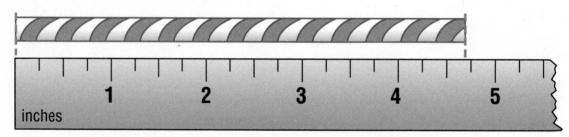

• To the nearest inch, the straw is about 5 in. long.

• To the nearest half inch, the straw is about
$4\frac{1}{2}$ in. long.

• To the nearest quarter inch, the straw is
about $4\frac{3}{4}$ in. long.

When you measure length, align the object
you are measuring with the beginning of the ruler.

Measure each to the nearest inch, nearest half inch, and nearest quarter inch.

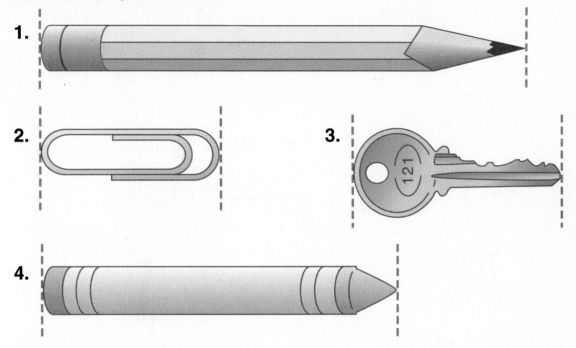

1.

2.

3.

4.

Draw a line for each length.

5. 3 in.

6. 2 in.

7. $1\frac{1}{2}$ in.

8. $4\frac{1}{2}$ in.

9. $5\frac{1}{2}$ in.

10. $3\frac{1}{4}$ in.

11. $6\frac{1}{4}$ in.

12. $2\frac{1}{4}$ in.

13. $3\frac{3}{4}$ in.

14. $1\frac{3}{4}$ in.

15. $4\frac{3}{4}$ in.

16. $6\frac{3}{4}$ in.

Estimate the length of each line to the nearest inch. Then measure each line to check your estimates.

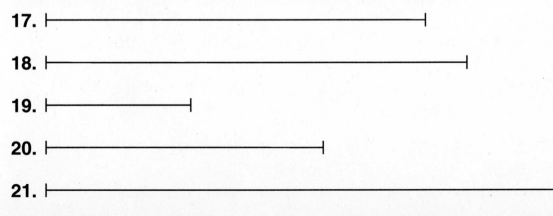

17.

18.

19.

20.

21.

7-2 Foot, Yard, and Mile

The **foot (ft)**, the **yard (yd)**, and the **mile (mi)** are also customary units of length.

12 inches (in.) = 1 foot (ft)
3 feet (ft) = 1 yard (yd)
5280 feet (ft) = 1 mile (mi)
1760 yards (yd) = 1 mile (mi)

▶ A license plate is about 1 foot long.

It takes about 25 minutes to walk 1 mile.

A door is about 1 yard wide.

Miles are used to measure long lengths called **distances**.

▶ Before you can compare measurements in different units, you need to **rename** units.

Compare: 4 ft _?_ 52 in.

You can make a table.　**or**　You can multiply the larger unit.

ft	1	2	3	4
in.	12	24	36	48

4 ft = 48 in.　　48 < 52
So 4 ft < 52 in.

4 ft = _?_ in.　　　1 ft = 12 in.
4 ft = (4 × 12) in.

4 ft = 48 in.　　48 < 52
So 4 ft < 52 in.

Write *in., ft, yd,* or *mi* for the unit you would use to measure each.

1. length of a football field
2. width of a desk

3. distance across town
4. length of your thumb

Write the letter of the best estimate.

5. length of a paintbrush   **a.** 9 ft   **b.** 9 yd   **c.** 9 in.

6. length of a bus   **a.** 40 mi   **b.** 40 ft   **c.** 40 yd

7. height of a wall   **a.** 3 in.   **b.** 3 yd   **c.** 3 ft

Compare. Write <, =, or >.

8. 6 yd _?_ 4 ft   9. 8 ft _?_ 95 in.   10. 2 mi _?_ 3000 yd

11. 7 ft _?_ 85 in.   12. 3 mi _?_ 15,000 ft   13. 3 ft _?_ 36 in.

Dividing to Rename Units

Divide to rename smaller units as larger units.
Use a calculator if you need to.

Compare: 72 in. _?_ 5 ft   Think: 1 ft = 12 in.
$$72 \text{ in.} = (72 \div 12) \text{ ft}$$
72 in. = 6 ft   6 > 5   So 72 in. > 5 ft

Compare. Write <, =, or >.

You may use a calculator.

14. 48 in. _?_ 4 ft   15. 18 ft _?_ 7 yd   16. 5280 yd _?_ 3 mi

17. 10,000 ft _?_ 2 mi   18. 64 in. _?_ 5 ft   19. 45 ft _?_ 20 yd

Computing Customary Units

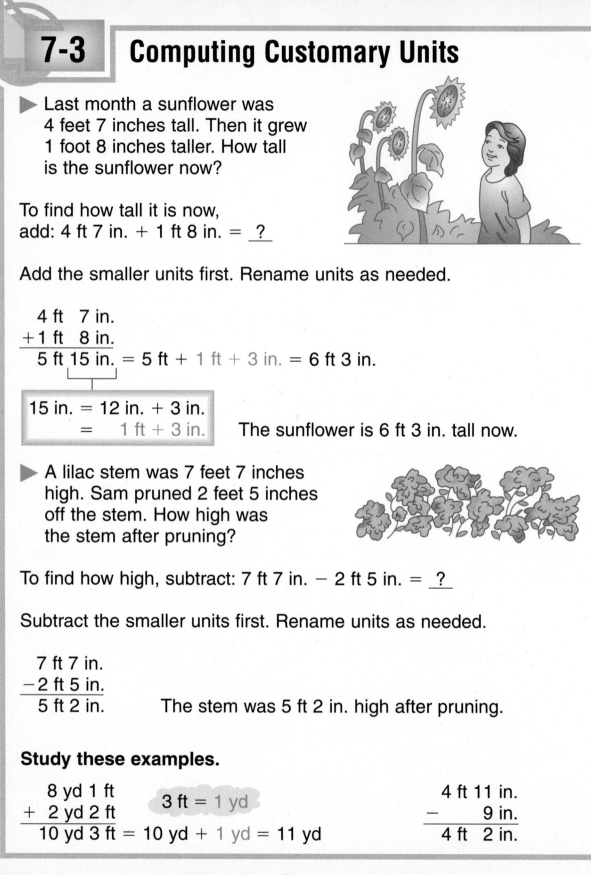

▶ Last month a sunflower was
4 feet 7 inches tall. Then it grew
1 foot 8 inches taller. How tall
is the sunflower now?

To find how tall it is now,
add: 4 ft 7 in. + 1 ft 8 in. = ?

Add the smaller units first. Rename units as needed.

```
  4 ft   7 in.
+ 1 ft   8 in.
  5 ft  15 in.  = 5 ft + 1 ft + 3 in. = 6 ft 3 in.
```

15 in. = 12 in. + 3 in.
      =   1 ft + 3 in.   The sunflower is 6 ft 3 in. tall now.

▶ A lilac stem was 7 feet 7 inches
high. Sam pruned 2 feet 5 inches
off the stem. How high was
the stem after pruning?

To find how high, subtract: 7 ft 7 in. − 2 ft 5 in. = ?

Subtract the smaller units first. Rename units as needed.

```
  7 ft 7 in.
− 2 ft 5 in.
  5 ft 2 in.
```
The stem was 5 ft 2 in. high after pruning.

Study these examples.

```
  8 yd 1 ft       3 ft = 1 yd
+ 2 yd 2 ft
 10 yd 3 ft = 10 yd + 1 yd = 11 yd
```

```
  4 ft 11 in.
−        9 in.
  4 ft  2 in.
```

Add.

1. 6 ft 2 in.
   $+$ 3 ft 5 in.

2. 7 yd 1 ft
   $+$ 1 yd 1 ft

3. 3 yd 2 ft
   $+$ 5 yd

4. 8 ft 6 in.
   $+$ 5 in.

5. 10 ft 3 in.
   $+$ 4 ft 10 in.

6. 5 ft 8 in.
   $+$ 7 ft 11 in.

7. 6 ft 9 in. $+$ 9 ft 5 in.

8. 4 yd 2 ft $+$ 3 yd 2 ft

Subtract.

9. 4 ft 8 in.
   $-$ 1 ft 3 in.

10. 9 ft 4 in.
   $-$ 9 ft 2 in.

11. 7 yd 2 ft
   $-$ 2 ft

12. 2 yd 2 ft
   $-$ 2 yd

13. 12 ft 9 in.
   $-$ 2 ft 4 in.

14. 8 ft 10 in.
   $-$ 5 ft 6 in.

15. 9 ft 7 in. $-$ 4 ft 3 in.

16. 4 ft 6 in. $-$ 2 ft 6 in.

Solve.

17. Amy's fence is 18 ft 10 in. long. She adds a 3 ft 5 in. section to the fence. How long is the fence now?

18. Joe painted 6 ft of a fence that is 20 ft 6 in. long. How many feet of fence are not painted?

Challenge

Subtract. Rename when necessary.

19. $\overset{3}{\cancel{4}}$ ft $\overset{16}{\cancel{4}}$ in.
   $-$ 1 ft 6 in.
   _____
   2 ft 10 in.

20. 3 yd 1 ft
   $-$ 1 yd 2 ft

21. 8 ft 6 in.
   $-$ 3 ft 11 in.

22. 9 yd 2 ft
   $-$ 8 yd 4 ft

23. 5 ft 1 in.
   $-$ 4 ft 11 in.

24. 12 ft
   $-$ 6 ft 8 in.

7-4 Customary Units of Capacity

The **fluid ounce (fl oz)**, the **cup (c)**, the **pint (pt)**, the **quart (qt)**, and the **gallon (gal)** are customary units of liquid capacity.

8 fluid ounces = 1 cup
2 cups = 1 pint
2 pints = 1 quart
2 quarts = 1 half gallon
4 quarts = 1 gallon

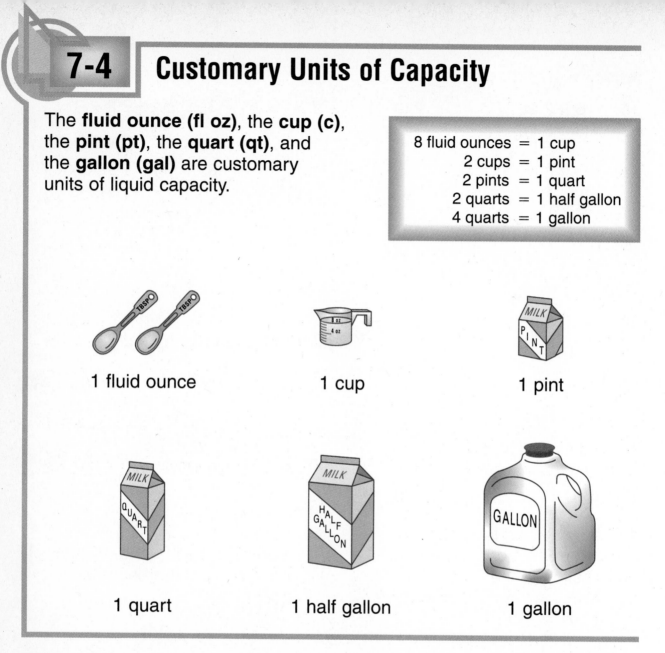

1 fluid ounce   1 cup   1 pint

1 quart   1 half gallon   1 gallon

Write *fl oz, c, pt, qt,* or *gal* for the unit you would use to measure the capacity of each.

1. water in a swimming pool

2. a melted ice cube

3. soup in a can

4. house paint in a can

5. pancake syrup in a plastic bottle

6. frozen yogurt in a small container

7. juice in a large glass

8. seltzer in a bottle

Copy and complete each table.

9.

gal	1	2	?	4	?
qt	4	8	?	?	20
pt	8	?	24	?	?

10.

pt	1	2	3	?	5
c	2	?	?	8	?
fl oz	16	32	?	?	?

Complete.

11. 2 pt = _?_ c

12. 8 c = _?_ pt

13. 16 qt = _?_ gal

14. 2 gal = _?_ qt

15. 10 pt = _?_ c

16. 48 pt = _?_ gal

Compare. Write <, =, or >. You may make a table, multiply the larger units, or divide the smaller units.

17. 7 c _?_ 50 fl oz

18. 5 gal _?_ 15 qt

19. 6 pt _?_ 11 c

20. 6 qt _?_ 16 pt

21. 90 fl oz _?_ 8 c

22. 20 c _?_ 10 pt

Solve.

23. Would you need 6 c, 6 pt, or 6 gal of paint to paint a room?

24. Would you drink 1 fl oz, 1 c, or 1 qt of milk at lunch?

25. Ted's pail holds 2 qt of water. He filled the pail 6 times to wash his mother's car. How many gallons of water did Ted use?

Finding Together

Estimate. Then check.

26. Find a container in your classroom that holds about 1 cup. Check by filling a measuring cup with rice, sand, or water and pouring it into the container.

7-5 Customary Units of Weight

The **ounce (oz)**, the **pound (lb)**, and the **ton (T)** are customary units of weight.

16 ounces (oz) = 1 pound (lb)
2000 pounds (lb) = 1 ton (T)

A letter weighs about 1 ounce.

A personal stereo weighs about 1 pound.

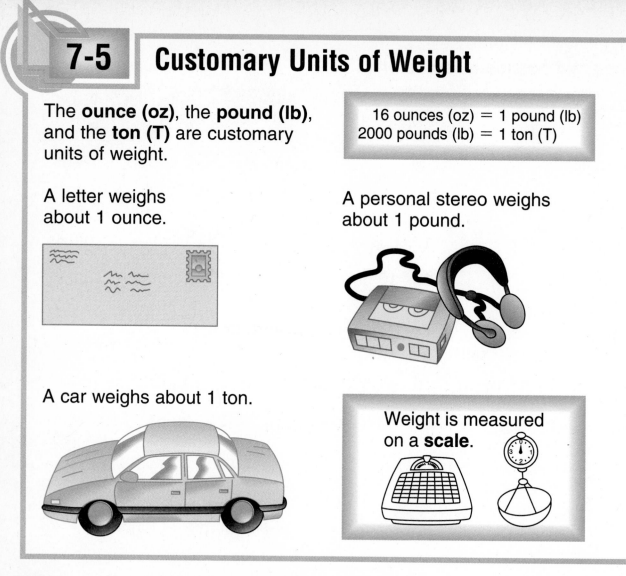

A car weighs about 1 ton.

Weight is measured on a **scale**.

Write _oz, lb,_ or _T_ for the unit you would use to measure the weight of each.

1. a carrot
2. an elephant
3. an electric guitar

4. a fire engine
5. a person
6. a toaster

7. a dog
8. a canary
9. a dump truck

Write the letter of the best estimate.

10. an orange
   a. 6 oz
   b. 1 lb
   c. 2 lb

11. a cat
   a. 30 lb
   b. 12 oz
   c. 12 lb

Copy and complete each table.

12.

oz	16	32	?	64	?	?
lb	1	2	3	?	5	6

13.

lb	2000	?	6000	?	?
T	1	2	?	4	?

Compare. Write <, =, or >. You may make a table, multiply larger units, or divide smaller units.

14. 5 lb _?_ 75 oz

15. 6 T _?_ 12,000 lb

16. 4 lb _?_ 58 oz

17. 8 lb _?_ 100 oz

18. 112 oz _?_ 6 lb

19. 8500 lb _?_ 5 T

Match. Write the letter of the tool you would use to measure each.

20. length of a pencil

21. water for a vase

22. length of the classroom

23. weight of your teacher

a. ruler

b. scale

c. measuring cup

d. yardstick

Solve.

24. Akeem has 5 sisters. He gives a 4-oz plum to each sister. In all do the plums weigh more or less than 1 lb?

25. A truck can carry 3000 lb of cargo. Can it carry two tractors that each weigh 1000 lb and a 625-lb plow?

Critical Thinking

26. Name two things that are small *and* heavy.

27. Name two things that are big *and* light.

28. Does the size of an object always give a clue to how much it weighs? Explain your answer.

7-6 Millimeter, Centimeter, and Decimeter

The **millimeter (mm)**, the **centimeter (cm)**, and the **decimeter (dm)** are metric units of length.

10 millimeters (mm) = 1 centimeter (cm)
10 centimeters (cm) = 1 decimeter (dm)

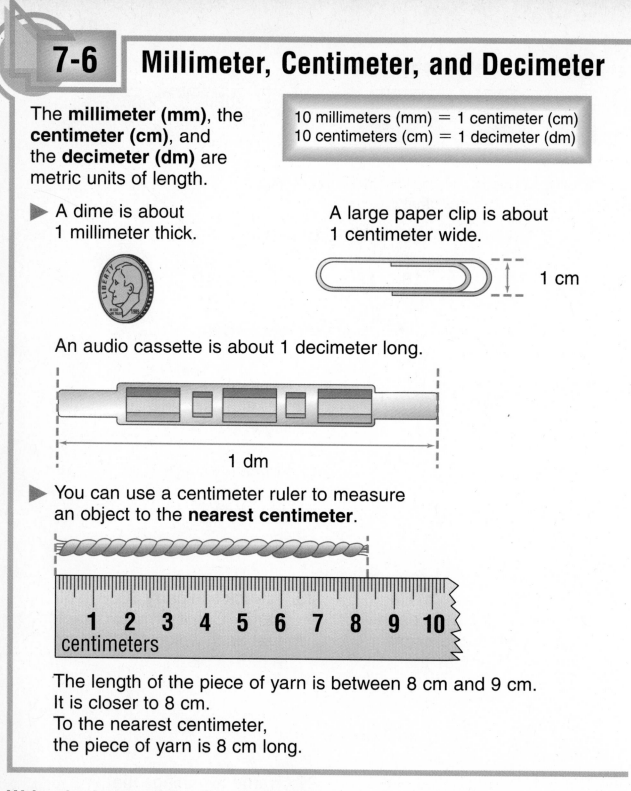

▶ A dime is about 1 millimeter thick.

A large paper clip is about 1 centimeter wide.

1 cm

An audio cassette is about 1 decimeter long.

1 dm

▶ You can use a centimeter ruler to measure an object to the **nearest centimeter**.

1 2 3 4 5 6 7 8 9 10
centimeters

The length of the piece of yarn is between 8 cm and 9 cm.
It is closer to 8 cm.
To the nearest centimeter,
the piece of yarn is 8 cm long.

Write the letter of the best estimate.

1. height of a mug   **a.** 1 dm   **b.** 1 cm   **c.** 1 mm

2. thickness of cardboard   **a.** 1 dm   **b.** 1 cm   **c.** 1 mm

Copy and complete each table.

3.

dm	1	?	3	?	5
cm	10	20	?	?	?

4.

cm	1	2	?	4	?
mm	10	?	30	?	?

Complete. You may make a table.

5. 7 cm = __?__ mm

6. 8 dm = __?__ cm

7. 10 cm = __?__ mm

8. 60 cm = __?__ dm

9. 200 mm = __?__ cm

10. 90 cm = __?__ dm

Compare. Write <, =, or >. You may make a table, multiply the larger units, or divide the smaller units.

11. 6 cm __?__ 59 mm

6 cm = (6 × 10) mm

12. 10 dm __?__ 100 cm

13. 8 cm __?__ 90 mm

14. 20 mm __?__ 20 cm

20 mm = (20 ÷ 10) cm

15. 400 cm __?__ 45 dm

16. 9 dm __?__ cm

Draw a line for each length.

17. 2 cm

18. 8 cm

19. 12 cm

20. 10 cm

21. 2 dm

Estimate each. Then measure to the nearest centimeter.

22. the length of your shoe

23. the length of your pencil

24. the width of your hand

25. the length of a dollar bill

26. the length of this book

27. the width of this book

Finding Together

28. Find the meanings of these prefixes commonly used in the metric system of measurement.

centi-   deci-   kilo-   milli-

7-7 Meter and Kilometer

The **meter (m)** and the **kilometer (km)** are also metric units of length.

100 centimeters (cm) = 1 meter (m)
10 decimeters (dm) = 1 meter (m)
1000 meters (m) = 1 kilometer (km)

A full-size baseball bat is about 1 meter long.

It takes about 15 minutes to walk 1 kilometer.

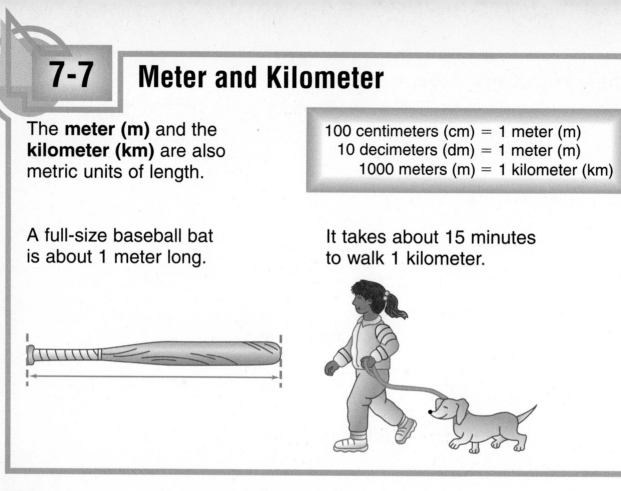

Write *mm, cm, dm, m,* or *km* for the unit you would use to measure each.

1. distance across your state

2. length of a soccer field

3. width of a nickel

4. height of a school desk

5. length of a room

6. height of a giraffe

7. length of a ladybug

8. distance from Maine to Florida

Copy and complete each table.

9.

km	1	2	?	?	?	6	?	?
m	1000	?	3000	?	?	?	7000	?

10.

m	1	?	3	?	5	?	?	?
cm	100	200	?	?	?	?	?	800

Compare. Write <, =, or >. You may make a table, multiply larger units, or divide smaller units.

11. 20 m _?_ 20 cm

12. 400 km _?_ 40 m

13. 6 m _?_ 600 cm

14. 3 km _?_ 3500 m

15. 8 m _?_ 700 cm

16. 15 km _?_ 150 m

17. 500 cm _?_ 4 m

18. 8000 m _?_ 5 km

19. 1000 cm _?_ 9 m

Solve. Use the map below.

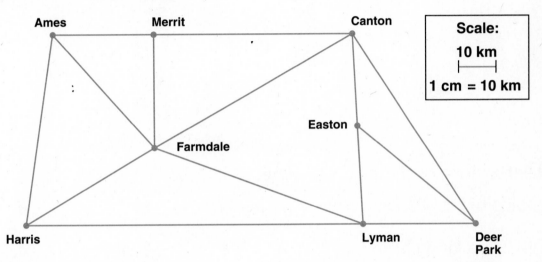

20. What is the shortest route from Ames to Lyman? How many kilometers long is this route?

21. Is the route from Canton to Deer Park longer or shorter than the route from Canton to Lyman?

22. Mr. Yuan wants to travel from Harris to Deer Park to Canton. About how many kilometers will he travel?

23. Ms. Rau must travel from Lyman to Merrit. Should she go through Farmdale or through Canton? Why?

24. Is the route from Ames to Canton to Farmdale longer or shorter than the route from Easton to Deer Park to Lyman to Farmdale?

25. What is the shortest route from Deer Park to Ames? from Easton to Harris? How long is each route?

7-8 Milliliter and Liter

The **milliliter (mL)** and the **liter (L)** are metric units of capacity.

> 1000 milliliters (mL) = 1 liter (L)

There are about 20 drops of water in 1 mL.

Seltzer and springwater are sold in bottles that hold 1 L.

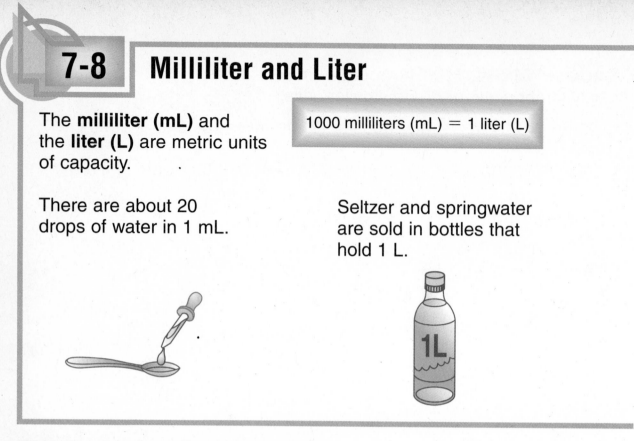

Write the letter of the best estimate.

1. bottle of liquid soap   **a.** 1 mL   **b.** 10 mL   **c.** 1 L

2. gasoline for a car   **a.** 48 mL   **b.** 48 L   **c.** 480 L

3. bowl of soup   **a.** 25 mL   **b.** 250 mL   **c.** 250 L

4. ladle of soup   **a.** 5 mL   **b.** 500 mL   **c.** 5 L

5. water in an aquarium   **a.** 60 mL   **b.** 600 mL   **c.** 60 L

Write *mL* or *L* for the unit you would use to measure the capacity of each.

6. large jug of apple cider   7. tablespoon of syrup

8. glass of juice   9. water in a bucket

10. water in a washing machine   11. cocoa in a cup

Copy and complete the table.

12.

L	1	2	?	?	?	6	?	?
mL	1000	?	3000	?	?	?	7000	?

Compare. Write <, =, or >. You may make a table, multiply larger units, or divide smaller units.

13. 2 L ? 200 mL   **14.** 5 L ? 6000 mL   **15.** 8 L ? 8000 mL

16. 10 L ? 1500 mL   **17.** 4000 mL ? 3 L   **18.** 9000 mL ? 10 L

Solve.

19. Mr. Wood's van can travel 5 km on 1 L of gasoline. How much gasoline does the van use to travel 50 kilometers?

20. Mrs. Wood's water jug holds 4 L of water. It has 500 mL of water in it now. How much more water is needed to fill the jug?

21. Ellen and Allen both carry small canteens. Each canteen holds 750 mL of water. How much water do they need to fill both canteens?

22. The Woods began their trip with 75 L of gasoline in their gas tank. They used 68 L of gasoline. How much gasoline was left in the tank?

23. Ellen filled her 750-mL canteen four times in one day. How many liters of water did she use?

Challenge

Write in order from the least amount to the greatest amount.

24. 4 L, 40 mL, 400 mL, 4 mL

25. 200 L, 20 mL, 20 L, 2 mL

26. 38 L, 380 mL, 380 L, 138 L

27. 24 L, 2400 mL, 240 mL, 240 L

7-9 Gram and Kilogram

The **gram (g)** and the **kilogram (kg)** are metric units of mass.

1000 grams (g) = 1 kilogram (kg)

A paper clip has a mass of about 1 gram.

A small bag of flour has a mass of about 1 kilogram.

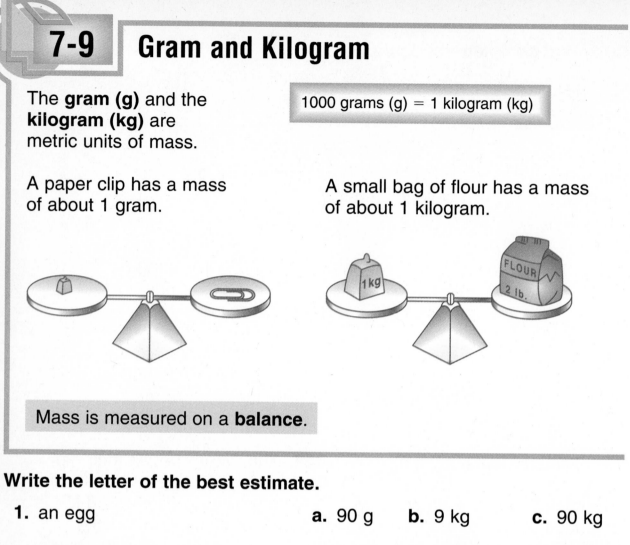

Mass is measured on a **balance**.

Write the letter of the best estimate.

1. an egg
   a. 90 g   **b.** 9 kg   **c.** 90 kg

2. a shark
   a. 100 g   **b.** 1000 g   **c.** 1000 kg

3. a worm
   a. 14 g   **b.** 14 000 g   **c.** 14 kg

4. a small dog
   a. 44 g   **b.** 44 kg   **c.** 440 kg

5. a slice of bread
   a. 2 g   **b.** 28 g   **c.** 28 kg

Write *g* or *kg* for the unit you would use to measure the mass of each.

6. a dinosaur   7. a mouse   8. a math book

9. a bag of oranges   10. a feather   11. a crayon

Copy and complete the table.

12.

kg	1	?	3	?	?	?	?	8
g	1000	?	?	4000	?	?	?	?

Compare. Write <, =, or >. You may make a table, multiply larger units, or divide smaller units.

13. 2 kg _?_ 20 g

14. 5 kg _?_ 5000 g

15. 9 kg _?_ 90 000 g

16. 8 kg _?_ 8324 g

17. 985 g _?_ 8 kg

18. 6000 g _?_ 5 kg

Solve.

19. A penny has a mass of about 3 g. About what is the mass of a roll of 50 pennies? of 2 rolls of 50 pennies?

20. Pete puts 150 g of turkey into each turkey sandwich. How many kilograms of turkey does he need for 20 sandwiches?

21. Each loaf of bread that Pete uses has a mass of 500 g. He orders 10 loaves of bread. Is this more than or less than 8 kilograms?

22. A carton holds up to 30 kg. Pete has 28 kg of canned goods and 4000 g of side dishes. Can he pack them all into the carton?

23. Pete cooks two turkeys. The first has a mass of 44 000 g. The second has a mass of 30 kg. Which turkey has the greater mass? How much greater?

Critical Thinking

Choose reasonable numbers so that each picture makes sense.

24.

25.

26.

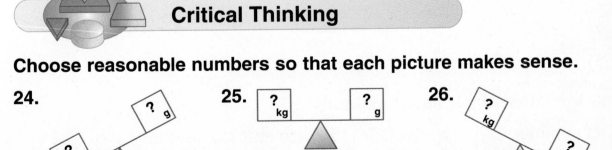

223

A **thermometer** is used to measure **temperature**.

Temperature can be measured in **degrees Fahrenheit (°F)** or in **degrees Celsius (°C)**.

▶ Each line on the Fahrenheit scale stands for 2°F. Room temperature in degrees Fahrenheit is about 68°F.

Each line on the Celsius scale stands for 1°C. Room temperature in degrees Celsius is about 20°C.

▶ Use a minus sign to write temperatures below zero.

Write: ⁻5°F
Read: 5 degrees Fahrenheit below zero

Write: ⁻10°C
Read: 10 degrees Celsius below zero

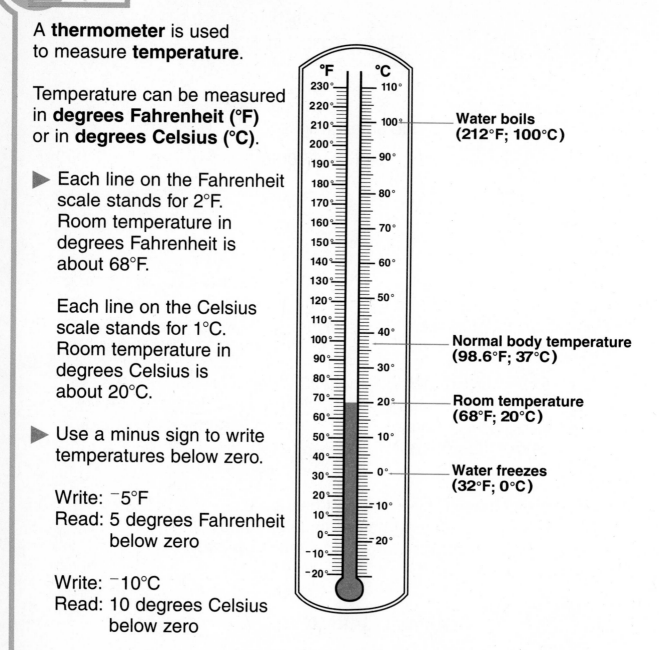

Water boils (212°F; 100°C)

Normal body temperature (98.6°F; 37°C)

Room temperature (68°F; 20°C)

Water freezes (32°F; 0°C)

Write the letter of the better estimate.

1. hot summer day
    a. 90°C
    b. 90°F

2. ice skating weather
    a. ⁻10°C
    b. 10°C

Write each temperature.

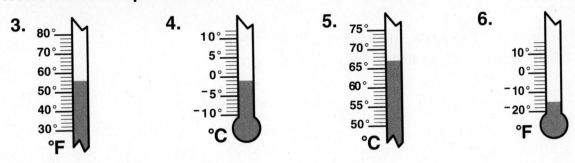

3. °F

4. °C

5. °C

6. °F

Compare. Write <, =, or >. You may use the thermometer on page 224.

7. 30°C _?_ 120°F

8. 100°C _?_ 212°F

9. 50°F _?_ 10°C

10. 140°F _?_ 60°C

11. ⁻10°F _?_ ⁻20°C

12. 100°F _?_ 50°C

Solve. You may use the thermometer on page 224.

13. At 6:00 A.M. the temperature was 45°F. It rose 13°F by noon. What was the temperature at noon?

14. The temperature was 22°C at 8:00 P.M. Overnight it dropped 9°C. What was the temperature in the morning?

15. The temperature was 36°F at 7:00 P.M. It dropped 10°F by midnight. What was the temperature at midnight?

16. At 5:00 A.M. the temperature was ⁻3°C. By noon it was 6°C. By how many degrees did the temperature rise?

17. The temperature rose 11°F from 5:30 A.M. to 10:00 A.M. It was ⁻17°F at 5:30 A.M. What was the temperature at 10:00 A.M.?

Write *true* or *false* for each statement.

18. You can swim outdoors at 39°C.

19. You can ice skate outside at 14°C.

20. You should turn on the air conditioner at 43°C.

21. You can take a bath in water that is 100°C.

You can read time after the half hour as minutes **past** the hour or as minutes **to** the next hour.

Read: 26 minutes **past** 6

Write: 6:26

Read: 43 minutes **past** 2

or

17 minutes **to** 3

Write: 2:43

Cesar is going to a movie that starts at 1:55. P.M. Will he see the movie in the morning or in the afternoon?

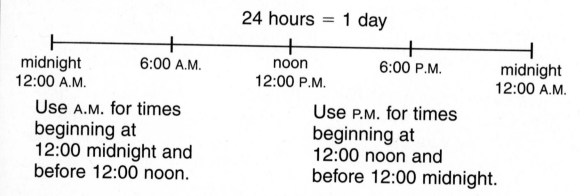

24 hours = 1 day

| midnight | 6:00 A.M. | noon | 6:00 P.M. | midnight |
| 12:00 A.M. | | 12:00 P.M. | | 12:00 A.M. |

Use A.M. for times beginning at 12:00 midnight and before 12:00 noon.

Use P.M. for times beginning at 12:00 noon and before 12:00 midnight.

Cesar will see the movie in the afternoon.

Write each time.

1.

2.

3.

Give the time in minutes past the hour and in minutes to the hour.

4.

5.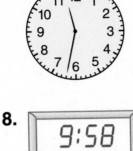

6.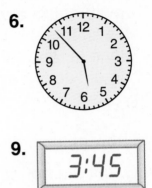

7. 4:39

8. 9:58

9. 3:45

Write A.M. or P.M. to make each statement reasonable.

10. Bill has breakfast at 7:15 _?_

11. School lets out at 3:00 _?_

12. Ahn goes to bed at 9:30 _?_

13. School begins at 8:00 _?_

Write the time. Use A.M. or P.M.

14. 10 minutes past 8 in the morning

15. 22 minutes to 10 at night

16. 36 minutes past 4 in the afternoon

17. 8 minutes to 9 in the morning

18. 18 minutes to noon

19. 45 minutes past midnight

Skills to Remember

Skip count to find each pattern.

20. by 2 from 12 to 30

21. by 10 from 9 to 59

22. by 5 from 0 to 25

23. by 5 from 30 to 60

7-12 Elapsed Time

Jody arrived at the airport at 11:10 A.M. to meet Lisa. Lisa's plane landed at 1:24 P.M. How long did Jody have to wait for Lisa?

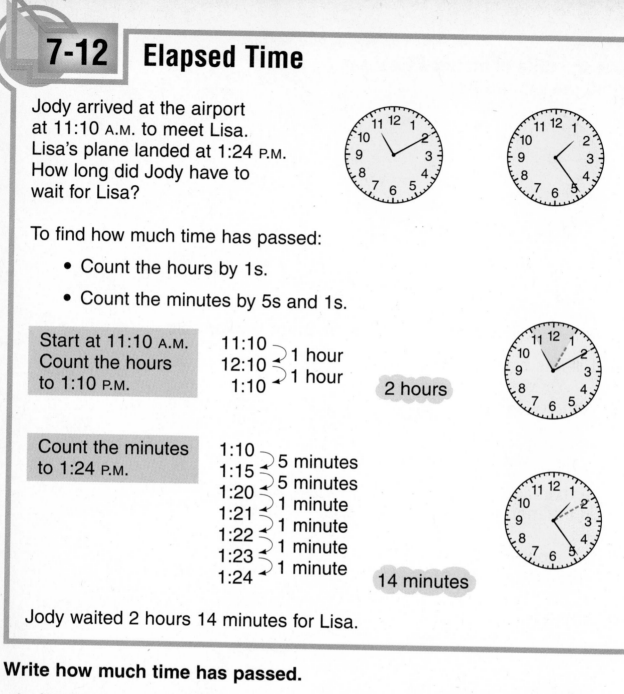

To find how much time has passed:

- Count the hours by 1s.
- Count the minutes by 5s and 1s.

Start at 11:10 A.M.
Count the hours to 1:10 P.M.

11:10
12:10 } 1 hour
1:10 } 1 hour

2 hours

Count the minutes to 1:24 P.M.

1:10
1:15 } 5 minutes
1:20 } 5 minutes
1:21 } 1 minute
1:22 } 1 minute
1:23 } 1 minute
1:24 } 1 minute

14 minutes

Jody waited 2 hours 14 minutes for Lisa.

Write how much time has passed.

1. from 8:05 A.M. to 8:30 A.M.

2. from 1:25 P.M. to 1:50 P.M.

3. from 6:30 A.M. to 6:51 A.M.

4. from 11:15 P.M. to 11:47 P.M.

5. from 11:45 P.M. to 12:04 A.M.

6. from 11:55 A.M. to 12:16 P.M.

7. from 3:25 P.M. to 4:40 P.M.

8. from 8:30 A.M. to 10:05 A.M.

Write how much time has passed.

9.

P.M.   to   A.M.

10.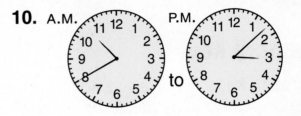

A.M.   to   P.M.

Solve.

11. Jody and Lisa left the airport at 2:05 P.M. They drove for 47 minutes before arriving at Jody's house. What time did they arrive at Jody's house?

12. Jody and Lisa will visit their cousin, who lives 1 hour and 10 minutes away. They want to get there at 11:00 A.M. What time should they leave?

Elapsed Time on a Calendar

Lisa arrived on June 26 and left on July 8.
How many days did she visit?

Count from June 26 to July 8. Count June 27 as day 1.

JUNE						
S	M	T	W	TH	F	S
			1	2	3	4
5	6	7	8	9	10	11
12	13	14	15	16	17	18
19	20	21	22	23	24	25
(26)	27	28	29	30		

JULY						
S	M	T	W	TH	F	S
					1	2
3	4	5	6	7	(8)	9
10	11	12	13	14	15	16
17	18	19	20	21	22	23
24/31	25	26	27	28	29	30

AUGUST						
S	M	T	W	TH	F	S
	1	2	3	4	5	6
7	8	9	10	11	12	13
14	15	16	17	18	19	20
21	22	23	24	25	26	27
28	29	30	31			

Lisa visited for 12 days.

Solve. Use the calendar.

13. What date is 10 days after July 22?

14. What date is 21 days before July 2?

15. What date is 4 weeks after June 15? before August 17?

TECHNOLOGY

Memory Keys

Memory keys are used to add, subtract, or recall a value stored in a calculator's memory.

M− → Subtracts a value from the value stored in memory.

M+ → Adds a value to the value stored in memory.

MR → Recalls the value stored in memory.

▶ Use memory keys to compute 21 ÷ 3 − 2 × 3 = _?_.

Remember: First multiply and divide, then add and subtract, in order from left to right.

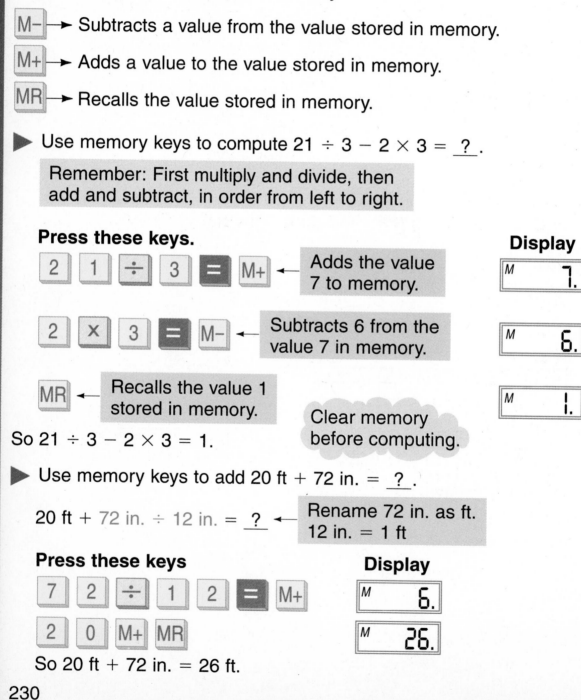

Press these keys.

2   1   ÷   3   =   M+   ← Adds the value 7 to memory.

Display

M   7.

2   ×   3   =   M−   ← Subtracts 6 from the value 7 in memory.

M   6.

MR   ← Recalls the value 1 stored in memory.

M   1.

So 21 ÷ 3 − 2 × 3 = 1.

Clear memory before computing.

▶ Use memory keys to add 20 ft + 72 in. = _?_.

20 ft + 72 in. ÷ 12 in. = _?_   ← Rename 72 in. as ft. 12 in. = 1 ft

Press these keys

7   2   ÷   1   2   =   M+

Display

M   6.

2   0   M+   MR

M   26.

So 20 ft + 72 in. = 26 ft.

230

Match each expression with the correct calculator keys.

1. $16 + 5 \times 2$ **2.** $5 \times 2 - 6$ **3.** $7 + 8 - 3 \times 5$ **4.** $3 \times 5 + 7 \times 4$

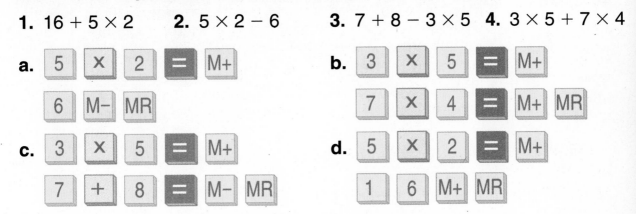

a. 5 × 2 = M+
6 M− MR

b. 3 × 5 = M+
7 × 4 = M+ MR

c. 3 × 5 = M+
7 + 8 = M− MR

d. 5 × 2 = M+
1 6 M+ MR

Use the memory keys on your calculator to compute.

5. $38 + 6 \times 3$ **6.** $5 \times 90 - 37$ **7.** $108 \div 12 - 2$

8. $19 \times 8 + 9 \times 41$ **9.** $34 \div 17 + 10 \times 3$ **10.** $4 \times 6 - 24 \div 8$

11. $54 \div 2 + 48 \div 6$ **12.** $12 \times 3 + 81 \div 9$ **13.** $64 \div 4 - 4 \times 4$

14. 4 ft + 36 in. = _?_ ft **15.** 96 in. + 9 ft = _?_ ft

16. 15 ft + 6 yd = _?_ yd **17.** 12 yd + 5 ft = _?_ ft

18. 60 in. + 2 ft = _?_ in. **19.** 180 yd − 180 ft = _?_ yd

20. $.45 + 3 \times \$8.01 - \$4.48$ **21.** $\$7.60 + \$25.10 \div 5 - \$.05$

22. $\$36.48 \div 6 + \$.09 \times 5$ **23.** $\$52.50 \times 3 - \$60.02 \div 2$

You can use a calculator to count by 5s.
Count by 5s to 30.

Press these keys: + 5 = = = = = =

24. Start at 25. Count by
2s to 37.

25. Start at 24 in. Count by
12 in. to 5 ft.

7-14 Problem Solving: Two-Step Problem

Problem: Maria has 3 packages to send to Hawaii in zone 8. One weighs 3 lb, the other 2 weigh 4 lb each. How much money will she save if she uses parcel post instead of priority mail?

Weight (lb)	Zone 8 Rates	
	Priority	Parcel Post
1	$2.90	—
2	$2.90	$2.85
3	$4.10	$4.05
4	$4.65	$4.60
5	$5.45	$5.40

1 IMAGINE Put yourself in the problem.

2 NAME *Facts:* 1—3-lb package
2—4-lb packages

Question: How much money is saved by using parcel post?

3 THINK Plan the steps to follow.

Step 1: Use the costs in the chart.
Add to find the cost of sending packages by priority mail or by parcel post.

3-lb cost + 4-lb cost = total cost

Step 2: Subtract to find the difference.

priority mail cost − parcel post cost = savings

4 COMPUTE Step 1: priority mail   parcel post   Step 2: savings

$$\begin{array}{r} \overset{1\ \ 1}{\ } \\ \$ \ \ 4.10 \\ 4.65 \\ + \ 4.65 \\ \hline \$13.40 \end{array} \qquad \begin{array}{r} \overset{1}{\ } \\ \$ \ \ 4.05 \\ 4.60 \\ + \ 4.60 \\ \hline \$13.25 \end{array} \qquad \begin{array}{r} \overset{3\ \ 10}{\ } \\ \$13.4\cancel{0} \\ - \ 13.25 \\ \hline \$ \ \ .15 \end{array}$$

Maria will save $.15 by using parcel post.

5 CHECK Use a calculator to check the computation in each step.
Remember to press the decimal point key.

232

Solve.

1. Paul sends his cousin three 28-oz fruit
cakes and 9 poppy seed muffins
that weigh 3 oz each. What is the
total weight of the package?

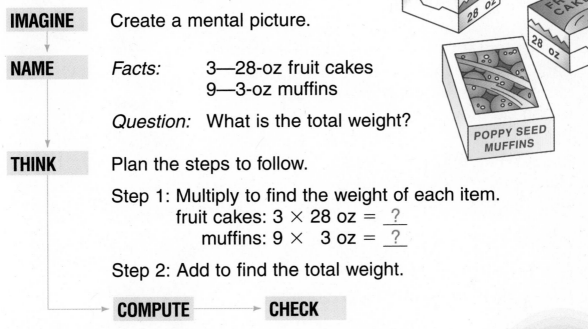

IMAGINE   Create a mental picture.

NAME   *Facts:*   3—28-oz fruit cakes
                          9—3-oz muffins

                Question: What is the total weight?

THINK   Plan the steps to follow.

                Step 1: Multiply to find the weight of each item.
                        fruit cakes: 3 × 28 oz = _?_
                           muffins: 9 ×   3 oz = _?_

                Step 2: Add to find the total weight.

        COMPUTE ⟶ **CHECK**

2. This year, Dan's wood-carving club includes
17 children, 23 teenagers, and 46 adults.
Last year, there were 54 members in all.
By how much has the membership changed?

3. Dan carves wood from 8:40 A.M. to 1:25 P.M.
each day. After lunch, he works from 2:30 P.M.
to 5:30 P.M. How many hours a day does
Dan work?

4. Ira sends six 2-lb parcel post packages to Hawaii.
How much change will he get from $20? Use the
zone 8 cost chart to find the answer.

5. Mr. Cheng bought 8 gallons of paint. Each gallon
cost $12.27. He also bought 2 paint rollers for
$4.75 each. What was the total cost?

7-15 Problem-Solving Applications

Solve.

Use these steps:

1. The sun set at 7:52 P.M. It rose the next morning at 5:02 A.M. How much time passed from sunset to sunrise?

2. Ray caught 3 fish that were about 4 pounds each. Mary caught 4 fish that were about the same size. About how many pounds of fish did they catch?

3. Mrs. O'Hara packed 2 pounds of trail mix. Her family ate 7 ounces of the mix. How much was left?

4. Mr. O'Hara brought 3 rolls of fishing line. Each roll holds 525 yards of line. Did he bring more than a mile of line?

5. Mrs. O'Hara caught a fish that weighed 12 kg. How much did the fish weigh in grams?

6. The O'Hara family left home at 8:25 A.M. Lunch at a rest stop took 45 minutes. They arrived at Loon Lake at 4:00 P.M. How long were they driving?

7. Mary's jug holds 3 L of water. It already has 500 mL in it. How much water should Mary add to fill it?

8. The hiking trail is 4 km long. There are signposts every 80 m. How many signposts are on the trail?

Solve.

9. A loon called at 7:48 A.M. It called again 13 minutes later. What time was the second call?

10. Mary glues 8 pine needles onto each postcard. She has 130 pine needles. How many postcards can she make?

USE THESE STRATEGIES:
Two-Step Problem
Extra Information
Choose the Operation
Logical Information
Interpret the Remainder
Guess and Test

11. The distance across Loon Lake is 2 miles. Mary rows the boat 2640 yards out on the lake. How much farther does she need to row to reach the other side?

12. The perimeter of Loon Lake is 3 km. There are lakefront cabins about every 95 m. About how many cabins are on the perimeter?

13. Ray's fishing reel has 325 yards of line. He cuts off 18 feet of line. How much line is left on the reel?

14. The family leaves Loon Lake at 9:00 A.M. and arrives home at 5:30 P.M. Mr. O'Hara drives the first half of the trip, then Mrs. O'Hara drives. About what time does Mrs. O'Hara start driving?

Use the map for problems 15 and 16.

15. About how long will it take to get from Loon Lake to Moon Lake at a rate of 50 miles per hour?

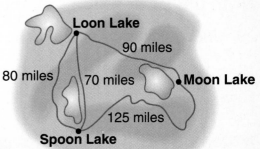

16. How long is the shortest route from Moon Lake to the other two lakes? How long is the longest route?

More Practice

Write *in.*, *ft*, *yd*, or *mi* for the unit you would use to measure each.

1. distance across the county

2. width of a creek

3. width of a book

4. length of a pool

Add.

5.   3 ft 2 in.
  + 4 ft 5 in.

6.   4 yd 1 ft
  + 6 yd 1 ft

7.   6 yd 2 ft
  + 7 yd

Complete.

8. 4 pt = ? c

9. 32 oz = ? lb

10. 6000 lb = ? T

11. 6 cm = ? mm

12. 4000 m = ? km

13. 300 mm = ? m

Compare. Write <, =, or >.

14. 6 kg ? 6000 g

15. 11 fl oz ? 2 c

16. 60 mm ? 6 m

17. 400 mL ? 4 L

18. 6 qt ? 1 gal

19. 5000 lb ? 1 T

20. 100 cm ? 10 m

21. 5 dm ? 50 m

22. 50 kg ? 1 g

Write the letter of the better estimate.

23. snow skiing weather   **a.** 25° F   **b.** 25° C

24. a day for a picnic   **a.** 32° C   **b.** 32° F

Write how much time has passed.

25. from 11:25 A.M. to 12:15 P.M.

26. from 11:30 P.M. to 7:15 A.M.

(See *Still More Practice,* p. 466.)

TIME ZONES

The clocks show the time in four different **time zones**
of the United States when it is 12:00 noon Central time.

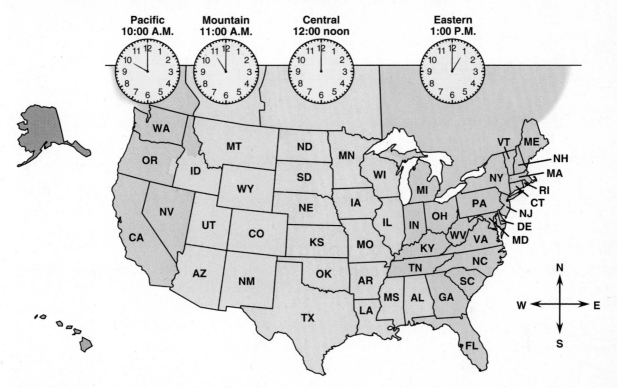

Solve. Use the time zone map.

1. What time is it in California
   when it is 2:00 P.M. in Maine?

2. What time is it in Georgia
   when it is 10:00 A.M. in Kansas?

3. Emily lives in Arizona. She
   will call Nat in Ohio at
   6:30 P.M. Eastern time.
   What is that time in Arizona?

4. Xue will call Chad in Nevada
   at 1:45 P.M. Eastern time
   from New York. What time
   is that in Nevada?

5. It is 2:07 A.M. in Arkansas.
   What time is it in
   a. Iowa?   **b.** Oregon?
   c. Vermont?   **d.** Idaho?

6. A 6-hour flight to Utah leaves
   Delaware at 1:27 P.M. Eastern
   time. What is the time in
   Utah when the plane arrives?

Check Your Mastery

Copy and complete each table.

See pp. 212–213, 220–221

1.

pt	1	2	?	4	5
c	2	?	6	8	?
fl oz	?	32	?	?	?

2.

gal	1	?	3	?	?
qt	4	?	12	?	?
pt	8	16	?	32	?

3.

L	1	?	3	?	?	?	7
mL	1000	2000	?	?	?	6000	?

Compare. Write <, =, or >.

See pp. 206–209, 214–215

4. 36 in. _?_ 4 ft

5. 62 in. _?_ 3 yd

6. 5750 yd _?_ 2 mi

7. 1T _?_ 2500 lb

8. 36 oz _?_ 1 lb

9. 14 lb _?_ 200 oz

Write *mL* or *L* for the unit you would use to measure the capacity of each.

See pp. 220–221

10. glass of milk

11. water in a pond

12. soda in a cup

13. gasoline in a car

Compare. Write <, =, or >.

See pp. 216–219, 222–223

14. 3 kg _?_ 30 g

15. 895 g _?_ 9 kg

16. 7000 g _?_ 6 kg

17. 6 cm _?_ 70 mm

18. 4 km _?_ 400 m

19. 10 dm _?_ 10 mm

Write *true* or *false* for each statement. See pp. 210–211, 224–227, 228–229

20. You can ice skate at 30° C.

21. You can wear shorts at 90° F.

22. You need a coat at 8° C.

23. 11:30 P.M. is school time.

24. Lunch is near 12:05 P.M.

25. Usually it is dark at 10:30 A.M.

26. The sum of 3 ft 10 in. and ?ft 10 in. is 8 ft 8 in.

27. 2 hours 15 minutes have passed from 11:15 A.M. to 2:30 P.M.

In this chapter you will:
Collect and organize data in tally charts, tables, bar graphs and pictographs
Read line and circle graphs
Predict the probability of dependent and independent events
Solve problems by making up a question

Do you remember?

The spinner is more likely to land on green.

Critical Thinking/ Finding Together
Each scoop stands for 100 ice cream cones. The picture shows the number of cones sold on Monday. Half that many cones were sold on Tuesday. Draw the scoops to show Tuesday's data.

239

Recording and Organizing Data

▶ Simon counted the different birds that came to his feeder. First he made a **tally** of each kind of bird in a **tally chart**. Then he found each total.

Kind of Bird	Tally	Total
House Sparrow	ҢЖ ҢЖ ҢЖ ҢЖ ҢЖ ҢЖ ІІ	32
House Finch	ҢЖ ҢЖ ҢЖ ҢЖ ҢЖ	25
Blue Jay	ҢЖ ҢЖ ІІІ	13
Chickadee	ҢЖ ҢЖ ҢЖ І	16
Nuthatch	ІІІІ	4
Junco	ҢЖ ҢЖ ҢЖ ҢЖ ІІІ	23

Remember:

/ = 1 and ҢЖ = 5

▶ Simon organized his information, or **data**, in a table. He organized the data in order from the greatest number of birds to the least number of birds.
Which kind of bird visited the feeder most often? least often?

Birds at My Feeder	
Kind	**Number**
House Sparrow	32
House Finch	25
Junco	23
Chickadee	16
Blue Jay	13
Nuthatch	4

Organizing information in a table from least to greatest or greatest to least makes it easier to find and compare data.

House sparrows visited the feeder most often.
Nuthatches visited least often.

The tally chart at the right shows the number of farm animals Alex and Rachel saw on a trip.

Copy and complete the chart.

	Animal	Tally	Total
1.	Cows	ҢЖ ҢЖ ҢЖ ҢЖ ҢЖ ҢЖ ҢЖ ҢЖ ІІ	?
2.	Pigs	?	11
3.	Goats	ҢЖ ҢЖ ҢЖ ІІІ	?
4.	Horses	ҢЖ ҢЖ ҢЖ ҢЖ І	?
5.	Sheep	?	26
6.	Chickens	ҢЖ ҢЖ ҢЖ ҢЖ ҢЖ ҢЖ ҢЖ ІІІ	?

Solve. Use the tally chart at the bottom of page 240.

7. Organize the data from least to greatest in a table.

8. What kind of animal was seen most often? least often?

9. How many more pigs would Alex and Rachel need to see to equal the number of horses?

10. Was the number of horses greater or less than the number of sheep? by how many?

11. How many more cows than pigs did Alex and Rachel see? how many fewer pigs than sheep?

12. Did Alex and Rachel see twice as many cows as horses? half as many goats as chickens?

Ms. Cruz took a survey. She asked 4th graders, "Which color is your favorite?" This is a list of the results.

Shirelle	– red	Nahn	– red	Kent	– purple	Steve	– green
Miguel	– purple	Nick	– purple	Lisa	– blue	Luis	– red
Mark	– blue	Tovah	– green	Cathy	– yellow	Bob	– green
Darla	– red	Maura	– red	Larry	– purple	Debi	– orange
Tony	– yellow	Adam	– purple	Maggie	– red	Tommy	– blue
Nilsa	– purple	John	– blue	Inez	– purple	Andrea	– purple

Use the list above to solve.

13. Make a tally chart and a table from the data in the list.

14. Which color is most popular? least popular?

15. Which color is the favorite of 6 students? of 3 students?

16. How many students did Ms. Cruz survey?

17. Which color did students like 4 times better than yellow? than orange?

Make Up Your Own

18. Ask 25 people, "What is your favorite fruit?" Make a tally to record their answers. Then organize the data in a table.

Graphing Sense

Graphs display data so that it can be easily understood. You can use graphs to compare sets of data.

▶ A **pictograph** uses pictures or symbols to represent different numbers of the same item. The **Key** tells how many each symbol stands for.

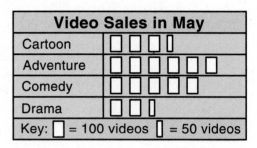

Video Sales in May	
Cartoon	□ □ □ ▯
Adventure	□ □ □ □ □ □
Comedy	□ □ □ □ □
Drama	□ □ ▯
Key: □ = 100 videos ▯ = 50 videos	

▶ A **bar graph** uses bars to represent measurements or numbers of different items. The **scale** on a bar graph tells how much or how many each bar stands for.

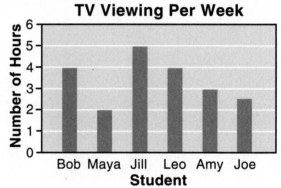

TV Viewing Per Week

▶ A **line graph** uses points and lines on a grid to show change over a period of time. A line graph also has a scale.

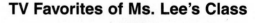
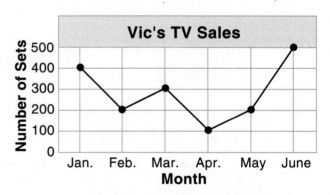

Vic's TV Sales

▶ A **circle graph** uses sections of a circle to compare the parts of a whole group.

TV Favorites of Ms. Lee's Class

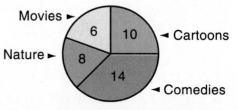

242

Solve. Use the graphs on page 242.

1. What is the title of the bar graph?

2. What is the title of the circle graph?

3. Which graph has a scale of 100?

4. Which graph has a key?

5. Which kind of video had the greatest sales in May? the least? How many of each were sold?

6. How many cartoon videos were sold in May?

7. Of which kind of video were 500 sold?

8. Which student watches TV the most hours per week? the fewest hours?

9. Which two students watch TV the same number of hours per week? How many hours is this?

10. Which student watches TV $2\frac{1}{2}$ hours per week?

11. In which month did Vic sell the fewest TVs? the most TVs? How many TVs did he sell in each of these months?

12. Did Vic sell more TVs in May or in January? How many more?

13. Which kind of TV show is most popular with Ms. Lee's class? least popular?

14. Are nature shows more popular with Ms. Lee's class than cartoons? than movies?

15. How many students are there in Ms. Lee's class? Explain how you found out.

Making Pictographs

Kai made a tally of the dogs that were in each category in the dog show.

Category	Tally	Total
Sporting	||||| ||||| ||||| ||||| ||||| ||||| |||||		36
Terriers	||||| ||||| ||||| |||||	20
Working	||||| ||||| ||||| ||||| ||||| ||||| ||||| ||||	39
Hounds	||||| ||||| ||||| ||||| ||||| |||||	30
Toy	|||||	5
Nonsporting	||||| |||||	10

Then Kai organized his data in a pictograph.

▶ To make a pictograph:

- List each category.

- If necessary, round the data to nearby numbers.
  $36 \rightarrow 35$ $39 \rightarrow 40$

- Choose a picture or symbol that can represent the number in each category.

- Choose a key.
  Let 🦴 = 10 dogs.

- Draw pictures to represent the number in each category.

- Label the pictograph. Write the title and the key.

Dogs in Dog Show	
Sporting	🦴 🦴 🦴 🦴
Terriers	🦴 🦴
Working	🦴 🦴 🦴 🦴
Hounds	🦴 🦴 🦴
Toy	🦴
Nonsporting	🦴

Key: 🦴 = 10 dogs 🦴 = 5 dogs

About how many of the dogs in the show were sporting dogs?

▶ To find about how many, count the number of pictures for the sporting dog category. Then use the key.

There are $3\frac{1}{2}$ pictures for the sporting dog category.

Use the key: 🦴 🦴 🦴 🦴
$$10 + 10 + 10 + 5 = 35$$

Of the dogs in the show, about 35 were sporting dogs.

The pictograph at the right shows the ice cream cones Ida sold at Ida's Ice Cream on a weekend in June.

Ice Cream Cones Sold	
Vanilla	🍦🍦🍦🍦🍦🍦
Chocolate	🍦🍦🍦🍦🍦🍦🍦🍦🍦
Strawberry	🍦🍦🍦🍦🍦
Butter Pecan	🍦🍦🍦🍦🍦🍦🍦
Pistachio	🍦🍦🍦🍦
Cherry	🍦🍦
Key: 🍦 = 50 cones 🍦 = 25 cones	

Use the pictograph to solve.

1. Which flavor was the most popular? How many cones of this flavor did Ida sell?

2. Ida sold 350 cones of one flavor. What flavor was this?

3. How many vanilla cones did Ida sell? how many cherry cones?

4. How many fewer cherry cones than strawberry cones did Ida sell?

5. How many ice cream cones did Ida sell altogether? List the flavors in order from greatest to least.

Use each to make a pictograph.

6.

Color of Car	Tally
Black	ⵀⵀ ⵀⵀ ⵀⵀ ⵀⵀ ⵀⵀ
Gray	ⵀⵀ ⵀⵀ ⵀⵀ ⵀⵀ ⵀⵀ ⵀⵀ ⵀⵀ
Blue	ⵀⵀ ⵀⵀ
Red	ⵀⵀ ⵀⵀ ⵀⵀ
White	ⵀⵀ ⵀⵀ ⵀⵀ ⵀⵀ ⵀⵀ ⵀⵀ
Green	ⵀⵀ

7.

Cats in the Cat Show	
Breed	**Number**
American Shorthair	275
Abyssinian	150
Siamese	200
Persian	250
Burmese	125
Manx	50
Rex	50
Himalayan	125

8. Write two questions for each of the pictographs you made.

Skills to Remember

Write the number that is halfway between each pair.

9. 100; 200   10. 0; 1000   11. 0; 500   12. 50; 100   13. 1000; 3000

245

8-4 Making Bar Graphs

Heidi found some information about the tallest tree of each species in the United States.

Heidi organized the data she found in a **vertical bar graph**.

Tallest Trees	
Tree	**Height in Feet**
Apple	70
Avocado	40
Mahogany	70
Mountain Ash	50
Pawpaw	60
Cypress	55

▶ To make a vertical bar graph:

- Use the data from the table to choose an appropriate scale. Start at 0.

- Draw and label the scale on the vertical line, or **axis**. (*Vertical* means "up and down.")

- Draw and label the horizontal axis. (*Horizontal* means "across.") List the name of each item.

- Draw vertical bars to represent each number.

- Title the graph.

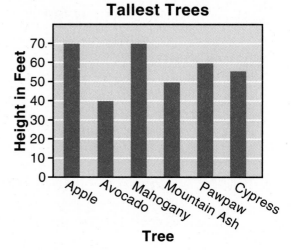

How tall is the tallest cypress tree in the United States?

▶ To find how tall, look at the bar labeled *Cypress*.

The top of the bar is *halfway* between 50 and 60.

The number that is *halfway* between 50 and 60 is 55.

So the tallest cypress tree in the United States is 55 feet tall.

Solve. Use the bar graph on page 246.

1. How many feet tall is the mountain ash tree?

2. Which two trees are the same height? How tall are they?

3. Which tree is 60 feet tall? How much taller is it than the shortest tree?

4. How much shorter is the cypress tree than the mahogany tree?

Copy and complete the horizontal bar graph. Use the table.

Top Speeds	
Animal	**Miles Per Hour**
Cat	30
Cheetah	70
Elephant	25
Grizzly Bear	30
Lion	50
Rabbit	35
Zebra	40

5.

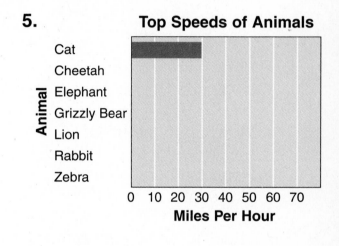

Solve. Use the completed horizontal bar graph.

6. Which animal has the shortest bar? the longest bar?

7. Which two animals have bars of the same length?

8. Which animals have bars that do not come to a ten?

9. Which animal has the second-longest bar?

Make a bar graph. Use the information below.

10.

Average Life Spans of Animals			
Baboon	– 20 years	Grizzly Bear	– 25 years
Bison	– 15 years	Pig	– 10 years
Elephant	– 40 years	Gray Squirrel	– 10 years
Hippopotamus	– 25 years	Rabbit	– 5 years

Line Graphs

Emmitt started doing sit-ups every day. The line graph shows Emmitt's progress the second week of his exercise program.

How many sit-ups did Emmitt do on Wednesday?

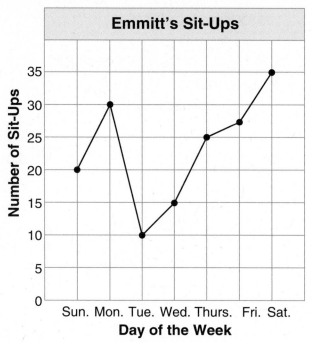

Emmitt's Sit-Ups

▶ To find how many:

- Find the day of the week on the horizontal axis.

- Move up to the point.

- Read the number on the vertical scale at the left.

Emmitt did 15 sit-ups on Wednesday.

About how many sit-ups did Emmitt do on Friday?

▶ To find *about* how many, move up to the point for Friday.

The point is *about* halfway between 25 and 30.

The number 27 is *about* halfway between 25 and 30.

So Emmitt did about 27 sit-ups on Friday.

Write how many sit-ups Emmitt did on the following days.

1. Monday   **2.** Thursday   **3.** Saturday   **4.** Sunday

Solve. Use the line graph on page 248.

5. On which day did Emmitt do the fewest sit-ups?

6. On which day did Emmitt do the most sit-ups?

7. On which days did Emmitt do more than 25 sit-ups?

8. On which days did Emmitt do less than 20 sit-ups?

9. Between which two days was there a difference of 20 sit-ups?

10. Between which two days was there a difference of about 8 sit-ups?

Solve. Use the line graph below.

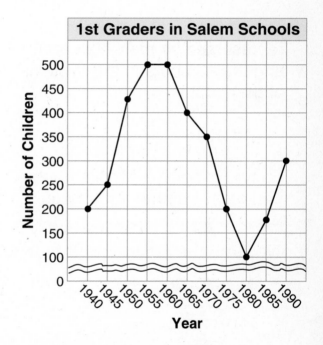

11. In which years were there the most 1st graders? How many 1st graders were there in these years?

12. In which years were there the fewest 1st graders? How many 1st graders was this?

13. About how many 1st graders were there in 1950? 1985?

14. In which year were there 350 first graders?

15. Is the difference in the number of 1st graders from 1985 to 1990 greater or less than that between 1975 and 1980?

16. In which 5-year period was the difference the same as the difference between 1960 and 1965?

17. In which 5-year period was the difference in the number of 1st graders the greatest?

18. In which 5-year period was there a difference of about 125 1st graders?

8-6 Circle Graphs

The town of Winterset held tryouts for a new community chorus.

The circle graph at the right shows the number of singers who were selected for the chorus.

How many singers make up the Winterset Community Chorus?

To find the number that is represented by the whole graph, add the numbers in the sections of the graph.

$$18 + 10 + 15 + 5 = 48$$

Forty-eight singers make up the Winterset Community Chorus.

Winterset Community Chorus

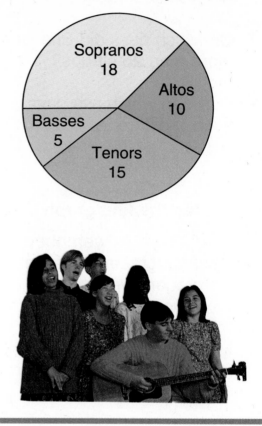

Solve. Use the circle graph below.

Jeremy's Budget

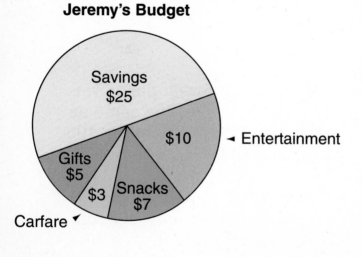

1. How much did Jeremy budget for savings? for carfare?

2. Did Jeremy budget more or less for entertainment than for gifts and snacks together? How much more or less?

3. How much money does the graph of Jeremy's budget represent in all?

250

Solve. Use the circle graph.

4. Which fruit is the favorite of 115 students?

5. How many students named melons as their favorite fruit?

6. Which two fruits were the favorites of the same number of students?

7. Which fruit was chosen as the favorite by the greatest number of students? How many students chose that fruit?

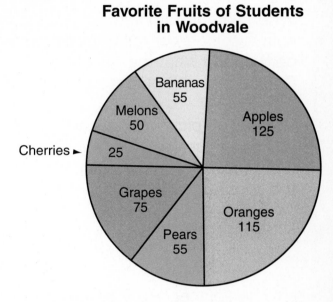

Favorite Fruits of Students in Woodvale

Bananas 55
Melons 50
Cherries ► 25
Apples 125
Grapes 75
Oranges 115
Pears 55

8. Which fruit was chosen as the favorite by the fewest students? Which fruit was chosen by double that number of students? by triple that number of students?

9. Were apples more or less popular than bananas and pears together? by how many votes?

10. How many students chose apples, oranges, *and* grapes? How many students in all chose apples, bananas, *and* pears?

11. How many students are there in Woodvale?

Critical Thinking

Solve.

Students' Pets

12. Which color section of the circle graph at the right represents each pet?
    a. cats–12   **b.** fish–4   **c.** birds–8   **d.** dogs–24

Predicting Probability

When you pick an item from a set of items without looking, spin a spinner, or roll number cubes, you do not know beforehand what the result, or **outcome**, will be. So you make the pick, spin, or roll **at random**.

Before you pick without looking, spin, or roll, you can figure out your chances of getting a particular result. This is called finding the **probability** of the event.

▶ What is the probability of the spinner landing on red? on blue? on white?

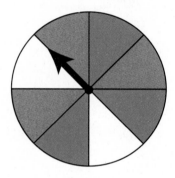

The spinner has 8 *equal* sections. Of the equal sections, 3 are red, 3 are blue, and 2 are white.

The probability of the spinner landing on

- red is 3 out of 8.

- blue is 3 out of 8.

- white is 2 out of 8.

▶ Is it equally likely that the spinner will land on

red or white?	white or blue?	blue or red?
3 > 2	2 < 3	3 = 3

So it is **more likely** that the spinner will land on red than on white.

So it is **less likely** that the spinner will land on white than on blue.

So it is **equally likely** that the spinner will land on blue or red.

Solve. Use the spinner at the right.

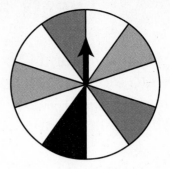

1. What is the probability of the spinner landing on
   - **a.** blue?
   - **b.** white?
   - **c.** black?
   - **d.** orange?

2. Is it *more likely*, *less likely*, or *equally likely* that the spinner will land on
   - **a.** orange than white?
   - **b.** blue or orange?
   - **c.** black than blue?
   - **d.** white than black?

Solve. Use the set of marbles.

3. At random, what is the probability that you would pick
   - **a.** green?
   - **b.** red?
   - **c.** orange?
   - **d.** blue?
   - **e.** black?
   - **f.** yellow?

4. Would you be more or less likely to pick yellow than green? black than yellow? red than blue? yellow than orange?

5. Would you be equally likely to pick black or green? orange or blue? orange or black? black or red? red or blue?

Challenge

Write the letter of the correct spinner.

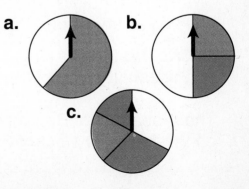

6. It is most likely to land on red.

7. It is most likely to land on blue.

8. It is equally likely to land on red or blue.

Events and Outcomes

Rae wrote A, B, and C on 3 slips of paper and put them into a bag. Then she picked a letter at random, tallied the outcome, and put the letter back into the bag.

Outcomes after 10 Tries

Letter	Tally
A	////
B	
C	#### /

Can Rae be sure of picking B on the 11th try?

▶ Rae began with 3 letters. The probability of picking B on the 1st try was 1 out of 3.

After each try, Rae put the letter back into the bag. So for each try, the probability of picking B was *still* 1 out of 3.

Rae has *the same chance* of picking B each time. She *cannot* be sure of picking B on the 11th try.

Ben wrote each of the even digits on slips of paper and put them into a bag. Then he picked a digit at random and put it in his pocket. He did this for each try.

Ben's Picks

Try	Digit
1st	8
2nd	6
3rd	

What is the probability of Ben picking 0 on the 3rd try?

▶ **1st Try:** 5 digits
Probability of picking 0: 1 out of 5

2nd Try: 4 digits
Probability of picking 0: 1 out of 4

3rd Try: 3 digits
Probability of picking 0: 1 out of 3

The probability changes as the number of possible outcomes changes.

The probability of Ben picking 0 on the 3rd try is 1 out of 3.

Solve. Use the information given on page 254.

1. Suppose Ben picks 4 on the 3rd try. What is the probability of his picking 0 on the 4th try?

2. If Ben picks 4 on the 3rd try, is it equally likely that he would pick 2 or 0 on the 4th try?

3. Suppose Rae started with A, B, C, D, E, and F. What would be the probability of her picking A on the 1st try? B on the 10th try? E on the 25th try? D on the 100th try?

Suppose you flip a quarter.

4. What is the probability of it landing heads up?

5. What is the probability of it landing tails up?

6. If it landed tails up four times in a row, could you tell whether it would land heads up or tails up the 5th time? Explain your answer.

Suppose there are 2 red marbles and 2 black marbles in a bag.

7. What is the probability of picking red? black?

8. On the 1st try you pick a red marble and put it in your pocket. On the 2nd try, what is the probability of picking red? of picking black?

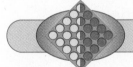 **Finding Together**

Make two spinners like the ones at the right. Decide which player is EVEN and which is ODD. Spin both spinners at the same time and find the sum. If the sum is odd, ODD scores 1 point. If the sum is even, EVEN scores 1 point. The winner is the first player to score 10 points. Switch roles and play again.

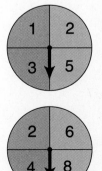

9. Is this game fair or unfair? Explain your answer.

8-9 Problem Solving: Make Up a Question

Problem: Penn School held an opinion poll about school dress codes. This bar graph shows the results of the voting. What questions can you answer?

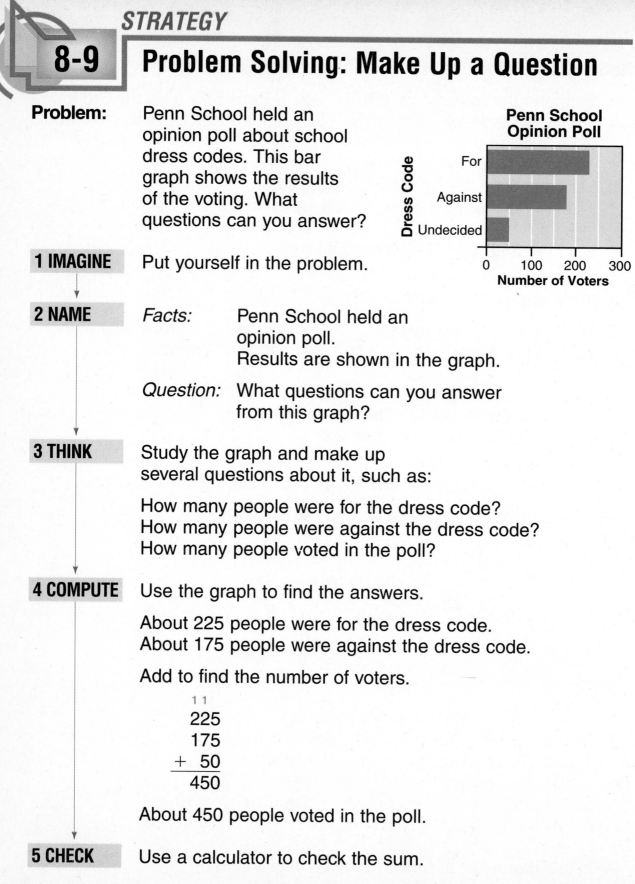

Penn School Opinion Poll

1 IMAGINE Put yourself in the problem.

2 NAME *Facts:* Penn School held an opinion poll. Results are shown in the graph.

Question: What questions can you answer from this graph?

3 THINK Study the graph and make up several questions about it, such as:

How many people were for the dress code?
How many people were against the dress code?
How many people voted in the poll?

4 COMPUTE Use the graph to find the answers.

About 225 people were for the dress code.
About 175 people were against the dress code.

Add to find the number of voters.

```
  11
  225
  175
+  50
  450
```

About 450 people voted in the poll.

5 CHECK Use a calculator to check the sum.

256

Solve.

1. Each earring Jenny makes has 3 beads. She uses a blue, a white, and a purple bead. The beads cost 47¢ each. What questions can you answer using this information?

IMAGINE Create a mental picture.

NAME *Facts:* Each earring has 3 beads.
The beads are blue, white, or purple.
The beads cost 47¢ each.

Question: What questions can you answer?

THINK You could ask about price:
- How much does it cost to make a pair of earrings?

You could ask about combinations:
- How many different earring patterns can Jenny make?

COMPUTE → **CHECK**

2. Michael spends 12 minutes exercising every day. He does 25 sit-ups and 10 push-ups. What questions can you answer about Michael's exercise schedule?

Exercise Schedule	
sit-ups	̶H̶H̶ ̶H̶H̶ ̶H̶H̶ ̶H̶H̶ ̶H̶H̶
push-ups	̶H̶H̶ ̶H̶H̶

3. A puppy is 6 pounds at birth and gains about 4 pounds every month for the first year.What questions can you answer about the puppy?

4. This graph shows the average daily temperature in Elmont. What questions can you answer based on the graph?

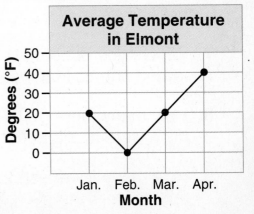

Average Temperature in Elmont

257

8-10 Problem-Solving Applications

Solve.

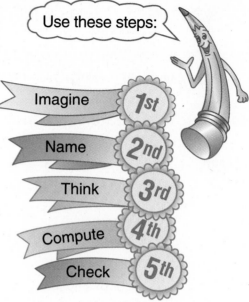

Use these steps:

Imagine — 1st

Name — 2nd

Think — 3rd

Compute — 4th

Check — 5th

1. There were 175 dogs at the Rosedale Pet Show. There were 50 small dogs and 85 medium dogs. The rest were large dogs. How many large dogs were in the show? Make a pictograph to show the answer.

2. Based on the numbers of each size of dog, was it more likely that a small, a medium, or a large dog would win the show? Use your pictograph to help find the answer.

Use the circle graph for problems 3–5.

3. Were more than half the pets entered dogs?

4. How many more dogs than cats entered?

5. How many pets entered the Rosedale Pet Show?

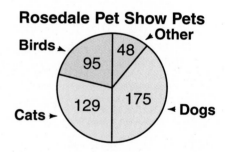

Rosedale Pet Show Pets

Other — 48

Birds — 95

Cats — 129

Dogs — 175

Use the bar graph for problems 6–9.

6. How many turtles were at the pet show?

7. Which type of pet had the fewest entries in the show?

8. How many more gerbils than mice were at the pet show?

9. How many fewer fish than rabbits were there?

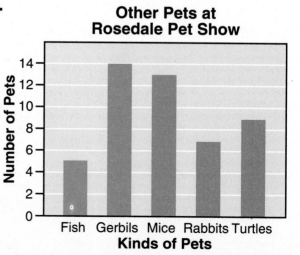

Other Pets at Rosedale Pet Show

Number of Pets

Fish Gerbils Mice Rabbits Turtles

Kinds of Pets

Solve.

10. There were 8 cats in the final round. There were twice as many in the semifinal round, and three times that many in the quarterfinals. How many cats were in the quarterfinals?

USE THESE STRATEGIES:
Make Up a Question
Two-Step Problem
Choose the Operation
Guess and Test
Logical Reasoning

11. Admission to the show was $3.75 for adults and $2.00 for children. Alana spent $13.25 for tickets. What tickets did she buy?

12. A dog-food supplier gave away 560 pounds of free food. The food was bundled in 4-ounce packages. How many packages were given away?

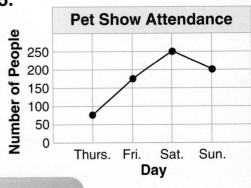

13. A collie, a turtle, and a canary won the top three prizes. The disappointed collie buried the winner's ribbon. The first- and third-place pets both had four feet. Who won the contest?

Use the line graph for problems 14 and 15.

14. About how many people attended the pet show in all?

15. Between which two days did attendance change the most?

Pet Show Attendance

Number of People

250
200
150
100
50
0

Thurs. Fri. Sat. Sun.
Day

Make Up Your Own

16. Write a problem using one of the graphs from pages 258 or 259. Have a classmate solve it.

More Practice

Mr. Singh asked the computer club, "Which is your favorite frozen yogurt flavor?" This is a list of his results.

Inez – vanilla	Nahn – vanilla	Luis – chocolate
Mark – chocolate	Tovah – vanilla	Debi – strawberry
Saul – mint	Maura – chocolate	Shannon – mint
Cathy – strawberry	Larry – strawberry	Juan – chocolate
Shirelle – chocolate	Kyle – vanilla	Lacey – chocolate

Use the list above to solve.

1. Make a tally chart and table from the data in the list.

2. Make a bar graph from the data in the list.

Use the line graph below to solve.

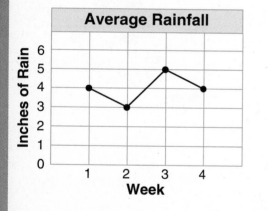

3. In which week was there the most rain?

4. How many inches of rain fell in week 2?

5. In which two weeks did the same amount of rain fall?

6. How many more inches of rain fell week 3 than week 2?

Solve. Use the spinner.

7. Is it equally likely that the spinner will land on
   a. red or yellow?   b. blue or red?

   c. yellow or white?   d. white or blue?

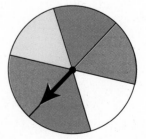

(See *Still More Practice*, p. 467.)

LINE PLOT

These are the math test scores of the students
in Mr. Fox's fourth-grade class.

Abby – 75	Dawn – 70	Nina – 85	Jaclyn – 65	Paul – 80
Joe – 70	Yukio – 85	Nora – 85	Lionel – 80	Lonette – 100
Nilsa – 90	Andy – 65	Sada – 75	Seiji – 85	Erika – 75
Tony – 85	Isaiah – 80	Zhou – 75	Kiri – 95	Nick – 85
Rob – 80	Carlo – 95	Greg – 90	Kate – 85	Chita – 80

Mr. Fox made a **line plot** to show the test
results. He wrote an X for each student
above the appropriate score.

```
                                          X
                                          X
                              X           X
                      X       X           X
                      X       X           X
              X       X       X       X       X
              X       X       X       X       X       X       X
           +-----+-----+-----+-----+-----+-----+-----+----
score:    65    70    75    80    85    90    95    100
```

The **range** is the difference between
the greatest and least scores.

$$\begin{array}{r} 100 \\ -\ 65 \\ \hline \end{array}$$

range ⟶ 35

The **mode** is the score
that appears most often.

mode ⟶ 85   7 students

Math Test Scores, Ms. Anton's Class

Alison – 60	Rick – 65	Julie – 80	Kim – 70	Ruth – 80
Wendell – 70	Joann – 80	Oscar – 70	Benazar – 65	Gabriel – 70
Joyce – 85	Tate – 70	Neil – 85	Dove – 75	Gary – 90
Bao – 75	Kathy – 90	Luz – 70	Hitoshi – 90	Seve – 60

Solve.

1. Use the scores above to make
   a line plot.

2. What is the range of the scores?

3. What is the mode of the scores?

261

Check Your Mastery

Solve. Use the pictograph below.

See pp. 242–245

Magazines Sold	
Theresa	□ □ □ □
Lyle	□ □ □ □ ▯
Colette	□ □ ▯
Everly	□ □ □ □
Key: □ = 10 magazines	
▯ = 5 magazines	

1. Who sold the most magazines?

2. How many more magazines did Lyle sell than Colette?

3. How many magazines were sold in all?

Copy and complete the bar graph.

See pp. 240–243, 246–247

Marble Collections	
Name	**Tally**
Mark	卌 卌 卌 卌 卌
Ray	卌 卌 卌 卌
Peggy	卌 卌 卌 //
Jane	卌 卌 卌 卌 卌 卌

4.

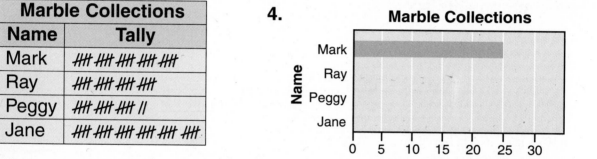

Marble Collections

Solve. Use the circle graph below.

See pp. 242–243, 250–251

5. How many students drank
a. milk?   **b.** juice?   **c.** soda?

6. How many more students drank milk than water? juice than soda?

7. Did fewer students drink milk than water and soda?

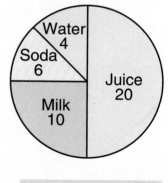

Number of Students

Solve. Use the spinner.

See pp. 254–255

8. What is the probability of the spinner landing on
a. white?   **b.** red?   **c.** blue?

262

⚡ Cumulative Test I

Choose the best answer.

1. The standard form of forty-six thousand, seven hundred thirty-nine is:
   - **a.** 46,398
   - **b.** 64,739
   - **c.** 46,000,739
   - **d.** 46,739

2. The value of the underlined digit in 68,325,784 is:
   - **a.** 10,000,000
   - **b.** 8,000,000
   - **c.** 800,000
   - **d.** 80,000,000

3. Round 3762 to the nearest thousand.
   - **a.** 3000
   - **b.** 3800
   - **c.** 4000
   - **d.** 5000

4. Make a front-end estimate: $12.29 + $61.95 + $19.50.
   - **a.** $90.00
   - **b.** $70.00
   - **c.** $100.00
   - **d.** $80.00

5. Estimate the product: 94 × 9.
   - **a.** 810
   - **b.** 1500
   - **c.** 100
   - **d.** 700

6. Which is normal room temperature?
   - **a.** 37°C
   - **b.** 20°C
   - **c.** 50°C
   - **d.** 68°C

7. From 6:45 P.M. to 7:12 P.M., how many minutes have passed?
   - **a.** 42
   - **b.** 15
   - **c.** 27
   - **d.** 47

Add or subtract.

8.
```
   9¢
   7¢
   1¢
 + 3¢
```

9.
```
   46
   24
 + 35
```

10.
```
  $2.14
   3.62
 + 5.37
```

11.
```
  7846
 +2685
```

12.
```
 $ 6.74
  12.28
  10.73
 + 9.50
```

13.
```
  38,261
 +56,398
```

14.
```
  524
  356
 +214
```

15.
```
  1041
  8162
 +3219
```

16.
```
  672
 - 40
```

17.
```
  6408
 -2139
```

18.
```
 $37.04
 - 17.82
```

19.
```
  57,639
 -29,862
```

20.
```
 $472.28
 - 185.39
```

21.
```
 $40.00
 - 23.79
```

22.
```
  6925
 -2368
```

23.
```
  982
 -694
```

24.
```
  4391
 - 861
```

25.
```
 $68.35
 - 23.86
```

26.
```
  1681
 - 798
```

27.
```
 $32.86
 - 19.98
```

Find the product or quotient.

28. 7
    ×8

29. 36
    × 4

30. $.49
    × 7

31. 3456
    × 5

32. $7.45
    × 63

33. 269
    × 29

34. 6321
    × 8

35. 7)56

36. 4)144

37. 6)1464

38. 5)3540

39. 8)$24.00

40. 7)6377

41. 5)800

42. $1.29 ÷ 3

Compare. Write <, =, or >.

43. 9 ft _?_ 3 yd

44. 6 lb _?_ 80 oz

45. 6000 lb _?_ 2 T

46. 36 in. _?_ 2 yd

47. 3 m _?_ 600 mm

48. 5 km _?_ 5000 m

49. 250 mL _?_ 25 L

50. 2 kg _?_ 200 g

Use the bar graph at the right for exercises 51–54.

51. Who had the most money in pledges?

52. How much did Steve and Lita have?

53. How much more than Lita did Paco have?

54. What was the total amount in pledges for all five students?

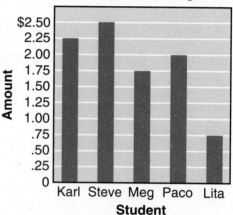

Walk-a-thon Pledges

Solve.

55. What is the probability of the spinner landing on blue? yellow?

56. Is it *more likely, less likely,* or *equally likely* that the spinner will land on yellow than green?

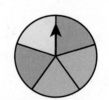

57. Carmen sold 23 tickets for the school play. Each ticket cost $13. How much money did she collect?

58. A box of 84 pens is packed in 7 layers. How many pens are in each layer?

59. Luz has test scores of 96, 85, 73, 76, and 95. What is her average on the 5 tests?

60. Desmond has a canvas that is 4 ft 12 in. wide. He cuts off $2\frac{1}{2}$ ft. How much is left?

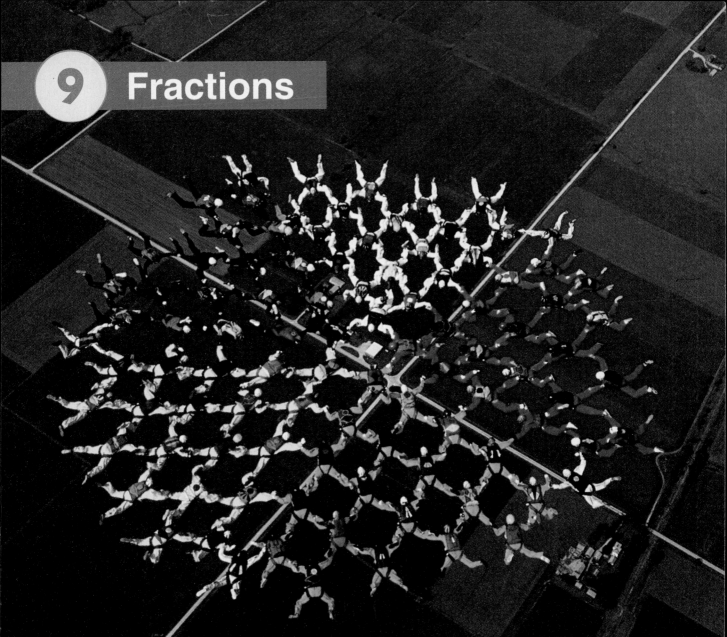

9 Fractions

In this chapter you will:

Recognize fractions as equal parts of
   regions or sets
Write equivalent fractions and
   fractions in lowest terms
Write mixed numbers
Identify common factors and greatest
   common factors
Estimate, compare, and order fractions
Use technology: probability programs
Solve problems using reasoning and
   analogies

Do you remember?

$$\frac{2}{3} = \frac{4}{6}$$

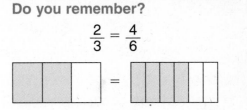

Critical Thinking/Finding Together
Think of the formation as a circle
graph. If there are about 100 sky
divers, estimate how many are in
yellow jump suits.

9-1 Parts of Regions

Tavon designed a flag on a sheet of paper. He folded the paper into 3 equal parts. Then he colored 2 parts green and 1 part yellow. What part of his design was yellow?

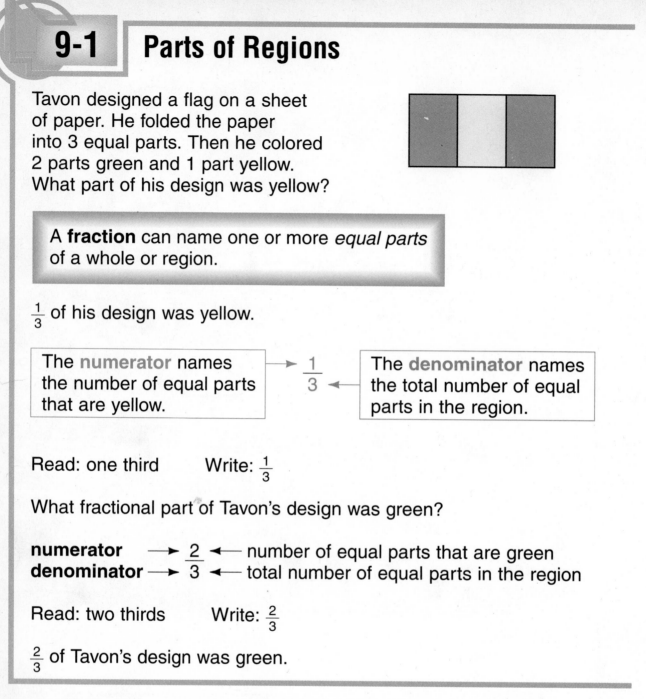

A **fraction** can name one or more *equal parts* of a whole or region.

$\frac{1}{3}$ of his design was yellow.

| The **numerator** names the number of equal parts that are yellow. | → $\frac{1}{3}$ ← | The **denominator** names the total number of equal parts in the region. |

Read: one third   Write: $\frac{1}{3}$

What fractional part of Tavon's design was green?

numerator ⟶ 2 ← number of equal parts that are green
denominator ⟶ 3 ← total number of equal parts in the region

Read: two thirds   Write: $\frac{2}{3}$

$\frac{2}{3}$ of Tavon's design was green.

Write the fraction for the shaded part. Then write the fraction for the part that is *not* shaded.

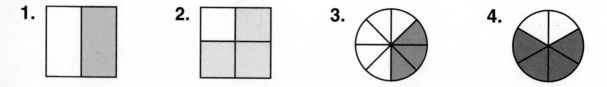

1.   2.   3.   4.

Write each as a fraction.

5. one fourth   **6.** two tenths   **7.** one half

8. four fifths   **9.** three fourths   **10.** five eighths

11. five sixths   **12.** three sevenths   **13.** one twelfth

Write each fraction in words.

14. $\frac{1}{10}$ **15.** $\frac{2}{5}$ **16.** $\frac{1}{6}$ **17.** $\frac{3}{8}$ **18.** $\frac{2}{7}$ **19.** $\frac{5}{12}$

Write the letter of the answer whose shaded part shows the fraction.

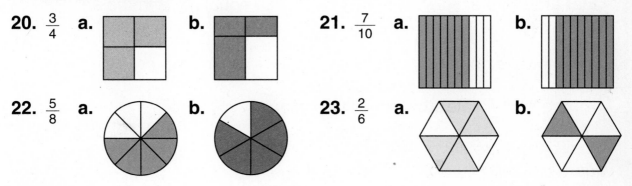

20. $\frac{3}{4}$ **a.**   **b.**   **21.** $\frac{7}{10}$ **a.**   **b.**

22. $\frac{5}{8}$ **a.**   **b.**   **23.** $\frac{2}{6}$ **a.**   **b.**

Solve.

24. Michelle designed a banner that was $\frac{7}{8}$ purple. Write this fraction in words.

25. Louis colored three tenths of a poster in red. Write this as a fraction.

Finding Together

Draw a picture to show each fraction.

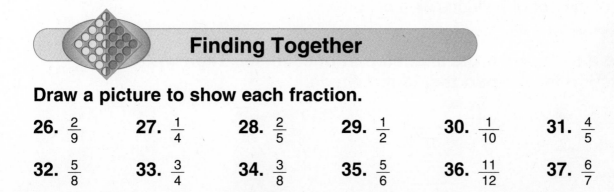

26. $\frac{2}{9}$ **27.** $\frac{1}{4}$ **28.** $\frac{2}{5}$ **29.** $\frac{1}{2}$ **30.** $\frac{1}{10}$ **31.** $\frac{4}{5}$

32. $\frac{5}{8}$ **33.** $\frac{3}{4}$ **34.** $\frac{3}{8}$ **35.** $\frac{5}{6}$ **36.** $\frac{11}{12}$ **37.** $\frac{6}{7}$

Parts of Sets

Of the 8 balloons that Nate bought at the parade, 3 were orange. What fractional part of the set of Nate's balloons was orange?

A fraction can name one or more *equal parts* of a set.

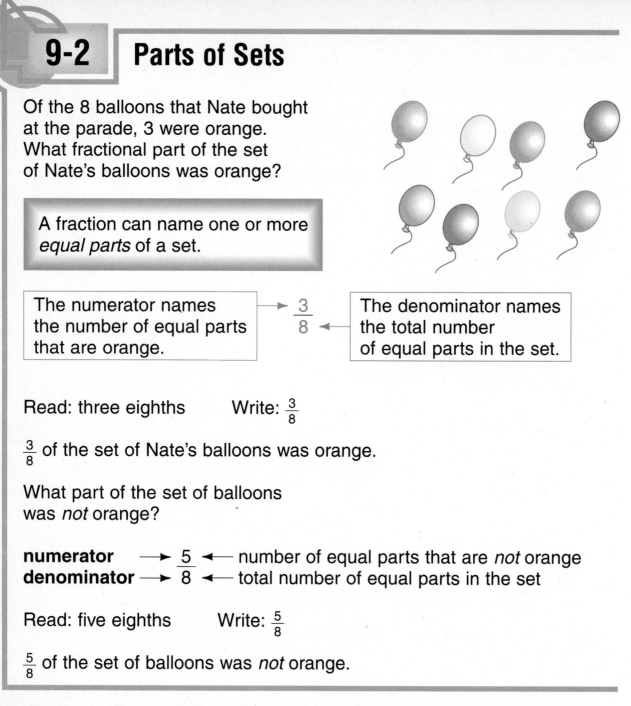

The numerator names the number of equal parts that are orange. → $\frac{3}{8}$ ← The denominator names the total number of equal parts in the set.

Read: three eighths   Write: $\frac{3}{8}$

$\frac{3}{8}$ of the set of Nate's balloons was orange.

What part of the set of balloons was *not* orange?

numerator → 5 ← number of equal parts that are *not* orange
denominator → 8 ← total number of equal parts in the set

Read: five eighths   Write: $\frac{5}{8}$

$\frac{5}{8}$ of the set of balloons was *not* orange.

Write a fraction for the shaded part of each set. Then write a fraction for the part that is *not* shaded.

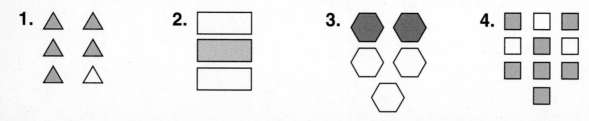

1.

2.

3.

4.

Write a fraction for the red part of each set. Then write a fraction for the yellow part.

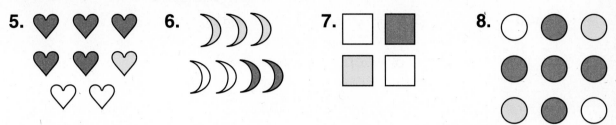

5. **6.** **7.** **8.**

Draw and shade a picture of a set to show each fraction.

9. $\frac{1}{2}$ **10.** $\frac{2}{3}$ **11.** $\frac{9}{10}$ **12.** $\frac{7}{8}$ **13.** $\frac{1}{12}$ **14.** $\frac{5}{7}$

Solve.

15. One tenth of the instruments in the Wildcat Marching Band were tubas. Write this as a fraction.

16. Of the baton twirlers in the parade, $\frac{7}{8}$ wore white boots. What fractional part of the set of twirlers did *not* wear white boots?

17. Of the horses in the parade, $\frac{7}{12}$ were palominos. Write this fraction in words.

Challenge

Use the pictures at the right to solve.

18. What part of the set of apples is *not* in the bowl?

19. What part of the set of bananas is on the plate?

20. What part of the set of all the fruit is on dishes? What part of the set of all the fruit is *not* on dishes?

9-3 Estimating Fractions

▶ You can use $\frac{1}{2}$ to estimate a fraction of a region.

About what fraction of each region is blue?

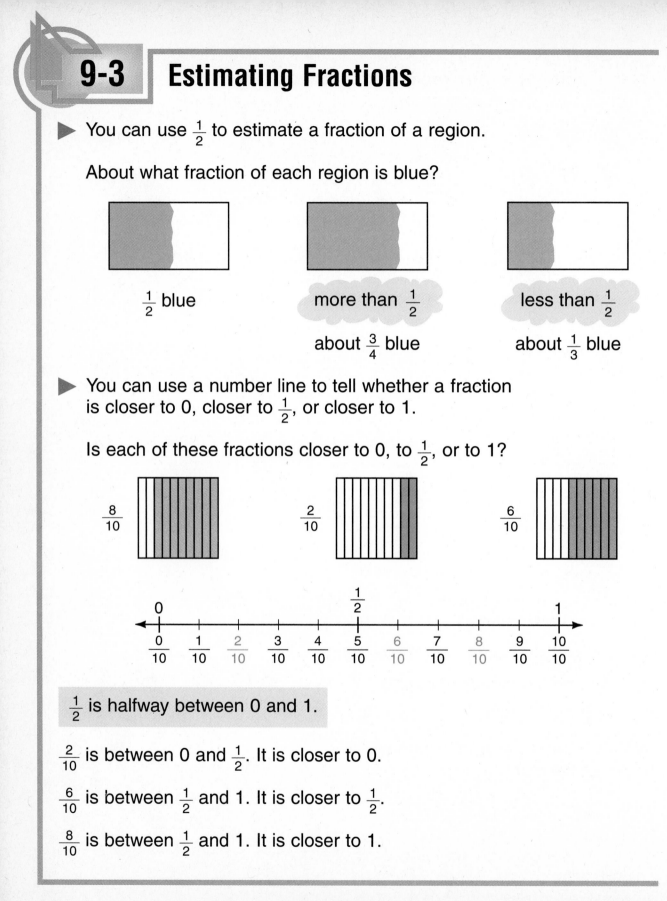

$\frac{1}{2}$ blue

more than $\frac{1}{2}$

about $\frac{3}{4}$ blue

less than $\frac{1}{2}$

about $\frac{1}{3}$ blue

▶ You can use a number line to tell whether a fraction is closer to 0, closer to $\frac{1}{2}$, or closer to 1.

Is each of these fractions closer to 0, to $\frac{1}{2}$, or to 1?

$\frac{8}{10}$

$\frac{2}{10}$

$\frac{6}{10}$

$\frac{1}{2}$ is halfway between 0 and 1.

$\frac{2}{10}$ is between 0 and $\frac{1}{2}$. It is closer to 0.

$\frac{6}{10}$ is between $\frac{1}{2}$ and 1. It is closer to $\frac{1}{2}$.

$\frac{8}{10}$ is between $\frac{1}{2}$ and 1. It is closer to 1.

Write *more than half* or *less than half*. Then tell about what fraction of each region is shaded.

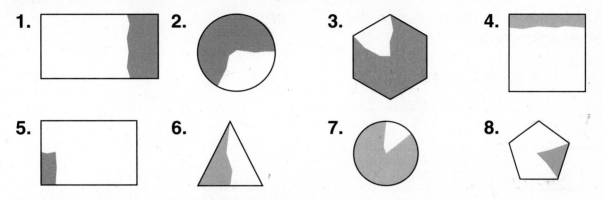

1.   2.   3.   4.

5.   6.   7.   8.

Use the number lines. Write whether each fraction is *closer to 0, closer to $\frac{1}{2}$*, or *closer to 1*.

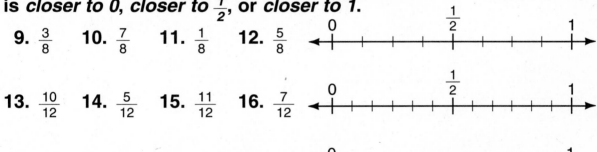

9. $\frac{3}{8}$ 10. $\frac{7}{8}$ 11. $\frac{1}{8}$ 12. $\frac{5}{8}$

13. $\frac{10}{12}$ 14. $\frac{5}{12}$ 15. $\frac{11}{12}$ 16. $\frac{7}{12}$

17. $\frac{2}{9}$ 18. $\frac{4}{9}$ 19. $\frac{7}{9}$ 20. $\frac{1}{9}$

Write whether each fraction is *closer to 0, closer to $\frac{1}{2}$*, or *closer to 1*. You may use number lines.

21. $\frac{3}{10}$ 22. $\frac{1}{8}$ 23. $\frac{4}{5}$ 24. $\frac{3}{7}$ 25. $\frac{1}{12}$ 26. $\frac{2}{3}$

Finding Together

About where on each number line is the arrow pointing?

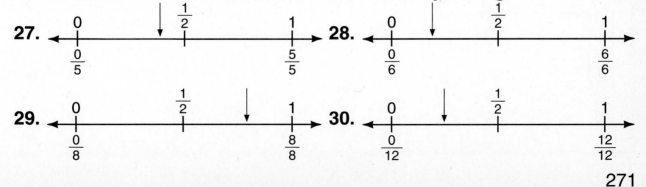

27.   28.

29.   30.

271

Equivalent Fractions

Equivalent fractions name the *same part* of a region or a set.

Equivalent Fraction Table

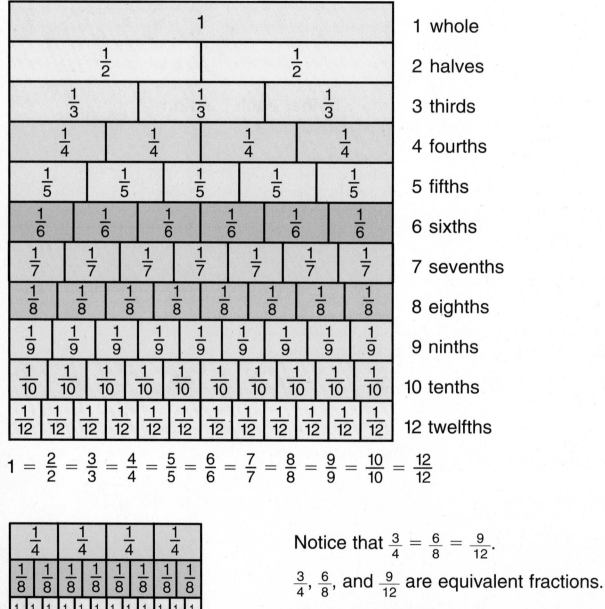

1		1 whole

$$1 = \frac{2}{2} = \frac{3}{3} = \frac{4}{4} = \frac{5}{5} = \frac{6}{6} = \frac{7}{7} = \frac{8}{8} = \frac{9}{9} = \frac{10}{10} = \frac{12}{12}$$

Notice that $\frac{3}{4} = \frac{6}{8} = \frac{9}{12}$.

$\frac{3}{4}$, $\frac{6}{8}$, and $\frac{9}{12}$ are equivalent fractions.

They all name the same part.

Write the equivalent fraction. Use the equivalent fraction table on page 272.

1. $\frac{1}{2} = \frac{?}{6}$
2. $\frac{1}{4} = \frac{?}{8}$
3. $\frac{2}{5} = \frac{?}{10}$
4. $\frac{4}{8} = \frac{?}{4}$

5. $\frac{2}{3} = \frac{?}{12}$
6. $\frac{5}{10} = \frac{?}{2}$
7. $\frac{3}{12} = \frac{?}{4}$
8. $\frac{2}{3} = \frac{?}{9}$

9. $\frac{1}{3} = \frac{?}{6}$
10. $\frac{2}{4} = \frac{?}{8}$
11. $\frac{2}{3} = \frac{?}{6}$
12. $\frac{1}{5} = \frac{?}{10}$

13. $\frac{1}{3} = \frac{?}{12}$
14. $\frac{2}{6} = \frac{?}{12}$
15. $\frac{3}{4} = \frac{?}{8}$
16. $\frac{3}{5} = \frac{?}{10}$

17. $\frac{1}{2} = \frac{?}{10}$
18. $\frac{3}{4} = \frac{?}{12}$
19. $\frac{2}{2} = \frac{?}{8}$
20. $\frac{1}{3} = \frac{?}{9}$

Does each pair show equivalent fractions? Write *yes* or *no*. Then write the equivalent fractions.

21.
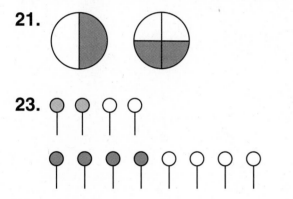

22.

23.

24.

Solve.

25. How many fifths are equal to four tenths?

26. How many twelfths are equal to five sixths?

Critical Thinking

27. Use the equivalent fraction table. Write all the fractions:
   a. that are equal to $\frac{1}{2}$.
   b. that are equal to 1.

28. Look at fifths and tenths. Then look at sixths and twelfths. Name a fraction that is equivalent to $\frac{2}{7}$.

Writing Equivalent Fractions

Suppose you did not have an equivalent fraction chart. How would you find equivalent fractions?

$\frac{1}{4}$			$\frac{1}{4}$			$\frac{1}{4}$			$\frac{1}{4}$	
$\frac{1}{8}$	$\frac{1}{8}$	$\frac{1}{8}$	$\frac{1}{8}$	$\frac{1}{8}$	$\frac{1}{8}$	$\frac{1}{8}$	$\frac{1}{8}$

To find equivalent fractions, multiply the numerator and the denominator by the same number.

$$\frac{3}{4} = \frac{?}{8} \qquad 4 \times \underline{?} = 8 \qquad 4 \times 2 = 8$$

$$\frac{3 \times 2}{4 \times 2} = \frac{6}{8}$$

So $\frac{3}{4} = \frac{6}{8}$ ⟵ These are equivalent fractions.

Study these examples.

$$\frac{1}{3} = \frac{?}{9} \qquad \begin{array}{l} 3 \times \underline{?} = 9 \\ 3 \times 3 = 9 \end{array}$$

$$\frac{1 \times 3}{3 \times 3} = \frac{3}{9}$$

So $\frac{1}{3} = \frac{3}{9}$

$$\frac{3}{5} = \frac{12}{?} \qquad \begin{array}{l} 3 \times \underline{?} = 12 \\ 3 \times 4 = 12 \end{array}$$

$$\frac{3 \times 4}{5 \times 4} = \frac{12}{20}$$

So $\frac{3}{5} = \frac{12}{20}$

Copy and complete.

1. $\frac{1 \times 2}{3 \times 2} = \frac{?}{?}$

2. $\frac{5 \times 3}{6 \times 3} = \frac{?}{?}$

3. $\frac{2 \times 2}{5 \times 2} = \frac{?}{?}$

4. $\frac{3 \times 4}{4 \times 4} = \frac{?}{?}$

5. $\frac{1 \times 3}{8 \times 3} = \frac{?}{?}$

6. $\frac{3 \times 2}{10 \times 2} = \frac{?}{?}$

7. $\frac{1 \times 3}{7 \times ?} = \frac{3}{?}$

8. $\frac{3 \times ?}{8 \times 2} = \frac{?}{?}$

9. $\frac{2 \times 4}{3 \times ?} = \frac{?}{?}$

10. $\frac{1 \times 5}{4 \times ?} = \frac{?}{?}$

11. $\frac{5 \times ?}{7 \times 2} = \frac{?}{?}$

12. $\frac{2 \times ?}{9 \times 2} = \frac{?}{?}$

Write the equivalent fraction.

13. $\dfrac{1 \times ?}{6 \times ?} = \dfrac{?}{12}$

14. $\dfrac{5 \times ?}{6 \times ?} = \dfrac{?}{12}$

15. $\dfrac{4 \times ?}{9 \times ?} = \dfrac{?}{27}$

16. $\dfrac{4 \times ?}{5 \times ?} = \dfrac{?}{20}$

17. $\dfrac{1 \times ?}{2 \times ?} = \dfrac{?}{10}$

18. $\dfrac{3 \times ?}{8 \times ?} = \dfrac{?}{32}$

19. $\dfrac{7 \times ?}{10 \times ?} = \dfrac{?}{30}$

20. $\dfrac{2 \times ?}{3 \times ?} = \dfrac{?}{18}$

21. $\dfrac{4 \times ?}{7 \times ?} = \dfrac{?}{21}$

22. $\dfrac{3}{4} = \dfrac{?}{12}$

23. $\dfrac{4}{5} = \dfrac{?}{10}$

24. $\dfrac{1}{12} = \dfrac{?}{36}$

25. $\dfrac{1}{2} = \dfrac{?}{10}$

26. $\dfrac{5}{6} = \dfrac{?}{12}$

27. $\dfrac{3}{8} = \dfrac{?}{24}$

28. $\dfrac{5}{9} = \dfrac{?}{27}$

29. $\dfrac{1}{4} = \dfrac{?}{16}$

30. $\dfrac{3}{7} = \dfrac{?}{14}$

31. $\dfrac{2}{5} = \dfrac{?}{25}$

32. $\dfrac{2}{3} = \dfrac{?}{18}$

33. $\dfrac{2}{4} = \dfrac{?}{12}$

34. $\dfrac{1}{6} = \dfrac{?}{30}$

35. $\dfrac{5}{8} = \dfrac{?}{40}$

36. $\dfrac{7}{10} = \dfrac{?}{20}$

37. $\dfrac{6}{10} = \dfrac{?}{20}$

38. $\dfrac{2}{4} = \dfrac{?}{12}$

39. $\dfrac{4}{6} = \dfrac{?}{18}$

40. $\dfrac{6}{8} = \dfrac{18}{?}$

41. $\dfrac{2}{7} = \dfrac{4}{?}$

42. $\dfrac{1}{9} = \dfrac{3}{?}$

43. $\dfrac{2}{3} = \dfrac{?}{12}$

44. $\dfrac{3}{10} = \dfrac{6}{?}$

45. $\dfrac{1}{8} = \dfrac{4}{?}$

46. $\dfrac{1}{5} = \dfrac{?}{15}$

47. $\dfrac{4}{9} = \dfrac{?}{18}$

48. $\dfrac{7}{10} = \dfrac{21}{?}$

Skills to Remember

Find the product or the missing factor.

49.
$$\begin{array}{r} ? \\ \times\ 1 \\ \hline 48 \end{array}$$

50.
$$\begin{array}{r} 24 \\ \times\ 2 \\ \hline ? \end{array}$$

51.
$$\begin{array}{r} 16 \\ \times\ ? \\ \hline 48 \end{array}$$

52.
$$\begin{array}{r} ? \\ \times\ 4 \\ \hline 48 \end{array}$$

53.
$$\begin{array}{r} 8 \\ \times 6 \\ \hline ? \end{array}$$

54. $6 \times \underline{\ ?\ } = 24$

55. $\underline{\ ?\ } \times 3 = 24$

56. $2 \times \underline{\ ?\ } = 24$

9-6 Factors

▶ Any number can be expressed as the product of two or more factors.

$$1 \times 24 = 24 \qquad 2 \times 3 \times 4 = 24$$

factors   factors

You can use multiplication sentences to find all the factors of a number.

Find all the factors of 24.

$1 \times 24 = 24$
$2 \times 12 = 24$ Factors of 24: 1, 2, 3, 4, 6, 8, 12, and 24
$3 \times 8 = 24$
$4 \times 6 = 24$

▶ **Common factors** are numbers that are factors of two or more products.

Find all the common factors of 24 and 18.

$$1 \times 24 = 24 \qquad 1 \times 18 = 18$$
$$2 \times 12 = 24 \qquad 2 \times 9 = 18$$
$$3 \times 8 = 24 \qquad 3 \times 6 = 18$$
$$4 \times 6 = 24$$

Common factors of 24 and 18: 1, 2, 3, and 6

▶ The **greatest common factor (GCF)** of two or more products is the greatest number that is a factor of those products.

Greatest common factor (GCF) of 24 and 18: 6

Find the missing factor.

1a. _?_ × 28 = 28 **b.** 2 × _?_ = 28 **c.** _?_ × 7 = 28

2a. 1 × _?_ = 12 **b.** _?_ × 6 = 12 **c.** 3 × _?_ = 12

3a. 16 = _?_ × 16 **b.** 16 = 2 × _?_ **c.** 16 = _?_ × 4

List all the factors of each. You may use multiplication sentences.

4. 5 **5.** 6 **6.** 8 **7.** 9 **8.** 4 **9.** 10

10. 21 **11.** 15 **12.** 14 **13.** 20 **14.** 32 **15.** 27

List all the common factors of each set of numbers. Then circle the GCF.

16. 2 and 6 **17.** 4 and 6 **18.** 6 and 8 **19.** 4 and 10

20. 8 and 12 **21.** 9 and 15 **22.** 6 and 15 **23.** 9 and 21

24. 10 and 30 **25.** 12 and 16 **26.** 12 and 18 **27.** 18 and 30

28. 24 and 36 **29.** 25 and 35 **30.** 36 and 42 **31.** 36 and 48

32. 8, 20, and 40 **33.** 12, 30, and 42 **34.** 10, 25, and 45

35. 18, 48, and 54 **36.** 15, 40, and 30 **37.** 20, 50, and 100

Critical Thinking

38. Look at the set of numbers at the right. Can the GCF be greater than 12? Explain why or why not. Then find the GCF.

12		42
	30	
18		
	36	

Fractions: Lowest Terms

▶ The **terms** of a fraction are its numerator and its denominator. A fraction is in **lowest terms**, or **simplest form**, when its numerator and denominator have no common factor other than 1.

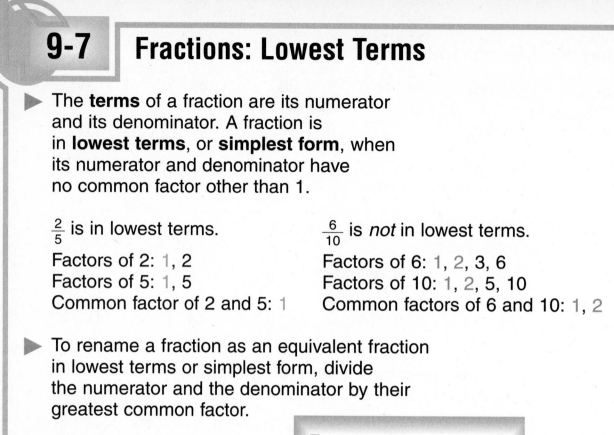

$\frac{2}{5}$ is in lowest terms.

Factors of 2: 1, 2
Factors of 5: 1, 5
Common factor of 2 and 5: 1

$\frac{6}{10}$ is *not* in lowest terms.

Factors of 6: 1, 2, 3, 6
Factors of 10: 1, 2, 5, 10
Common factors of 6 and 10: 1, 2

▶ To rename a fraction as an equivalent fraction in lowest terms or simplest form, divide the numerator and the denominator by their greatest common factor.

Write $\frac{6}{10}$ in lowest terms.

Factors of 6: 1, 2, 3, 6
Factors of 10: 1, 2, 5, 10

The GCF of 6 and 10 is 2.

$$\frac{6 \div 2}{10 \div 2} = \frac{3}{5}$$

Factors of 3: 1, 6
Factors of 5: 1, 5

So $\frac{6}{10}$ in lowest terms is $\frac{3}{5}$.

Copy and complete.

1. $\frac{4 \div 4}{8 \div 4} = \frac{?}{?}$

2. $\frac{3 \div 3}{9 \div 3} = \frac{?}{?}$

3. $\frac{6 \div 2}{8 \div 2} = \frac{?}{?}$

4. $\frac{8 \div 2}{10 \div 2} = \frac{?}{?}$

5. $\frac{9 \div ?}{12 \div 3} = \frac{?}{?}$

6. $\frac{14 \div 7}{21 \div ?} = \frac{?}{?}$

7. $\frac{10 \div ?}{25 \div ?} = \frac{?}{5}$

8. $\frac{12 \div ?}{42 \div ?} = \frac{?}{7}$

9. $\frac{15 \div ?}{45 \div ?} = \frac{3}{?}$

Is each fraction in lowest terms? Write *yes* or *no*.

10. $\frac{4}{7}$ 11. $\frac{6}{9}$ 12. $\frac{11}{12}$ 13. $\frac{7}{10}$ 14. $\frac{2}{10}$ 15. $\frac{8}{12}$

Write each fraction in lowest terms.

16. $\frac{2}{6}$ 17. $\frac{4}{24}$ 18. $\frac{9}{18}$ 19. $\frac{3}{12}$ 20. $\frac{2}{4}$ 21. $\frac{12}{20}$

22. $\frac{6}{18}$ 23. $\frac{10}{20}$ 24. $\frac{8}{24}$ 25. $\frac{9}{15}$ 26. $\frac{15}{20}$ 27. $\frac{4}{10}$

28. $\frac{6}{24}$ 29. $\frac{8}{14}$ 30. $\frac{6}{15}$ 31. $\frac{10}{12}$ 32. $\frac{7}{21}$ 33. $\frac{5}{15}$

34. $\frac{8}{18}$ 35. $\frac{9}{27}$ 36. $\frac{15}{18}$ 37. $\frac{10}{15}$ 38. $\frac{9}{15}$ 39. $\frac{12}{18}$

Solve. Express each answer in simplest form.

40. The chorus sang 12 songs at open house. Four of the songs were folk songs. What fractional part of the songs were folk songs?

41. Of 35 paintings on display in the school lobby, 7 were done in water colors. What fractional part of the paintings were water colors?

42. Jamie's parents looked at his notebook. Ten of the 40 pages were filled with math problems. Write this as a fraction in simplest form.

43. Glenda cut out the 26 letters of the alphabet to decorate the classroom. She cut 13 letters from green paper. What fractional part of the letters were green?

44. Writing awards were presented to 30 students. Of the awards, 6 were for poetry and 10 were for essays. What fractional part of the awards were for poetry? for essays?

45. There were 80 fourth-graders in Hadley School. Of these, 35 were boys. What fractional part of the fourth-graders were girls?

Mixed Numbers

Darryl is baking bread. His recipe calls for three and two thirds cups of whole-wheat flour.

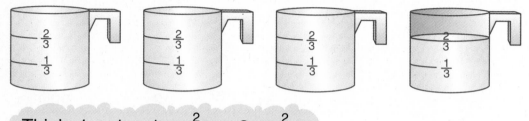

Think: $1 + 1 + 1 + \frac{2}{3}$, or $3 + \frac{2}{3}$

Read: three and two thirds   Write: $3\frac{2}{3}$

$3\frac{2}{3}$ is a mixed number.

A **mixed number** is made up of a whole number and a fraction.

whole number $\longrightarrow 3\frac{2}{3} \longleftarrow$ fraction

Study these examples.

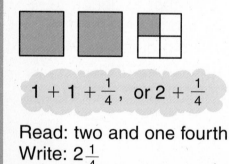

$1 + 1 + \frac{1}{4}$, or $2 + \frac{1}{4}$

Read: two and one fourth
Write: $2\frac{1}{4}$

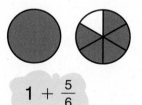

$1 + \frac{5}{6}$

Read: one and five sixths
Write: $1\frac{5}{6}$

Write as a mixed number.

1. four and three tenths

2. seven and two fifths

3. ten and one ninth

4. eight and five twelfths

5. twelve and three eighths

6. six and one half

Write a mixed number for each.

7.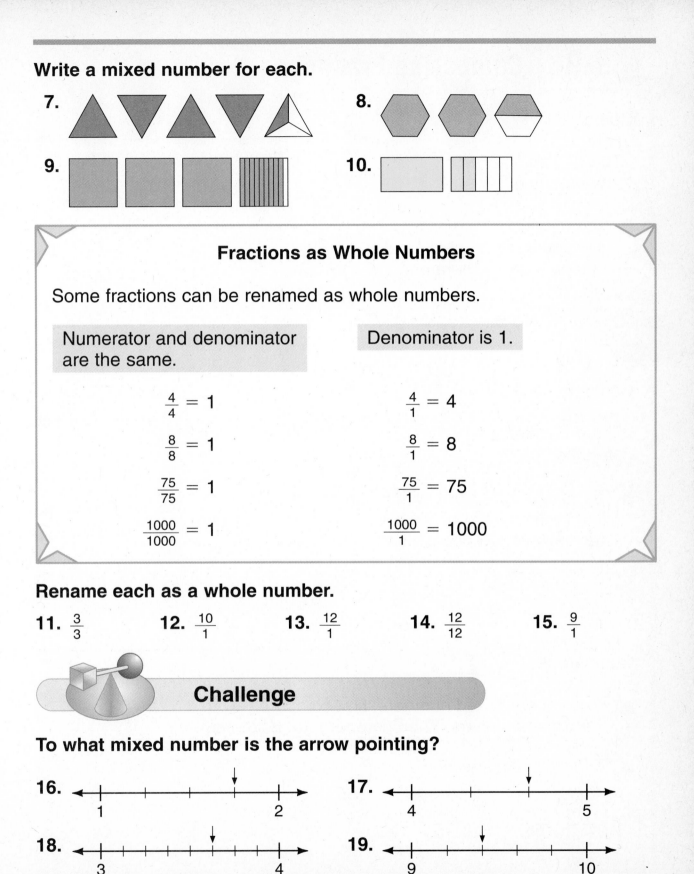

8.

9.

10.

Fractions as Whole Numbers

Some fractions can be renamed as whole numbers.

Numerator and denominator are the same.	Denominator is 1.
$\frac{4}{4} = 1$	$\frac{4}{1} = 4$
$\frac{8}{8} = 1$	$\frac{8}{1} = 8$
$\frac{75}{75} = 1$	$\frac{75}{1} = 75$
$\frac{1000}{1000} = 1$	$\frac{1000}{1} = 1000$

Rename each as a whole number.

11. $\frac{3}{3}$ **12.** $\frac{10}{1}$ **13.** $\frac{12}{1}$ **14.** $\frac{12}{12}$ **15.** $\frac{9}{1}$

Challenge

To what mixed number is the arrow pointing?

16.

17.

18.

19.

281

Comparing Fractions

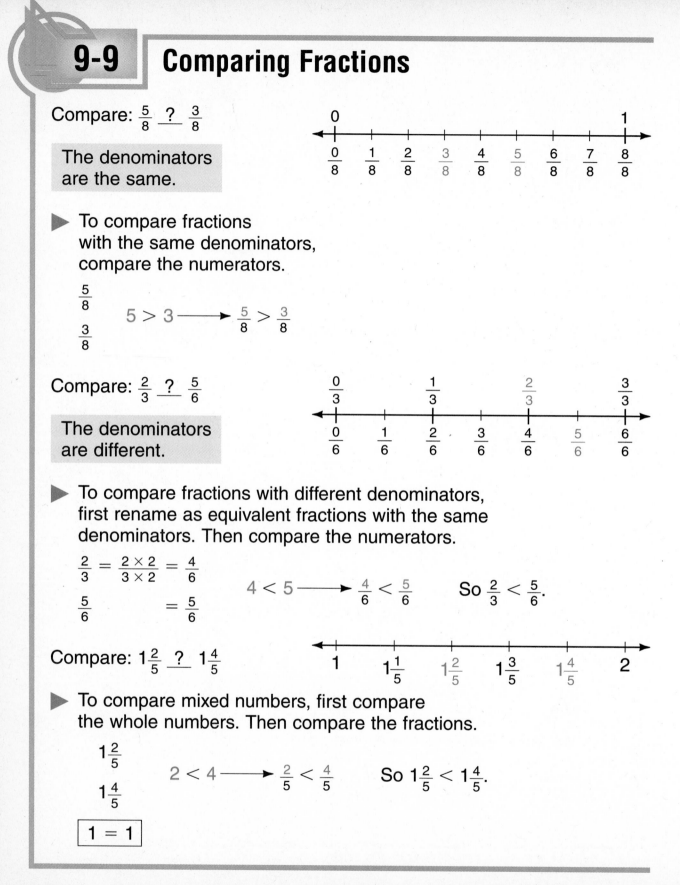

Compare: $\frac{5}{8}$ __?__ $\frac{3}{8}$

The denominators are the same.

▶ To compare fractions with the same denominators, compare the numerators.

$\frac{5}{8}$

$\frac{3}{8}$

$5 > 3 \longrightarrow \frac{5}{8} > \frac{3}{8}$

Compare: $\frac{2}{3}$ __?__ $\frac{5}{6}$

The denominators are different.

▶ To compare fractions with different denominators, first rename as equivalent fractions with the same denominators. Then compare the numerators.

$\frac{2}{3} = \frac{2 \times 2}{3 \times 2} = \frac{4}{6}$

$\frac{5}{6} \qquad = \frac{5}{6}$

$4 < 5 \longrightarrow \frac{4}{6} < \frac{5}{6} \qquad$ So $\frac{2}{3} < \frac{5}{6}$.

Compare: $1\frac{2}{5}$ __?__ $1\frac{4}{5}$

▶ To compare mixed numbers, first compare the whole numbers. Then compare the fractions.

$1\frac{2}{5}$

$1\frac{4}{5}$

$2 < 4 \longrightarrow \frac{2}{5} < \frac{4}{5} \qquad$ So $1\frac{2}{5} < 1\frac{4}{5}$.

$\boxed{1 = 1}$

Compare. Write <, =, or >.

1. $\frac{3}{4}$? $\frac{1}{4}$ _____

2. $\frac{5}{8}$? $\frac{7}{8}$ _____

3. $\frac{2}{7}$? $\frac{4}{7}$ _____

4. $\frac{7}{9}$? $\frac{5}{9}$ _____

5. $\frac{1}{6}$? $\frac{5}{6}$ _____

6. $\frac{4}{5}$? $\frac{4}{5}$ _____

7. $\frac{7}{10}$? $\frac{3}{10}$ _____

8. $\frac{11}{12}$? $\frac{5}{12}$ _____

9. $\frac{8}{12}$? $\frac{3}{4}$ _____

10. $\frac{2}{3}$? $\frac{6}{9}$ _____

11. $\frac{1}{2}$? $\frac{4}{6}$ _____

12. $\frac{1}{4}$? $\frac{2}{8}$ _____

13. $\frac{1}{3}$? $\frac{1}{6}$ _____

14. $\frac{3}{5}$? $\frac{3}{10}$ _____

15. $\frac{7}{8}$? $\frac{2}{4}$ _____

16. $\frac{7}{12}$? $\frac{5}{6}$ _____

17. $\frac{6}{10}$? $\frac{3}{5}$ _____

18. $\frac{1}{2}$? $\frac{4}{8}$ _____

19. $\frac{3}{4}$? $\frac{10}{12}$ _____

20. $\frac{3}{10}$? $\frac{1}{2}$ _____

21. $4\frac{3}{4}$? $4\frac{1}{4}$ _____

22. $1\frac{2}{3}$? $2\frac{1}{3}$ _____

23. $5\frac{1}{9}$? $2\frac{1}{9}$ _____

24. $6\frac{2}{5}$? $6\frac{4}{5}$ _____

25. $3\frac{3}{10}$? $3\frac{7}{10}$ _____

26. $8\frac{5}{8}$? $8\frac{3}{8}$ _____

27. $2\frac{4}{9}$? $4\frac{2}{9}$ _____

28. $1\frac{3}{6}$? $1\frac{3}{6}$ _____

Solve.

29. Of the fir trees in the park, $\frac{3}{10}$ were pines and $\frac{1}{10}$ were spruce. Were there more pines or more spruce in the park?

30. At the feeding station, $\frac{1}{3}$ of the birds were sparrows and $\frac{3}{12}$ were finches. Were there more sparrows or finches at the feeding station?

31. The northern sector of the park had $3\frac{3}{4}$ mi of trails. The eastern sector had $3\frac{1}{4}$ mi of trails. Which sector had more miles of trails?

32. On Monday, $\frac{3}{4}$ of the park's visitors were schoolchildren. On Tuesday $\frac{5}{8}$ of the visitors were schoolchildren. Did more schoolchildren visit the park on Monday or on Tuesday?

Challenge

Copy and complete.

33. $1\frac{2}{3} > 1\frac{?}{?}$

34. $5\frac{3}{8} < 5\frac{?}{?}$

35. $2\frac{3}{5} < 2\frac{?}{?}$

36. $4\frac{3}{4} > 4\frac{?}{?}$

9-10 Ordering Fractions

Order from least to greatest: $\frac{1}{2}, \frac{7}{10}, \frac{3}{10}$

> The denominators are different.

To order fractions with different denominators:

- Rename as equivalent fractions with the same denominator.

$$\frac{1}{2} = \frac{1 \times 5}{2 \times 5} = \frac{5}{10} \quad 2 \times 5 = 10$$

$$\frac{7}{10} = \frac{7}{10}$$

$$\frac{3}{10} = \frac{3}{10}$$

- Compare the fractions by comparing the numerators.

$$\frac{3}{10} < \frac{5}{10} \quad 3 < 5$$

$$\frac{5}{10} < \frac{7}{10} \quad 5 < 7$$

- Arrange in order from least to greatest.

$$\frac{3}{10}, \frac{5}{10}, \frac{7}{10}$$

The order from least to greatest: $\frac{3}{10}, \frac{1}{2}, \frac{7}{10}$

Study this example.

Order from greatest to least: $\frac{3}{8}, \frac{1}{8}, \frac{7}{8}$

> The denominators are the same.

> Compare the fractions by comparing the numerators.

$$\frac{7}{8} > \frac{3}{8} \quad 7 > 3$$

$$\frac{3}{8} > \frac{1}{8} \quad 3 > 1$$

> Arrange in order from greatest to least.

$$\frac{7}{8}, \frac{3}{8}, \frac{1}{8}$$

The order from greatest to least: $\frac{7}{8}, \frac{3}{8}, \frac{1}{8}$

Write in order from least to greatest.

1. $\frac{4}{6}, \frac{2}{6}, \frac{3}{6}$

2. $\frac{1}{5}, \frac{4}{5}, \frac{2}{5}$

3. $\frac{5}{12}, \frac{9}{12}, \frac{1}{12}$

4. $\frac{1}{8}, \frac{6}{8}, \frac{4}{8}$

5. $\frac{8}{9}, \frac{5}{9}, \frac{7}{9}$

6. $\frac{3}{7}, \frac{5}{7}, \frac{2}{7}$

7. $\frac{8}{10}, \frac{2}{10}, \frac{6}{10}$

8. $\frac{2}{4}, \frac{1}{4}, \frac{3}{4}$

9. $\frac{1}{2}, \frac{1}{4}, \frac{3}{4}$

10. $\frac{5}{6}, \frac{2}{3}, \frac{2}{6}$

11. $\frac{3}{8}, \frac{5}{8}, \frac{1}{4}$

12. $\frac{5}{12}, \frac{1}{6}, \frac{3}{12}$

13. $\frac{3}{10}, \frac{9}{10}, \frac{2}{5}$

14. $\frac{1}{2}, \frac{1}{8}, \frac{6}{8}$

15. $\frac{2}{3}, \frac{5}{12}, \frac{11}{12}$

16. $\frac{7}{9}, \frac{1}{3}, \frac{4}{9}$

Write in order from greatest to least.

17. $\frac{1}{7}, \frac{6}{7}, \frac{4}{7}$

18. $\frac{4}{9}, \frac{8}{9}, \frac{2}{9}$

19. $\frac{1}{10}, \frac{7}{10}, \frac{8}{10}$

20. $\frac{5}{8}, \frac{2}{8}, \frac{7}{8}$

21. $\frac{9}{12}, \frac{3}{12}, \frac{6}{12}$

22. $\frac{3}{6}, \frac{5}{6}, \frac{1}{6}$

23. $\frac{3}{5}, \frac{1}{5}, \frac{4}{5}$

24. $\frac{3}{10}, \frac{9}{10}, \frac{2}{10}$

25. $\frac{1}{6}, \frac{1}{2}, \frac{2}{6}$

26. $\frac{5}{12}, \frac{9}{12}, \frac{1}{2}$

27. $\frac{2}{3}, \frac{2}{9}, \frac{5}{9}$

28. $\frac{3}{12}, \frac{3}{4}, \frac{7}{12}$

29. $\frac{6}{10}, \frac{9}{10}, \frac{1}{2}$

30. $\frac{2}{12}, \frac{1}{12}, \frac{2}{3}$

31. $\frac{1}{8}, \frac{3}{4}, \frac{5}{8}$

32. $\frac{3}{6}, \frac{7}{12}, \frac{2}{12}$

Solve.

33. Marie cut three lengths of ribbon. They were $\frac{1}{2}$ yd, $\frac{3}{8}$ yd, and $\frac{5}{8}$ yd long. Which was the longest length? Which was the shortest?

34. Brad lives $\frac{3}{4}$ mi from school. Donna lives $\frac{1}{4}$ mi from school, and Chris lives $\frac{1}{2}$ mi from school. Who lives closest to school?

35. Jack bought $\frac{5}{8}$ lb turkey, $\frac{1}{2}$ lb ham, $\frac{3}{8}$ lb roast beef, and $\frac{1}{8}$ lb salami. Write these fractions in order from least to greatest. Then write them in order from greatest to least.

TECHNOLOGY

Probability Programs

If you tossed a coin 50 times, about how many times would you expect the coin to land on tails?

To find how many times, toss a coin or use a computer program.

The computer program below simulates a coin toss. It lets the numbers 1 and 2 stand for heads and tails. The program uses a **FOR...NEXT loop** to repeat the coin toss a given number of times.

```
10 PRINT "How many times do you want to toss a coin?"
20 INPUT T
30 FOR X = 1 to T
40 LET N = INT(RND(1)*2) + 1
50 PRINT N;
60 NEXT X
70 END
```

Waits for you to enter a number.

Assigns the numbers 1 or 2 to N.

Tells the computer to store a number in X. The first number will be 1. The last will be what you input in line 20.

Tells the computer to loop back to line 30 and store the next number in X.

Sample Output for T = 50

```
1 2 2 2 2 1 1 1 1 2 2 2 2 1 2 2 2 2 2 2 2 2 1 1 1 2
2 1 1 2 2 2 2 2 1 1 1 1 1 1 2 2 1 2 2 1 2 2 2 1
```

Solve. Use the computer program above.

1. If T = 5, how many times will the program run lines 40 and 50?

2. Suppose line 30 was FOR X = 3 to 9. What value would be stored in X after lines 40 and 50 are repeated twice?

286

Solve. Use the program on page 286.

3. Toss a coin 10 times. Write the output. How many 2s were printed?

4. Toss a coin 20 times. Then 30 times. Write the output for each. How many 2s were printed for each?

5. Predict the number of times a coin will land on tails if you toss it 40 times. 50 times. Run the program to check your predictions.

Write the output for each program.

6.
```
10 FOR X = 1 to 5
20 PRINT X
30 NEXT X
40 END
```

7.
```
10 FOR I = 2 to 10
20 PRINT 40 – I
30 NEXT I
40 END
```

8.
```
10 FOR H = 3 to 12
20 PRINT H + H
30 NEXT H
40 END
```

The program below will find the **average**, or **mean**, of a set of data.

```
 5 LET Total = 0
10 PRINT "How many numbers are in the set of data?"
20 INPUT N
30 FOR X = 1 to N
40 PRINT "Enter a number from the set of data."
50 INPUT D
60 LET Total = Total + D
70 NEXT X
80 PRINT "The mean of this set of data is " Total/N
90 END
```

Find the average for each set of data. Use the program above.

9. 12, 15, 18, 16, 21, 14

10. 124, 202, 96, 106

9-12 Problem Solving: Logic and Analogies

Problem: Gwen, Maraya, and Sonia each buy a bracelet. One is $6\frac{3}{4}$ in., one is $6\frac{1}{2}$ in., and the third is $6\frac{4}{8}$ in.

Gwen's bracelet is longer than Sonia's. How long is Maraya's bracelet?

1 IMAGINE Put yourself in the problem.

2 NAME *Facts:* Bracelets are $6\frac{3}{4}$ in., $6\frac{1}{2}$ in., and $6\frac{4}{8}$ in.

Gwen's bracelet is longer than Sonia's.

Question: How long is Maraya's bracelet?

3 THINK To compare mixed numbers:

First, compare whole number parts. $6 = 6 = 6$

Next, compare fraction parts. $\frac{3}{4}\ \underset{\_\_\_}{?}\ \frac{1}{2}\qquad \frac{1}{2}\ \underset{\_\_\_}{?}\ \frac{4}{8}$

Write equivalent fractions with like denominators.

$$\frac{3\times 2}{4\times 2}=\frac{?}{8}\qquad \frac{1\times 4}{2\times 4}=\frac{?}{8}\qquad \frac{4}{8}$$

Think: The common denominator is 8.

4 COMPUTE $\dfrac{3\times 2}{4\times 2}=\dfrac{6}{8}\qquad \dfrac{1\times 4}{2\times 4}=\dfrac{4}{8}\qquad \dfrac{4}{8}$

$$6\frac{3}{4}=6\frac{6}{8}\qquad 6\frac{1}{2}=6\frac{4}{8}\qquad 6\frac{4}{8}$$

$$6\frac{6}{8}>6\frac{4}{8}\qquad\qquad \text{equivalent}$$

Two bracelets are the same length.

Gwen's is longer than Sonia's, so Gwen's bracelet is $6\frac{6}{8}$ in. long.

Sonia's and Maraya's must be equal in length. $6\frac{1}{2}$ in. $= 6\frac{4}{8}$ in.

5 CHECK Draw 3 lines: $6\frac{3}{4}$ in., $6\frac{1}{2}$ in., $6\frac{4}{8}$ in. Then compare.

Solve.

USE THESE STRATEGIES:
Logical Reasoning
Guess and Test
Make Up a Question
Extra Information
Make a Table
Organized List

9. For every sunflower seed Deven plants, he also plants 4 zinnia seeds. Deven plants 45 seeds in all. How many zinnia seeds does he plant?

10. Diego has 10 pots. He puts marigolds in $\frac{2}{5}$ of the pots and daisies in $\frac{1}{2}$ of the pots. Are there more pots with daisies or marigolds?

11. Ms. Tallchief plants 2 red and 2 pink geraniums in a row in her window box. How many different arrangements can she make?

12. Kito plants a garden in $8\frac{1}{2}$ hours. When he is finished, $\frac{1}{4}$ of the rows are corn, $\frac{1}{3}$ are lettuce, $\frac{3}{12}$ are squash, and $\frac{1}{6}$ are zucchini. What questions can you answer about Kito's garden?

13. A fraction has a denominator that is 8 greater than its numerator. It is equivalent to $\frac{1}{3}$. What is the fraction?

14. Two fractions are equivalent. The denominator of one is the same as the numerator of the other. What are some possibilities for the two fractions?

15. Lila plants 16 bulbs: some lilies, some tulips, and some daffodils. One eighth of the bulbs are daffodils. One half of the bulbs are lilies. Order the types of bulbs from least to greatest.

291

More Practice

Write each as a fraction.

1. one half

2. three eighths

3. five sevenths

Write a fraction to show the shaded part of each set.

4.

5.

6.

About what fraction of each region is shaded?

7.

8.

9.

Write the equivalent fraction.

10. $\frac{1}{9} = \frac{5}{?}$

11. $\frac{7}{10} = \frac{14}{?}$

12. $\frac{6}{9} = \frac{?}{54}$

13. $\frac{3}{4} = \frac{18}{?}$

**Find the common factors for each set of numbers.
Then find the greatest common factor.**

14. 8, 12

15. 6, 16

16. 12, 20

Write each fraction in lowest terms.

17. $\frac{10}{15}$

18. $\frac{6}{12}$

19. $\frac{8}{24}$

20. $\frac{4}{20}$

21. $\frac{15}{40}$

Write in order from least to greatest.

22. $\frac{4}{10}, \frac{7}{10}, \frac{6}{5}$

23. $\frac{11}{12}, \frac{3}{4}, \frac{2}{12}$

Write in order from greatest to least.

24. $\frac{6}{9}, \frac{2}{3}, \frac{4}{9}$

25. $\frac{4}{5}, \frac{3}{10}, \frac{1}{10}$

Compare. Write <, =, or >.

26. $2\frac{7}{14}$ _?_ $3\frac{4}{14}$

27. $6\frac{10}{12}$ _?_ $7\frac{1}{12}$

28. $1\frac{2}{3}$ _?_ $2\frac{1}{3}$

292

(See *Still More Practice,* p. 468.)

RATIO AND PERCENT

You can use a **ratio** to compare the number of violins to the number of trombones.

The ratio of violins to trombones is 6 to 2.

▶ You can write a ratio in three ways.

| violins | ► 6 to 2 ◄ | trombones |

| violins | ► 6 : 2 ◄ | trombones |

| violins | ► 6/2 ◄ | trombones |

When you write a ratio, be sure to write the numbers in the correct order.

The ratio of violins to trombones: 6 to 2, 6:2, or $\frac{6}{2}$

The ratio of trombones to violins: 2 to 6, 2:6, or $\frac{2}{6}$

▶ If you write a ratio as a fraction with a denominator of 100, you can express that ratio as a **percent (%)**.

| fraction | $\frac{8}{100}$ | $\frac{10}{100}$ | $\frac{85}{100}$ | $\frac{100}{100}$ |

| percent | 8% | 10% | 85% | 100% |

Write each ratio three ways.

1. 4 clarinets to 7 trumpets
2. 10 oboes to 1 piano
3. 5 cellos to 8 tubas
4. 9 bassoons to 6 saxophones

Write each ratio as a percent.

5. $\frac{50}{100}$
6. $\frac{1}{100}$
7. $\frac{75}{100}$
8. 25:100
9. 99:100

Write each percent as a fraction.

10. 30%
11. 5%
12. 62%
13. 48%
14. 150%

Check Your Mastery

Write each as a fraction.

See pp. 266–269

1. five sixths

2. seven eighths

3.

Write the equivalent fraction.

See pp. 272–275

4. $\frac{3}{4} = \frac{?}{12}$

5. $\frac{1}{5} = \frac{5}{?}$

6. $\frac{1}{3} = \frac{3}{?}$

7. $\frac{2}{7} = \frac{?}{21}$

Find the common factors for each set. Then find the greatest common factor.

See pp. 276–277

8. 12, 24

9. 18, 36, 12

Write each in simplest form.

See pp. 278–281

10. $\frac{8}{12}$

11. $\frac{6}{10}$

12. $\frac{12}{36}$

13. $\frac{14}{28}$

14. $7\frac{8}{10}$

Write in order from least to greatest.

See pp. 282–285

15. $\frac{7}{10}, \frac{3}{5}, \frac{2}{10}$

16. $\frac{3}{20}, \frac{5}{20}, \frac{7}{5}$

Write in order from greatest to least.

See pp. 282–285

17. $\frac{14}{21}, \frac{3}{7}, \frac{3}{21}$

18. $\frac{11}{22}, \frac{6}{11}, \frac{12}{22}$

Solve.

See pp. 270–271, 284–285

19. Chet walked $\frac{5}{10}$ mile. Juanita walked $\frac{3}{5}$ mile. Toya walked $\frac{2}{5}$ mile. Who walked the longest distance? Who walked the shortest distance?

20. Mike poured this glass of juice. Is it about $\frac{1}{3}$ full or $\frac{2}{3}$ full?

In this chapter you will:

Add and subtract fractions with like and unlike denominators

Find common multiples and greatest common multiples

Add and subtract mixed numbers

Write sums and differences in simplest form

Estimate: sums and differences of mixed numbers

Find fractional parts of numbers

Solve problems using simpler numbers

Do you remember?

$$\frac{1}{5} + \frac{3}{5} = \frac{4}{5}$$

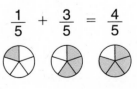

Critical Thinking/Finding Together

What fractional part of the set of piggy banks is green? Is the fraction in lowest terms?

10-1 Adding: Like Denominators

Pam walked $\frac{3}{10}$ mile from her house to school. Then she walked $\frac{5}{10}$ mile from school to the bus stop. How far did Pam walk?

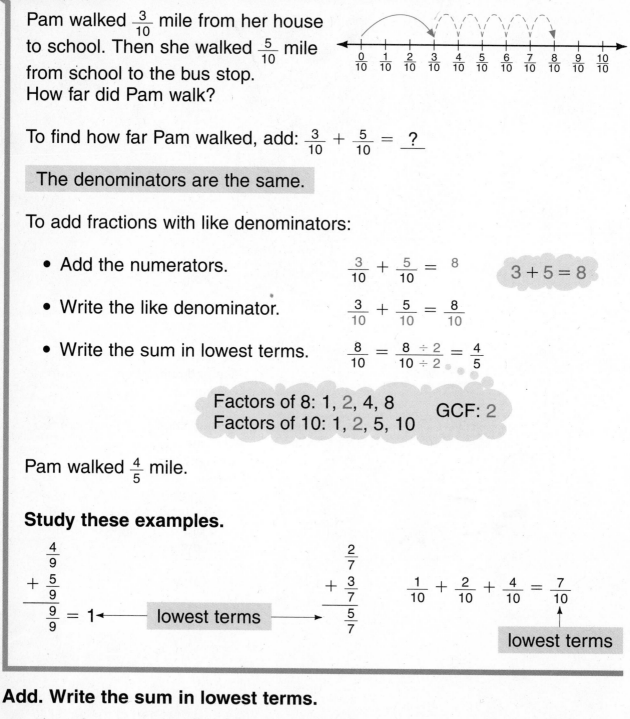

To find how far Pam walked, add: $\frac{3}{10} + \frac{5}{10} = \underline{\ ?\ }$

> The denominators are the same.

To add fractions with like denominators:

- Add the numerators. $\frac{3}{10} + \frac{5}{10} = \ 8$ $3 + 5 = 8$

- Write the like denominator. $\frac{3}{10} + \frac{5}{10} = \frac{8}{10}$

- Write the sum in lowest terms. $\frac{8}{10} = \frac{8 \div 2}{10 \div 2} = \frac{4}{5}$

> Factors of 8: 1, 2, 4, 8
> Factors of 10: 1, 2, 5, 10   GCF: 2

Pam walked $\frac{4}{5}$ mile.

Study these examples.

$$\begin{array}{r} \frac{4}{9} \\ + \frac{5}{9} \\ \hline \frac{9}{9} = 1 \end{array} \longleftarrow \text{lowest terms} \longrightarrow \begin{array}{r} \frac{2}{7} \\ + \frac{3}{7} \\ \hline \frac{5}{7} \end{array}$$

$$\frac{1}{10} + \frac{2}{10} + \frac{4}{10} = \frac{7}{10}$$

lowest terms

Add. Write the sum in lowest terms.

1. $\frac{1}{4} + \frac{2}{4}$ 2. $\frac{5}{8} + \frac{2}{8}$ 3. $\frac{1}{3} + \frac{1}{3}$ 4. $\frac{2}{7} + \frac{4}{7}$

Find the sum in lowest terms.

5. $\frac{2}{9} + \frac{1}{9}$

6. $\frac{1}{6} + \frac{2}{6}$

7. $\frac{2}{10} + \frac{4}{10}$

8. $\frac{2}{5} + \frac{3}{5}$

9. $\frac{1}{8} + \frac{5}{8}$

10. $\frac{3}{7} + \frac{4}{7}$

11. $\frac{4}{12} + \frac{6}{12}$

12. $\frac{2}{6} + \frac{2}{6}$

13. $\frac{3}{4} + \frac{1}{4}$

14. $\frac{2}{9} + \frac{4}{9}$

15. $\frac{4}{10} + \frac{4}{10}$

16. $\frac{2}{8} + \frac{2}{8}$

17. $\begin{array}{r} \frac{1}{9} \\ + \frac{3}{9} \\ \hline \end{array}$

18. $\begin{array}{r} \frac{3}{5} \\ + \frac{1}{5} \\ \hline \end{array}$

19. $\begin{array}{r} \frac{2}{10} \\ + \frac{3}{10} \\ \hline \end{array}$

20. $\begin{array}{r} \frac{3}{8} \\ + \frac{5}{8} \\ \hline \end{array}$

21. $\begin{array}{r} \frac{5}{12} \\ + \frac{3}{12} \\ \hline \end{array}$

22. $\begin{array}{r} \frac{1}{2} \\ + \frac{1}{2} \\ \hline \end{array}$

23. $\begin{array}{r} \frac{5}{7} \\ + \frac{2}{7} \\ \hline \end{array}$

24. $\begin{array}{r} \frac{2}{8} \\ + \frac{4}{8} \\ \hline \end{array}$

25. $\begin{array}{r} \frac{3}{12} \\ + \frac{3}{12} \\ \hline \end{array}$

26. $\begin{array}{r} \frac{1}{12} \\ + \frac{3}{12} \\ \hline \end{array}$

27. $\frac{2}{12} + \frac{1}{12} + \frac{7}{12}$

28. $\frac{3}{10} + \frac{2}{10} + \frac{5}{10}$

29. $\frac{1}{8} + \frac{5}{8} + \frac{2}{8}$

Solve. Write each answer in simplest form.

30. Mr. Lom rode his exercycle for $\frac{1}{4}$ hour before breakfast and $\frac{1}{4}$ hour after supper. For how much time did he ride his exercycle?

31. Jake cycled $\frac{3}{8}$ mile from his house to Rick's. Then he cycled $\frac{5}{8}$ mile from Rick's to Hal's. How far did Jake cycle?

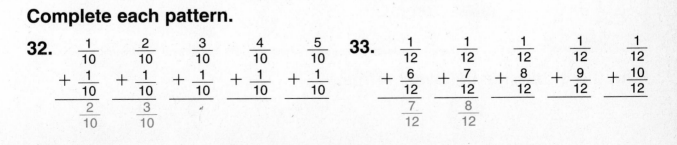

Mental Math

Complete each pattern.

32. $\begin{array}{r} \frac{1}{10} \\ + \frac{1}{10} \\ \hline \frac{2}{10} \end{array}$ $\begin{array}{r} \frac{2}{10} \\ + \frac{1}{10} \\ \hline \frac{3}{10} \end{array}$ $\begin{array}{r} \frac{3}{10} \\ + \frac{1}{10} \\ \hline \end{array}$ $\begin{array}{r} \frac{4}{10} \\ + \frac{1}{10} \\ \hline \end{array}$ $\begin{array}{r} \frac{5}{10} \\ + \frac{1}{10} \\ \hline \end{array}$

33. $\begin{array}{r} \frac{1}{12} \\ + \frac{6}{12} \\ \hline \frac{7}{12} \end{array}$ $\begin{array}{r} \frac{1}{12} \\ + \frac{7}{12} \\ \hline \frac{8}{12} \end{array}$ $\begin{array}{r} \frac{1}{12} \\ + \frac{8}{12} \\ \hline \end{array}$ $\begin{array}{r} \frac{1}{12} \\ + \frac{9}{12} \\ \hline \end{array}$ $\begin{array}{r} \frac{1}{12} \\ + \frac{10}{12} \\ \hline \end{array}$

10-2 Subtracting: Like Denominators

Kevin had $\frac{7}{8}$ yard of felt. He used
$\frac{3}{8}$ yard to make a pirate's hat.
How much felt was left?

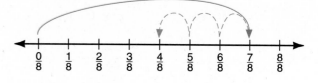

To find how much was left, subtract: $\frac{7}{8} - \frac{3}{8} = $ _?_

The denominators are the same.

To subtract fractions with like denominators:

- Subtract the numerators. $\qquad \frac{7}{8} - \frac{3}{8} = \frac{}{}4 \qquad\qquad 7 - 3 = 4$

- Write the like denominator. $\qquad \frac{7}{8} - \frac{3}{8} = \frac{4}{8}$

- Write the difference
  in lowest terms. $\qquad\qquad \frac{4}{8} = \frac{4 \div 4}{8 \div 4} = \frac{1}{2}$

Factors of 4: 1, 2, 4 $\qquad$ GCF: 4
Factors of 8: 1, 2, 4, 8

There was $\frac{1}{2}$ yard of felt left.

Study these examples.

$$\begin{array}{r} \frac{3}{4} \\ -\ \frac{3}{4} \\ \hline \frac{0}{4} = 0 \end{array} \longleftarrow \text{lowest terms} \longrightarrow \begin{array}{r} \frac{7}{9} \\ -\ \frac{5}{9} \\ \hline \frac{2}{9} \end{array}$$

Find the difference in lowest terms.

1. $\frac{9}{10} - \frac{2}{10}$ $\qquad$ **2.** $\frac{3}{5} - \frac{2}{5}$ $\qquad$ **3.** $\frac{4}{7} - \frac{2}{7}$ $\qquad$ **4.** $\frac{3}{4} - \frac{1}{4}$

298

Subtract. Write the difference in lowest terms.

5. $\frac{6}{9} - \frac{3}{9}$

6. $\frac{2}{3} - \frac{1}{3}$

7. $\frac{5}{6} - \frac{4}{6}$

8. $\frac{5}{8} - \frac{5}{8}$

9. $\frac{11}{12} - \frac{5}{12}$

10. $\frac{8}{10} - \frac{2}{10}$

11. $\frac{4}{5} - \frac{4}{5}$

12. $\frac{6}{8} - \frac{2}{8}$

13. $\frac{8}{9} - \frac{2}{9}$

14. $\frac{10}{12} - \frac{1}{12}$

15. $\frac{3}{6} - \frac{1}{6}$

16. $\frac{7}{10} - \frac{3}{10}$

17. $\begin{array}{r} \frac{3}{4} \\ -\frac{2}{4} \\ \hline \end{array}$

18. $\begin{array}{r} \frac{7}{9} \\ -\frac{1}{9} \\ \hline \end{array}$

19. $\begin{array}{r} \frac{11}{12} \\ -\frac{8}{12} \\ \hline \end{array}$

20. $\begin{array}{r} \frac{9}{10} \\ -\frac{7}{10} \\ \hline \end{array}$

21. $\begin{array}{r} \frac{1}{2} \\ -\frac{1}{2} \\ \hline \end{array}$

22. $\begin{array}{r} \frac{2}{7} \\ -\frac{2}{7} \\ \hline \end{array}$

23. $\begin{array}{r} \frac{4}{5} \\ -\frac{1}{5} \\ \hline \end{array}$

24. $\begin{array}{r} \frac{5}{6} \\ -\frac{1}{6} \\ \hline \end{array}$

25. $\begin{array}{r} \frac{10}{12} \\ -\frac{6}{12} \\ \hline \end{array}$

26. $\begin{array}{r} \frac{6}{10} \\ -\frac{2}{10} \\ \hline \end{array}$

Solve. Write the answer in simplest form.

27. Nora bought $\frac{5}{6}$ yard of calico. Wayne bought $\frac{2}{6}$ yard of calico. How much more calico did Nora buy than Wayne?

28. Jo used $\frac{5}{8}$ yard of red linen to make a skirt. She used $\frac{1}{8}$ yard of blue linen for a scarf. Did she use more red or blue linen? How much more?

29. Ben has $\frac{1}{4}$ yard of denim. He needs $\frac{3}{4}$ yard for a school project. How much more denim does he need?

Skills to Remember

Divide.

30. $6\overline{)8}$ **31.** $4\overline{)13}$ **32.** $8\overline{)43}$ **33.** $5\overline{)27}$ **34.** $2\overline{)11}$ **35.** $3\overline{)20}$

36. $48 \div 7$ **37.** $89 \div 12$ **38.** $65 \div 9$ **39.** $76 \div 10$

Improper Fractions

An **improper fraction** is a fraction greater than one. Its numerator is greater than its denominator.

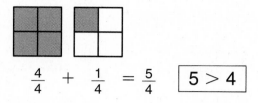

$\frac{4}{4}$ + $\frac{1}{4}$ = $\frac{5}{4}$ $\boxed{5 > 4}$

Write as a mixed number in simplest form: $\frac{20}{8}$ = __?__

To write an improper fraction as a mixed number:

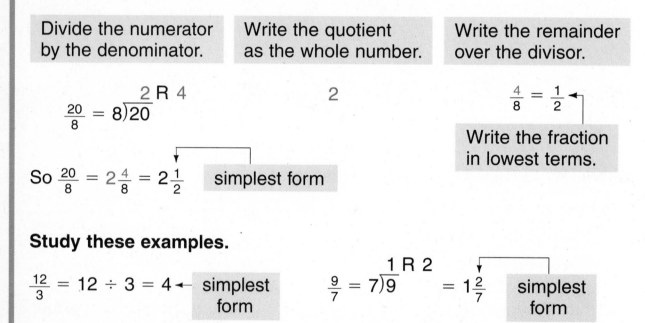

| Divide the numerator by the denominator. | Write the quotient as the whole number. | Write the remainder over the divisor. |

$$\frac{20}{8} = 8\overline{)20}^{\,2\ R\ 4}$$

2

$$\frac{4}{8} = \frac{1}{2}$$

Write the fraction in lowest terms.

So $\frac{20}{8} = 2\frac{4}{8} = 2\frac{1}{2}$ simplest form

Study these examples.

$\frac{12}{3} = 12 \div 3 = 4$ ← simplest form

$\frac{9}{7} = 7\overline{)9}^{\,1\ R\ 2} = 1\frac{2}{7}$ simplest form

---

Write as a whole number or mixed number in simplest form.

1.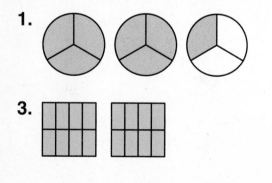

2.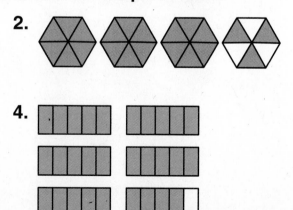

3.

4.

Write as a whole number or mixed number in simplest form.

5. $\frac{24}{5}$ 6. $\frac{17}{3}$ 7. $\frac{7}{2}$ 8. $\frac{9}{4}$ 9. $\frac{13}{6}$ 10. $\frac{27}{3}$

11. $\frac{30}{10}$ 12. $\frac{15}{9}$ 13. $\frac{32}{12}$ 14. $\frac{20}{6}$ 15. $\frac{10}{5}$ 16. $\frac{14}{4}$

17. $\frac{70}{12}$ 18. $\frac{58}{10}$ 19. $\frac{42}{8}$ 20. $\frac{33}{6}$ 21. $\frac{92}{8}$ 22. $\frac{26}{10}$

Add. Write each sum in simplest form.

23. $\frac{3}{5} + \frac{4}{5}$ 24. $\frac{2}{3} + \frac{2}{3}$ 25. $\frac{4}{6} + \frac{2}{6}$ 26. $\frac{2}{4} + \frac{3}{4}$

27. $\frac{4}{6} + \frac{5}{6}$ 28. $\frac{7}{8} + \frac{5}{8}$ 29. $\frac{4}{7} + \frac{5}{7}$ 30. $\frac{7}{9} + \frac{8}{9}$

31. $\frac{10}{12} + \frac{8}{12}$ 32. $\frac{3}{10} + \frac{7}{10}$ 33. $\frac{1}{2} + \frac{1}{2}$ 34. $\frac{7}{8} + \frac{3}{8}$

35. $\frac{14}{5} + \frac{16}{5}$ 36. $\frac{20}{8} + \frac{30}{8}$ 37. $\frac{25}{10} + \frac{20}{10}$ 38. $\frac{23}{12} + \frac{57}{12}$

Solve. Write each answer in simplest form.

39. What is fifteen thirds in simplest form?

40. What is twenty-two eighths in simplest form?

41. Steve walked $\frac{25}{10}$ miles to the county fair. How many miles did he walk?

42. Kelvin sold $\frac{110}{12}$ egg cartons at the fair. How many egg cartons did he sell?

43. Sue ate $\frac{5}{2}$ pies at the pie-eating contest. How many pies did she eat? Was this more or less than 3 pies?

10-4 Estimating with Mixed Numbers

John brought $5\frac{1}{8}$ lb of apples, $2\frac{1}{4}$ lb of bananas, and $8\frac{1}{2}$ lb of melons to a picnic. About how many pounds of fruit did he bring to the picnic?

To find about how many pounds, estimate the sum: $5\frac{1}{8} + 2\frac{1}{4} + 8\frac{1}{2}$

▶ To estimate sums with mixed numbers, add the whole numbers.

$$\begin{array}{r} 5\frac{1}{8} \\ 2\frac{1}{4} \\ +\,8\frac{1}{2} \\ \hline 15 \end{array}$$

John brought about 15 lb of fruit to the picnic.

About how many more pounds of melons than bananas did John bring?

To find about how many more, estimate the difference: $8\frac{1}{2} - 2\frac{1}{4}$

▶ To estimate differences with mixed numbers, subtract the whole numbers.

$$\begin{array}{r} 8\frac{1}{2} \\ -\,2\frac{1}{4} \\ \hline 6 \end{array}$$

John brought about 6 more pounds of melons than bananas.

Estimate the sum.

1. $6\frac{1}{5} + 9\frac{2}{10}$

2. $8\frac{1}{4} + 8\frac{4}{12}$

3. $3\frac{1}{2} + 7\frac{2}{6}$

4. $1\frac{4}{9} + 4\frac{1}{6}$

5. $5\frac{2}{3} + 2\frac{4}{9}$

6. $4\frac{3}{4} + 9\frac{3}{8}$

7. $7\frac{2}{10} + 5\frac{1}{2}$

8. $6\frac{3}{8} + 4\frac{1}{4}$

Estimate the sum.

9. $3\frac{1}{3}$
$4\frac{2}{6}$
$+\ 7\frac{1}{9}$

10. $5\frac{3}{4}$
$9\frac{1}{8}$
$+\ 6\frac{1}{4}$

11. $2\frac{1}{2}$
$8\frac{4}{10}$
$+\ 6\frac{9}{10}$

12. $9\frac{1}{4}$
$4\frac{1}{2}$
$+\ 4\frac{3}{12}$

13. $8\frac{2}{3}$
$4\frac{5}{6}$
$+\ 7\frac{1}{3}$

14. $10\frac{4}{10}$
$8\frac{1}{5}$
$+\ 10\frac{1}{10}$

15. $7\frac{3}{4}$
$12\frac{1}{4}$
$+\ 1\frac{1}{2}$

16. $14\frac{2}{3}$
$10\frac{1}{6}$
$+\ 12\frac{5}{9}$

17. $24\frac{2}{10}$
$16\frac{8}{10}$
$+\ 10\frac{3}{5}$

18. $15\frac{1}{8}$
$25\frac{3}{8}$
$+\ 6\frac{1}{4}$

Estimate the difference.

19. $18\frac{2}{3}$
$-\ 9\frac{6}{9}$

20. $9\frac{3}{4}$
$-\ 7\frac{4}{8}$

21. $13\frac{1}{5}$
$-\ 8\frac{5}{10}$

22. $7\frac{1}{2}$
$-\ 4\frac{3}{4}$

23. $11\frac{6}{9}$
$-\ 5\frac{1}{6}$

24. $15\frac{8}{12}$
$-\ 8\frac{2}{3}$

25. $6\frac{7}{8}$
$-\ 3\frac{3}{4}$

26. $14\frac{8}{10}$
$-\ 7\frac{4}{5}$

27. $13\frac{1}{2}$
$-\ 6\frac{6}{12}$

28. $12\frac{5}{6}$
$-\ 4\frac{1}{3}$

29. $22\frac{3}{9} - 12\frac{2}{3}$
30. $48\frac{1}{2} - 30\frac{7}{10}$
31. $19\frac{11}{12} - 11\frac{3}{4}$
32. $25\frac{7}{12} - 15\frac{4}{6}$

Solve.

33. David brought $5\frac{2}{10}$ lb of potato salad to the picnic. Sue brought $7\frac{1}{2}$ lb of potato salad. About how many pounds of potato salad were there?

34. Jerry traveled $15\frac{3}{4}$ mi to get to the picnic. Emmy traveled $6\frac{1}{2}$ mi less. About how far did Emmy have to travel?

35. Nan brought a watermelon that weighed $20\frac{1}{4}$ lb. The picnickers ate $15\frac{3}{4}$ lb of watermelon. About how many pounds of watermelon were left?

36. Sal needed 35 lb of turkey to feed the picnickers. He bought turkeys that weighed $10\frac{7}{10}$ lb, $16\frac{1}{2}$ lb, and $11\frac{3}{10}$ lb. Did Sal buy enough turkey?

Add and Subtract Mixed Numbers

Akers' Farms displays plants in trays of ten. Lucy buys $2\frac{6}{10}$ trays of plants and her brother buys $1\frac{2}{10}$ trays. How many trays of plants do they buy in all? How many more trays does Lucy buy than her brother?

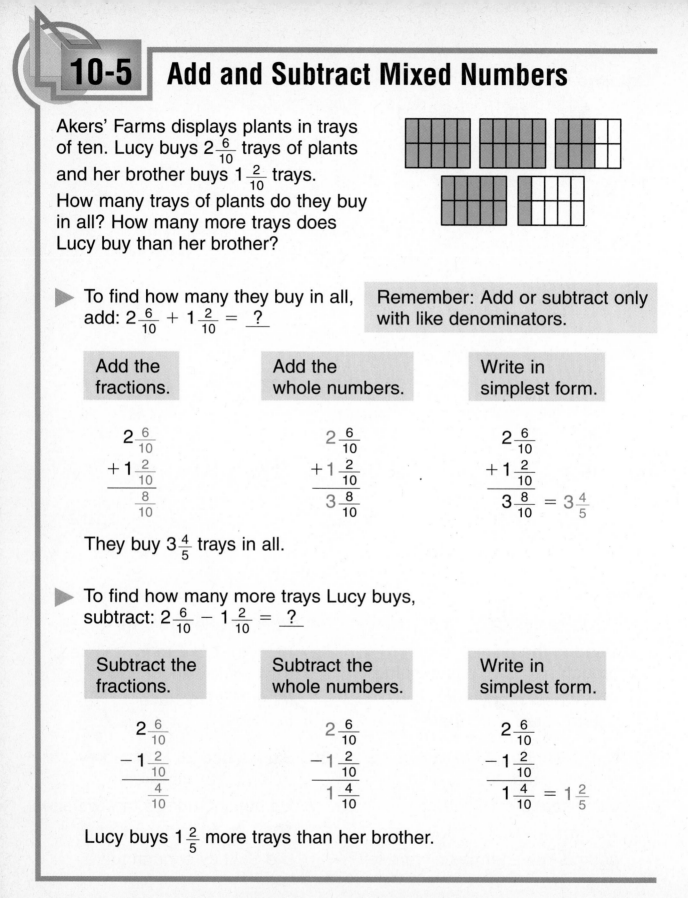

▶ To find how many they buy in all, add: $2\frac{6}{10} + 1\frac{2}{10} = \underline{\ ?\ }$

Remember: Add or subtract only with like denominators.

Add the fractions.	Add the whole numbers.	Write in simplest form.
$2\frac{6}{10}$ $+1\frac{2}{10}$ $\overline{\ \ \frac{8}{10}}$	$2\frac{6}{10}$ $+1\frac{2}{10}$ $\overline{3\frac{8}{10}}$	$2\frac{6}{10}$ $+1\frac{2}{10}$ $\overline{3\frac{8}{10}} = 3\frac{4}{5}$

They buy $3\frac{4}{5}$ trays in all.

▶ To find how many more trays Lucy buys, subtract: $2\frac{6}{10} - 1\frac{2}{10} = \underline{\ ?\ }$

Subtract the fractions.	Subtract the whole numbers.	Write in simplest form.
$2\frac{6}{10}$ $-1\frac{2}{10}$ $\overline{\ \ \frac{4}{10}}$	$2\frac{6}{10}$ $-1\frac{2}{10}$ $\overline{1\frac{4}{10}}$	$2\frac{6}{10}$ $-1\frac{2}{10}$ $\overline{1\frac{4}{10}} = 1\frac{2}{5}$

Lucy buys $1\frac{2}{5}$ more trays than her brother.

Add. Write the sum in simplest form.

1. $6\frac{2}{6}$
$+ 7\frac{1}{6}$

2. $8\frac{1}{4}$
$+ 5\frac{1}{4}$

3. $4\frac{3}{5}$
$+ 3\frac{1}{5}$

4. $2\frac{3}{8}$
$+ 1\frac{1}{8}$

5. $9\frac{2}{7}$
$+ 6\frac{4}{7}$

6. $5\frac{4}{12}$
$+ 5\frac{6}{12}$

7. $7\frac{2}{9}$
$+ 8\frac{4}{9}$

8. $26\frac{2}{4}$
$+ 17\frac{1}{4}$

9. $36\frac{3}{10}$
$+ 28\frac{5}{10}$

10. $47\frac{3}{8}$
$+ 54\frac{3}{8}$

Subtract. Write the difference in simplest form.

11. $9\frac{10}{12}$
$- 7\frac{7}{12}$

12. $5\frac{2}{3}$
$- 1\frac{1}{3}$

13. $8\frac{3}{4}$
$- 3\frac{1}{4}$

14. $6\frac{4}{5}$
$- 4\frac{2}{5}$

15. $10\frac{7}{8}$
$- 2\frac{5}{8}$

16. $57\frac{5}{6}$
$- 48\frac{2}{6}$

17. $32\frac{6}{7}$
$- 27\frac{1}{7}$

18. $40\frac{8}{9}$
$- 18\frac{5}{9}$

19. $23\frac{9}{10}$
$- 23\frac{3}{10}$

20. $12\frac{1}{2}$
$- 7\frac{1}{2}$

Align and add or subtract. Watch the signs.

21. $18\frac{11}{12} - 9\frac{1}{12}$ **22.** $14\frac{7}{10} - 8\frac{3}{10}$ **23.** $21\frac{2}{6} + 5\frac{2}{6}$ **24.** $31\frac{6}{8} - 9\frac{2}{8}$

25. $1\frac{1}{8} + 19\frac{2}{8}$ **26.** $6\frac{2}{9} + 17\frac{1}{9}$ **27.** $30\frac{9}{10} - 2\frac{1}{10}$ **28.** $42\frac{1}{5} + 8\frac{3}{5}$

Solve.

29. The fence around Lucy's garden was $7\frac{4}{12}$ ft high. She put chicken wire at the top so it is now $10\frac{7}{12}$ ft high. How many feet of wire did she add to the height of the fence?

Mental Math

Add or subtract. Watch the signs.

30. $8\frac{7}{8} - 4$ **31.** $9 + 5\frac{2}{3}$ **32.** $7\frac{9}{10} + 6$ **33.** $10\frac{3}{4} - 9$

10-6 Multiples

▶ The **multiples** of a number are all the products that have that number as a factor.

factors
	0	1	2	3	4	5	6	7	8	9
	×2	×2	×2	×2	×2	×2	×2	×2	×2	×2

Multiples of 2: 0 2 4 6 8 10 12 14 16 18 . . .

factors
	0	1	2	3	4	5	6	7	8	9
	×3	×3	×3	×3	×3	×3	×3	×3	×3	×3

Multiples of 3: 0 3 6 9 12 15 18 21 24 27 . . .

> You can find the multiples of a number by multiplying or by skip counting.

▶ **Common multiples** are all the numbers other than 0 that are multiples of two or more numbers.

Multiples of 2: 0, 2, 4, 6, 8, 10, 12, 14, 16, 18, 20, 22, 24 . . .

Multiples of 3: 0, 3, 6, 9, 12, 15, 18, 21, 24, . . .

Common multiples of 2 and 3: 6, 12, 18, 24, . . .

▶ The **least common multiple (LCM)** of two or more numbers is the least number that is a multiple of those numbers.

Least common multiple (LCM) of 2 and 3: 6

Is each a multiple of 2? Write *yes* or *no*.

1. 5　　　　**2.** 40　　　　**3.** 62　　　　**4.** 0　　　　**5.** 29　　　　**6.** 88

Is each a multiple of 3? Write *yes* or *no*.

7. 33   **8.** 1   **9.** 29   **10.** 60   **11.** 48   **12.** 100

List the first eleven multiples of each.

13. 6   **14.** 4   **15.** 9   **16.** 10   **17.** 8   **18.** 5

Write the first four common multiples for each set of numbers. Then write the least common multiple (LCM).

19. 2, 4   **20.** 3, 9   **21.** 4, 8   **22.** 6, 3   **23.** 5, 10

24. 2, 8   **25.** 6, 9   **26.** 8, 12   **27.** 7, 2   **28.** 2, 10

29. 4, 5   **30.** 8, 10   **31.** 4, 6   **32.** 9, 12   **33.** 3, 5

34. 2, 4, and 10   **35.** 3, 9, and 12   **36.** 2, 3, and 9

37. 6, 8, and 12   **38.** 4, 6, and 8   **39.** 5, 6, and 10

Critical Thinking

Write *true* or *false* for each statement.

40. All multiples of 3 are divisible by 3.

41. All multiples of 4 are multiples of 8.

42. No multiples of 9 are multiples of 3.

43. Some multiples of 6 are multiples of 12.

44. All multiples of 2 are even numbers.

45. No multiples of 5 are even numbers.

46. Some multiples of 3 are odd numbers.

47. All multiples of 7 are odd numbers.

10-7 Adding: Unlike Denominators

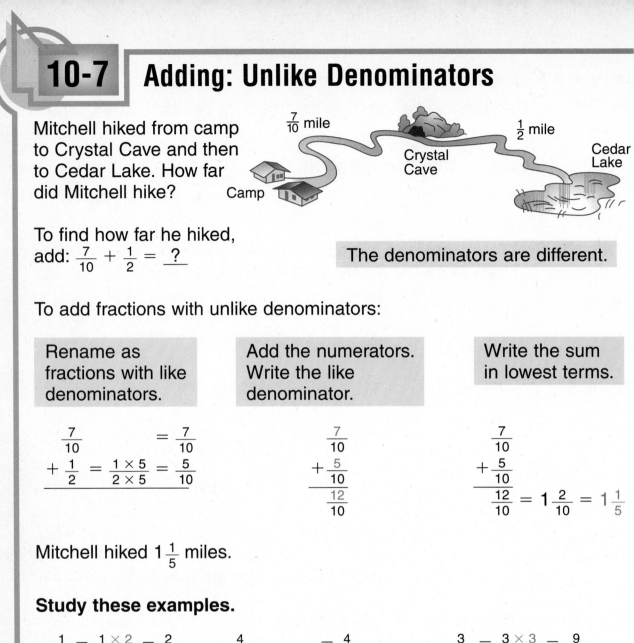

Mitchell hiked from camp to Crystal Cave and then to Cedar Lake. How far did Mitchell hike?

$\frac{7}{10}$ mile   Crystal Cave $\frac{1}{2}$ mile   Cedar Lake   Camp

To find how far he hiked,
add: $\frac{7}{10} + \frac{1}{2} = \underline{\ ?\ }$

The denominators are different.

To add fractions with unlike denominators:

| Rename as fractions with like denominators. | Add the numerators. Write the like denominator. | Write the sum in lowest terms. |

$$\begin{array}{r} \frac{7}{10} \qquad = \frac{7}{10} \\ +\ \frac{1}{2} = \frac{1\times5}{2\times5} = \frac{5}{10} \\ \hline \end{array}$$

$$\begin{array}{r} \frac{7}{10} \\ +\ \frac{5}{10} \\ \hline \frac{12}{10} \end{array}$$

$$\begin{array}{r} \frac{7}{10} \\ +\ \frac{5}{10} \\ \hline \frac{12}{10} = 1\frac{2}{10} = 1\frac{1}{5} \end{array}$$

Mitchell hiked $1\frac{1}{5}$ miles.

Study these examples.

$$\begin{array}{r} \frac{1}{4} = \frac{1\times2}{4\times2} = \frac{2}{8} \\ +\ \frac{3}{8} \qquad = \frac{3}{8} \\ \hline \frac{5}{8} \end{array}$$

$$\begin{array}{r} \frac{4}{6} \qquad = \frac{4}{6} \\ +\ \frac{1}{3} = \frac{1\times2}{3\times2} = \frac{2}{6} \\ \hline \frac{6}{6} = 1 \end{array}$$

$$\begin{array}{r} \frac{3}{4} = \frac{3\times3}{4\times3} = \frac{9}{12} \\ +\ \frac{1}{12} \qquad = \frac{1}{12} \\ \hline \frac{10}{12} = \frac{5}{6} \end{array}$$

Add. Write the sum in lowest terms.

1. $\frac{1}{2}$
$+\frac{1}{4}$

2. $\frac{1}{3}$
$+\frac{1}{6}$

3. $\frac{3}{4}$
$+\frac{1}{8}$

4. $\frac{2}{3}$
$+\frac{1}{9}$

5. $\frac{3}{8}$
$+\frac{1}{2}$

Find the sum in lowest terms.

6. $\dfrac{6}{8}$
$+\dfrac{1}{4}$

7. $\dfrac{1}{3}$
$+\dfrac{5}{12}$

8. $\dfrac{2}{3}$
$+\dfrac{4}{9}$

9. $\dfrac{1}{2}$
$+\dfrac{5}{8}$

10. $\dfrac{3}{5}$
$+\dfrac{3}{10}$

11. $\dfrac{7}{9}$
$+\dfrac{1}{3}$

12. $\dfrac{8}{10}$
$+\dfrac{1}{5}$

13. $\dfrac{7}{8}$
$+\dfrac{3}{4}$

14. $\dfrac{5}{12}$
$+\dfrac{1}{6}$

15. $\dfrac{2}{3}$
$+\dfrac{5}{6}$

16. $\dfrac{1}{4}$
$+\dfrac{5}{12}$

17. $\dfrac{6}{9}$
$+\dfrac{1}{3}$

18. $\dfrac{11}{12}$
$+\dfrac{3}{4}$

19. $\dfrac{1}{2}$
$+\dfrac{4}{8}$

20. $\dfrac{4}{5}$
$+\dfrac{6}{10}$

21. $\dfrac{2}{3} + \dfrac{1}{6}$

22. $\dfrac{1}{2} + \dfrac{5}{10}$

23. $\dfrac{1}{3} + \dfrac{5}{9}$

24. $\dfrac{3}{4} + \dfrac{2}{12}$

25. $\dfrac{2}{5} + \dfrac{9}{10}$

26. $\dfrac{5}{8} + \dfrac{1}{4}$

27. $\dfrac{3}{4} + \dfrac{7}{12}$

28. $\dfrac{2}{9} + \dfrac{2}{3}$

Solve. Write each answer in simplest form.

29. Diego spent $\dfrac{1}{2}$ hour playing water polo and $\dfrac{3}{4}$ hour swimming. How much time did he spend on water sports?

30. Carlene hiked $\dfrac{4}{5}$ mi. Freddie hiked $\dfrac{9}{10}$ mi farther than Carlene. How far did Freddie hike?

31. Travis paddled a canoe upriver for $\dfrac{7}{8}$ mi. Then Linda paddled it upriver for $\dfrac{3}{4}$ mi more. How far did Travis and Linda paddle upriver?

Challenge

Add. Write the sum in simplest form.

32. $\dfrac{1}{2} + \dfrac{2}{8} + \dfrac{5}{8}$

33. $\dfrac{4}{5} + \dfrac{9}{10} + \dfrac{3}{10}$

34. $\dfrac{7}{12} + \dfrac{2}{3} + \dfrac{5}{12}$

10-8 Subtracting: Unlike Denominators

Lila had $\frac{11}{12}$ ft of balsa wood. She used $\frac{1}{4}$ ft of the wood to make a miniature chair for her dollhouse. How much wood did Lila have left?

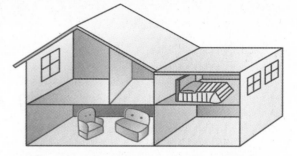

To find how much she had left, subtract: $\frac{11}{12} - \frac{1}{4} = \underline{?}$

The denominators are different.

To subtract fractions with unlike denominators:

| Rename as fractions with like denominators. | Subtract the numerators. Write the like denominator. | Write the difference in lowest terms. |

$$\frac{11}{12} = \frac{11}{12}$$
$$-\frac{1}{4} = \frac{1 \times 3}{4 \times 3} = \frac{3}{12}$$

$$\frac{11}{12}$$
$$-\frac{3}{12}$$
$$\frac{8}{12}$$

$$\frac{11}{12}$$
$$-\frac{3}{12}$$
$$\frac{8}{12} = \frac{2}{3}$$

Lila had $\frac{2}{3}$ ft of wood left.

Study these examples.

$$\frac{3}{4} = \frac{3}{4}$$
$$-\frac{1}{2} = \frac{1 \times 2}{2 \times 2} = \frac{2}{4}$$
$$\frac{1}{4}$$

$$\frac{2}{3} = \frac{2 \times 3}{3 \times 3} = \frac{6}{9}$$
$$-\frac{6}{9} = \frac{6}{9}$$
$$\frac{0}{9} = 0$$

Subtract. Write the difference in lowest terms.

1. $\frac{1}{4} - \frac{1}{8}$

2. $\frac{5}{8} - \frac{1}{4}$

3. $\frac{5}{6} - \frac{1}{3}$

4. $\frac{4}{5} - \frac{1}{10}$

Find the difference in lowest terms.

5. $\frac{2}{3}$
$-\frac{1}{6}$

6. $\frac{9}{10}$
$-\frac{1}{2}$

7. $\frac{7}{9}$
$-\frac{2}{3}$

8. $\frac{9}{12}$
$-\frac{3}{4}$

9. $\frac{7}{8}$
$-\frac{1}{2}$

10. $\frac{7}{10}$
$-\frac{1}{5}$

11. $\frac{7}{8}$
$-\frac{3}{4}$

12. $\frac{5}{6}$
$-\frac{2}{12}$

13. $\frac{2}{3}$
$-\frac{2}{9}$

14. $\frac{3}{4}$
$-\frac{6}{8}$

15. $\frac{10}{12}$
$-\frac{2}{6}$

16. $\frac{6}{8}$
$-\frac{1}{2}$

17. $\frac{1}{2}$
$-\frac{3}{12}$

18. $\frac{3}{5}$
$-\frac{1}{10}$

19. $\frac{8}{9}$
$-\frac{2}{3}$

20. $\frac{3}{4}$
$-\frac{8}{12}$

21. $\frac{9}{10}$
$-\frac{3}{5}$

22. $\frac{8}{9}$
$-\frac{1}{3}$

23. $\frac{7}{10}$
$-\frac{1}{2}$

24. $\frac{1}{3}$
$-\frac{2}{6}$

Solve. Write each answer in simplest form.

25. Kyle worked on his model airplane for $\frac{3}{4}$ hour. Lief worked on his model ship for $\frac{1}{2}$ hour. Who worked on his model longer? How much longer?

26. Sharon decorated a valentine with pieces of ribbon. She used $\frac{2}{6}$ ft of red ribbon and $\frac{8}{12}$ ft of white ribbon. How much more white than red ribbon did Sharon use?

27. Clint had a large sheet of paper that was $\frac{9}{12}$ yd long. He trimmed $\frac{1}{3}$ yd from it. How long was the sheet of paper after trimming?

28. $\frac{7}{10}$ minus $\frac{1}{5}$ equals what number?

29. What is the sum of $\frac{1}{6}$ and $\frac{8}{12}$?

30. What is the difference between $\frac{8}{9}$ and $\frac{2}{3}$?

31. $\frac{3}{4}$ plus $\frac{3}{8}$ equals what number?

Computing Probability

There are 10 marbles in the jar: 1 is purple, 2 are white, 3 are red, and 4 are yellow. What is the probability that, without looking, you would pick a marble of each color?

The probability that you would pick:

- purple is 1 out of 10, or $\frac{1}{10}$.

- white is 2 out of 10, or $\frac{2}{10}$.

- red is 3 out of 10, or $\frac{3}{10}$.

- yellow is 4 out of 10, or $\frac{4}{10}$.

The probability of picking any given color is the probability of that **event**.

Probability of picking a red marble: $\frac{3}{10}$ Write: $P(\text{red}) = \frac{3}{10}$

What is the probability that you would pick a red *or* a purple marble?

To find the probability of picking red *or* purple, add the two probabilities by adding the fractions.

$$\frac{3}{10} + \frac{1}{10} = \frac{4}{10}$$

Probability of picking red *or* purple: $\frac{4}{10}$ Write: $P(\text{red or purple}) = \frac{4}{10}$

Find the probability of each event. Use the spinner.

1. $P(\text{green})$

2. $P(\text{yellow})$

3. $P(\text{red})$

4. $P(\text{blue})$

5. $P(\text{green or yellow})$

6. $P(\text{red or blue})$

7. $P(\text{green or yellow or red})$

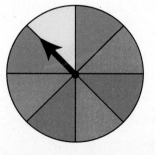

Find the probability of each event. Use the cards.

8. $P(B)$

9. $P(E)$

10. $P(C)$

11. $P(D)$

12. $P(A \text{ or } C)$

13. $P(B \text{ or } D)$

14. $P(A \text{ or } B \text{ or } E)$

15. $P(B \text{ or } C \text{ or } D)$

16. $P(\text{not } D)$

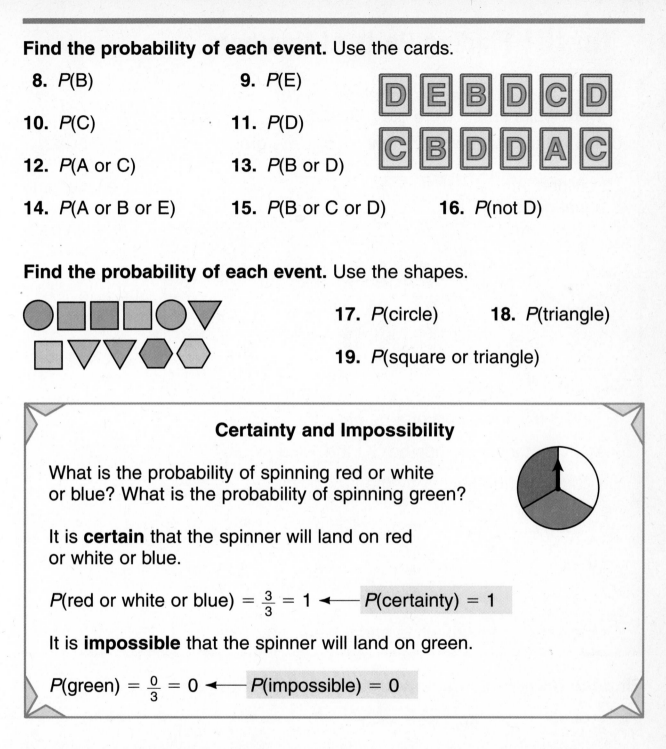

Find the probability of each event. Use the shapes.

17. $P(\text{circle})$

18. $P(\text{triangle})$

19. $P(\text{square or triangle})$

Certainty and Impossibility

What is the probability of spinning red or white or blue? What is the probability of spinning green?

It is **certain** that the spinner will land on red or white or blue.

$P(\text{red or white or blue}) = \frac{3}{3} = 1 \longleftarrow P(\text{certainty}) = 1$

It is **impossible** that the spinner will land on green.

$P(\text{green}) = \frac{0}{3} = 0 \longleftarrow P(\text{impossible}) = 0$

Find the probability of each event. Use the marbles on page 312.

20. $P(\text{red or yellow or white})$

21. $P(\text{orange or green})$

22. $P(\text{red or purple or white or yellow})$

10-10 Finding Parts of Numbers

Of 12 kittens at the animal shelter,
$\frac{1}{3}$ were white and $\frac{2}{3}$ were gray. How many
of the kittens were white? How many were gray?

12 divided into
3 equal parts;
4 in each part

$12 \div 3 = 4$

$\frac{1}{3}$ of 12 = 4

12 divided into
3 equal parts;
4 in each part;
8 in 2 parts

$12 \div 3 = 4$
$2 \times 4 = 8$

$\frac{2}{3}$ of 12 = 8

To find a fractional part of a number:

- **Divide** the whole number by the denominator.

- **Multiply** the quotient by the numerator.

$\frac{1}{3}$ of 12: $12 \div 3 = 4 \longrightarrow 1 \times 4 = 4$ So $\frac{1}{3}$ of 12 = 4

$\frac{2}{3}$ of 12: $12 \div 3 = 4 \longrightarrow 2 \times 4 = 8$ So $\frac{2}{3}$ of 12 = 8

Of the kittens, 4 were white and 8 were gray.

Find the part of each number. You may draw a picture.

1. $\frac{1}{5}$ of 15   2. $\frac{1}{3}$ of 9   3. $\frac{1}{2}$ of 14   4. $\frac{1}{8}$ of 40

5. $\frac{1}{4}$ of 24   6. $\frac{1}{9}$ of 36   7. $\frac{1}{7}$ of 42   8. $\frac{1}{5}$ of 50

9. $\frac{1}{6}$ of 30   10. $\frac{1}{6}$ of 24   11. $\frac{1}{8}$ of 16   12. $\frac{1}{2}$ of 8

Find the missing number.

13. $\frac{2}{3}$ of 15 = _?_   **14.** $\frac{5}{8}$ of 16 = _?_   **15.** $\frac{5}{6}$ of 18 = _?_

16. $\frac{3}{7}$ of 21 = _?_   **17.** $\frac{3}{8}$ of 40 = _?_   **18.** $\frac{2}{5}$ of 25 = _?_

19. $\frac{3}{4}$ of 32 = _?_   **20.** $\frac{2}{9}$ of 27 = _?_   **21.** $\frac{5}{7}$ of 14 = _?_

22. $\frac{4}{5}$ of 45 = _?_   **23.** $\frac{3}{8}$ of 64 = _?_   **24.** $\frac{8}{9}$ of 9 = _?_

25. $\frac{3}{4}$ of 20 = _?_   **26.** $\frac{6}{7}$ of 28 = _?_   **27.** $\frac{3}{5}$ of 35 = _?_

28. $\frac{4}{6}$ of 54 = _?_   **29.** $\frac{2}{3}$ of 33 = _?_   **30.** $\frac{3}{4}$ of 40 = _?_

31. $\frac{7}{8}$ of 72 = _?_   **32.** $\frac{2}{5}$ of 50 = _?_   **33.** $\frac{4}{9}$ of 99 = _?_

Solve.

34. Jamail raised 28 rabbits. Of these, $\frac{3}{4}$ were black and white. How many of the rabbits were black and white?

35. Of 30 retrievers at the kennel, $\frac{4}{5}$ were golden retrievers. How many of the retrievers were golden retrievers?

36. Farmer Green has 64 chickens. Of these, $\frac{3}{8}$ are Rhode Island Reds. How many of his chickens are Rhode Island Reds?

37. Of 150 birds that came to the feeder, $\frac{2}{3}$ were finches. How many of the birds were finches?

38. There are 32 black and white cows and 16 brown cows in the pasture. $\frac{3}{8}$ of all the cows are lying down. Of these, $\frac{1}{6}$ are brown. How many brown cows are lying down?

10-11 Problem Solving: Use Simpler Numbers

Problem: A piece of ribbon is $12\frac{7}{8}$ ft long. Tatsu cuts off two pieces that are $4\frac{3}{8}$ ft each. Does she have enough ribbon left to cut one more piece the same length?

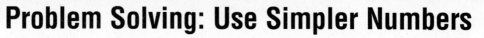

1 IMAGINE   Draw and label a picture.

2 NAME   *Facts:* $12\frac{7}{8}$ ft of ribbon
  Two $4\frac{3}{8}$ ft pieces cut from it

  Question: Is there $4\frac{3}{8}$ ft left?

3 THINK   Use simpler numbers like 12 and 4.
  Use 12 for the $12\frac{7}{8}$ ft length.

  Use 4 for the $4\frac{3}{8}$ ft length.

  First add to find the amount of ribbon cut.
  4 ft + 4 ft = 8 ft
  Then subtract to find the amount of ribbon left.
  12 ft − 8 ft = 4 ft

4 COMPUTE   Now use the numbers in the problem.

$$
\begin{array}{r}
4\frac{3}{8}\text{ ft} \\
+\,4\frac{3}{8}\text{ ft} \\
\hline
8\frac{6}{8}\text{ ft cut}
\end{array}
\qquad
\begin{array}{r}
12\frac{7}{8}\text{ ft} \\
-\;\;8\frac{6}{8}\text{ ft} \\
\hline
4\frac{1}{8}\text{ ft left}
\end{array}
$$

Compare. $4\frac{1}{8} < 4\frac{3}{8}$ so Tatsu does *not* have enough ribbon to cut another piece.

5 CHECK   Add the pieces. Do the pieces equal $12\frac{7}{8}$ ft?
$4\frac{3}{8} + 4\frac{3}{8} + 4\frac{1}{8} = 12\frac{7}{8}$
The answer checks.

Solve.

1. Frank checked his kitten's weight on the first day of each month. He kept the information on a chart. How much weight did the kitten gain between April 1 and June 1?

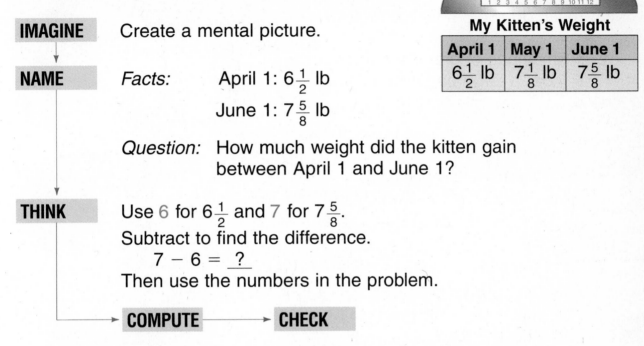

My Kitten's Weight

April 1	May 1	June 1
$6\frac{1}{2}$ lb	$7\frac{1}{8}$ lb	$7\frac{5}{8}$ lb

IMAGINE   Create a mental picture.

NAME   *Facts:*   April 1: $6\frac{1}{2}$ lb

June 1: $7\frac{5}{8}$ lb

Question: How much weight did the kitten gain between April 1 and June 1?

THINK   Use 6 for $6\frac{1}{2}$ and 7 for $7\frac{5}{8}$.

Subtract to find the difference.

$7 - 6 = \underline{\ ?\ }$

Then use the numbers in the problem.

COMPUTE ⟶ **CHECK**

2. One paper-clip chain is $24\frac{1}{4}$ in. long. Another is $41\frac{1}{4}$ in. long. How long will the chain be if the two chains are connected?

3. Ms. Hanley is running a $26\frac{5}{10}$ mile race. She stops for water after $17\frac{3}{10}$ miles. How much farther does she have to run?

4. A bread recipe calls for $4\frac{1}{2}$ c of white flour, $2\frac{1}{4}$ c of wheat flour, and 1 c of rye flour. How much flour does this recipe use?

Make Up Your Own

5. Write a problem with fractions or mixed numbers. Use simpler numbers. Then solve it using the original numbers.

Problem-Solving Applications

Solve.

Use these steps:

1. Regina's class has a healthy snack sale. Each oatmeal bar weighs $4\frac{1}{4}$ oz. How much do two oatmeal bars weigh?

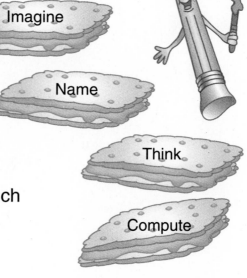

Imagine

Name

2. A small bag of granola weighs $6\frac{1}{8}$ oz. A large bag weighs $12\frac{3}{8}$ oz. How much heavier is the large bag of granola?

Think

3. Apples weigh about $3\frac{3}{4}$ oz each. Pears weigh about $4\frac{1}{4}$ oz each. About how much do an apple and a pear weigh together?

Compute

4. Todd uses about $\frac{1}{8}$ oz of peanut butter on each cracker sandwich he makes. How many crackers will 1 oz of peanut butter cover?

Check

5. Of the 10 kinds of bread at the sale, $\frac{1}{5}$ have sesame seeds. How many kinds of bread have sesame seeds?

6. The carrot bread has 100 calories per slice. About $\frac{7}{10}$ of the calories come from carbohydrates. About how many calories come from carbohydrates?

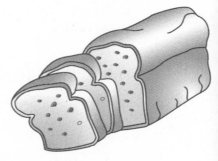

7. A loaf of banana bread is 8 in. long. How many $\frac{1}{2}$ in. slices can be cut from the loaf?

8. A carrot is $10\frac{1}{4}$ in. long. Regina cuts it in half. About how long is each half?

Solve.

9. There are 24 muffins for sale. Half the muffins are bran and $\frac{1}{4}$ are corn. How many corn muffins are for sale?

10. Jan bought half of a loaf of rye bread. She gave half of her piece to Ramon. Ramon's piece weighs $\frac{3}{4}$ lb. How much did the original loaf of bread weigh?

11. A carrot stick has fewer calories than an apple. An oat bar has more calories than an apple. Does a carrot stick or an oat bar have more calories?

12. Sue uses $\frac{1}{2}$ oz toasted oats, $\frac{1}{4}$ oz raisins, and $\frac{1}{4}$ oz carob drops for her trail mix. She makes 16 oz of mix. How many ounces of raisins does she use?

13. Wes ate a snack of 150 calories. The low-fat yogurt had half the calories of the oatmeal cookies. How many calories did the yogurt have?

USE THESE STRATEGIES:
Choose the Operation
Guess and Test
Use Simpler Numbers
Extra Information
Working Backwards
Logical Reasoning
Use a Graph

Use the pictograph for problems 14–16.

14. What fractional part of the mini-muffins were corn muffins?

15. What fractional part of the mini-muffins were fruit muffins?

16. What fractional part of the mini-muffins were spice-flavored muffins?

Mini-Muffin Menu	
apple	⬡ ⬡ ⬡
blueberry	⬡ ⬡
cinnamon	⬡ ⬡ ⬡ ⬡
corn	⬡
Key: Each ⬡ = 5 mini-muffins	

More Practice

Add or subtract. Write the answer in simplest form.

1. $\begin{array}{r} \frac{1}{5} \\ +\frac{2}{5} \\ \hline \end{array}$

2. $\begin{array}{r} \frac{5}{8} \\ -\frac{3}{8} \\ \hline \end{array}$

3. $\begin{array}{r} \frac{5}{6} \\ +\frac{1}{2} \\ \hline \end{array}$

4. $\begin{array}{r} \frac{8}{9} \\ -\frac{2}{3} \\ \hline \end{array}$

5. $\begin{array}{r} \frac{7}{10} \\ -\frac{2}{20} \\ \hline \end{array}$

6. $\begin{array}{r} 4\frac{1}{10} \\ +3\frac{1}{10} \\ \hline \end{array}$

7. $\begin{array}{r} 8\frac{2}{6} \\ -4\frac{1}{6} \\ \hline \end{array}$

8. $\begin{array}{r} 5\frac{3}{16} \\ -3\frac{3}{16} \\ \hline \end{array}$

9. $\begin{array}{r} 12\frac{12}{25} \\ +2\frac{3}{25} \\ \hline \end{array}$

10. $\begin{array}{r} 5\frac{3}{8} \\ +4\frac{1}{8} \\ \hline \end{array}$

11. $\frac{1}{2} + \frac{1}{2}$

12. $\frac{6}{10} - \frac{1}{5}$

13. $\frac{1}{4} + \frac{7}{8}$

14. $\frac{5}{6} - \frac{1}{3}$

Write as a whole number or mixed number in simplest form.

15. $\frac{16}{8}$

16. $\frac{13}{4}$

17. $\frac{15}{6}$

18. $\frac{20}{5}$

19. $\frac{17}{3}$

Is each a multiple of 4? Write *yes* or *no*.

20. 24

21. 38

22. 16

23. 48

24. 46

Write the least common multiple of each set.

25. 4, 10

26. 9, 12

27. 9, 6

28. 5, 6

Find the probability of each event.

△○□□○□□ ○△△□○○○

29. $P(\triangle)$

30. $P(\square)$

31. $P(\bigcirc)$

Find the part of each number.

32. $\frac{1}{3}$ of 18

33. $\frac{1}{8}$ of 24

34. $\frac{1}{10}$ of 100

35. $\frac{1}{6}$ of 42

36. $\frac{2}{5}$ of 45

37. $\frac{4}{9}$ of 72

38. $\frac{3}{4}$ of 40

39. $\frac{5}{12}$ of 24

(See *Still More Practice*, p. 469.)

LEAST COMMON DENOMINATOR

Rafael's cookie recipe called for
$\frac{1}{3}$ cup of brown sugar and $\frac{3}{4}$ cup
of white sugar. How much sugar
did Rafael use?

Add: $\frac{1}{3} + \frac{3}{4} = \underline{\quad ? \quad}$

To add $\frac{1}{3} + \frac{3}{4}$, rename *both fractions* as fractions
with the least common denominator.

The **least common denominator (LCD)**
is the least common multiple of the denominators.

Multiples of 3: 0, 3, 6, 9, 12, 15, 18, 21, 24, . . .
Multiples of 4: 0, 4, 8, 12, 16, 20, 24, . . .

So the LCD
of $\frac{1}{3}$ and $\frac{3}{4}$ is 12.

Rename the fractions.

$$\frac{1}{3} = \frac{1 \times 4}{3 \times 4} = \frac{4}{12}$$
$$+\frac{3}{4} = \frac{3 \times 3}{4 \times 3} = \frac{9}{12}$$

Add.

$$\frac{4}{12}$$
$$+\frac{9}{12}$$
$$\frac{13}{12} = 1\frac{1}{12} \leftarrow \boxed{\text{simplest form}}$$

Rafael used $1\frac{1}{12}$ cups of sugar.

Write the LCD for each set of fractions.

1. $\frac{1}{2}, \frac{2}{5}$ **2.** $\frac{3}{4}, \frac{1}{6}$ **3.** $\frac{2}{3}, \frac{3}{8}$ **4.** $\frac{1}{5}, \frac{1}{6}$

5. $\frac{3}{10}, \frac{1}{4}$ **6.** $\frac{4}{5}, \frac{3}{4}$ **7.** $\frac{1}{3}, \frac{1}{5}, \frac{1}{6}$ **8.** $\frac{1}{3}, \frac{1}{4}, \frac{1}{5}$

Add or subtract. Use the LCD. Write the answer in simplest form.

9. $\frac{1}{2} + \frac{2}{7}$ **10.** $\frac{1}{4} + \frac{3}{5}$ **11.** $\frac{5}{6} - \frac{1}{9}$ **12.** $\frac{2}{3} - \frac{1}{2}$

13. $\frac{7}{8} - \frac{3}{10}$ **14.** $\frac{9}{10} + \frac{1}{6}$ **15.** $\frac{7}{9} - \frac{3}{8}$ **16.** $\frac{5}{8} + \frac{2}{3}$

Check Your Mastery

Add or subtract. Write the answer in lowest terms.

See pp. 296–299, 308–311

1. $\frac{3}{10} + \frac{1}{5}$

2. $\frac{1}{6} + \frac{2}{6}$

3. $\frac{7}{8} - \frac{5}{8}$

4. $\frac{2}{3} - \frac{1}{6}$

5. $\frac{4}{5} - \frac{3}{10}$

6. $\frac{7}{8} + \frac{1}{4}$

7. $\frac{8}{10} - \frac{1}{2}$

8. $\frac{2}{3} + \frac{11}{12}$

Write as a whole number or mixed number in simplest form.

See pp. 300–301

9. $\frac{7}{2}$

10. $\frac{16}{5}$

11. $\frac{21}{8}$

12. $\frac{30}{6}$

13. $\frac{38}{7}$

Estimate the sum or the difference.

See pp. 302–303

14. $3\frac{2}{3}$ $+8\frac{1}{3}$

15. $7\frac{1}{10}$ $+8\frac{3}{5}$

16. $8\frac{7}{9}$ $-1\frac{3}{9}$

17. $24\frac{7}{8}$ $-14\frac{3}{4}$

Write the least common multiple.

See pp. 306–307

18. 2, 6

19. 4, 3

20. 4, 12

21. 5, 7

Find the part of each number.

See pp. 314–315

22. $\frac{1}{2}$ of 26

23. $\frac{2}{3}$ of 21

24. $\frac{3}{5}$ of 25

25. $\frac{5}{8}$ of 64

Solve.

See pp. 312–313, 318–319

26. There are 7 puppies in the pet shop. Four are black, 2 are black and white, and 1 is brown. What is the probability that the first one sold will be black? black and white? brown?

27. Of 24 apples, $\frac{1}{3}$ are green. How many are green?

Choose the best answer.

1. five sevenths

   a. $\frac{5}{7}$ **b.** $\frac{1}{2}$

   c. $\frac{7}{5}$ **d.** not given

2. $18 = 2 \times \underline{\ ?\ }$

   a. 36   **b.** 9

   c. 8   **d.** not given

3. What is $\frac{6}{24}$ in lowest terms?

   a. $\frac{1}{6}$ **b.** $\frac{1}{2}$

   c. $\frac{1}{4}$ **d.** not given

4. $\frac{1}{2} = \frac{?}{6}$ **a.** 12

                  b. 4

                  c. 8

                  d. not given

5. $\frac{7}{9} - \frac{2}{9}$ **a.** $\frac{5}{9}$

                  b. 5

                  c. $\frac{4}{9}$

                  d. not given

6. What is $\frac{17}{4}$ as a mixed number?

   a. $3\frac{1}{4}$ **b.** $4\frac{1}{4}$

   c. $2\frac{1}{2}$ **d.** not given

7. $\frac{3}{10} + \frac{1}{5}$ **a.** $\frac{1}{2}$

                  b. $\frac{1}{3}$

                  c. $\frac{4}{15}$

                  d. not given

8. $\frac{3}{4} - \frac{1}{2}$ **a.** $\frac{1}{6}$

                  b. $\frac{1}{4}$

                  c. $\frac{1}{2}$

                  d. not given

9. $\frac{1}{2}$ of 20   **a.** 40

                  b. 10

                  c. 12

                  d. not given

10. $\frac{2}{3} = \frac{?}{9}$ **a.** 6

                  b. 8

                  c. 10

                  d. not given

11. What is the GCF of 8 and 12?

   a. 8   **b.** 6

   c. 4   **d.** not given

12. What is $\frac{9}{18}$ in lowest terms?

   a. $\frac{3}{4}$ **b.** $\frac{1}{9}$

   c. $\frac{1}{3}$ **d.** not given

13. $\frac{3}{5} + \frac{1}{5}$ **a.** $\frac{4}{5}$

                  b. $\frac{4}{10}$

                  c. $\frac{1}{2}$

                  d. not given

14. $\frac{7}{8} - \frac{3}{8}$ **a.** $\frac{1}{3}$

                  b. $\frac{3}{4}$

                  c. $\frac{1}{2}$

                  d. not given

15. six and one third

   a. $3\frac{1}{6}$ **b.** $6\frac{1}{3}$

   c. $6\frac{1}{4}$ **d.** not given

16. $\frac{1}{3} + \frac{4}{9}$ **a.** $\frac{5}{12}$

                  b. $\frac{5}{9}$

                  c. $\frac{7}{9}$

                  d. not given

17. $\frac{7}{9} - \frac{1}{3}$ **a.** $\frac{5}{6}$

                  b. $\frac{2}{3}$

                  c. $\frac{4}{9}$

                  d. not given

18. $\frac{3}{4}$ of 36   **a.** 48

                  b. 27

                  c. 9

                  d. not given

19. What is the GCF of 7 and 21?

   a. 7   **b.** 21

   c. 14   **d.** not given

20. $\frac{5}{6} = \frac{?}{18}$ **a.** 8

                  b. 10

                  c. 15

                  d. not given

21. $\begin{array}{r} 3\frac{1}{7} \\ + 2\frac{4}{7} \\ \hline \end{array}$ **a.** $5\frac{6}{7}$

                  b. $6\frac{5}{7}$

                  c. $5\frac{4}{7}$

                  d. not given

Choose the best answer.

22. About what fractional part is shaded?

  a. $\frac{1}{2}$
  b. $\frac{1}{3}$
  c. $\frac{1}{4}$

23. What mixed number is shown?

  a. $3\frac{1}{2}$
  b. $4\frac{1}{3}$
  c. $3\frac{1}{3}$

24. Compare.

$\frac{2}{5} \; ? \; \frac{3}{5}$

  a. $<$
  b. $=$
  c. $>$

25. Compare.

$\frac{1}{2} \; ? \; \frac{4}{8}$

  a. $<$
  b. $=$
  c. $>$

26. What part is shaded?

  a. $\frac{7}{15}$
  b. $\frac{1}{3}$
  c. $\frac{3}{4}$
  d. $\frac{8}{15}$

27. Estimate the sum.

$4\frac{1}{3} + 6\frac{1}{3}$

  a. 10
  b. 12
  c. 2
  d. 24

28. Estimate the difference.

$16\frac{1}{6} - 9\frac{1}{6}$

  a. 14
  b. 7
  c. 25
  d. 13

29. Which is a multiple of 3?

  a. 20
  b. 16
  c. 25
  d. 24

30.

$P(\text{green}) = \underline{} ?$

  a. $\frac{3}{4}$
  b. $\frac{5}{8}$
  c. $\frac{1}{8}$
  d. $\frac{2}{8}$

31. What mixed number is shown?

  a. $4\frac{1}{3}$
  b. $5\frac{1}{3}$
  c. $5\frac{1}{2}$
  d. $4\frac{1}{2}$

32. Nora has $1\frac{3}{5}$ yards of denim. She needs $2\frac{4}{5}$ yards for a skirt. How many more yards does she need?

  a. $4\frac{2}{5}$
  b. $\frac{1}{5}$
  c. $1\frac{2}{5}$
  d. $1\frac{1}{5}$

33. Juan used $\frac{1}{2}$ yd of wire for his project. Rory used $\frac{1}{4}$ yd more. How many yards of wire did Rory use?

  a. $\frac{2}{6}$
  b. $\frac{2}{8}$
  c. $\frac{3}{4}$
  d. $\frac{1}{6}$

34. Sally grew $3\frac{2}{4}$ inches. Mae grew $1\frac{1}{4}$ inches. How much more than Mae did Sally grow?

  a. $4\frac{1}{2}$ in.
  b. $2\frac{1}{4}$ in.
  c. 5 in.
  d. 3 in.

35. Of 45 birds in the cage, $\frac{4}{5}$ are robins. How many of the birds in the cage are robins?

  a. 32
  b. 9
  c. 13
  d. 36

11 Geometry

In this chapter you will:

Identify rays, angles, lines, and line
   segments; and parallel, intersecting,
   and perpendicular lines
Name the parts of a circle
Identify polygons and classify
   quadrilaterals and triangles
Study congruent, similar, and
   symmetrical figures
Plot and name ordered pairs
Use technology: LOGO
Solve problems by finding a pattern

Do you remember?

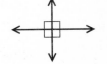

Parallel lines   Perpendicular lines

Critical Thinking/Finding Together
How many rectangles do the windows
in the pink building form?

11-1 Points, Lines, and Line Segments

▶ A **plane** is a flat surface that never ends. The surface of a table or a sheet of paper are both parts of planes.

▶ A, B, and X are **points** in a plane. A• B• •X

Read: point A, point B, point X
Write: A, B, X

▶ A **line segment** is a straight figure. It has two **endpoints**.

D ●————————————————● E

Read: line segment DE **or** line segment ED
Write: $\overline{DE}$ **or** $\overline{ED}$

▶ A **line** is a straight figure with *no* endpoints. A line goes on forever in both directions.

←————— G •———————————•H —————→

Line segment GH is part of line GH.

Read: line GH **or** line HG
Write: $\overleftrightarrow{GH}$ **or** $\overleftrightarrow{HG}$

Identify each as a *point*, *line*, or *line segment*. Use symbols.

1. •R

2. Y–Z

3. F •———• G

4. M–N

5. H–J

6. L•

7. P–Q

8. V–W

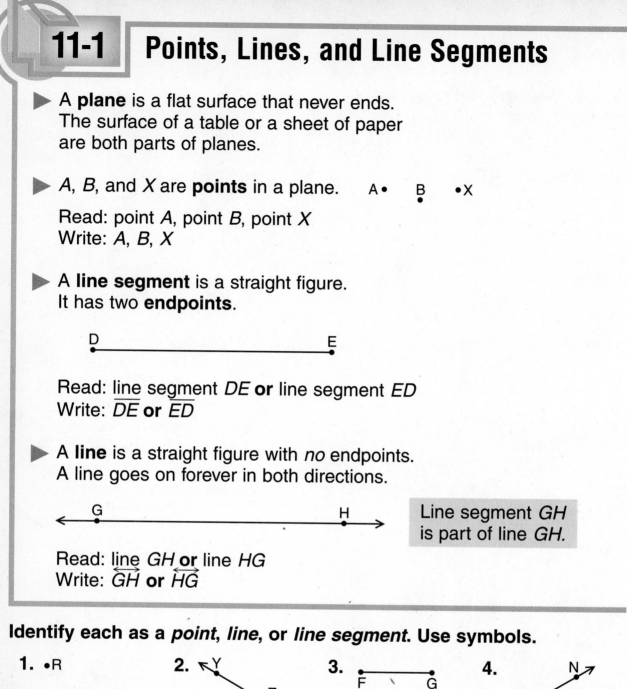

Draw and label each.

9. $\overline{TV}$ 10. K 11. $\overleftrightarrow{ST}$ 12. $\overline{FG}$

13. D 14. $\overrightarrow{PQ}$ 15. $\overline{LM}$ 16. Z

Write the letter of each line segment.

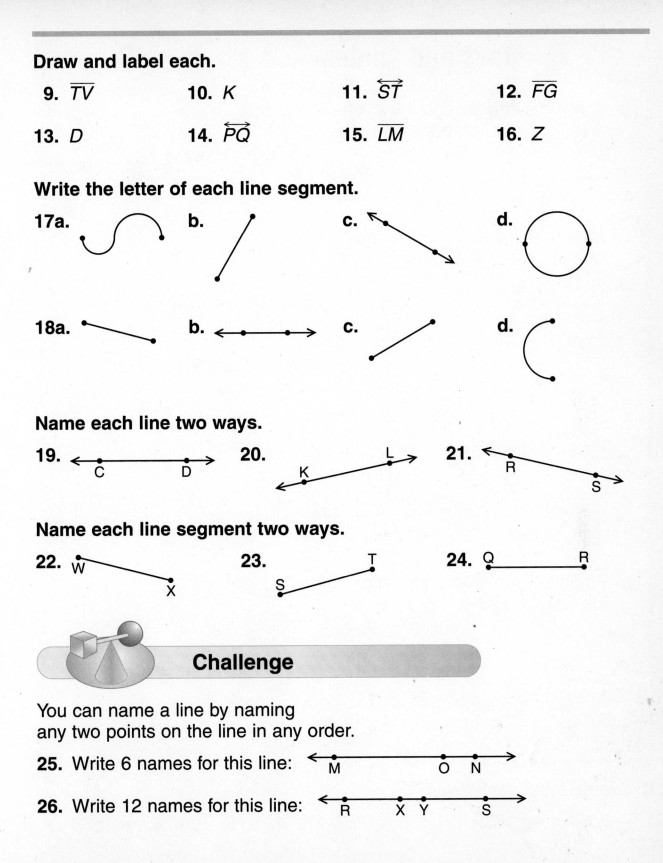

17a.   b.   c.   d.

18a.   b.   c.   d.

Name each line two ways.

19.   20.   21.
C   D   K   L   R   S

Name each line segment two ways.

22.   23.   24. Q   R
W   X   S   T

Challenge

You can name a line by naming
any two points on the line in any order.

25. Write 6 names for this line: M   O   N

26. Write 12 names for this line: R   X   Y   S

327

11-2 Rays and Angles

▶ A **ray** is a straight figure with one endpoint.
A ray goes on forever in one direction.

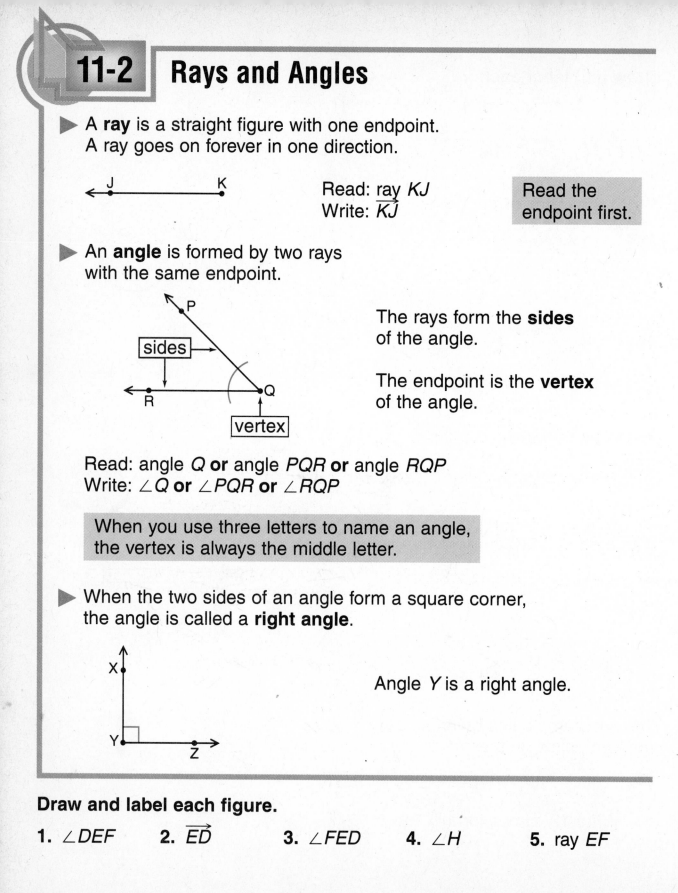

Read: ray *KJ*
Write: $\overrightarrow{KJ}$

Read the endpoint first.

▶ An **angle** is formed by two rays with the same endpoint.

The rays form the **sides** of the angle.

The endpoint is the **vertex** of the angle.

Read: angle *Q* **or** angle *PQR* **or** angle *RQP*
Write: $\angle Q$ **or** $\angle PQR$ **or** $\angle RQP$

When you use three letters to name an angle, the vertex is always the middle letter.

▶ When the two sides of an angle form a square corner, the angle is called a **right angle**.

Angle *Y* is a right angle.

Draw and label each figure.

1. $\angle DEF$ 2. $\overrightarrow{ED}$ 3. $\angle FED$ 4. $\angle H$ 5. ray *EF*

328

Name each figure.

6. 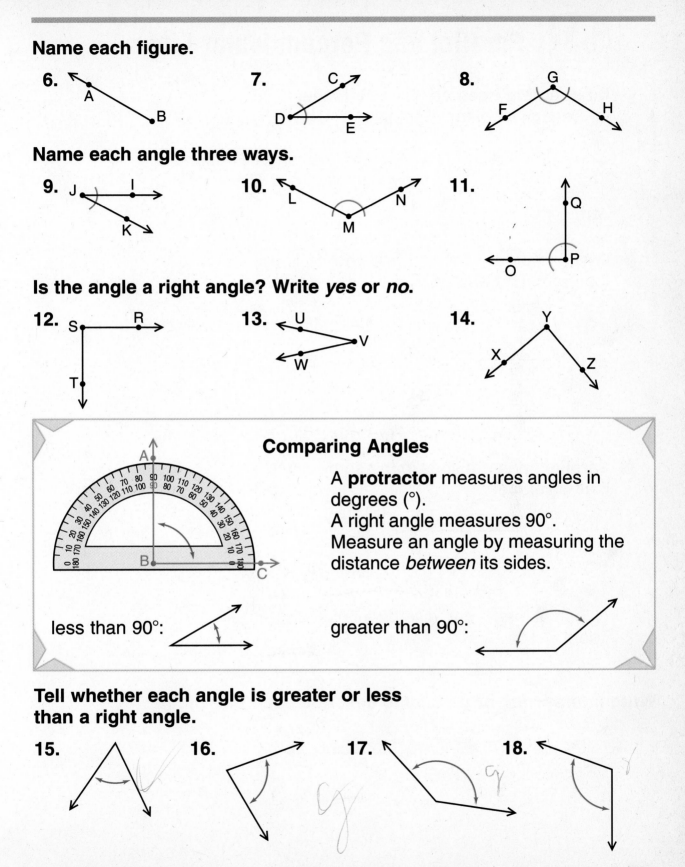A ⟶ B

7. C, D, E

8. F, G, H

Name each angle three ways.

9. J, I, K

10. L, M, N

11. Q, O, P

Is the angle a right angle? Write *yes* or *no*.

12. S, R, T

13. U, V, W

14. Y, X, Z

Comparing Angles

A **protractor** measures angles in degrees (°).
A right angle measures 90°.
Measure an angle by measuring the distance *between* its sides.

less than 90°:

greater than 90°:

Tell whether each angle is greater or less than a right angle.

15.

16.

17.

18.

11-3   Parallel and Perpendicular Lines

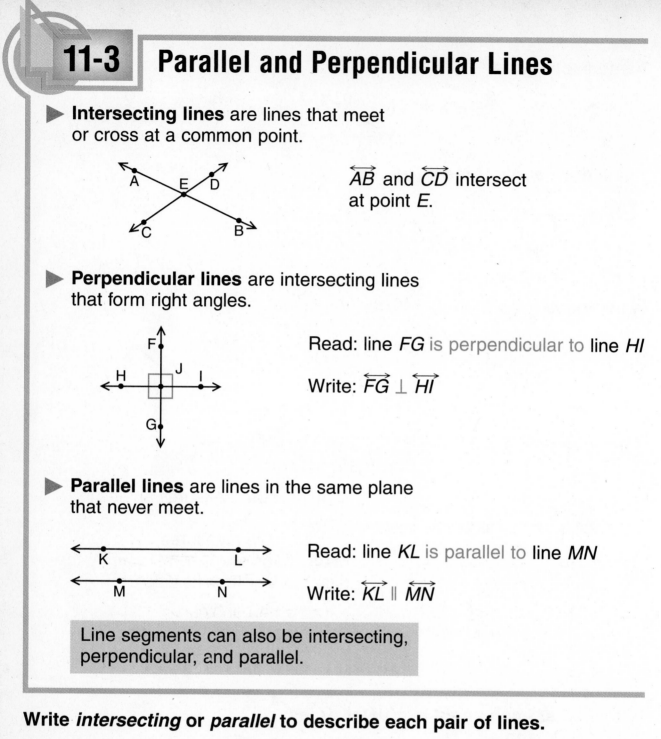

▶ **Intersecting lines** are lines that meet or cross at a common point.

$\overleftrightarrow{AB}$ and $\overleftrightarrow{CD}$ intersect at point *E*.

▶ **Perpendicular lines** are intersecting lines that form right angles.

Read: line *FG* is perpendicular to line *HI*

Write: $\overleftrightarrow{FG} \perp \overleftrightarrow{HI}$

▶ **Parallel lines** are lines in the same plane that never meet.

Read: line *KL* is parallel to line *MN*

Write: $\overleftrightarrow{KL} \parallel \overleftrightarrow{MN}$

Line segments can also be intersecting, perpendicular, and parallel.

Write *intersecting* or *parallel* to describe each pair of lines.

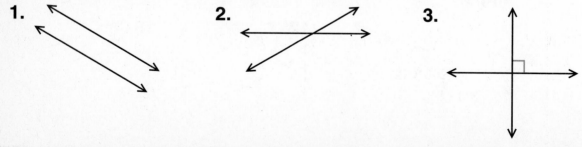

1.

2.

3.

Use the figure to solve.

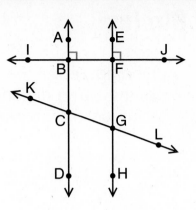

4. At what point does $\overleftrightarrow{EH}$ intersect $\overleftrightarrow{KL}$?

5. Name the pair of parallel lines.

6. What kind of angle is ∠*IBA*?

7. Name two pairs of perpendicular lines.

8. Is ∠*FGL* greater or less than a right angle?

Copy these lines on dot paper.

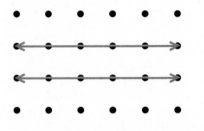

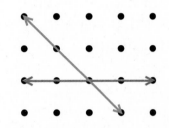

Draw a line segment that:

9. is perpendicular to both red lines.

10. is parallel to the green line and intersects the blue line.

11. intersects one red line but not the other.

12. is perpendicular to the green line.

Critical Thinking

Solve.

13. Are $\overleftrightarrow{RS}$ and $\overleftrightarrow{XY}$ parallel, intersecting, or neither? Explain your answer.

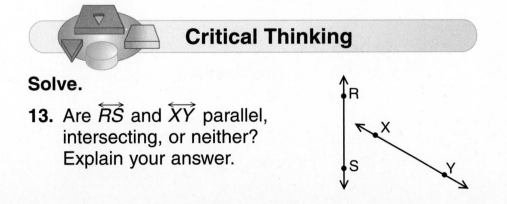

▶ A **circle** is a plane figure. All the points on the circle are the same distance from another point, called the **center**.

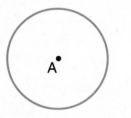

Point *A* is the center of circle *A*.

A circle is named by its center point.

▶ The parts of a circle have special names.

Any line segment with endpoints at the *center* of the circle and *on* the circle is a **radius**.

$\overline{BE}$ is a radius. $\overline{BC}$ and $\overline{BD}$ are also radii (plural of radius).

Any line segment that passes *through* the center of the circle and has *both* endpoints on the circle is a **diameter**.

$\overline{CD}$ is a diameter.

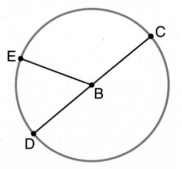

The length of the diameter is always twice the length of the radius.

Solve. Use the circle below.

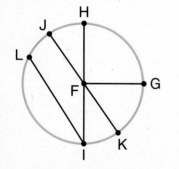

1. Name 6 points on the circle.

2. Name five line segments that are radii.

3. Suppose $\overline{FG}$ is 5 in. long. How long is $\overline{JF}$? How long is $\overline{HI}$?

Solve. Use the circle at the right.

4. Name the circle and its center.

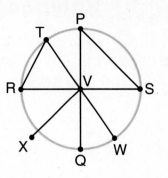

5. How many diameters are shown? Name the diameters.

6. Is $\overline{TR}$ a radius? Explain why or why not.

7. Is $\overline{VX}$ a radius? Explain why or why not.

8. How many radii are shown? Name the radii.

Curves

A **simple closed curve** is a path that begins and ends at the same point and does not cross itself.

Not Simple   Not Closed

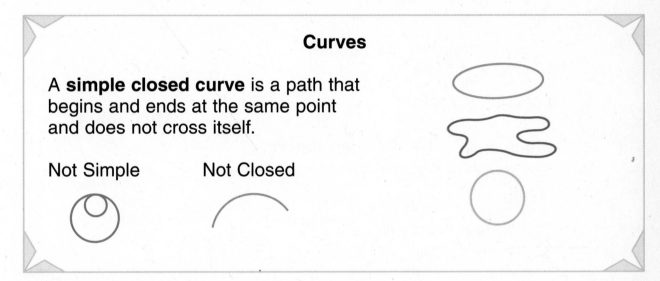

Write *true* or *false*. Use the picture below.

9. Some of the simple closed curves are green.

10. None of the simple closed curves are blue.

11. All circles are simple closed curves.

333

Polygons

▶ A **polygon** is any closed plane figure formed by connected line segments that do not cross.

The line segments are the **sides** of the polygon.

Two sides of a polygon meet at a point called a **vertex** (plural: vertices).

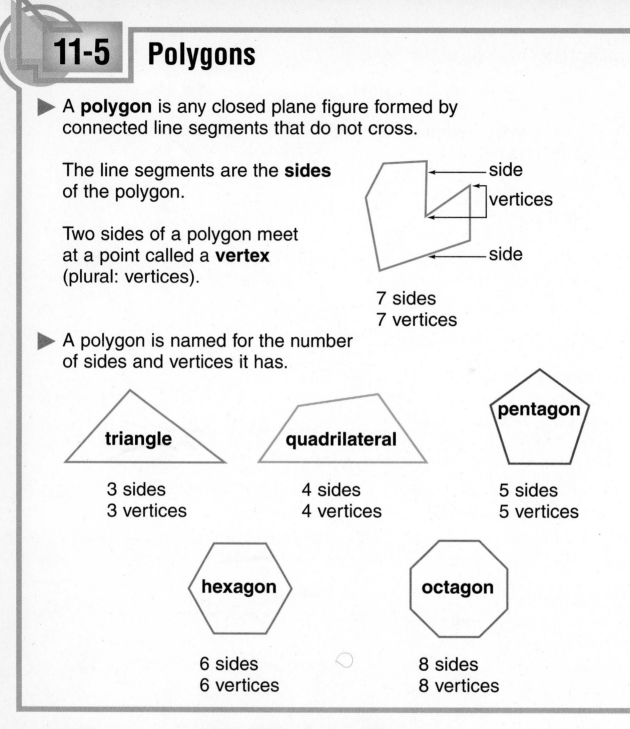

side

vertices

side

7 sides
7 vertices

▶ A polygon is named for the number of sides and vertices it has.

triangle

3 sides
3 vertices

quadrilateral

4 sides
4 vertices

pentagon

5 sides
5 vertices

hexagon

6 sides
6 vertices

octagon

8 sides
8 vertices

Is each figure a polygon? Write *yes* or *no*.

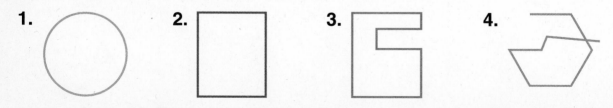

1.

2.

3.

4.

Write the name of each polygon.

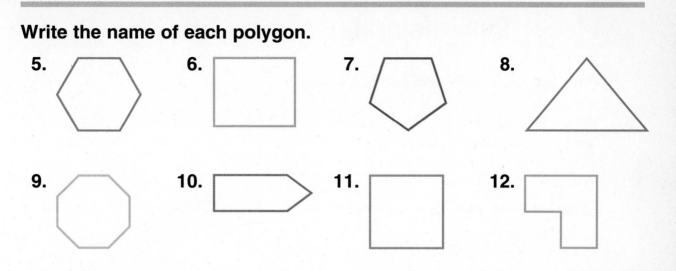

5.　　　　6.　　　　7.　　　　8.

9.　　　　10.　　　　11.　　　　12.

Solve.

13. What is the name of the polygon that has 8 sides and 8 vertices?

14. What is the name of the polygon that has 5 sides and 5 vertices?

15. What is the name of the polygon that has 3 sides? How many vertices does it have?

16. What is the name of the polygon that has 6 vertices? How many sides does it have?

17. Use dot paper. Draw five different quadrilaterals.

18. Use dot paper. Draw four different hexagons.

19. Is a circle a polygon? Explain your answer.

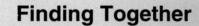

Finding Together

Make a pattern, design, or picture with polygons.

20. Use the same polygon in different sizes. Color your pattern.

21. Use the same polygon in the same size. Color your pattern.

22. Use different polygons. Color your pattern.

Quadrilaterals

Some quadrilaterals have special names.

▶ A **parallelogram** has opposite sides that are parallel *and* that are the same length.

Quadrilateral *ABCD* is a parallelogram.

▶ A **rectangle** also has opposite sides that are parallel *and* that are the same length. All the angles of a rectangle are right angles.

Quadrilateral *EFGH* is a rectangle.

▶ A **square** has opposite sides that are parallel. *All* its sides are the same length. All the angles of a square are right angles.

Quadrilateral *JKLM* is a square.

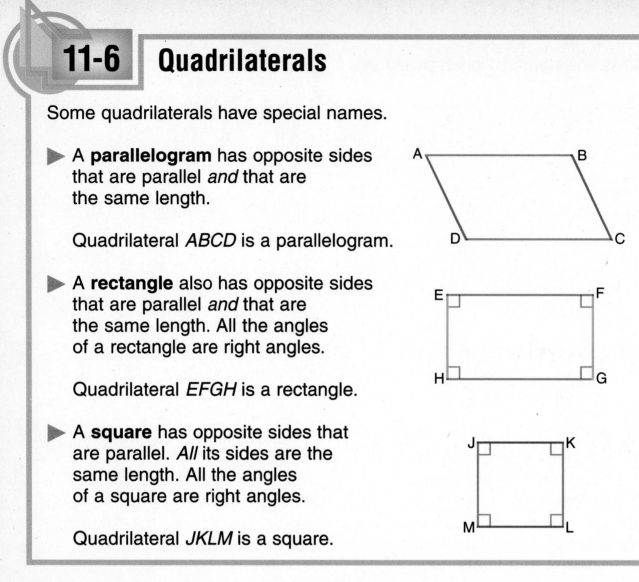

Is each figure a quadrilateral? Write *yes* or *no*.

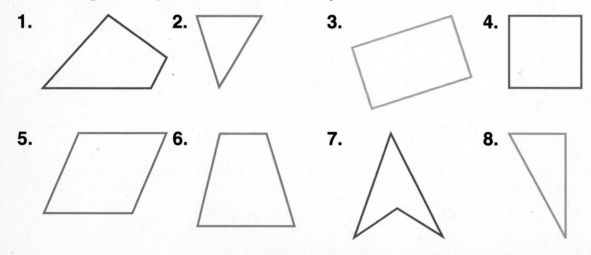

1.
2.
3.
4.
5.
6.
7.
8.

Solve. Use the figure below.

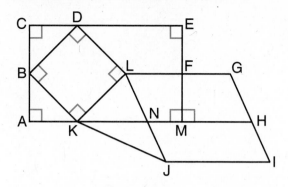

9. What kind of polygon is figure *DEFL*?

10. What is the special name for figure *BDLK*? figure *JLGI*? figure *ACEM*?

11. Which side is opposite $\overline{CA}$? opposite $\overline{DL}$? $\overline{BD}$? $\overline{LJ}$? $\overline{LG}$?

12. Name 5 quadrilaterals other than those named in questions **9** and **10**.

Use dot paper to draw each quadrilateral described.

13. with 4 right angles; with 2 right angles; with 1 right angle

14. with 0 right angles and 1 pair of opposite sides that are parallel

15. whose sides are all equal in length and is *not* a square

16. with 0 right angles and 0 pairs of opposite sides that are parallel

Write *true* or *false* for each statement.

17. A quadrilateral never has 4 sides.

18. A square always has 4 right angles.

19. No triangles are quadrilaterals.

20. No quadrilateral has parallel opposite sides.

21. All rectangles are parallelograms.

22. All squares are also rectangles.

23. All quadrilaterals are parallelograms.

24. Some parallelograms are also squares.

Triangles

These polygons are all triangles.

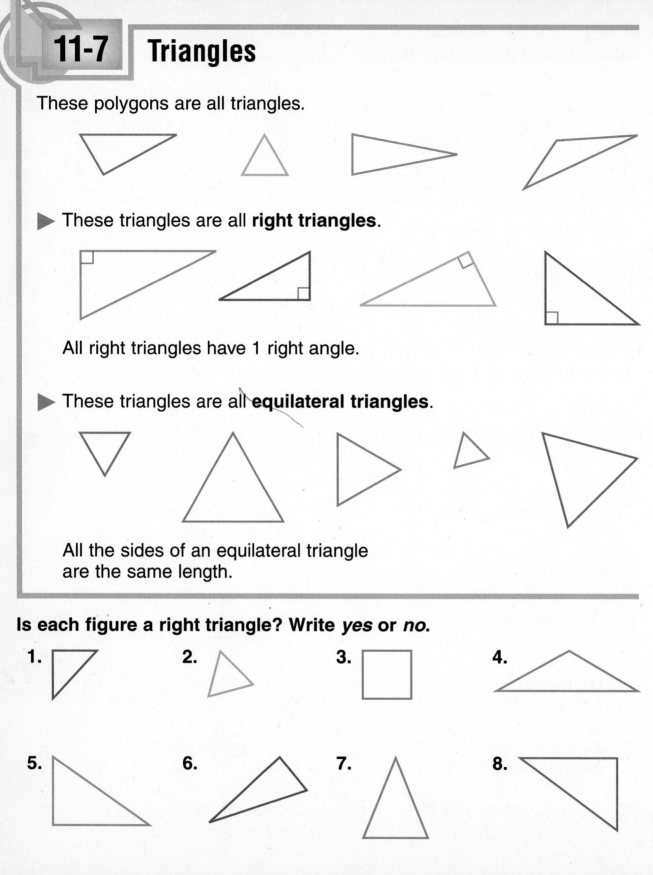

▶ These triangles are all **right triangles**.

All right triangles have 1 right angle.

▶ These triangles are all **equilateral triangles**.

All the sides of an equilateral triangle
are the same length.

Is each figure a right triangle? Write *yes* or *no*.

1.

2.

3.

4.

5.

6.

7.

8.

Is each figure an equilateral triangle? Write *yes* or *no*.

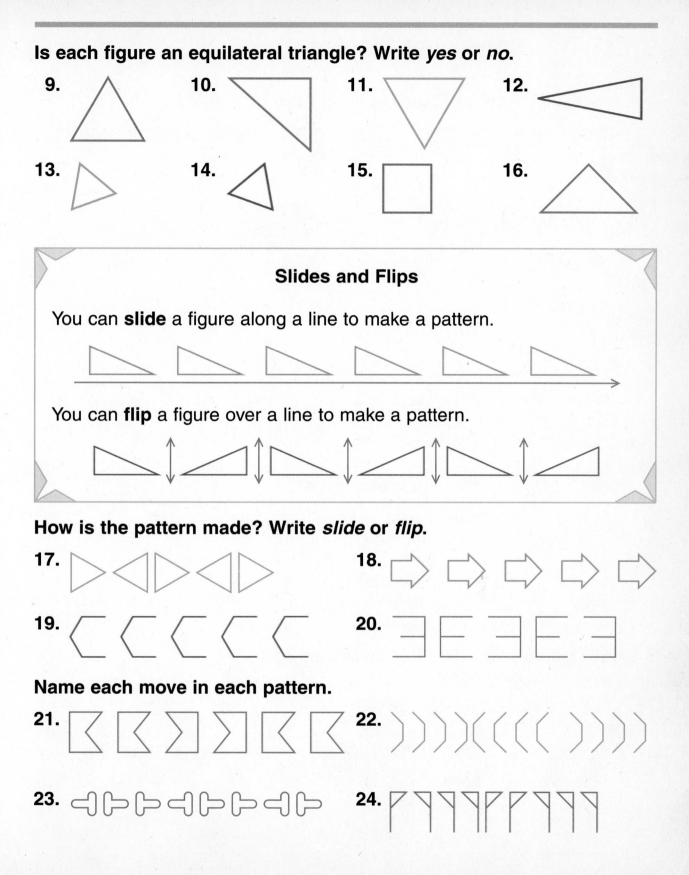

9.

10.

11.

12.

13.

14.

15.

16.

Slides and Flips

You can **slide** a figure along a line to make a pattern.

You can **flip** a figure over a line to make a pattern.

How is the pattern made? Write *slide* or *flip*.

17.

18.

19.

20.

Name each move in each pattern.

21.

22.

23.

24.

Congruent Figures

Elena used congruent figures to make each pattern.

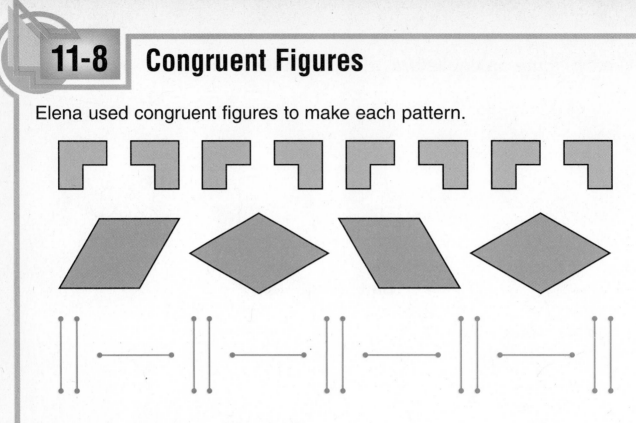

Congruent figures have exactly
the same size and the same shape.

To find whether two figures are congruent:

- Carefully trace one figure onto tracing paper.
- Lay the tracing over the other figure.

If the tracing and the figure match,
the two figures are congruent.

Are the figures congruent? Write *yes* or *no*.
You may use tracing paper.

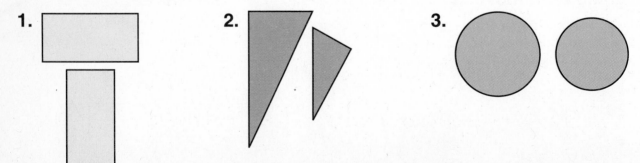

1.

2.

3.

Write the letter of the figure that is congruent to the first figure.

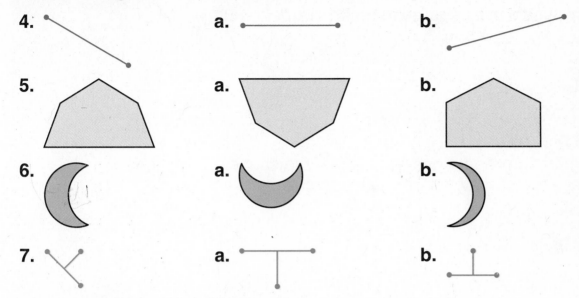

4.   a.   b.

5.   a.   b.

6.   a.   b.

7.   a.   b.

Use dot paper. Draw a figure that is congruent to each figure below.

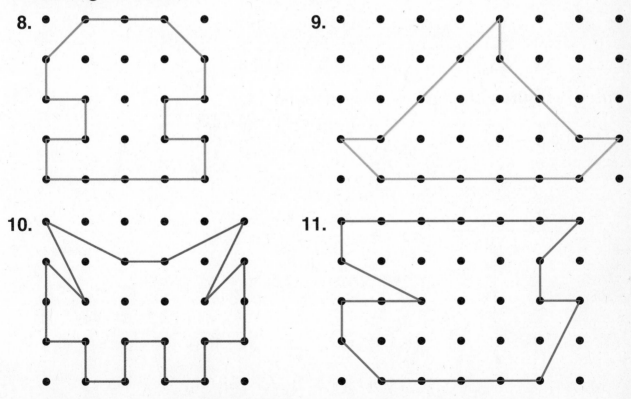

8.

9.

10.

11.

Similar Figures

Billy used similar figures to make this pattern.

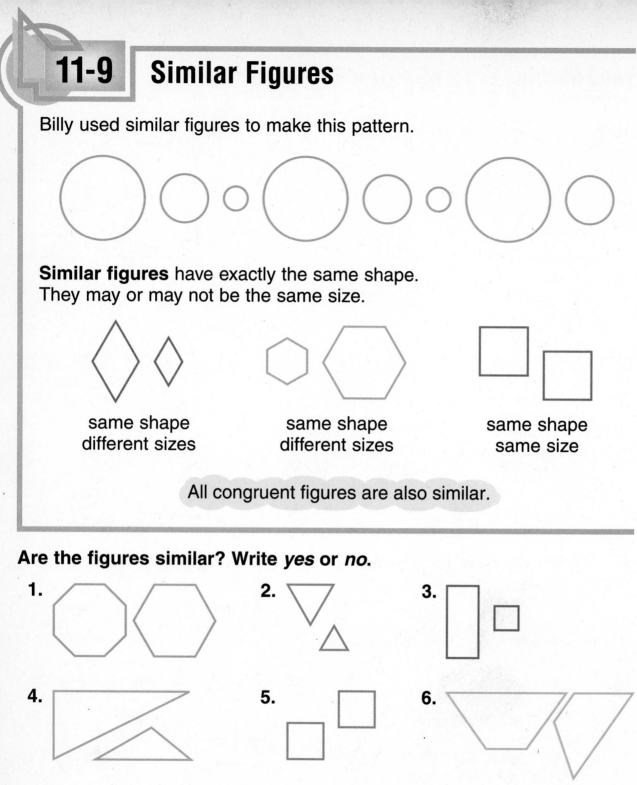

Similar figures have exactly the same shape.
They may or may not be the same size.

same shape
different sizes

same shape
different sizes

same shape
same size

All congruent figures are also similar.

Are the figures similar? Write *yes* or *no*.

1.

2.

3.

4.

5.

6.

7.

8.

9.

Write the letter of the figure that is similar to the first figure.

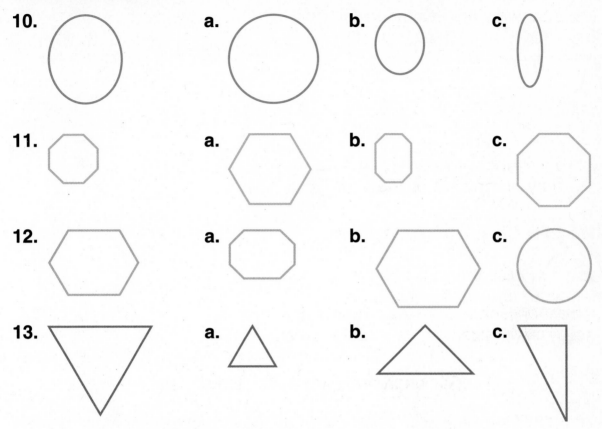

10.   a.   b.   c.

11.   a.   b.   c.

12.   a.   b.   c.

13.   a.   b.   c.

Copy each figure onto dot paper. Then draw a figure that is twice as large.

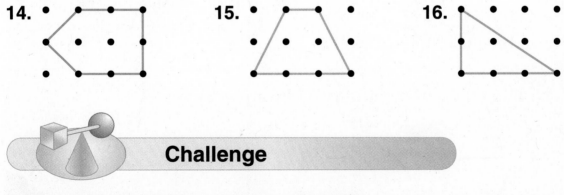

14.   15.   16.

Challenge

Copy and cut out four of these triangles.

17. Fit the triangles together to form a similar triangle.

Symmetry

If you can fold a figure in half so that the two halves match exactly, the figure is **symmetrical**.

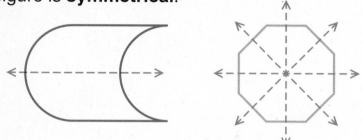 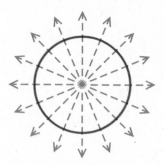

The fold line is a **line of symmetry**.

If you can turn a tracing of a figure halfway around so that the tracing and the figure match exactly, the figure has **half-turn symmetry**.

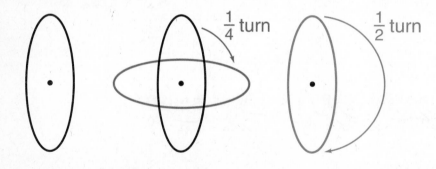

$\frac{1}{4}$ turn

$\frac{1}{2}$ turn

This figure has half-turn symmetry.

Is each red line a line of symmetry? Write *yes* or *no*.

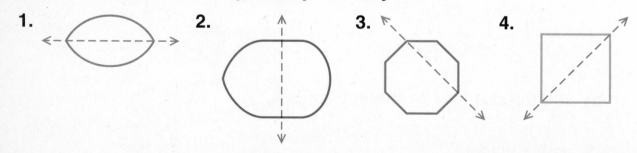

1.

2.

3.

4.

Is each figure symmetrical? Write *yes* or *no*.

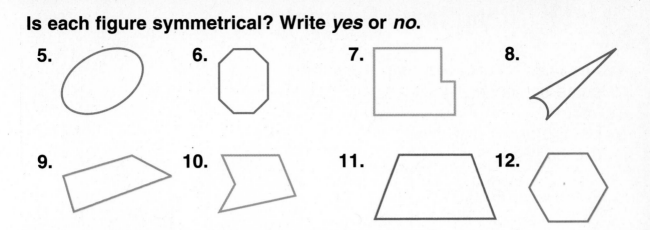

5.　　　　　6.　　　　　7.　　　　　8.

9.　　　　　10.　　　　　11.　　　　　12.

**Make two copies of each figure on dot paper.
Cut out one of each figure. Turn it around on the
first figure. Does each figure have half-turn
symmetry? Write *yes* or *no*.**

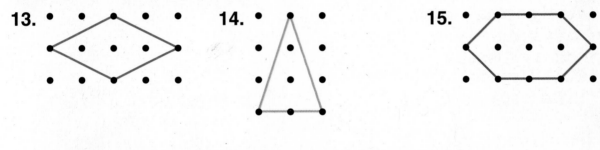

13.　　　　　14.　　　　　15.

Skills to Remember

Solve. Use the graph.

16. On what day was the
    temperature 55°F?

17. On which two days was
    the temperature the same?

18. What was the temperature
    on Tuesday?

19. What was the highest
    temperature of the week?

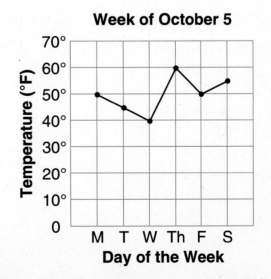

Week of October 5

Temperature (°F)

70°
60°
50°
40°
30°
20°
10°
0

M　T　W　Th　F　S
Day of the Week

Coordinate Geometry

You can use an **ordered pair** of numbers to locate points on a grid.

▶ What ordered pair gives the location of point *A*?

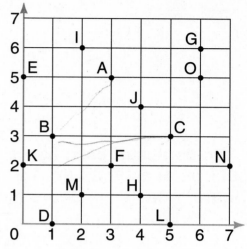

Point *A* is:
   3 spaces to the right. →
   5 spaces up. ↑

The ordered pair (3, 5) gives the location of point *A*.

▶ What point is located at (5, 3)?

Move 5 spaces to the right. →
Move 3 spaces up. ↑

Point *C* is located at (5, 3).

In an ordered pair, the *first number* tells you to move to the right. The *second number* tells you to move up.

Use the grid to answer each question.

1. What ordered pair gives the location of point *B*?

2. What ordered pair gives the location of point *H*?

3. What point is located at (2, 6)?

4. What point is located at (4, 4)?

5. What ordered pair gives the location of point *D*?

6. What point is located at (0, 5)?

Write the name of the figure at each point.

7. (1, 8)   **8.** (6, 7)

9. (9, 1)   **10.** (4, 9)

11. (7, 3)   **12.** (1, 0)

Write the ordered pair for each figure.

13. heart

14. sunburst

15. right triangle

16. parallelogram

17. crescent moon

Make and label three 8 by 8 grids on graph paper. Draw each point. Then connect the points in order with line segments.

18. (3, 7) (5, 7) (6, 5) (6, 3) (5, 1) (3, 1) (2, 3) (2, 5)

19. (1, 1) (7, 1) (7, 7)   **20.** (1, 6) (5, 6) (8, 2) (3, 2)

21. Name the figures you have drawn.

Make Up Your Own

22. Give a list of ordered pairs that, when connected by line segments, form a polygon.

TECHNOLOGY

LOGO

LOGO is a computer language that can be used to draw figures. **Commands** are used to tell a small triangle called a turtle how to move around the computer screen.

LOGO turtle

Below are some commands used to move the turtle.

Command	What you enter	How the turtle moves
FORWARD	FD 20	Forward 2 steps
BACK	BK 20	Back 2 steps
RIGHT	RT 90	Makes a right angle turn (90°)
LEFT	LT 45	Makes half of a right angle turn
REPEAT	REPEAT 3[FD 20]	Repeats the command(s) in brackets 3 times
PENUP	PU	Turtle moves without drawing
PENDOWN	PD	Puts the turtle back in drawing mode

These commands tell the turtle to draw this figure.

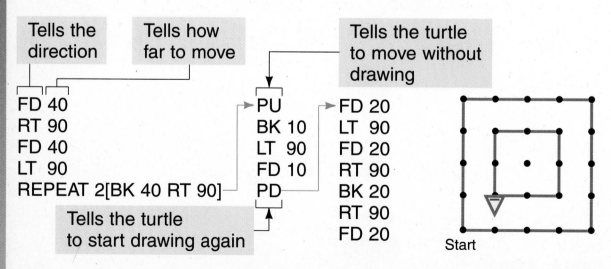

Tells the direction

Tells how far to move

Tells the turtle to move without drawing

```
FD 40        PU      FD 20
RT 90        BK 10   LT  90
FD 40        LT  90  FD 20
LT  90       FD 10   RT 90
REPEAT 2[BK 40 RT 90]  PD   BK 20
                            RT 90
                            FD 20
```

Tells the turtle to start drawing again

Start

348

Match each movement with the correct LOGO commands.

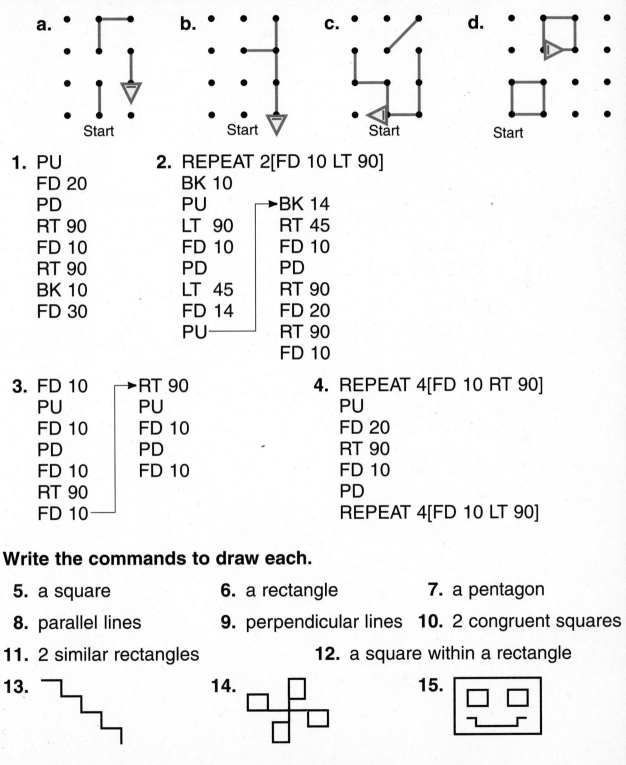

a.   Start

b.   Start

c.   Start

d.   Start

1. PU
FD 20
PD
RT 90
FD 10
RT 90
BK 10
FD 30

2. REPEAT 2[FD 10 LT 90]
BK 10
PU   →BK 14
LT 90   RT 45
FD 10   FD 10
PD   PD
LT 45   RT 90
FD 14   FD 20
PU⌐   RT 90
         FD 10

3. FD 10 →RT 90
PU   PU
FD 10   FD 10
PD   PD
FD 10   FD 10
RT 90
FD 10⌐

4. REPEAT 4[FD 10 RT 90]
PU
FD 20
RT 90
FD 10
PD
REPEAT 4[FD 10 LT 90]

Write the commands to draw each.

5. a square   **6.** a rectangle   **7.** a pentagon

8. parallel lines   **9.** perpendicular lines   **10.** 2 congruent squares

11. 2 similar rectangles   **12.** a square within a rectangle

13.   **14.**   **15.**

11-13 | Problem Solving: Find a Pattern

Problem: Tyrell draws a spiral on graph
paper. He draws 4 segments.
Then he draws 5 more continuing
the pattern. How long is the
finished spiral?

1 cm
4 cm
2 cm
3 cm

1 IMAGINE Create a mental picture
of the finished spiral.

2 NAME *Facts:* Spiral has 4 line segments.
Spiral will have 5 more.

Question: How long is the finished spiral?

3 THINK Look for sums of ten.
Measure the length of each segment.

$$1 + 2 + 3 + 4 + 5 + 6 + 7 + 8 + 9 = \underline{\ ?\ }$$

4 COMPUTE Add to find the total length.

The sum has 4 tens:

$1 + 9$, $2 + 8$, $3 + 7$, and $4 + 6$ or 40.

$40 + 5 = 45$

The spiral is 45 cm long.

5 CHECK Cut a 45-cm string and use it
to measure the spiral.
Use a calculator to check addition.

350

Solve.

1. Jessie makes this drawing. She adds one more square. Her finished drawing has 2 lines of symmetry. Where does she add the square?

Original Drawing

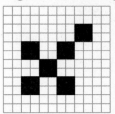

IMAGINE	Put yourself in the problem.

NAME	*Facts:*	Jessie draws this shape. She adds one square. The finished shape has 2 lines of symmetry.
	Question:	Where does she add the last square?

THINK	Find the line of symmetry in the original drawing. Then think of other ways to fold the shape in half.

COMPUTE → **CHECK**

2. Jacques paints on a belt these shapes in order: triangle, square, triangle, pentagon, triangle, hexagon. What do the ninth and tenth shapes look like?

3. Can you cut this shape into 2 congruent hexagons? 2 congruent octagons?

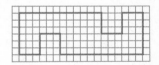

4. Troy is making a cage for pet guinea pigs. The floor of the cage must have an area of 4 square units. How many different shapes can Troy make with the 4 square units?

2 ft

5. A brick border follows this pattern. How many bricks are used in a 10-ft border?

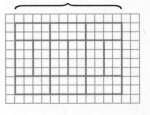

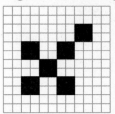

Make Up Your Own

6. Write a problem using a pattern. Have a classmate solve it.

Solve.

1. Sylvia's Sign Shop made an octagonal sign. How many sides does it have? How many angles?

2. The sign shop made the neon sign **HI**. Where are the parallel lines in the sign? Where are the perpendicular lines?

3. The Dilly Deli ordered a sign in the shape of a pickle. Is the sign a simple closed curve?

4. Roy orders a square sign from the sign shop. How many lines of symmetry does his sign have?

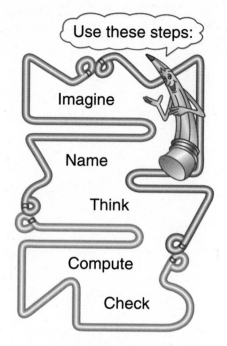

Use these steps:

Imagine

Name

Think

Compute

Check

5. 4 is to square as 8 is to ? .

6. The sign for Trex Tires is a circle. Name the radii shown on the sign at the right.

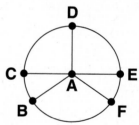

7. Draw 5 square shapes so that any two squares touch along one entire side. In how many different ways can the shapes be arranged?

Use the table for problems 8–10.

8. How much is a hexagonal sign?

9. How much more expensive is a pentagonal sign than a triangular sign?

10. What is the cost of 2 rectangular signs and 1 triangular sign?

Sign Prices

Number of Sides (4 ft each)	Price per Side
3	$25
4	$20
5	$45
6	$60

Solve.

11. Hank, Don, and Ned are waiting in line. Don is ahead of Ned. Hank has been waiting longer than the others. What is their order in line?

12. A tool measures 16 cm. A plastic tube measures 71 cm. How much longer is the plastic tube?

13. Sylvia cuts a triangle, a square, and a pentagon out of wood. The first shape she cuts has more sides than the second but fewer sides than the third. In what order does she cut the shapes?

14. Marcy cut an equilateral triangle to make 4 congruent signs. Each side of the triangle is 2 ft long. How did Marcy cut the triangle?

15. Sylvia's shop has 8 rows of paint cans. There are 10 cans in the first row, 9 cans in the second row, 8 in the third, and so on. How many cans of paint are there in all?

16. How would you describe the shape of this sign for the Food Barn? How many angles does it have? What other questions can you answer about this sign?

USE THESE STRATEGIES:
Find a Pattern
Logical Reasoning
Choose the Operation
Extra Information
Make Up a Question
Draw a Picture

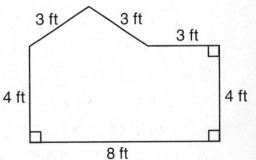

Make Up Your Own

17. Write a problem modeled on problem 12. Have a classmate solve it.

More Practice

Identify each.

1. __?__ ray

2. __?__ line segment

3. __?__ perpendicular lines

4. __?__ pentagon

5. __?__ line

6. __?__ right triangle

7. __?__ circle

8. __?__ parallel lines

9. __?__ point

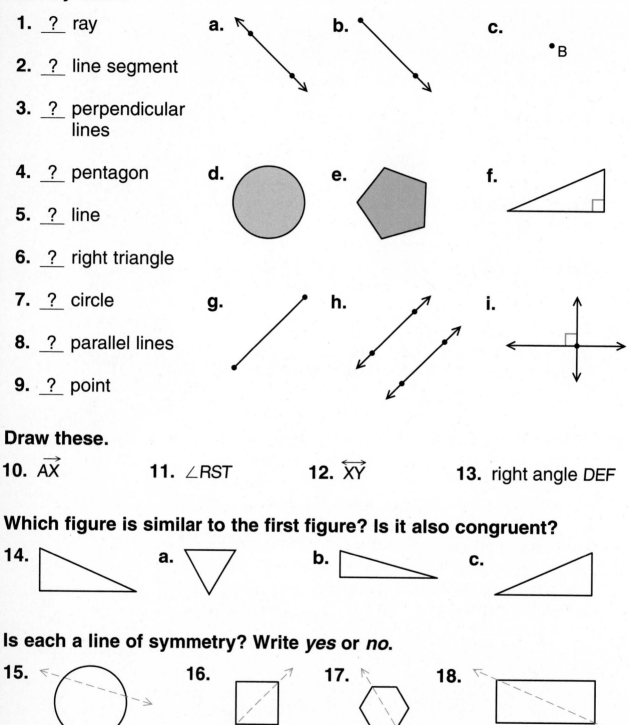

Draw these.

10. $\overrightarrow{AX}$

11. $\angle RST$

12. $\overleftrightarrow{XY}$

13. right angle *DEF*

Which figure is similar to the first figure? Is it also congruent?

14.   a.   b.   c.

Is each a line of symmetry? Write *yes* or *no*.

15.   16.   17.   18.

(See *Still More Practice*, pp. 469–470.)

TANGRAMS

Copy the **tangram** puzzle on grid paper. Then cut it out.

Flip, slide, or turn the puzzle pieces to solve.

1. Name the shape of each puzzle piece.

2. Which two pieces cover piece 6? Which two cover piece 4?

3. Which three pieces cover piece 1? Cover piece 1 in a different way. Which pieces did you use?

4. Use pieces 1 and 2. How many different figures can you make? Name them.

5. Make the largest possible triangle you can. How many pieces did you use?

6. Make two similar parallelograms. Which pieces did you use for the large parallelogram? Which did you use for the small parallelogram?

7. A **trapezoid** is a quadrilateral with only one pair of opposite sides that are parallel. Use different pairs of puzzle pieces to make trapezoids. How many trapezoids did you make? Which two pieces did you use for each?

8. Make trapezoids from 3 pieces, 4 pieces, 5 pieces, and 6 pieces. Record the puzzle pieces you used for each.

9. Use all seven tangram pieces to make a rectangle and then a parallelogram.

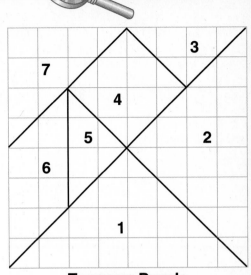

Tangram Puzzle

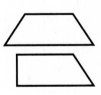

Identify each.

See pp. 326–339

1. __?__ parallelogram
2. __?__ perpendicular lines
3. __?__ diameter
4. __?__ radius
5. __?__ octagon
6. __?__ line segment
7. __?__ ray
8. __?__ equilateral triangle

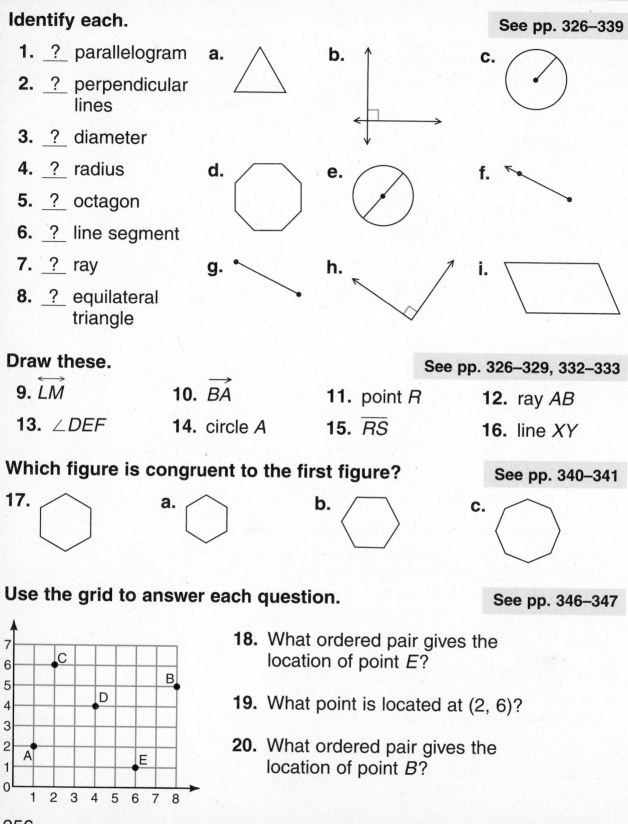

Draw these.

See pp. 326–329, 332–333

9. $\overleftrightarrow{LM}$
10. $\overrightarrow{BA}$
11. point R
12. ray AB
13. $\angle DEF$
14. circle A
15. $\overline{RS}$
16. line XY

Which figure is congruent to the first figure?

See pp. 340–341

17.   a.   b.   c.

Use the grid to answer each question.

See pp. 346–347

18. What ordered pair gives the location of point E?

19. What point is located at (2, 6)?

20. What ordered pair gives the location of point B?

12 Perimeter, Area, and Volume

In this chapter you will:
Find perimeter and area by
counting and using formulas
Identify space figures and relate
them to plane figures
Investigate volume
Solve problems by using a
drawing or a model

Do you remember?

1 square unit

1 cubic unit

Critical Thinking/Finding Together
How many quadrilaterals can you
find in the picture?

12-1 Perimeter

Ms. Wade wants to build a fence around her property. How many feet of fencing should she buy?

To find how many feet of fencing she should buy, you need to find the perimeter of the property.

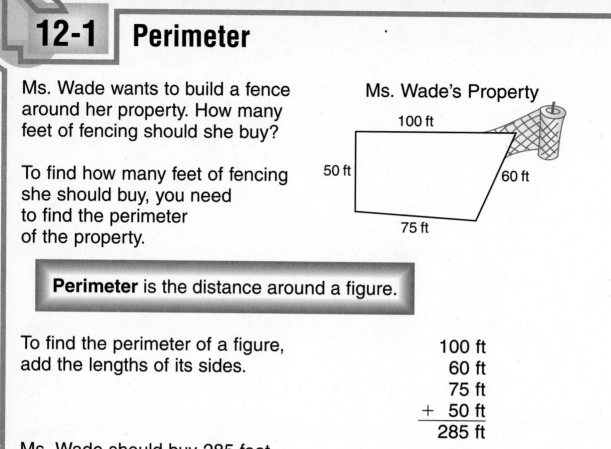

Ms. Wade's Property

100 ft

50 ft   60 ft

75 ft

Perimeter is the distance around a figure.

To find the perimeter of a figure, add the lengths of its sides.

```
   100 ft
    60 ft
    75 ft
+   50 ft
   285 ft
```

Ms. Wade should buy 285 feet of fencing.

Find the perimeter of each figure.

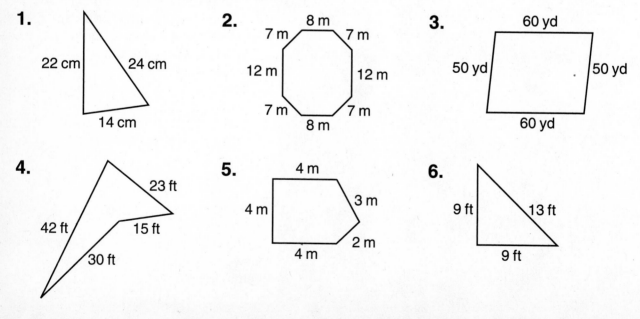

1.
22 cm   24 cm
14 cm

2.
8 m
7 m   7 m
12 m   12 m
7 m   7 m
8 m

3.
60 yd
50 yd   50 yd
60 yd

4.
23 ft
42 ft   15 ft
30 ft

5.
4 m
4 m   3 m
        2 m
4 m

6.
9 ft   13 ft
9 ft

Find the perimeter of each.

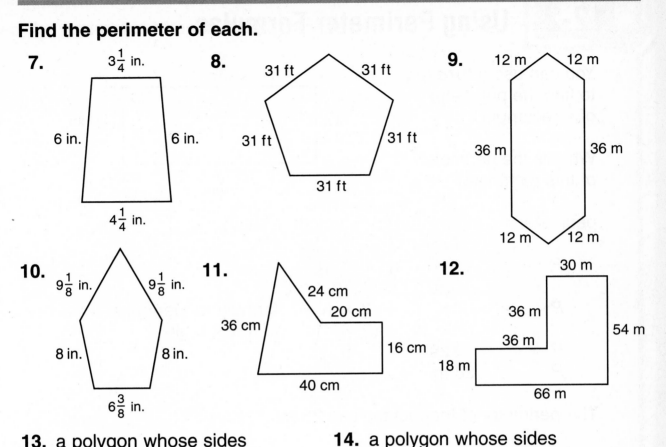

7. $3\frac{1}{4}$ in.   6 in.   6 in. $4\frac{1}{4}$ in.

8. 31 ft   31 ft   31 ft   31 ft   31 ft

9. 12 m   12 m   36 m   36 m   12 m   12 m

10. $9\frac{1}{8}$ in. $9\frac{1}{8}$ in.   8 in.   8 in. $6\frac{3}{8}$ in.

11. 24 cm   20 cm   36 cm   16 cm   40 cm

12. 30 m   36 m   36 m   54 m   18 m   66 m

13. a polygon whose sides measure 100 ft, 142 ft, 68 ft, and 127 ft

14. a polygon whose sides measure 92 m, 109 m, and 92 m

Solve.

15. What is the perimeter of a playground with sides of 49 m, 36 m, 42 m, 38 m, and 45 m?

16. What is the perimeter of a banner with sides of 16 in., 6 in., and 16 in.?

17. What is the perimeter of a wall hanging with sides of 24 in., 36 in., 12 in., and 12 in.?

Finding Together

Use centimeter grid paper.

18. How many rectangles can you make with a perimeter of 10 cm?

12-3 Area

Area is the number of square units
needed to cover a flat surface.

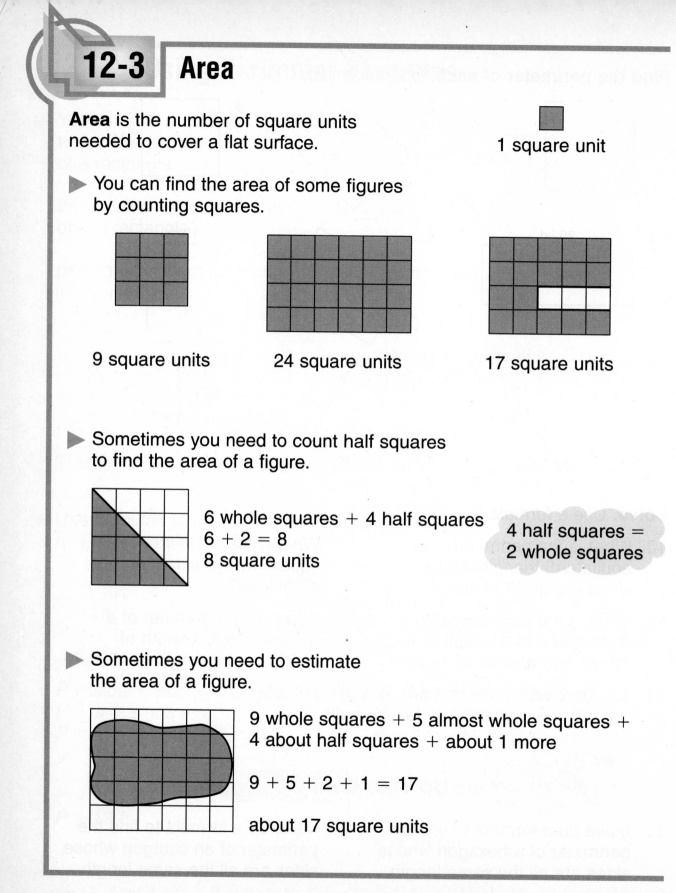

1 square unit

▶ You can find the area of some figures
by counting squares.

9 square units   24 square units   17 square units

▶ Sometimes you need to count half squares
to find the area of a figure.

6 whole squares + 4 half squares
6 + 2 = 8
8 square units

4 half squares =
2 whole squares

▶ Sometimes you need to estimate
the area of a figure.

9 whole squares + 5 almost whole squares +
4 about half squares + about 1 more

9 + 5 + 2 + 1 = 17

about 17 square units

Find the area of each figure.

1.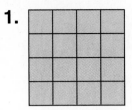

2.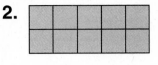

3.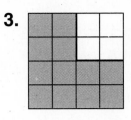

4.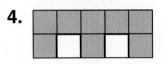

5.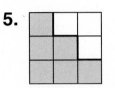

6.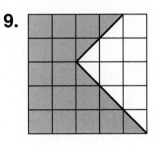

7.

8.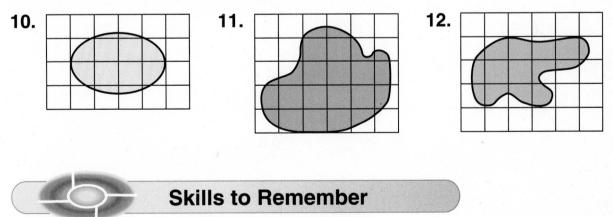

9.

Estimate the area of each figure.

10.

11.

12.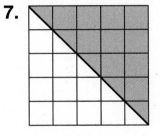

Multiply.

13.	14.	15.	16.	17.	18.
14 × 4	29 × 3	72 × 7	54 ×48	95 ×12	63 ×25

Using the Area Formula

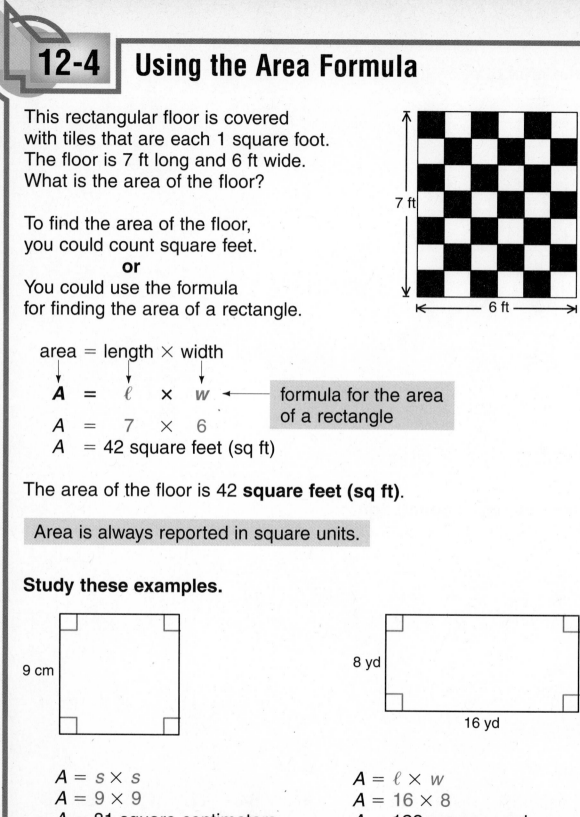

This rectangular floor is covered with tiles that are each 1 square foot. The floor is 7 ft long and 6 ft wide. What is the area of the floor?

To find the area of the floor, you could count square feet.

or

You could use the formula for finding the area of a rectangle.

area = length × width

$A = \ell \times w$ ← formula for the area of a rectangle

$A = 7 \times 6$

$A = 42$ square feet (sq ft)

The area of the floor is 42 **square feet (sq ft)**.

Area is always reported in square units.

Study these examples.

$A = s \times s$
$A = 9 \times 9$
$A = 81$ square centimeters
(sq cm)

$A = \ell \times w$
$A = 16 \times 8$
$A = 128$ square yards
(sq yd)

Find the area. Use the area formula.

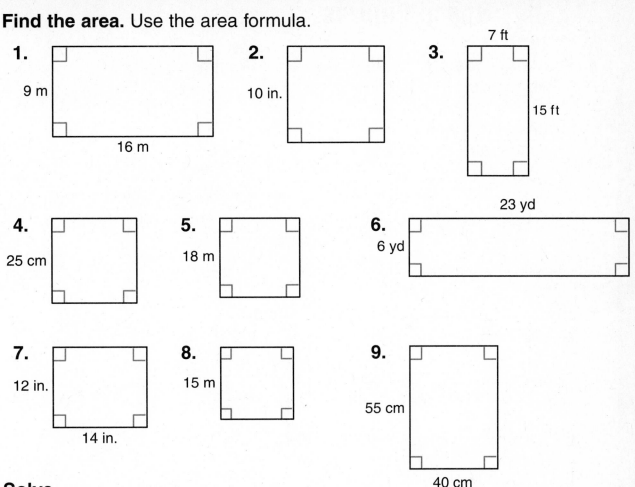

1.
9 m
16 m

2.
10 in.

3.
7 ft
15 ft

4.
25 cm

5.
18 m

6.
23 yd
6 yd

7.
12 in.
14 in.

8.
15 m

9.
55 cm
40 cm

Solve.

10. A football field is 120 yd long (including the end zones) and 55 yd wide. What is the area of a football field?

11. A baseball infield is a square that is 90 ft along each side, or base line. What is its area?

12. A tennis court is a rectangle that is 78 ft long and 27 ft wide. What is the area of a tennis court?

Challenge

Use graph paper to solve.

13. Draw two different figures that each have an area of 18 square units.

14. Draw as many rectangles as you can that each have an area of 24 square units.

Space Figures

▶ **Space figures** are not flat. They are sometimes called **solids**.

A **cube** is a space figure with 6 faces, 12 edges, and 8 vertices.

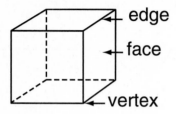

edge

face

vertex

A **face** is a flat surface of a space figure. Two faces meet at a line segment called an **edge**. Two or more edges meet at a **vertex**.

▶ These space figures have faces, edges, and vertices.

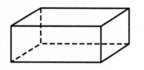   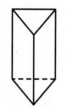   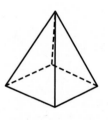

rectangular prism	**triangular prism**	**square pyramid**
6 faces	5 faces	5 faces
12 edges	9 edges	8 edges
8 vertices	6 vertices	5 vertices

▶ These space figures have 0 edges. Each has a curved surface.

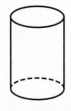      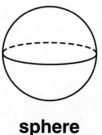

cylinder	**cone**	**sphere**
2 circular faces	1 circular face	0 faces

Write the name of the space figure each is most like.

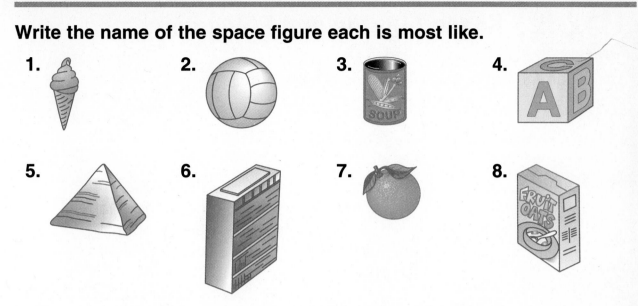

1.

2.

3.

4.

5.

6.

7.

8.

Copy and complete. You need not draw the space figures.

9. name	cube	?	?	?	?	?	?
10. faces	?	?	?	6	?	?	?
11. edges	12	?	?	?	?	?	?
12. vertices	?	?	?	?	?	?	6

Solve.

13. I have 2 faces, 0 edges, and 0 vertices. Which space figure am I?

14. I have 1 face and a curved surface. Which space figure am I?

15. I have 5 faces and 5 vertices. How many edges do I have? Which space figure am I?

16. I am shaped like a ball. How many faces, edges, and vertices do I have? Which space figure am I?

17. I have 6 faces and 12 edges. I am not a rectangular prism. Which space figure am I?

18. I have 9 edges and 6 vertices. How many faces do I have? Which space figure am I?

Space Figures and Polygons

▶ Each face of a space figure is a plane figure.

triangular
prism

net of a triangular
prism

A **net** is the shape
made by opening
a solid figure and
laying it flat.

The net shows that a triangular prism
is made up of 5 polygons: 2 triangles
and 3 rectangles.

▶ If you could cut a space figure,
the new faces you create would
also be plane figures.

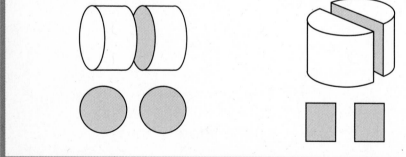

Name the shape of each shaded face.

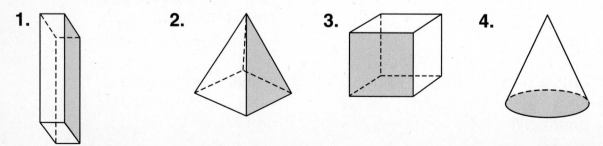

1.   2.   3.   4.

**Use dot paper. Copy each net. Name each polygon.
Then cut, fold, and tape each net to make
a space figure.**

5.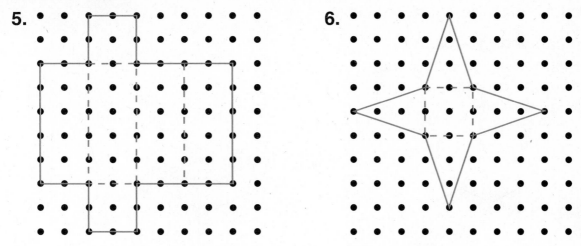

6.

Name the shape of the new faces made by each cut.

7.

8.

9.

10.

11.

12.

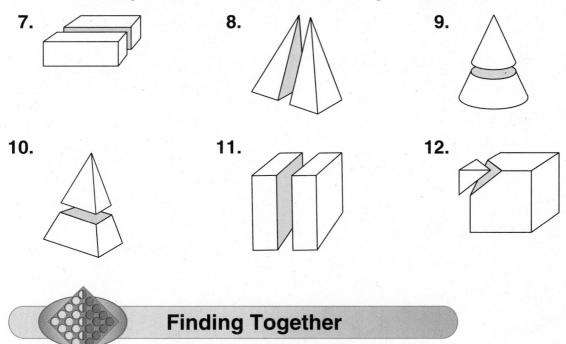

Finding Together

13. Press models of space figures into clay.
    Name the plane figures you have made.

14. Use dot paper. Draw a net of a cube. Cut out and
    fold the net. Tape the edges together.

12-7 Volume

The **volume** of a space figure is the number of cubic units the figure contains.

You can find the volume of a space figure by counting the number of cubic units needed to fill it.

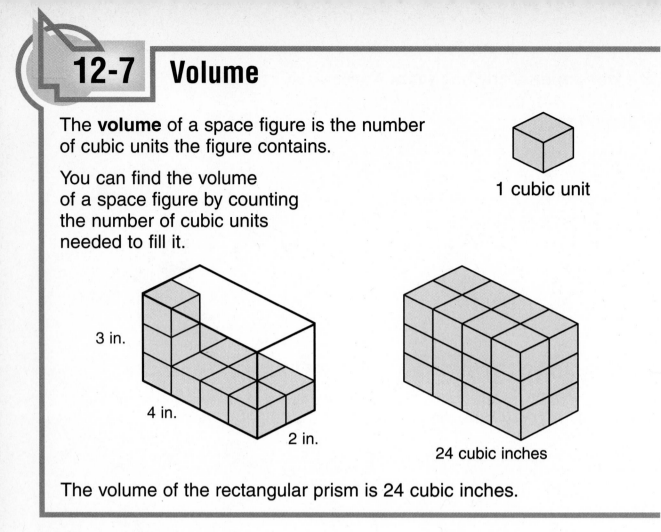

1 cubic unit

3 in.

4 in.

2 in.

24 cubic inches

The volume of the rectangular prism is 24 cubic inches.

Find the volume of each.

1.
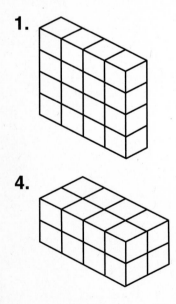

2.
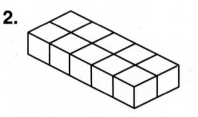

3.
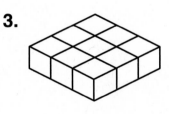

4.

5.

6.
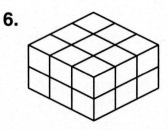

Find the volume of each in cubic feet.

7.   **8.**   **9.**

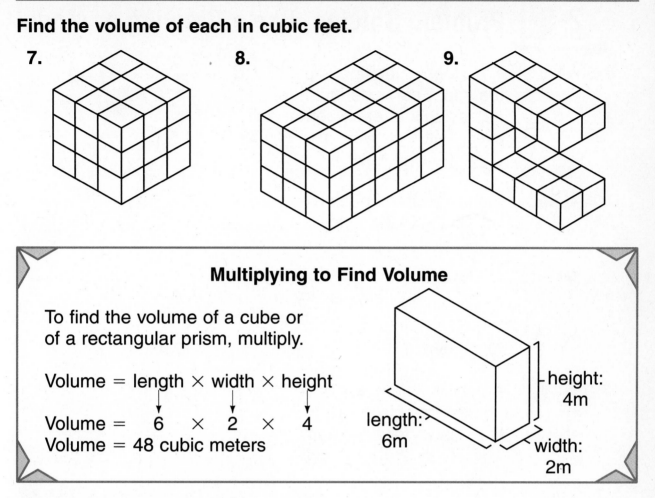

Multiplying to Find Volume

To find the volume of a cube or of a rectangular prism, multiply.

Volume = length × width × height

Volume =   6   ×   2   ×   4

Volume = 48 cubic meters

length: 6m
width: 2m
height: 4m

Multiply to find the volume of each.

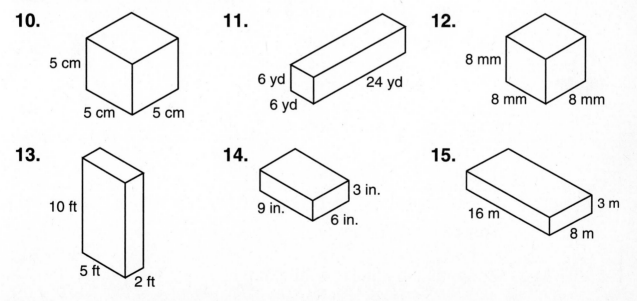

10. 5 cm, 5 cm, 5 cm

11. 6 yd, 6 yd, 24 yd

12. 8 mm, 8 mm, 8 mm

13. 10 ft, 5 ft, 2 ft

14. 9 in., 3 in., 6 in.

15. 16 m, 3 m, 8 m

371

12-8 Problem Solving: Use a Drawing or Model

Problem: The Hobby Hut sign is a triangle. Each side is 2 ft long. It has lights at each corner and every half foot. How many lights does the sign have?

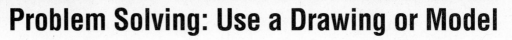

1 IMAGINE Picture yourself putting light bulbs in the sign.

2 NAME *Facts:*   1 light—at each corner
                 1 light—every half foot along
                          each side

Question: How many lights does the sign have?

3 THINK Equilateral triangles have 3 equal sides.
Draw a triangle.
Use marks for each light.
Multiply to find the number
of lights:

     at each corner ⟶ $3 \times 1 = \underline{\ ?\ }$
     along each side ⟶ $3 \times 3 = \underline{\ ?\ }$

Then add to find the total.

4 COMPUTE 1 light at each corner
     $3 \times 1 = 3$
3 lights along each side
     $3 \times 3 = 9$
The total number of lights
     $3 + 9 = 12$

The sign has 12 lights.

5 CHECK Count all the lights on the sign.

Solve.

1. A shape made up of tiles that are
1 cm square has an area of
9 sq cm and a perimeter of
12 cm. Describe the shape.

A = 9 sq cm

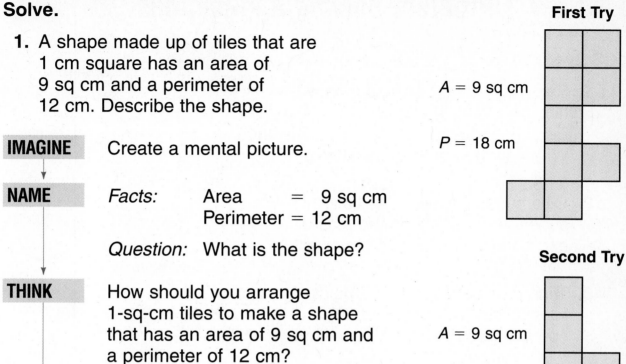

| **IMAGINE** | Create a mental picture. |

P = 18 cm

| **NAME** | *Facts:* | Area | = | 9 sq cm |
| | | Perimeter | = | 12 cm |

| | *Question:* | What is the shape? |

| **THINK** | How should you arrange
1-sq-cm tiles to make a shape
that has an area of 9 sq cm and
a perimeter of 12 cm? |

A = 9 sq cm

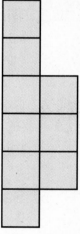

COMPUTE → **CHECK**

P = 16 cm

2. The area of a rectangle is 32
square inches. One of the sides
is 4 inches. How long are the
other sides?

3. The volume of a rectangular prism
is 24 cubic cm. The base of the prism
is 2 cm by 4 cm. How tall is it?

4. How many triangles can you find
in the puzzle on the right?

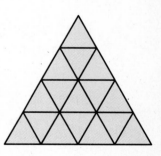

5. Bill draws a square with each side 4 cm long.
He draws a dot in the center of each
side and connects the dots to draw
another square. About how long are
the sides of the new square?

Solve.

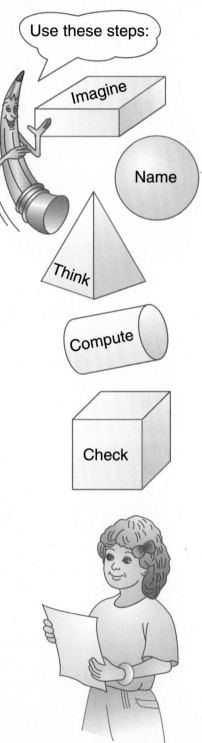

Use these steps:

Imagine

Name

Think

Compute

Check

1. Sara babysits for Ollie and shows him how to build a tower with 27 cubes. Each cube has a volume of 1 cubic inch. What is the volume of the tower?

2. Ollie builds a tower with his 1-inch cubes. What shape is the face of each 1-inch cube in Ollie's tower?

3. Trina brings crayons. The point of the blue crayon is rubbed flat. What space figure does the crayon look like?

4. Benji's crib mattress is 34 in. by 30 in. What is the perimeter of the mattress?

5. Sara draws a hexagon. Each side is 9 cm. What is the perimeter of the hexagon?

6. Trina shows Benji a shape. It has 2 circular faces. What might the shape be?

7. Three children work together to build a large rectangular prism. It has a width of 7 in., a length of 8 in., and a height of 10 in. What is the volume of this prism?

8. Trina has a sheet of paper that is $8\frac{1}{4}$ in. by 11 in. What is the perimeter of the paper?

Solve.

9. Ralph has a photo in his wallet. The area of the photo is 6 square inches. How long might each side be?

10. Trina made this bead pattern: 1 sphere, 2 cylinders, 3 cones, 2 spheres, 3 cylinders, 4 cones, and so on. What is the shape of the 20th figure?

11. The smallest side of a quadrilateral is 5 cm. The next side is 10 cm. The length of each succeeding side increases by 5 cm. What is the shape's perimeter?

12. Ralph's rectangular quilt has a perimeter of 14 feet. One side is 3 feet long. What is the area of the quilt?

13. Angie makes giant pillows. The table tells about each pillow. What space figure does Benji's pillow look like?

14. Did Sara or Trina get a pillow in the shape of a sphere?

15. Draw five 1-centimeter squares to make a shape so that any 2 squares touch along at least one entire side. How many different arrangements are possible?

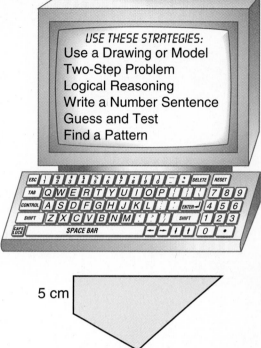

USE THESE STRATEGIES:
Use a Drawing or Model
Two-Step Problem
Logical Reasoning
Write a Number Sentence
Guess and Test
Find a Pattern

5 cm

	Benji's Pillow	Sara's Pillow	Trina's Pillow
faces	6	0	1
edges	12	0	0
curved surface	0	1	1

 **Make Up Your Own**

16. Write a problem that needs a drawing or model. Have a classmate solve it.

More Practice

Find the perimeter. Use a perimeter formula when you can.

1.

8 m

3 m   3 m

8 m

2.

10 yd   10 yd

6 yd

3.

3 cm

4 cm   4 cm

3 cm   3 cm

Find the area.

4.

5.

15 in.

6.

10 m

24 m

Name each space figure.

7.

8.

9.

Name the shape of each shaded face.

10.

11.

12.

Find the volume.

13.

14.

15.

4 cm

6 cm

4 cm

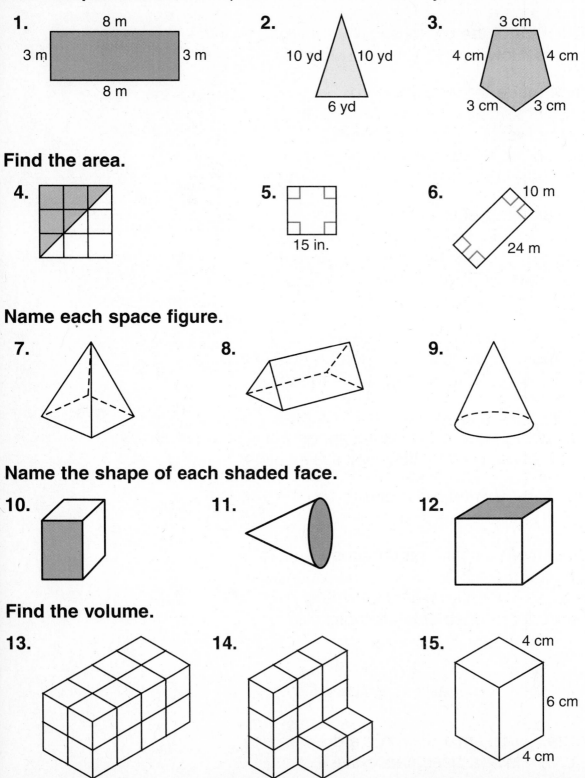

376

(See *Still More Practice*, p. 470.)

13 Dividing by Two Digits

In this chapter you will:
- Estimate quotients
- Divide 2-, 3-, and 4-digit dividends by 2 digits
- Use trial quotients in division
- Use technology: calculating with fractions
- Solve problems with hidden facts

Do you remember?
Divide to find the number in each set.
Divide to find the number of equal sets.

Critical Thinking/Finding Together
What is the greatest number of people a waiter can serve if each serves the same number? There are 12 tables in each of 2 sections. Each table seats 4 people, and there are 6 waiters.

Division Patterns

Use division facts and patterns with zero
to divide tens, hundreds, and
thousands by multiples of 10.

Study these division patterns.

Fact: $8 \div 1 = 8$

$80 \div 10 = 8$
$800 \div 10 = 80$
$8000 \div 10 = 800$

Fact: $9 \div 3 = 3$

$90 \div 30 = 3$
$900 \div 30 = 30$
$9000 \div 30 = 300$

Fact: $28 \div 7 = 4$

$280 \div 70 = 4$
$2800 \div 70 = 40$
$28,000 \div 70 = 400$

Fact: $10 \div 2 = 5$

$100 \div 20 = 5$
$1000 \div 20 = 50$
$10,000 \div 20 = 500$

Copy and complete.

1.
$9 \div 1 = \underline{?}$
$90 \div 10 = \underline{?}$
$900 \div 10 = \underline{?}$
$9000 \div 10 = \underline{?}$

2.
$8 \div 4 = \underline{?}$
$80 \div 40 = \underline{?}$
$800 \div 40 = \underline{?}$
$8000 \div 40 = \underline{?}$

3.
$6 \div 3 = \underline{?}$
$60 \div 30 = \underline{?}$
$600 \div 30 = \underline{?}$
$6000 \div 30 = \underline{?}$

4.
$32 \div 8 = \underline{?}$
$320 \div 80 = \underline{?}$
$3200 \div 80 = \underline{?}$
$32,000 \div 80 = \underline{?}$

5.
$40 \div 5 = \underline{?}$
$400 \div 50 = \underline{?}$
$4000 \div 50 = \underline{?}$
$40,000 \div 50 = \underline{?}$

6.
$30 \div 6 = \underline{?}$
$300 \div 60 = \underline{?}$
$3000 \div 60 = \underline{?}$
$30,000 \div 60 = \underline{?}$

Divide mentally.

7. $40 \div 20$ **8.** $20 \div 10$ **9.** $60 \div 20$ **10.** $70 \div 10$

11. $360 \div 90$ **12.** $420 \div 60$ **13.** $560 \div 80$ **14.** $250 \div 50$

15. $200 \div 40$ **16.** $300 \div 50$ **17.** $400 \div 80$ **18.** $100 \div 50$

19. $8000 \div 20$ **20.** $4000 \div 80$ **21.** $3000 \div 60$ **22.** $2000 \div 50$

23. $4500 \div 90$ **24.** $6400 \div 80$ **25.** $1200 \div 30$ **26.** $1800 \div 20$

27. $30\overline{)21{,}000}$ **28.** $40\overline{)80{,}000}$ **29.** $70\overline{)35{,}000}$ **30.** $90\overline{)81{,}000}$

31. $50\overline{)60{,}000}$ **32.** $60\overline{)54{,}000}$ **33.** $30\overline{)24{,}000}$ **34.** $40\overline{)36{,}000}$

Solve.

35. The dividend is 50.
The quotient is 5.
What is the divisor?

36. The quotient is 90.
The dividend is 3600.
What is the divisor?

37. The quotient is 400.
The dividend is 20,000.
What is the divisor?

38. The dividend is 56,000.
The quotient is 800.
What is the divisor?

39. The quotient is 70.
The divisor is 50.
What is the dividend?

40. The divisor is 90.
The quotient is 800.
What is the dividend?

41. How many zeros are in
the quotient when you
divide 500 by 10?

42. How many zeros are in
the quotient when you
divide 4800 by 60?

43. How many zeros are in
the quotient when you
divide 540 by 90?

44. How many zeros are in
the quotient when you
divide 40,000 by 8?

13-2 Divisors: Multiples of Ten

Forty students share 137 stickers equally. How many stickers does each student get? How many stickers are left over?

To find how many each gets, divide: $137 \div 40 = \underline{\ ?\ }$

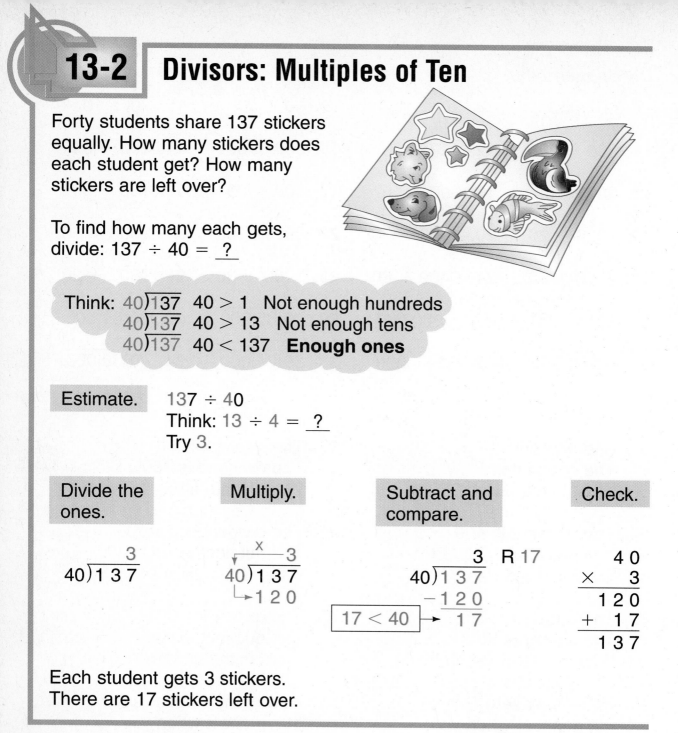

Think:
$40\overline{)137}$ $40 > 1$ Not enough hundreds
$40\overline{)137}$ $40 > 13$ Not enough tens
$40\overline{)137}$ $40 < 137$ **Enough ones**

Estimate.

$137 \div 40$
Think: $13 \div 4 = \underline{\ ?\ }$
Try 3.

Divide the ones.	Multiply.	Subtract and compare.	Check.
$\begin{array}{r} 3 \\ 40\overline{)137} \end{array}$	$\begin{array}{r} \times\ 3 \\ 40\overline{)137} \\ \rightarrow 120 \end{array}$	$\begin{array}{r} 3\ \text{R }17 \\ 40\overline{)137} \\ -120 \\ \hline 17 \end{array}$ $17 < 40$	$\begin{array}{r} 40 \\ \times\ \ 3 \\ \hline 120 \\ +\ \ 17 \\ \hline 137 \end{array}$

Each student gets 3 stickers.
There are 17 stickers left over.

Copy and complete.

1. $\begin{array}{r} 4\ \text{R }\underline{\ ?\ } \\ 20\overline{)85} \\ -?? \\ \hline ? \end{array}$

2. $\begin{array}{r} 5\ \text{R }\underline{\ ?\ } \\ 50\overline{)258} \\ -??? \\ \hline ? \end{array}$

3. $\begin{array}{r} ?\ \text{R }\underline{\ ?\ } \\ 20\overline{)166} \\ -??? \\ \hline ? \end{array}$

4. $\begin{array}{r} ?\ \text{R }35 \\ 80\overline{)675} \\ -??? \\ \hline ?? \end{array}$

Divide and check.

5. $40\overline{)66}$ **6.** $80\overline{)98}$ **7.** $20\overline{)78}$ **8.** $50\overline{)85}$ **9.** $30\overline{)77}$

10. $70\overline{)356}$ **11.** $90\overline{)548}$ **12.** $80\overline{)567}$ **13.** $40\overline{)283}$ **14.** $50\overline{)454}$

15. $20\overline{)175}$ **16.** $50\overline{)349}$ **17.** $30\overline{)199}$ **18.** $70\overline{)501}$ **19.** $90\overline{)317}$

20. $647 \div 80$ **21.** $485 \div 60$ **22.** $278 \div 90$ **23.** $256 \div 30$

24. $430 \div 70$ **25.** $312 \div 50$ **26.** $250 \div 40$ **27.** $197 \div 60$

28. $395 \div 90$ **29.** $244 \div 70$ **30.** $138 \div 20$ **31.** $256 \div 30$

32. $599 \div 80$ **33.** $384 \div 60$ **34.** $672 \div 90$ **35.** $358 \div 40$

Solve.

36. Mariah will give an equal number of pencils to each of 60 students. She has 122 pencils. At most, how many pencils can she give to each student? How many pencils will she have left?

37. Brendan is sorting 150 pieces of chalk into boxes. Each box holds 20 pieces of chalk. How many boxes can he fill? How many pieces of chalk will be in the box that is not full?

38. The media center ordered 495 booklets on different health topics. Each of 80 fourth-graders will read the same number of booklets. How many booklets will each fourth-grader read?

39. Dionne is helping Mr. Rau to stack 256 magazines. They put 30 magazines into each stack. How many stacks of 30 magazines are there? How many magazines are in the last stack?

40. Sixty students pledged to read a total of 268 books. What is the least number of books each student could read if each reads the same number of books?

13-3 Estimating Quotients

To estimate quotients with 2-digit divisors, think of nearby numbers that are compatible.

Estimate: 664 ÷ 24

664 ÷ 24

about 600   about 20

> When one number divides another evenly, the two numbers are **compatible**.

Think: 20)$\overline{600}$ with 30 on top

So 664 ÷ 24 is about 30.

Study these examples.

Estimate: 96 ÷ 31

Think: 30)$\overline{90}$ with 3 on top

So 96 ÷ 31 is about 3.

Estimate: $86.43 ÷ 38

Think: 40)$\overline{\$80.00}$ with $2.00 on top

So $86.43 ÷ 38 is about $2.00.

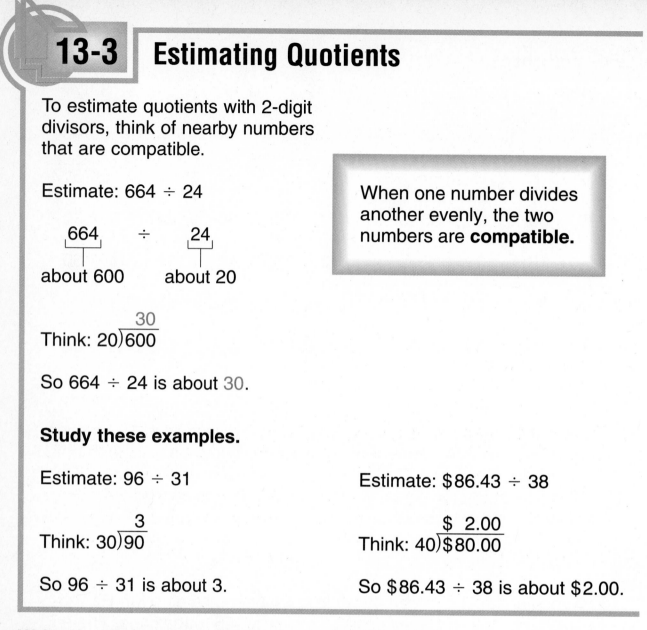

Write the divisor and dividend you would use to estimate the quotient.

1. 63 ÷ 21   **2.** 89 ÷ 32   **3.** 78 ÷ 19   **4.** 47 ÷ 22

5. 58 ÷ 33   **6.** 67 ÷ 11   **7.** 81 ÷ 44   **8.** 92 ÷ 36

9. 594 ÷ 26   **10.** 905 ÷ 38   **11.** 825 ÷ 18   **12.** 652 ÷ 21

13. 452 ÷ 17   **14.** 395 ÷ 24   **15.** 6475 ÷ 36   **16.** 7959 ÷ 43

Estimate the quotient.

17. 95 ÷ 35   **18.** 87 ÷ 43   **19.** 62 ÷ 12   **20.** 59 ÷ 28

21. 49 ÷ 25   **22.** 81 ÷ 21   **23.** 91 ÷ 29   **24.** 67 ÷ 22

25. 644 ÷ 24   **26.** 841 ÷ 19   **27.** 919 ÷ 29   **28.** 592 ÷ 31

29. 799 ÷ 46   **30.** 652 ÷ 38   **31.** 401 ÷ 22   **32.** 423 ÷ 16

33. 8743 ÷ 36   **34.** 7921 ÷ 45   **35.** 5932 ÷ 24   **36.** 6417 ÷ 38

37. $59.75 ÷ 27   **38.** $4.21 ÷ 19   **39.** $91.39 ÷ 34   **40.** $5.56 ÷ 17

Solve.

41. Last week 896 students came to the Folk Art Museum in buses. About the same number of students traveled on each of 28 buses. About how many students were there on each bus?

42. One class spent $75.05 for lunch in the museum cafeteria. There were 19 students in the class, and each student spent about the same amount. About how much money did each student spend for lunch at the museum?

Skills to Remember

Divide.

43. 7)58   **44.** 5)49   **45.** 3)36   **46.** 6)87

47. 3)745   **48.** 4)936   **49.** 8)277   **50.** 9)545

51. 2)$1.28   **52.** 7)$7.14   **53.** 9)$74.43   **54.** 6)$54.12

Two-Digit Dividends

Terry had 92 flower seeds. He planted 22 seeds in each of his flower boxes. How many flower boxes did Terry have? How many extra seeds were there?

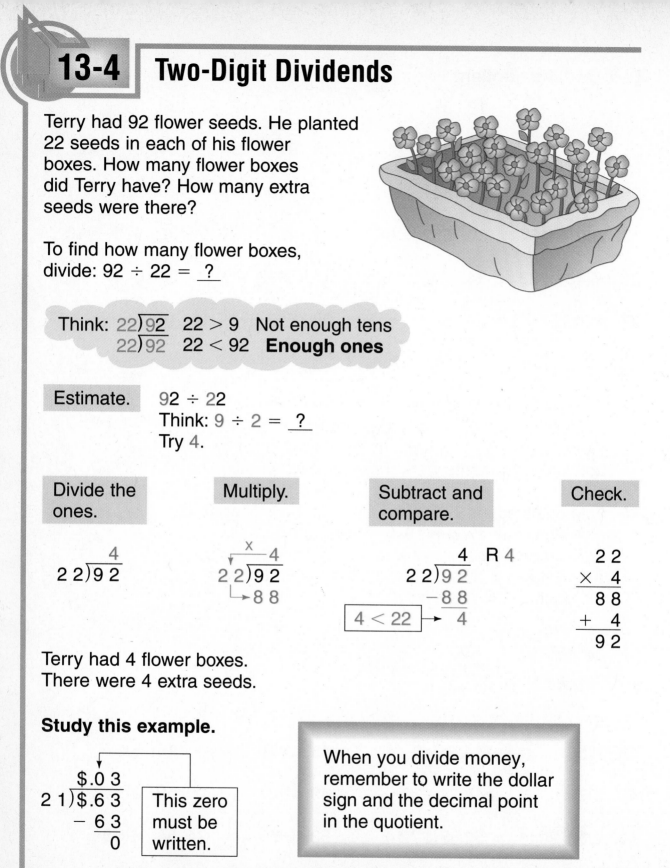

To find how many flower boxes, divide: 92 ÷ 22 = _?_

Think: 22)92   22 > 9   Not enough tens
       22)92   22 < 92   **Enough ones**

Estimate.   92 ÷ 22
            Think: 9 ÷ 2 = _?_
            Try 4.

Divide the ones.	Multiply.	Subtract and compare.	Check.

Divide the ones.

$$\begin{array}{r} 4 \\ 22\overline{)92} \end{array}$$

Multiply.

$$\begin{array}{r} \times\ 4 \\ 22\overline{)92} \\ 88 \end{array}$$

Subtract and compare.

$$\begin{array}{r} 4\ \text{R } 4 \\ 22\overline{)92} \\ -88 \\ \hline 4 \end{array}$$ 4 < 22

Check.

$$\begin{array}{r} 22 \\ \times\ 4 \\ \hline 88 \\ +\ 4 \\ \hline 92 \end{array}$$

Terry had 4 flower boxes.
There were 4 extra seeds.

Study this example.

$$\begin{array}{r} \$.03 \\ 21\overline{)\$.63} \\ -63 \\ \hline 0 \end{array}$$

This zero must be written.

When you divide money, remember to write the dollar sign and the decimal point in the quotient.

388

Copy and complete.

1. $\begin{array}{r} 2 \\ 24\overline{)48} \\ -48 \\ \hline ? \end{array}$

2. $\begin{array}{r} 3 \text{ R }\underline{\quad?\quad} \\ 25\overline{)96} \\ -?? \\ \hline 21 \end{array}$

3. $\begin{array}{r} 2 \text{ R }\underline{\quad?\quad} \\ 44\overline{)89} \\ -88 \\ \hline ? \end{array}$

4. $\begin{array}{r} ? \text{ R }\underline{\quad?\quad} \\ 21\overline{)94} \\ -84 \\ \hline ?? \end{array}$

Divide and check.

5. $31\overline{)62}$ 6. $23\overline{)46}$ 7. $42\overline{)84}$ 8. $33\overline{)99}$ 9. $22\overline{)88}$

10. $32\overline{)64}$ 11. $33\overline{)66}$ 12. $41\overline{)82}$ 13. $23\overline{)92}$ 14. $43\overline{)86}$

15. $22\overline{)45}$ 16. $42\overline{)88}$ 17. $31\overline{)96}$ 18. $22\overline{)73}$ 19. $34\overline{)69}$

20. $21\overline{)98}$ 21. $41\overline{)89}$ 22. $32\overline{)95}$ 23. $24\overline{)89}$ 24. $42\overline{)70}$

25. $51\overline{)65}$ 26. $22\overline{)98}$ 27. $42\overline{)99}$ 28. $21\overline{)96}$ 29. $31\overline{)78}$

30. $22\overline{)\$.66}$ 31. $45\overline{)\$.90}$ 32. $31\overline{)\$.93}$ 33. $26\overline{)\$.78}$ 34. $33\overline{)\$.66}$

Solve.

35. Chris set out 96 tomato plants in a vegetable garden. She placed 24 tomato plants in each row. How many rows of tomato plants were there?

36. Mike was putting 95 seed packets in a display. He wanted to put the same number of packets into each of 22 slots. How many packets could he have put into each slot? How many packets would he have had left over?

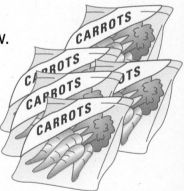

Challenge

Compare. Write <, =, or >.

37. $64 \div 32 \underline{\ ?\ } 72 \div 24$

38. $84 \div 21 \underline{\ ?\ } 96 \div 32$

39. $72 \div 36 \underline{\ ?\ } 96 \div 48$

40. $58 \div 29 \underline{\ ?\ } 90 \div 45$

13-5 Three-Digit Dividends

There are 158 people who want to take a boat ride on the lake. How many trips with 45 passengers can the tour boat make? How many passengers will be on the last trip?

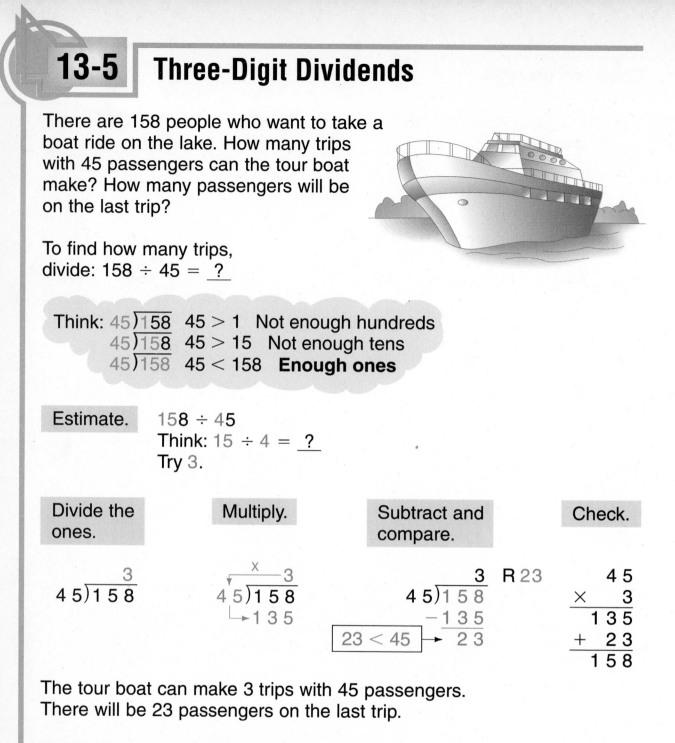

To find how many trips,
divide: 158 ÷ 45 = _?_

Think: $45\overline{)158}$ 45 > 1 Not enough hundreds
$45\overline{)158}$ 45 > 15 Not enough tens
$45\overline{)158}$ 45 < 158 **Enough ones**

Estimate. 158 ÷ 45
Think: 15 ÷ 4 = _?_
Try 3.

Divide the ones.	Multiply.	Subtract and compare.	Check.

$$\begin{array}{r} 3 \\ 45\overline{)158} \end{array}$$

$$\begin{array}{r} ^{\times}\quad 3 \\ 45\overline{)158} \\ \rightarrow 135 \end{array}$$

$$\begin{array}{r} 3 \ \text{R}\,23 \\ 45\overline{)158} \\ -135 \\ \hline \boxed{23 < 45} \rightarrow 23 \end{array}$$

$$\begin{array}{r} 45 \\ \times\quad 3 \\ \hline 135 \\ +\quad 23 \\ \hline 158 \end{array}$$

The tour boat can make 3 trips with 45 passengers.
There will be 23 passengers on the last trip.

Study these examples.

$$\begin{array}{r} 6 \\ 63\overline{)378} \\ -378 \\ \hline 0 \end{array}$$

$$\begin{array}{r} \$\,.05 \\ 72\overline{)\$3.60} \\ -360 \\ \hline 0 \end{array}$$

Copy and complete.

$$\begin{array}{r} 6 \\ 51\overline{)306} \\ -??? \\ \hline ? \end{array}$$ **1.**   **2.** $$\begin{array}{r} 9 \;\; R\;\underline{\;?\;} \\ 46\overline{)419} \\ -??? \\ \hline ? \end{array}$$ **3.** $$\begin{array}{r} 4 \;\; R\;\underline{\;?\;} \\ 83\overline{)392} \\ -??? \\ \hline ?? \end{array}$$ **4.** $$\begin{array}{r} ? \;\; R\;\underline{\;?\;} \\ 64\overline{)533} \\ -512 \\ \hline ?? \end{array}$$

Divide and check.

5. $22\overline{)176}$ **6.** $32\overline{)160}$ **7.** $43\overline{)258}$ **8.** $57\overline{)285}$ **9.** $74\overline{)222}$

10. $61\overline{)122}$ **11.** $95\overline{)380}$ **12.** $34\overline{)238}$ **13.** $62\overline{)248}$ **14.** $81\overline{)648}$

15. $42\overline{)146}$ **16.** $72\overline{)236}$ **17.** $51\overline{)489}$ **18.** $24\overline{)109}$ **19.** $91\overline{)476}$

20. $63\overline{)456}$ **21.** $54\overline{)237}$ **22.** $83\overline{)229}$ **23.** $75\overline{)474}$ **24.** $32\overline{)266}$

25. $67\overline{)\$1.34}$ **26.** $92\overline{)\$4.60}$ **27.** $71\overline{)\$6.39}$ **28.** $83\overline{)\$3.32}$ **29.** $44\overline{)\$3.08}$

Solve.

30. Each ticket seller sold 82 tickets to a total of 574 passengers. How many ticket sellers were there?

31. The tickets came in rolls of 150. The ticket sellers sold 35 rolls of tickets. How many tickets did they sell?

32. Each tour bus can carry 64 passengers. What is the least number of buses needed for 595 passengers?

Calculator Activity

Divide. Then use a calculator to check.

$$\begin{array}{r} 4 \;\; R\;19 \\ 41\overline{)183} \\ -164 \\ \hline 19 \end{array}$$

$$\boxed{4}\;\boxed{\times}\;\boxed{4}\;\boxed{1}\;\boxed{+}\;\boxed{1}\;\boxed{9}\;\boxed{=}\;\boxed{\quad 183.\quad}$$

33. $174 \div 42$ **34.** $218 \div 43$ **35.** $119 \div 23$

36. $213 \div 52$ **37.** $199 \div 62$ **38.** $326 \div 51$

13-6 | Trial Quotients

Sometimes the quotient you try is too large. When this happens, you need to change the estimate.

Divide: 172 ÷ 27 = ?

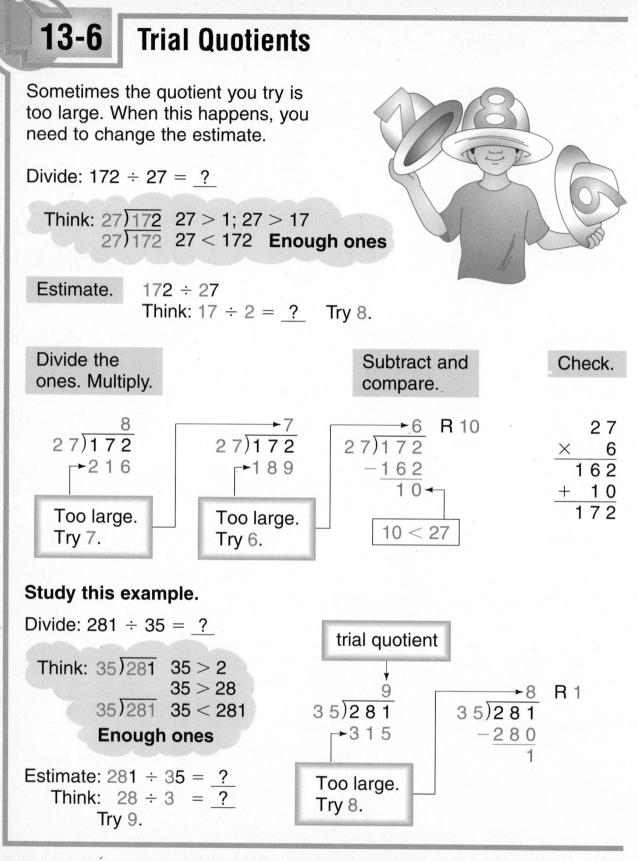

Think: 27)172 27 > 1; 27 > 17
27)172 27 < 172 **Enough ones**

Estimate. 172 ÷ 27
Think: 17 ÷ 2 = ? Try 8.

Divide the ones. Multiply.

```
        8
27)1 7 2
   →2 1 6
```
Too large.
Try 7.

```
        →7
27)1 7 2
   →1 8 9
```
Too large.
Try 6.

Subtract and compare.

```
       →6 R 10
27)1 7 2
  −1 6 2
     1 0←
```
10 < 27

Check.

```
      2 7
   ×    6
    1 6 2
  +   1 0
    1 7 2
```

Study this example.

Divide: 281 ÷ 35 = ?

Think: 35)281 35 > 2
35 > 28
35)281 35 < 281
Enough ones

Estimate: 281 ÷ 35 = ?
Think: 28 ÷ 3 = ?
Try 9.

trial quotient
↓
```
        9
35)2 8 1
  →3 1 5
```
Too large.
Try 8.

```
       →8 R 1
35)2 8 1
  −2 8 0
       1
```

Copy and complete.

1.
$$\begin{array}{r} 4 \\ 27\overline{)82} \\ 108 \end{array}$$
Try 3. →
$$\begin{array}{r} 3 \ \text{R} \ \underline{?} \\ 27\overline{)82} \\ -81 \\ \hline ? \end{array}$$

2.
$$\begin{array}{r} \$\ .07 \\ 48\overline{)\$2.88} \\ 3\ 36 \end{array}$$
Try $.06. →
$$\begin{array}{r} \$\ .06 \\ 48\overline{)\$2.88} \\ -?\ ?? \\ \hline ? \end{array}$$

3.
$$\begin{array}{r} 5 \\ 64\overline{)310} \\ ??? \end{array}$$
Try 4. →
$$\begin{array}{r} ? \ \text{R} \ \underline{?} \\ 64\overline{)310} \\ -??? \\ \hline 54 \end{array}$$

4.
$$\begin{array}{r} 8 \\ 86\overline{)657} \\ 688 \end{array}$$
Try ? . →
$$\begin{array}{r} ? \ \text{R} \ \underline{?} \\ 86\overline{)657} \\ -??? \\ \hline ?? \end{array}$$

Divide.

5. $27\overline{)52}$
6. $36\overline{)91}$
7. $45\overline{)82}$
8. $29\overline{)75}$
9. $35\overline{)68}$

10. $35\overline{)124}$
11. $48\overline{)165}$
12. $54\overline{)260}$
13. $79\overline{)221}$
14. $29\overline{)116}$

15. $66\overline{)542}$
16. $94\overline{)638}$
17. $87\overline{)569}$
18. $49\overline{)202}$
19. $58\overline{)346}$

20. $27\overline{)124}$
21. $39\overline{)277}$
22. $76\overline{)571}$
23. $99\overline{)828}$
24. $85\overline{)483}$

25. $28\overline{)\$.84}$
26. $59\overline{)\$3.54}$
27. $78\overline{)\$6.24}$
28. $69\overline{)\$5.52}$
29. $49\overline{)\$3.43}$

Solve.

30. Mr. Dean has signed up 180 students for a field trip to the zoo. Each bus will carry 36 students and 4 teachers. How many buses are needed for the field trip?

31. There are 115 monkeys at the zoo. There are at least 25 monkeys in each environment. How many environments are there at the zoo?

32. There are 325 animal spoons in the store. Each display holds 48 spoons. How many displays are there? How many extra animal spoons are there?

Greater Quotients

Divide: 995 ÷ 22 = _?_

Think: 22)995 22 > 9 Not enough hundreds
22)995 22 < 99 **Enough tens**

Estimate.   995 ÷ 22
Think: 9 ÷ 2 = _?_
Try 4.

Divide the tens.	Multiply.	Subtract and compare.	Bring down the ones.
4 22)995	×4 22)995 88	4 22)995 −88 11 11 < 22	4 22)995 −88 115 partial dividend

Repeat the steps.

Estimate.   115 ÷ 22
Think: 11 ÷ 2 = _?_
Try 5.

Divide the ones.	Multiply.	Subtract and compare.	Check.
45 22)995 −88 115	×45 22)995 −88 115 110	45 R5 22)995 −88 115 −110 5 5 < 22	45 × 22 90 900 990 + 5 995

Copy and complete.

$$
\begin{array}{r}
26 \\
1.\ 34\overline{)884} \\
-\ ?? \\
\hline
204 \\
-\ ??? \\
\hline
?
\end{array}
$$

$$
\begin{array}{r}
2?\quad R\ \underline{\ ?\ } \\
2.\ 42\overline{)890} \\
-\ ?? \\
\hline
50 \\
-\ ?? \\
\hline
?
\end{array}
$$

$$
\begin{array}{r}
?9 \\
3.\ 26\overline{)489} \\
-\ ?? \\
\hline
229 \\
\rightarrow 234
\end{array}
$$

$$
\boxed{\text{Try}\ \underline{\ ?\ }.}
$$

$$
\begin{array}{r}
??\quad R\ \underline{\ ?\ } \\
26\overline{)489} \\
-\ ?? \\
\hline
229 \\
-\ 208 \\
\hline
??
\end{array}
$$

Divide and check.

4. $40\overline{)840}$ 5. $70\overline{)920}$ 6. $60\overline{)954}$ 7. $30\overline{)629}$ 8. $50\overline{)850}$

9. $42\overline{)882}$ 10. $23\overline{)552}$ 11. $31\overline{)899}$ 12. $45\overline{)630}$ 13. $34\overline{)578}$

14. $35\overline{)721}$ 15. $45\overline{)678}$ 16. $59\overline{)620}$ 17. $51\overline{)801}$ 18. $21\overline{)892}$

19. $61\overline{)827}$ 20. $82\overline{)963}$ 21. $35\overline{)745}$ 22. $52\overline{)856}$ 23. $44\overline{)999}$

24. $938 \div 21$ 25. $875 \div 33$ 26. $882 \div 41$ 27. $676 \div 53$

28. $764 \div 65$ 29. $770 \div 42$ 30. $900 \div 64$ 31. $535 \div 25$

32. $\$7.04 \div 32$ 33. $\$5.52 \div 24$ 34. $\$6.82 \div 22$ 35. $\$9.02 \div 41$

Solve.

36. Carey picked 865 pears. He put 42 pears into each box. How many boxes did Carey fill? How many pears were left over?

37. Wendell sold one peach to each of 33 customers for a total of $8.25. What was the cost of each peach?

38. Jo picked 535 apples. She put the same number of apples into each of 24 baskets. What is the greatest number of apples Jo could have put into each basket? How many apples would be left over?

13-8 Teens as Divisors

You may have to change your estimate more than once when the divisor is a number from 11 through 19.

Divide: $926 \div 15 = \underline{?}$

Think: $15\overline{)926}$ $15 > 9$ Not enough hundreds
$15\overline{)926}$ $15 < 92$ **Enough tens**

Estimate. $926 \div 15 =$
Think: $9 \div 1 = \underline{?}$
Try 9.

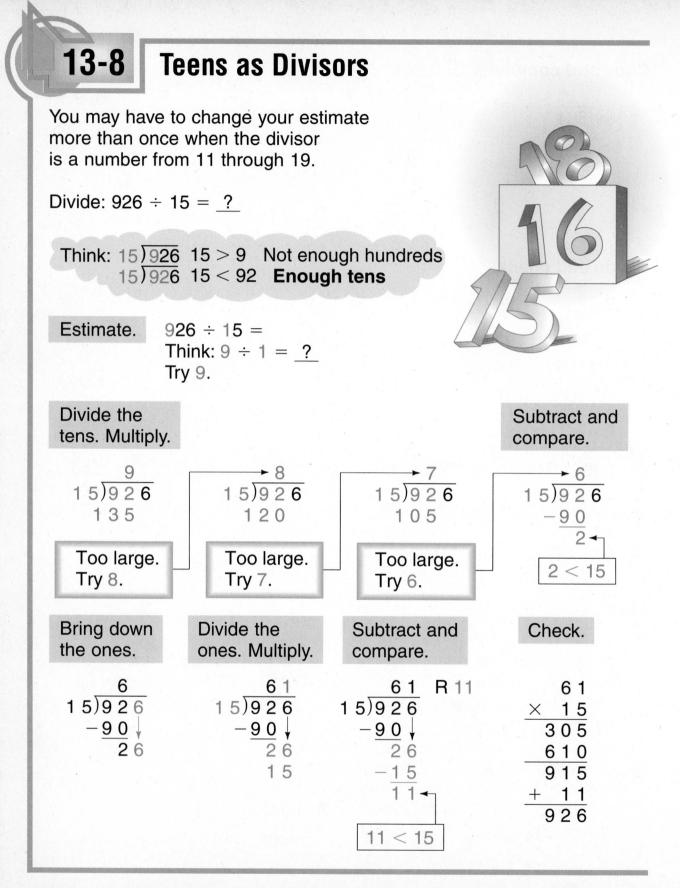

Divide the tens. Multiply.

$$\begin{array}{r} 9 \\ 15\overline{)926} \\ 135 \end{array}$$

Too large. Try 8.

$$\begin{array}{r} 8 \\ 15\overline{)926} \\ 120 \end{array}$$

Too large. Try 7.

$$\begin{array}{r} 7 \\ 15\overline{)926} \\ 105 \end{array}$$

Too large. Try 6.

Subtract and compare.

$$\begin{array}{r} 6 \\ 15\overline{)926} \\ -90 \\ \hline 2 \end{array}$$

$2 < 15$

Bring down the ones.

$$\begin{array}{r} 6 \\ 15\overline{)926} \\ -90\downarrow \\ \hline 26 \end{array}$$

Divide the ones. Multiply.

$$\begin{array}{r} 61 \\ 15\overline{)926} \\ -90\downarrow \\ \hline 26 \\ 15 \end{array}$$

Subtract and compare.

$$\begin{array}{r} 61 \ \text{R} 11 \\ 15\overline{)926} \\ -90\downarrow \\ \hline 26 \\ -15 \\ \hline 11 \end{array}$$

$11 < 15$

Check.

$$\begin{array}{r} 61 \\ \times\ 15 \\ \hline 305 \\ 610 \\ \hline 915 \\ +\ 11 \\ \hline 926 \end{array}$$

Copy and complete.

1.
$$\begin{array}{r} 8 \\ 12\overline{)96} \\ -?? \\ \hline ? \end{array}$$

2.
$$\begin{array}{r} 9 \text{ R } \underline{?} \\ 14\overline{)127} \\ -??? \\ \hline ? \end{array}$$

3.
$$\begin{array}{r} 2? \\ 17\overline{)357} \\ -?? \\ \hline ?? \\ -?? \\ \hline ? \end{array}$$

4.
$$\begin{array}{r} ?8 \text{ R } \underline{?} \\ 19\overline{)536} \\ -?? \\ \hline ??? \\ -??? \\ \hline ? \end{array}$$

Divide and check.

5. $15\overline{)95}$
6. $12\overline{)92}$
7. $18\overline{)79}$
8. $16\overline{)68}$
9. $11\overline{)74}$

10. $14\overline{)112}$
11. $16\overline{)128}$
12. $17\overline{)139}$
13. $14\overline{)127}$
14. $15\overline{)146}$

15. $13\overline{)641}$
16. $19\overline{)309}$
17. $14\overline{)456}$
18. $17\overline{)195}$
19. $12\overline{)252}$

20. $11\overline{)316}$
21. $18\overline{)723}$
22. $16\overline{)522}$
23. $15\overline{)187}$
24. $19\overline{)799}$

25. $17\overline{)435}$
26. $12\overline{)651}$
27. $18\overline{)563}$
28. $13\overline{)286}$
29. $16\overline{)344}$

30. $11\overline{)\$1.21}$
31. $15\overline{)\$1.80}$
32. $19\overline{)\$3.99}$
33. $14\overline{)\$4.90}$
34. $12\overline{)\$5.04}$

Solve.

35. The divisor is 13.
The quotient is 64.
The remainder is 10.
What is the dividend?

36. The quotient is 55.
The divisor is 17.
The remainder is 7.
What is the dividend?

37. The divisor is 16.
The quotient is 36.
What is the dividend?

38. The quotient is 42.
The divisor is 18.
What is the dividend?

39. The divisor is 11.
The dividend is 852.
How many digits will the
quotient contain?

40. The dividend is 747. The
divisor is 16. What is
the first digit of the
quotient? the second digit?

Four-Digit Dividends

Divide: 5481 ÷ 64 = _?_

Think: 64)5481 64 > 5   Not enough thousands
       64)5481 64 > 54   Not enough hundreds
       64)5481 64 < 548 **Enough tens**

Estimate.   5481 ÷ 64
            Think: 54 ÷ 6 = _?_
            Try 9.

Divide the tens. Multiply.	Subtract and compare.	Bring down the ones.

$$\begin{array}{r} 9 \\ 64\overline{)5481} \\ 576 \end{array}$$

Too large.
Try 8.

$$\begin{array}{r} 8 \\ 64\overline{)5481} \\ 512 \end{array}$$

$$\begin{array}{r} 8 \\ 64\overline{)5481} \\ -512 \\ \hline 36 \end{array}$$

36 < 64

$$\begin{array}{r} 8 \\ 64\overline{)5481} \\ -512\downarrow \\ \hline 361 \end{array}$$

Repeat the steps.

Divide the ones. Multiply.	Subtract and compare.	Check.

$$\begin{array}{r} 86 \\ 64\overline{)5481} \\ -512\downarrow \\ \hline 361 \\ 384 \end{array}$$

Too large.
Try 5.

$$\begin{array}{r} 85 \\ 64\overline{)5481} \\ -512\downarrow \\ \hline 361 \\ 320 \end{array}$$

$$\begin{array}{r} 85 \quad \text{R }41 \\ 64\overline{)5481} \\ -512 \\ \hline 361 \\ -320 \\ \hline 41 \end{array}$$

41 < 64

$$\begin{array}{r} 85 \\ \times \quad 64 \\ \hline 340 \\ 5100 \\ \hline 5440 \\ +\quad 41 \\ \hline 5481 \end{array}$$

Copy and complete.

$$\begin{array}{r} 24 \text{ R } \underline{?} \\ \textbf{1. } 51\overline{)1273} \\ -102 \\ \hline 253 \\ -??? \\ \hline ? \end{array}$$

$$\begin{array}{r} 46 \text{ R } \underline{?} \\ \textbf{2. } 24\overline{)1107} \\ -96 \\ \hline 147 \\ -??? \\ \hline ? \end{array}$$

$$\begin{array}{r} ?? \text{ R } \underline{?} \\ \textbf{3. } 33\overline{)2179} \\ -198 \\ \hline 199 \\ -??? \\ \hline ? \end{array}$$

Divide and check.

4. $40\overline{)2459}$ **5.** $80\overline{)5346}$ **6.** $70\overline{)6842}$ **7.** $50\overline{)4779}$

8. $34\overline{)1180}$ **9.** $52\overline{)3115}$ **10.** $44\overline{)2106}$ **11.** $63\overline{)4914}$

12. $72\overline{)4594}$ **13.** $96\overline{)7128}$ **14.** $22\overline{)1550}$ **15.** $84\overline{)5285}$

16. $64\overline{)5084}$ **17.** $48\overline{)4128}$ **18.** $38\overline{)2242}$ **19.** $55\overline{)3226}$

20. $22\overline{)1810}$ **21.** $73\overline{)5808}$ **22.** $14\overline{)1248}$ **23.** $18\overline{)1200}$

24. $92\overline{)\$21.16}$ **25.** $51\overline{)\$16.83}$ **26.** $88\overline{)\$22.00}$ **27.** $67\overline{)\$56.95}$

Solve.

28. Each of 45 students bought a copy of *The Great Dinosaurs.* They paid a total of $42.75. How much did one copy of *The Great Dinosaurs* cost?

29. There are 1565 books at the Elmford book fair. If each table can hold 55 books, what is the least number of tables needed for the fair?

30. Each home room in Elmford Middle School can seat 36 students. There are 1256 students in the school. How many home rooms are needed for all the students?

31. Students bought 32 copies of *Amazing Science.* Each copy cost $2.98. What was the total amount the students spent to buy *Amazing Science?*

13-10 Zero in the Quotient

Divide: 2865 ÷ 14 = __?__

Think: $14\overline{)2865}$ 14 > 2   Not enough thousands
$14\overline{)2865}$ 14 < 28   **Enough hundreds**

Estimate.   2865 ÷ 14
Think: 2 ÷ 1 = __?__
Try 2.

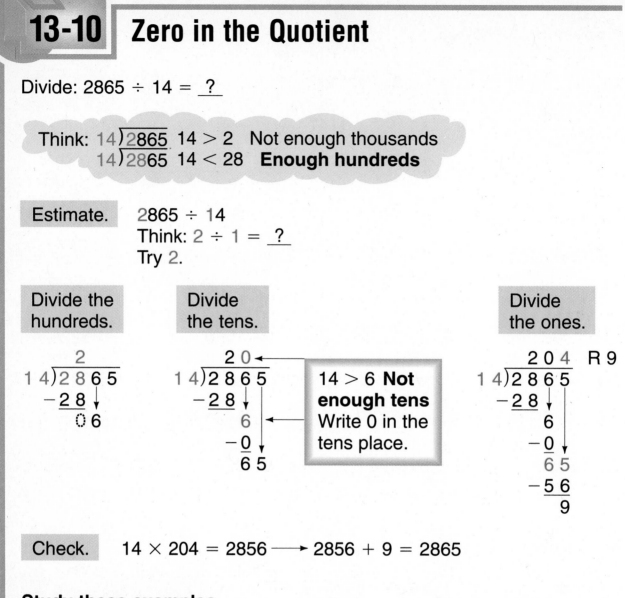

Divide the hundreds.

$$\begin{array}{r} 2 \\ 14\overline{)2865} \\ -28\downarrow \\ \hline 06 \end{array}$$

Divide the tens.

$$\begin{array}{r} 20 \\ 14\overline{)2865} \\ -28\downarrow \\ \hline 6 \\ -0\downarrow \\ \hline 65 \end{array}$$

14 > 6 **Not enough tens**
Write 0 in the tens place.

Divide the ones.

$$\begin{array}{r} 204 \quad R\,9 \\ 14\overline{)2865} \\ -28\downarrow \\ \hline 6 \\ -0\downarrow \\ \hline 65 \\ -56 \\ \hline 9 \end{array}$$

Check.   14 × 204 = 2856 ⟶ 2856 + 9 = 2865

Study these examples.

$$\begin{array}{r} 300 \quad R\,5 \\ 21\overline{)6305} \\ -63\downarrow \\ \hline 0 \\ -0\downarrow \\ \hline 5 \\ -0 \\ \hline 5 \end{array}$$

$$\begin{array}{r} \$3.06 \\ 26\overline{)\$79.56} \\ -78\downarrow \\ \hline 15 \\ -0\downarrow \\ \hline 156 \\ -156 \\ \hline 0 \end{array}$$

Copy and complete.

$$
\begin{array}{r}
60 \\
35\overline{)2100} \\
-210 \\
\hline ?
\end{array}
$$
1.

$$
\begin{array}{r}
102 \\
57\overline{)5814} \\
-57 \\
\hline 11 \\
-\ ? \\
\hline 1?4 \\
-??? \\
\hline
\end{array}
$$
2.

$$
\begin{array}{r}
\$\ 2.0? \\
18\overline{)\$36.90} \\
-36 \\
\hline 9 \\
-\ ? \\
\hline ?0 \\
-?? \\
\hline
\end{array}
$$
3.

$$
\begin{array}{r}
3??\ \ R\ \underline{\ ?} \\
24\overline{)7231} \\
-72 \\
\hline 3 \\
-\ ? \\
\hline ?1 \\
-?? \\
\hline ?
\end{array}
$$
4.

Divide and check.

5. $45\overline{)3600}$ **6.** $32\overline{)1600}$ **7.** $24\overline{)2166}$ **8.** $56\overline{)3930}$

9. $17\overline{)6800}$ **10.** $25\overline{)5000}$ **11.** $41\overline{)8214}$ **12.** $33\overline{)9927}$

13. $21\overline{)2247}$ **14.** $19\overline{)5852}$ **15.** $32\overline{)9856}$ **16.** $46\overline{)9246}$

17. $15\overline{)9097}$ **18.** $51\overline{)5576}$ **19.** $28\overline{)8538}$ **20.** $34\overline{)7068}$

21. $43\overline{)8735}$ **22.** $13\overline{)9175}$ **23.** $62\overline{)6736}$ **24.** $74\overline{)7904}$

25. $18\overline{)\$37.44}$ **26.** $23\overline{)\$70.61}$ **27.** $85\overline{)\$92.65}$ **28.** $56\overline{)\$60.48}$

Solve.

29. Damon bought a 12-yard length of cloth for $48.72. What was the cost per yard?

Challenge

Find the quotient and any remainder.

30. $22\overline{)22,154}$ **31.** $32\overline{)64,128}$ **32.** $17\overline{)61,085}$

33. $42\overline{)84,378}$ **34.** $51\overline{)51,408}$ **35.** $24\overline{)96,088}$

TECHNOLOGY

Calculating with Fractions

You can use a fraction calculator
to express an improper fraction
as a mixed number in simplest form.

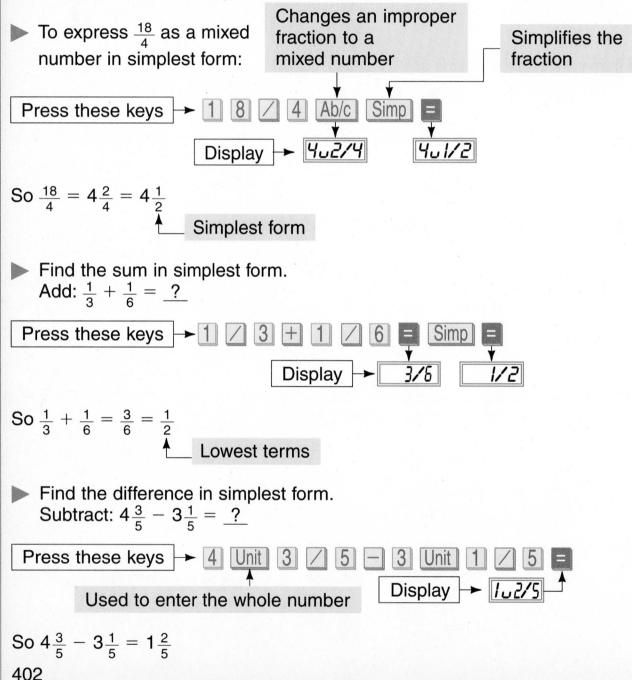

▶ To express $\frac{18}{4}$ as a mixed
number in simplest form:

Changes an improper fraction to a mixed number

Simplifies the fraction

Press these keys ➔ 1 8 ⁄ 4 Ab/c Simp =

Display ➔ 4⌐2/4   4⌐1/2

So $\frac{18}{4} = 4\frac{2}{4} = 4\frac{1}{2}$

Simplest form

▶ Find the sum in simplest form.
Add: $\frac{1}{3} + \frac{1}{6} = \underline{}$

Press these keys ➔ 1 ⁄ 3 + 1 ⁄ 6 = Simp =

Display ➔ 3/6   1/2

So $\frac{1}{3} + \frac{1}{6} = \frac{3}{6} = \frac{1}{2}$

Lowest terms

▶ Find the difference in simplest form.
Subtract: $4\frac{3}{5} - 3\frac{1}{5} = \underline{}$

Press these keys ➔ 4 Unit 3 ⁄ 5 − 3 Unit 1 ⁄ 5 =

Used to enter the whole number

Display ➔ 1⌐2/5

So $4\frac{3}{5} - 3\frac{1}{5} = 1\frac{2}{5}$

402

Write as a mixed number in simplest form. Use a calculator.

1. $\frac{37}{3}$　　2. $\frac{99}{7}$　　3. $\frac{82}{6}$　　4. $\frac{46}{4}$　　5. $\frac{57}{8}$　　6. $\frac{71}{3}$

7. $\frac{51}{9}$　　8. $\frac{28}{6}$　　9. $\frac{56}{18}$　　10. $\frac{33}{9}$　　11. $\frac{99}{27}$　　12. $\frac{20}{12}$

Use the $\boxed{\text{Simp}}$ **key to tell if the fractions are equivalent. Write** *Yes* **or** *No*.

13. $\frac{6}{8}, \frac{3}{4}$　　　14. $\frac{9}{12}, \frac{3}{4}$　　　15. $\frac{18}{30}, \frac{6}{15}$　　　16. $\frac{32}{64}, \frac{4}{6}$

17. $\frac{3}{8}, \frac{27}{72}$　　　18. $\frac{16}{28}, \frac{2}{3}$　　　19. $\frac{3}{8}, \frac{45}{120}$　　　20. $\frac{12}{15}, \frac{144}{180}$

Add or subtract. Write your answer in simplest form.

21. $\frac{4}{7}$ $+\frac{2}{7}$　　22. $\frac{5}{9}$ $+\frac{3}{9}$　　23. $\frac{7}{10}$ $-\frac{2}{10}$　　24. $\frac{9}{12}$ $-\frac{3}{12}$　　25. $\frac{1}{4}$ $+\frac{3}{8}$

26. $\frac{7}{10}$ $-\frac{1}{2}$　　27. $1\frac{1}{4}$ $+4\frac{1}{4}$　　28. $9\frac{7}{12}$ $-5\frac{1}{12}$　　29. $28\frac{3}{8}$ $+52\frac{3}{8}$　　30. $41\frac{1}{3}$ $-9\frac{1}{3}$

Use a calculator.

$\frac{3}{4}$ of 32 = ___?___

$\boxed{\text{Press these keys}}$ ➡ $\boxed{3}$ $\boxed{2}$ $\boxed{\div}$ $\boxed{4}$ $\boxed{=}$ $\boxed{\times}$ $\boxed{3}$ $\boxed{=}$

$\boxed{\text{Display}}$ ➡ $\boxed{24}$

So $\frac{3}{4}$ of 32 = 24

31. $\frac{1}{8}$ of 72　　　32. $\frac{2}{5}$ of 25　　　33. $\frac{3}{7}$ of 49　　　34. $\frac{4}{6}$ of 54

13-12 | Problem Solving: Hidden Information

Problem: Andre needs 14 ft of rope to make a plant hanger. He buys a spool that has 175 in. of rope. Does he have enough rope?

1 IMAGINE Put yourself in the problem.

2 NAME *Facts:* Andre needs 14 ft of rope. The spool has 175 in.

Question: Does he have enough rope?

3 THINK To solve the problem, you need information that is not stated.

Remember: 12 in. = 1 ft

To find whether he has enough rope:
First divide. 175 in. ÷ 12 in. = _?_ ft
Then compare. 14 ft _?_ _?_ ft

4 COMPUTE

```
      1 4   R 7
1 2)1 7 5
    -1 2
      5 5
    -4 8
       7
```

Think: 14 R 7 means 14 ft 7 in.

Compare. 14 ft < 14 ft 7 in.
Yes, Andre has enough rope.

5 CHECK Multiply and add to check division.

```
      14          168
    × 12         +  7
      28          175
    14
    168
```

The answer checks.

Solve.

1. Winnie made 136 yogurt sundaes. How many quarts of yogurt were used for these pint-sized sundaes?

IMAGINE   Create a mental picture.

NAME   *Facts:*   136 yogurt sundaes
1 pint for each sundae

Question: How many quarts of yogurt were used?

THINK   Is there hidden information in the problem?   Yes.

> Remember: 2 pints = 1 quart

Since there were 136 sundaes, 136 pints of yogurt were used.
To find out how many quarts were used, divide: 136 ÷ 2 = ?

COMPUTE ──→ CHECK

2. A nature video is 148 minutes long. Can Saundra watch the video in $2\frac{1}{2}$ hours?

3. Paulo earns the same amount every week for delivering newspapers. He earns $1196 a year. How much does he earn each week?

4. In one full day a satellite transmits 9600 messages. About how many messages can it transmit in 1 hour?

5. Byron deposits $30 in quarters in the bank. How many coins does he turn in at the bank?

Solve.

Use these steps:

Imagine

Name

Think

Compute

Check

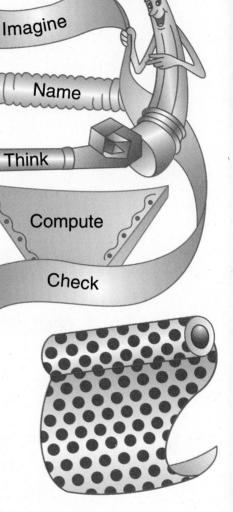

1. A store displays 252 different wrapping papers on 14 racks. How many papers fit equally on each rack?

2. There are 180 green stripes on a 20-inch sheet of wrapping paper. How many stripes are there per inch?

3. Wrap It Up shop sells 10 ft of ribbon for $1.60. How much does 1 ft of ribbon cost?

4. A pack of 24 party invitations costs $1.98. About how much does each invitation cost?

5. Wrap It Up decorates its window with 18-in. strips of ribbon. They cut as many as could be cut from a 100 in. roll. How much ribbon is left over?

6. Crepe paper streamers are sold in 28-ft rolls. To decorate the gym for a party, 150 ft of crepe paper are needed. How many rolls should be bought?

7. The store sells ready-made bows in packs of 15. Each pack costs $4.20. How much does each bow cost?

8. There are 2892 purple dots on a 12-ft roll of wrapping paper. About how many dots are on 1 ft of paper?

9. A complete party package costs $75.90. If 22 friends share the cost, how much will each friend spend?

Solve.

USE THESE STRATEGIES:
Make a Table
Choose the Operation
Hidden Information
Find a Pattern
Use a Graph
Interpret the Remainder

10. Birthday candles are sold in packs of 12. How many packs should you buy to put 35 candles on a cake?

11. One wrapping paper shows cats and dogs in 8 rows. The first 5 rows follow this pattern: 2 cats, 4 dogs, 3 cats, 5 dogs, 4 cats. How does the pattern look in the last 3 rows?

12. A 48-in. sheet of the safari pattern shows 20 lions. About how many lions would show on a 1-ft sheet of safari paper?

13. The store window is filled with 350 balloons. They came in packs of 24. How many packs were needed?

14. Helium balloons are $11.28 a dozen. How much is one helium balloon?

15. On Mondays the store deducts 10¢ from every dollar spent. Ted spent $14 on Friday. How much would he have saved if he had shopped on Monday?

16. Allie spent $16.28 at Wrap It Up. Julia spent 4 times that amount. How much money did Julia spend?

Use the graph for problems 17 and 18.

17. Of which patterns did the store sell more than 20 but fewer than 40 packs?

18. Of which pattern did the store sell about 15 fewer packs than teddy bears?

Wrapping Paper Sales

Patterns of Paper: Teddy Bears, Stars, Horses, Flowers, Dinosaurs

Number of Packs: 0, 10, 20, 30, 40

More Practice

Divide and check.

1. $20\overline{)66}$ **2.** $30\overline{)75}$ **3.** $70\overline{)351}$ **4.** $50\overline{)299}$ **5.** $90\overline{)319}$

6. $395 \div 70$ **7.** $312 \div 70$ **8.** $139 \div 20$ **9.** $256 \div 20$

Estimate the quotient.

10. $48 \div 20$ **11.** $82 \div 39$ **12.** $99 \div 47$ **13.** $497 \div 19$

14. $4011 \div 38$ **15.** $\$69.03 \div 9$ **16.** $7482 \div 47$ **17.** $\$5.79 \div 19$

Divide and check.

18. $22\overline{)66}$ **19.** $45\overline{)90}$ **20.** $31\overline{)\$.93}$ **21.** $13\overline{)\$.65}$ **22.** $17\overline{)85}$

23. $56\overline{)280}$ **24.** $37\overline{)222}$ **25.** $76\overline{)342}$ **26.** $42\overline{)\$3.36}$ **27.** $75\overline{)\$97.75}$

28. $17\overline{)435}$ **29.** $14\overline{)456}$ **30.** $13\overline{)286}$ **31.** $15\overline{)\$1.80}$ **32.** $12\overline{)\$5.04}$

33. $34\overline{)1180}$ **34.** $96\overline{)7128}$ **35.** $14\overline{)1248}$ **36.** $67\overline{)5690}$ **37.** $73\overline{)5808}$

38. $17\overline{)6800}$ **39.** $19\overline{)5852}$ **40.** $13\overline{)9175}$ **41.** $28\overline{)8536}$ **42.** $74\overline{)7904}$

Solve.

43. There are 257 sheets of lined paper for 24 students to share equally. How many sheets of paper does each student get? How many sheets are left over?

44. The rental of a school bus for a field trip is $56.00. Thirty-two students are going on the trip. How much money does each student have to pay?

45. The dividend is 80. The quotient is 4. What is the divisor?

46. The quotient is 8. The divisor is 31. What is the dividend?

(See *Still More Practice*, p. 471.)

LOGIC

You have to read carefully to be sure you do not draw a false conclusion from true statements.

Read these statements and conclusions. All the statements are true.

statements: All dogs have ears.
Sparky is a dog.

conclusion: Sparky has ears.   TRUE

statements: All dogs have ears.
My cat has ears.

conclusion: My cat is a dog.   FALSE

Read the true statements carefully. Then write
true or *false* **for each conclusion.**

1. All ducks have feathers.
   A chicken has feathers.
   A chicken is a duck.

2. All fish can swim.
   A salmon is a fish.
   A salmon can swim.

3. Ralph is a 4th grade boy.
   All the 4th grade boys
   wore sneakers on Monday.
   Ralph wore sneakers
   on Monday.

4. All the 4th grade boys wore
   sneakers on Monday.
   Maria wore sneakers
   on Monday.
   Maria is a 4th grade boy.

5. All triangles are polygons.
   A pentagon is a polygon.
   A pentagon is a triangle.

6. All squares are parallelograms.
   All rectangles are parallelograms.
   All rectangles are squares.

7. Triangle *A* has one right
   angle. All right triangles
   have one right angle.
   Triangle *A* is a right triangle.

Check Your Mastery

Divide and check. See pp. 382–385

1. $200 \div 20$ **2.** $6400 \div 80$ **3.** $395 \div 90$ **4.** $250 \div 40$

5. $90\overline{)548}$ **6.** $30\overline{)199}$ **7.** $50\overline{)312}$ **8.** $60\overline{)485}$ **9.** $20\overline{)138}$

Estimate the quotient. See pp. 386–387

10. $58 \div 33$ **11.** $825 \div 18$ **12.** $395 \div 24$ **13.** $7959 \div 43$

14. $29\overline{)919}$ **15.** $45\overline{)7921}$ **16.** $27\overline{)5975}$ **17.** $19\overline{)841}$ **18.** $38\overline{)6417}$

Divide and check. See pp. 388–401

19. $33\overline{)66}$ **20.** $31\overline{)96}$ **21.** $24\overline{)89}$ **22.** $41\overline{)\$.82}$ **23.** $23\overline{)\$.92}$

24. $42\overline{)146}$ **25.** $34\overline{)\$2.38}$ **26.** $83\overline{)\$2.49}$ **27.** $24\overline{)109}$ **28.** $54\overline{)237}$

29. $66\overline{)542}$ **30.** $76\overline{)\$5.32}$ **31.** $49\overline{)202}$ **32.** $31\overline{)\$1.24}$ **33.** $99\overline{)828}$

34. $45\overline{)678}$ **35.** $35\overline{)745}$ **36.** $42\overline{)770}$ **37.** $25\overline{)\$9.00}$ **38.** $41\overline{)882}$

39. $18\overline{)723}$ **40.** $15\overline{)\$1.80}$ **41.** $15\overline{)187}$ **42.** $88\overline{)2200}$ **43.** $73\overline{)\$58.40}$

Solve. See pp. 406–407

44. There are 2242 students at P.S. 124. If they are divided equally in 59 classrooms, how many students are there in each classroom?

45. The parents' organization bought lunch for the 32 students in Mr. Perez's class. All the lunches cost $95.36. What was the cost of each lunch?

46. A bus seats 52 passengers. How many buses are needed to carry 795 passengers from the hotel to the state fair?

14 Decimals: Addition and Subtraction

In this chapter you will:

Read and write decimals to hundredths

Understand decimal place value

Add or subtract decimals

Compare, order and round decimals

Estimate decimal sums and differences

Divide money

Solve multi-step problems

Do you remember?

$$\frac{2}{10} = \frac{2 \times 10}{10 \times 10} = \frac{20}{100}$$

Critical Thinking/ Finding Together

Some hummingbirds weigh about six hundredths of an ounce. Would two adult hummingbirds and two of their babies weigh more or less than twelve hundredths of an ounce?

14-1 Tenths and Hundredths

▶ You can write tenths as a fraction or as a **decimal**.

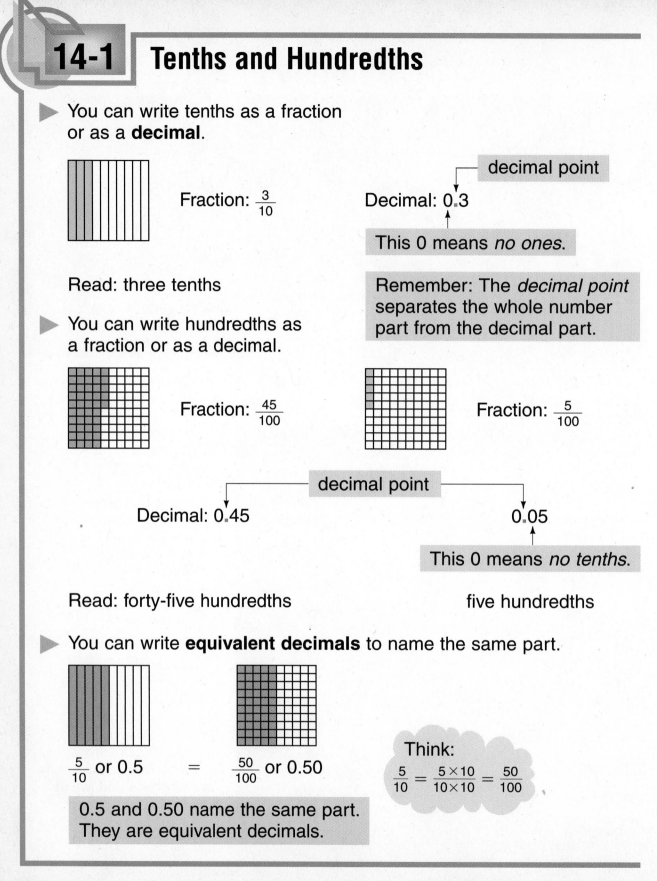

Fraction: $\frac{3}{10}$

decimal point

Decimal: 0.3

This 0 means *no ones*.

Read: three tenths

▶ You can write hundredths as a fraction or as a decimal.

Fraction: $\frac{45}{100}$

Remember: The *decimal point* separates the whole number part from the decimal part.

Fraction: $\frac{5}{100}$

decimal point

Decimal: 0.45

0.05

This 0 means *no tenths*.

Read: forty-five hundredths

five hundredths

▶ You can write **equivalent decimals** to name the same part.

$\frac{5}{10}$ or 0.5   = $\frac{50}{100}$ or 0.50

Think:
$\frac{5}{10} = \frac{5 \times 10}{10 \times 10} = \frac{50}{100}$

0.5 and 0.50 name the same part. They are equivalent decimals.

Write as a fraction. Then write as a decimal.

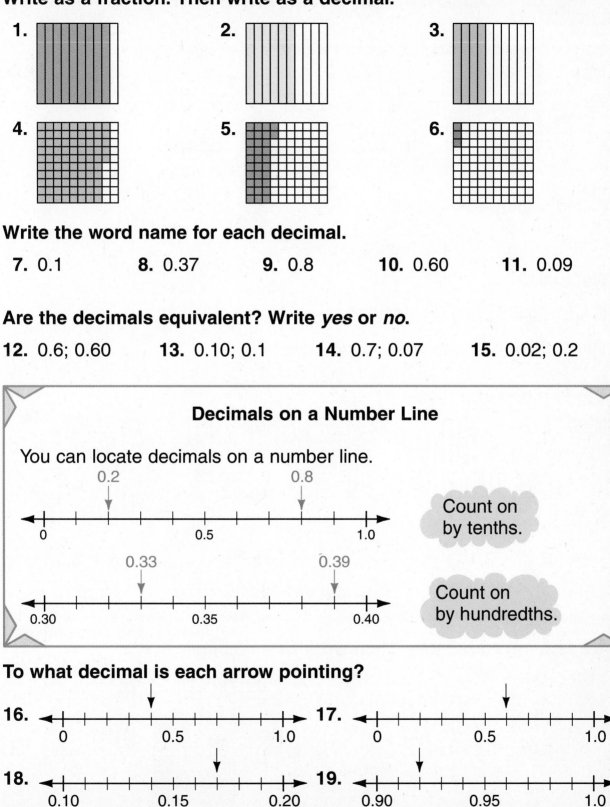

1.
2.
3.
4.
5.
6.

Write the word name for each decimal.

7. 0.1   **8.** 0.37   **9.** 0.8   **10.** 0.60   **11.** 0.09

Are the decimals equivalent? Write *yes* or *no*.

12. 0.6; 0.60   **13.** 0.10; 0.1   **14.** 0.7; 0.07   **15.** 0.02; 0.2

Decimals on a Number Line

You can locate decimals on a number line.

0.2   0.8

0   0.5   1.0

Count on by tenths.

0.33   0.39

0.30   0.35   0.40

Count on by hundredths.

To what decimal is each arrow pointing?

16.
0   0.5   1.0

17.
0   0.5   1.0

18.
0.10   0.15   0.20

19.
0.90   0.95   1.0

413

14-2   Decimals Greater Than One

You can write a mixed number or a whole number as a decimal.

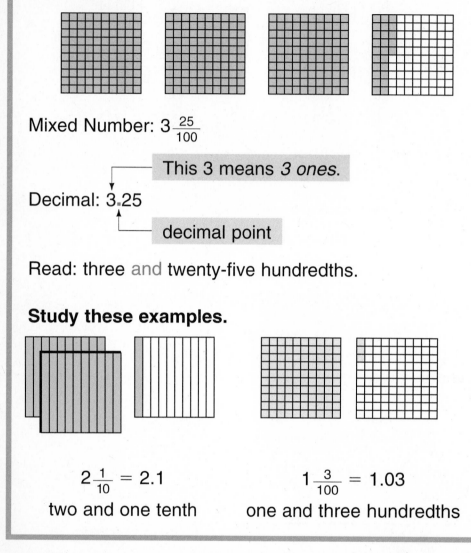

Mixed Number: $3\frac{25}{100}$

This 3 means *3 ones*.

Decimal: 3.25

decimal point

Read: three and twenty-five hundredths.

Study these examples.

$2\frac{1}{10} = 2.1$

two and one tenth

$1\frac{3}{100} = 1.03$

one and three hundredths

$3 = 3.0$

three

Write as a mixed number. Then write as a decimal.

1.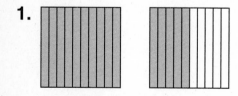

2.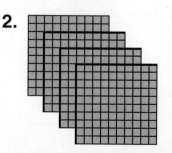

Write each as a decimal.

3. $5\frac{3}{10}$ **4.** $8\frac{7}{10}$ **5.** $4\frac{2}{10}$ **6.** $7\frac{5}{10}$

7. $9\frac{21}{100}$ **8.** 10 **9.** $3\frac{6}{100}$ **10.** $2\frac{1}{100}$

11. $24\frac{6}{10}$ **12.** $97\frac{17}{100}$ **13.** 50 **14.** $100\frac{9}{100}$

15. three and eight tenths **16.** nine and nineteen hundredths

17. twelve and one hundredth **18.** one hundred fifty-seven

Write the word name for each decimal.

19. 6.4 **20.** 4.30 **21.** 8.08 **22.** 5.00 **23.** 60.02

To what decimal is each arrow pointing?

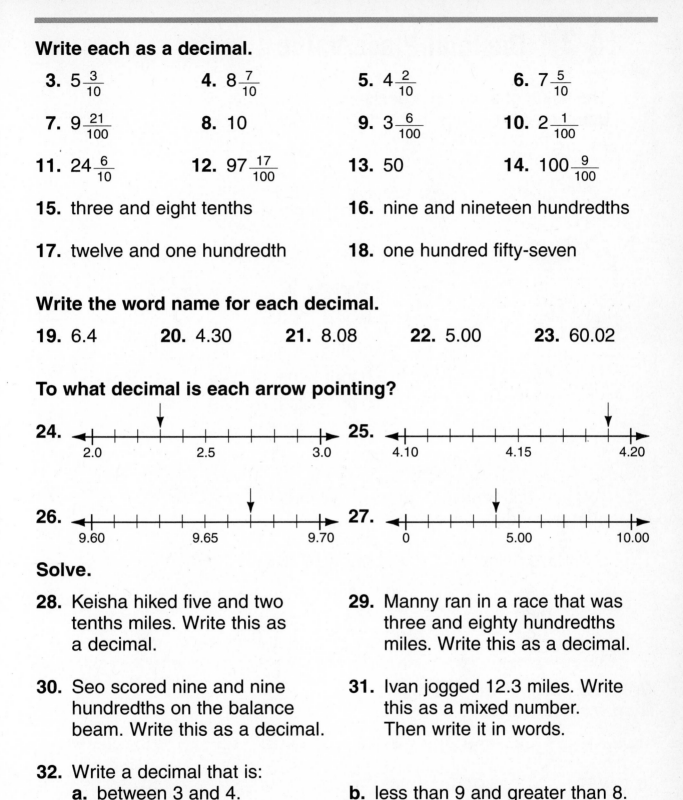

24.
2.0 2.5 3.0

25.
4.10 4.15 4.20

26.
9.60 9.65 9.70

27.
0 5.00 10.00

Solve.

28. Keisha hiked five and two tenths miles. Write this as a decimal.

29. Manny ran in a race that was three and eighty hundredths miles. Write this as a decimal.

30. Seo scored nine and nine hundredths on the balance beam. Write this as a decimal.

31. Ivan jogged 12.3 miles. Write this as a mixed number. Then write it in words.

32. Write a decimal that is:
a. between 3 and 4.
b. less than 9 and greater than 8.
c. between 11 and 12.
d. greater than 1 and less than 2.

Decimal Place Value

▶ The value of a digit in a decimal depends on its place in the decimal.

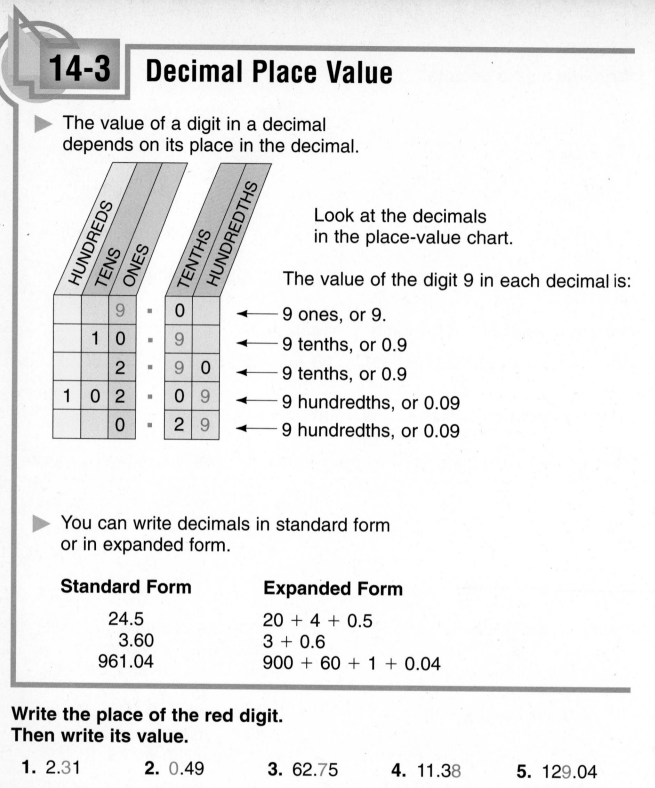

Look at the decimals in the place-value chart.

The value of the digit 9 in each decimal is:

◀—— 9 ones, or 9.

◀—— 9 tenths, or 0.9

◀—— 9 tenths, or 0.9

◀—— 9 hundredths, or 0.09

◀—— 9 hundredths, or 0.09

▶ You can write decimals in standard form or in expanded form.

Standard Form	Expanded Form
24.5	20 + 4 + 0.5
3.60	3 + 0.6
961.04	900 + 60 + 1 + 0.04

Write the place of the red digit.
Then write its value.

1. 2.31
2. 0.49
3. 62.75
4. 11.38
5. 129.04

6. 21.59
7. 5.04
8. 30.03
9. 25.15
10. 53.96

11. 4.10
12. 8.56
13. 509.88
14. 9.14
15. 18.03

Write in expanded form.

16. 0.23 **17.** 4.07 **18.** 9.94 **19.** 1.8 **20.** 205.6

21. 91.05 **22.** 30.8 **23.** 84.73 **24.** 670.01 **25.** 700.60

Write in standard form. Then write each word name.

26. 40 + 2 + 0.9 + 0.07 **27.** 500 + 70 + 5 + 0.2 + 0.06

28. 6 + 0.9 + 0.01 **29.** 8 + 0.2

30. 0.4 + 0.06 **31.** 0.1 + 0.01

32. 800 + 5 + 0.03 **33.** 300 + 20 + 0.8

34. 100 + 0.5 + 0.07 **35.** 50 + 0.3 + 0.04

Write in words.

36. 200 + 30 + 0.6 **37.** 50 + 7 + 0.01

38. 90 + 0.1 + 0.2 **39.** 400 + 9 + 0.09

Challenge

The third place to the right of the decimal point is the **thousandths place**.

Ones	Tenths	Hundredths	Thousandths
0	0	0	2

$$\frac{2}{1000} = 0.002$$

Read: two thousandths

Write as a decimal.

40. $\frac{6}{1000}$ **41.** $\frac{1}{1000}$ **42.** $\frac{9}{1000}$ **43.** $\frac{12}{1000}$ **44.** $\frac{25}{1000}$

45. $\frac{99}{1000}$ **46.** $\frac{702}{1000}$ **47.** $\frac{811}{1000}$ **48.** $\frac{450}{1000}$ **49.** $\frac{940}{1000}$

Comparing Decimals

Who rode the greater distance
in the bike-a-thon?

Bike-A-Thon Distances	
Sheena	17.5 km
Noemi	17.58 km

To find who rode the greater distance,
compare: 17.5 _?_ 17.58

To compare decimals:

- Align the digits
  by their place value.

  17.5
  17.58

- Start at the left. Compare
  the digits in the greatest place.

  17.5
  17.58 $1 = 1$

- If these are the same,
  compare the next digits.

  17.5
  17.58 $7 = 7$

- Keep comparing digits until
  you find two digits that
  are *not* the same.

  17.5
  17.58 $5 = 5$

                 Think:
  17.50 $0.5 = 0.50$
  17.58 $0 < 8$

So 17.5 < 17.58

The greater distance is 17.58 km.
So Noemi rode the greater distance.

Study these examples.

$.96 _?_ $.92   42.7 _?_ 4.7

$.96 $9 = 9$ 42.7
$.92 $6 > 2$ 4.7   There are no tens
                                               in 4.7.
So $.96 > $.92 $4 > 0$

                          So 42.7 > 4.7

Compare. Write <, =, or >.

1. 0.4 _?_ 0.9

2. 0.22 _?_ 0.18

3. 0.35 _?_ 0.38

4. 0.65 _?_ 0.6

5. 0.7 _?_ 0.70

6. 0.84 _?_ 0.8

7. 2.7 _?_ 1.8

8. 7.5 _?_ 7.9

9. 5.6 _?_ 5.9

10. 5.47 _?_ 5.77

11. 8.03 _?_ 8.30

12. 2.35 _?_ 1.99

13. 23.05 _?_ 8.79

14. 2.17 _?_ 62.1

15. 14.9 _?_ 1.49

16. 100.1 _?_ 100.10

17. 235.0 _?_ 23.5

18. 604.04 _?_ 604.40

19. 839.00 _?_ 839.10

20. 147.5 _?_ 145.7

21. 252.01 _?_ 225.1

22. $5.65 _?_ $3.65

23. $.76 _?_ $.76

24. $20.19 _?_ $2.09

25. $1.04 _?_ $1.40

26. $10.00 _?_ $10.25

27. $3.09 _?_ $3.90

Solve.

28. Ken's top speed in the bike-a-thon was 32.6 kilometers per hour. Vijay's top speed was 32.65 kilometers per hour. Which boy had the greater top speed?

29. Each week before the bike-a-thon, Misha rode his bike 112.5 km and Luke rode his bike 121.5 km. Who rode his bike the lesser distance each week?

30. Elise had a total of $42.75 in pledges for the bike-a-thon and Andres had a total of $42.05. Who had the greater total pledges?

31. This year the bike-a-thon raised $726.50 for charity. The bike-a-thon last year raised $725.75. Was the greater amount raised this year or last year?

14-5 Ordering Decimals

Order the winning times from fastest to slowest.

▶ You can use place value to order decimals from least to greatest.

Winning Times	
Olympic Speed Skating, 500 Meters	
1964 McDermott, U.S.A.	40.1 seconds
1968 Keller, W. Ger.	40.3 seconds
1976 Kulikov, U.S.S.R.	39.17 seconds
1980 Heiden, U.S.A.	38.03 seconds

Align by place value.	Compare tens. Rearrange.	Compare ones. Rearrange.	Compare tenths. Rearrange if necessary.
40.1	39.17	38.03 ← least	38.03
40.3	38.03	39.17	39.17
39.17	40.1	40.1	40.1
38.03	40.3	40.3	40.3 ← greatest
	30 < 40	8 < 9	0.1 < 0.3
		0 = 0	

The order from fastest to slowest: 38.03; 39.17; 40.1; 40.3

or

The order from slowest to fastest: 40.3; 40.1; 39.17; 38.03

▶ You can use a number line to order decimals.

Order from least to greatest: 0.6; 0.4; 0.78; 0.65

The order from least to greatest: 0.4; 0.6; 0.65; 0.78

or

The order from greatest to least: 0.78; 0.65; 0.6; 0.4

Write in order from least to greatest. You may use a number line.

1. 0.2; 0.9; 0.5

2. 3.5; 3.3; 3.35

3. 1.12; 1.02; 1.2

4. 5; 0.5; 0.05

5. 6.7; 6.77; 6.07; 7.67

6. 2.4; 4.2; 2.44; 4.02

7. 10.03; 1.30; 10.3; 1.33

8. 52.6; 62.5; 6.52; 56.2

9. 83.7; 87.37; 87.3; 83.07

10. 13.3; 33.31; 13.33; 130

Write in order from greatest to least. You may use a number line.

11. 0.1; 0.01; 0.11

12. 2.6; 2.06; 6.26

13. 4.04; 4.40; 4.0

14. 9.99; 9.19; 9.9

15. 1.18; 1.8; 1.81; 1.08

16. 17.6; 16.7; 61.7; 17.76

17. 59.03; 59; 53.9; 53.09

18. 44; 4.04; 40.4; 44.04

19. 90.3; 30.93; 30.09; 39.3

20. 75.01; 75.1; 75.11; 7.51

Copy and complete.

21. 2.32, 2.33, 2.34, _?_ , 2.36, _?_

22. 16.1, 16.2, 16.3, _?_ , _?_ , _?_

23. 0.07, 0.08, 0.09, _?_ , _?_ , _?_

24. 1.99, 1.98, 1.97, _?_ , _?_ , _?_

25. 8.5, 8.4, _?_ , 8.2, _?_ , _?_

26. 6.3, 6.2, 6.1, _?_ , _?_ , _?_

14-6 Rounding Decimals

A number line can help you to round decimals.

Round to the nearest tenth: 0.42, 0.45, and 0.48.

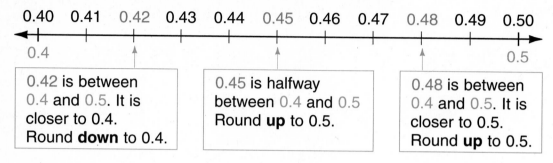

0.42 is between 0.4 and 0.5. It is closer to 0.4. Round **down** to 0.4.		0.45 is halfway between 0.4 and 0.5 Round **up** to 0.5.	0.48 is between 0.4 and 0.5. It is closer to 0.5. Round **up** to 0.5.

To round decimals:

* Find the place you are rounding to.

* Look at the digit to its right.

Round to the nearest tenth: 1.35, 5.62, and 2.48.

1.35 → 1.4
5 = 5
Round **up** to 1.4.

5.62 → 5.6
2 < 5
Round **down** to 5.6.

2.48 → 2.5
8 > 5
Round **up** to 2.5.

Round to the nearest one: 4.09, 6.7, and 8.54.

4.09 → 4
0 < 5
Round **down** to 4.

6.7 → 7
7 > 5
Round **up** to 7.

8.54 → 9
5 = 5
Round **up** to 9.

Do not write zeros to the right of the place you are rounding to.

Round to the nearest one.

1. 7.3   **2.** 9.2   **3.** 3.9   **4.** 1.5   **5.** 12.8

6. 16.2   **7.** 28.5   **8.** 62.4   **9.** 30.8   **10.** 19.7

11. 4.64   **12.** 15.35   **13.** 25.78   **14.** 41.23   **15.** 20.91

16. 17.52   **17.** 71.18   **18.** 49.62   **19.** 24.03   **20.** 3.95

Round to the nearest tenth.

21. 6.27   **22.** 4.64   **23.** 9.75   **24.** 2.20   **25.** 1.11

26. 31.37   **27.** 25.65   **28.** 85.06   **29.** 24.75   **30.** 38.33

31. 9.47   **32.** 13.53   **33.** 27.13   **34.** 82.75   **35.** 63.08

36. 52.71   **37.** 30.59   **38.** 81.11   **39.** 55.05   **40.** 44.89

Solve.

41. What is ten and three tenths rounded to the nearest one?

42. What is six and five tenths rounded to the nearest one?

43. What is seventeen hundredths rounded to the nearest tenth?

44. What is nine and five hundredths rounded to the nearest tenth?

45. Is two and fifteen hundredths rounded to the nearest one: 2, 2.2, or 3?

46. Is one and fifty hundredths rounded to the nearest tenth: 20, 2.0, or 1.5?

 **Critical Thinking**

47. Round 49.92 to the nearest one. Explain how you got your answer.

48. Round 87.99 to the nearest tenth. Explain how you got your answer.

14-7 Adding Decimals

At a gymnastics meet, Shogi scored 9.1 on the parallel bars and 8.95 on the rings. How many points did Shogi score altogether?

To find how many, add: $9.1 + 8.95 = $ _?_

Think of how you add money.

Line up the decimal points.	Add the hundredths.	Add the tenths. Regroup.	Add the ones.

9.1 0 ←
 + 8.9 5
	9.1 0
	 + 8.9 5
	       5
		1
		 9.1 0
		 + 8.9 5
		     0 5
			1
			 9.1 0
			 + 8.9 5
			 1 8.0 5

Remember: 9.1 = 9.10

Write the decimal point in the sum.

Shogi scored 18.05 points altogether.

Study these examples.

```
   1              1 1                1       1          1
   0.8            5.7 5          $2 7.0 8          7 5.0 0
 + 0.6            0.9 0        +    6.6 5        +    6.4 2
   1.4          + 2 8.3 2        $3 3.7 3          8 1.4 2
                  3 4.9 7
```

Add.

1.   0.3
 + 0.6

2.   1.4
 + 6.2

3.   0.9
 + 0.7

4.   5.6
 + 9.8

5.   8.5
 + 10.5

6.   0.12
 + 0.43

7.   3.01
 + 0.57

8.   0.84
 + 0.77

9. $2.09
 +   7.83

10. $24.55
 +   2.86

Find the sum.

11. 5.03
    + 8.9

12. 83.8
    + 47.65

13. 90.41
    + 62.7

14. 17.54
    + 5.9

15. 45
    + 9.24

16. 16.75
     4.32
    + 10.08

17. 0.7
     1.2
    + 8.9

18. 92.3
     48.05
    + 18.39

19. 74.32
     10.1
    + 0.8

20. 59.11
      0.98
    + 100.2

Align and add.

21. 0.3 + 8.44

22. 4.25 + 0.7

23. 12.87 + 34

24. 0.95 + 22.6

25. 44.73 + 0.9

26. 62 + 0.8

27. 7.5 + 16.92 + 0.56

28. 133.04 + 0.8 + 3.47

29. 32.5 + 575 + 0.4

30. 367.92 + 0.09 + 5.1

Solve.

31. Val ran the first 100 meters of a 200-meter dash in 15.34 seconds. She ran the next 100 meters in 16.9 seconds. What was Val's time in the 200-meter dash?

32. Xavier swam the 100-meter freestyle in 58.95 seconds. If he could keep up that pace for another 100 meters, what would be his time in the 200-meter freestyle?

33. The times for the 4 legs of a relay race were 10.9 seconds, 12.74 seconds, 11.08 seconds, and 10.06 seconds. How long did it take to run the race?

Mental Math

Add.

34. 5
    + 1.75

35. 4.3
    + 2

36. 10.91
    + 10

37. 15
    + 5.83

38. 50
    + 50.06

425

14-8 Subtracting Decimals

How much farther is it from the Village to Black Rock than from Old Farm to Sam's Beach?

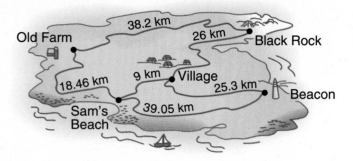

To find how much farther, subtract: 26 − 18.46 = __?__

Think of how you subtract money.

Line up the decimal points. Regroup.	Subtract the hundredths.	Subtract the tenths.	Regroup. Subtract the ones.

$$
\begin{array}{r}
9\\
5\ \cancel{10}\ 10\\
2\ \cancel{6}.\cancel{0}\ \cancel{0}\\
-\ 1\ 8.4\ 6\\
\hline
\end{array}
$$

Remember: 26 = 26.00

$$
\begin{array}{r}
9\\
5\ \cancel{10}\ 10\\
2\ \cancel{6}.\cancel{0}\ \cancel{0}\\
-\ 1\ 8.4\ 6\\
\hline
4
\end{array}
$$

$$
\begin{array}{r}
9\\
5\ \cancel{10}\ 10\\
2\ \cancel{6}.\cancel{0}\ \cancel{0}\\
-\ 1\ 8.4\ 6\\
\hline
5\ 4
\end{array}
$$

$$
\begin{array}{r}
15\ 9\\
1\ \cancel{5}\ \cancel{10}\ 10\\
2\ \cancel{6}.\cancel{0}\ \cancel{0}\\
-\ 1\ 8.4\ 6\\
\hline
7.5\ 4
\end{array}
$$

Write the decimal point in the difference.

It is 7.54 km farther.

Study these examples.

$$
\begin{array}{r}
0\ 16\\
\cancel{1}.\cancel{6}\\
-\ 0.8\\
\hline
0.8
\end{array}
\qquad
\begin{array}{r}
9\\
\cancel{10}\ 10\\
\cancel{1}\ \cancel{0}.\cancel{0}\ 5\\
-\ \ \ 8.2\ 0\\
\hline
1.8\ 5
\end{array}
\qquad
\begin{array}{r}
7\ 10\\
9.\cancel{8}\ \cancel{0}\\
-\ 3.4\ 2\\
\hline
6.3\ 8
\end{array}
\qquad
\begin{array}{r}
\$0.6\ 6\\
-\ 0.6\ 1\\
\hline
\$0.0\ 5
\end{array}
$$

Subtract.

1.   0.9
       −0.6

2.   0.35
       −0.02

3.   8.7
       −1.4

4.   1.48
       −1.03

5. $5.65
       − 2.43

Find the difference.

6. 18.7 $-$ 13.9	**7.** 24.2 $-$ 16.7	**8.** 3.43 $-$ 2.84	**9.** 62.19 $-$ 48.75	**10.** $75.11 $-$ 27.25
11. 23.16 $-$ 15.9	**12.** 82.6 $-$ 56.75	**13.** 64.5 $-$ 56.48	**14.** 10 $-$ 9.07	**15.** 16 $-$ 15.5
16. 17 $-$ 7.4	**17.** 92.1 $-$ 0.77	**18.** 76 $-$ 8.32	**19.** 58 $-$ 9.09	**20.** 31.2 $-$ 0.99

Align and subtract.

21. 90.17 $-$ 9.07   **22.** 40.6 $-$ 2.04   **23.** 8.34 $-$ 0.5

24. 88 $-$ 12.56   **25.** 62.1 $-$ 61.02   **26.** 34.7 $-$ 25.38

27. 100 $-$ 55.5   **28.** 99 $-$ 0.09   **29.** 76.1 $-$ 75.06

Solve. Use the map on page 426.

30. How much closer to the Village is the Beacon than Black Rock?

31. How much farther from Old Farm is Black Rock than Sam's Beach?

32. Is the route from Sam's Beach to the Beacon longer or shorter than the distance from Black Rock to Old Farm? How much longer or shorter?

33. How many kilometers would you travel if you went from Old Farm to the Beacon by way of Sam's Beach and the Village?

Calculator Activity

Subtract. Then check by adding.

34. 506.2 $-$ 175.35	**35.** 239.07 $-$ 86.6	**36.** 400.02 $-$ 0.8	**37.** 604 $-$ 64.91

Estimating with Decimals

You can use rounding to estimate decimal sums and differences.

To estimate sums or differences with decimals:
- Round the decimals to the greatest *nonzero* place of the smaller number.
- Then add or subtract.

Estimate: 123.6 + 8.43

$$123.6 \longrightarrow 124$$
$$+ \ \ \ 8.43 \longrightarrow + \ \ \ 8$$
$$\text{about} \ \ \ 132$$

Estimate: 78.61 − 0.45

$$78.61 \longrightarrow 78.6$$
$$+ \ 0.45 \longrightarrow - \ \ 0.5$$
$$\text{about} \ \ \ 78.1$$

Study these examples.

$$0.92 \longrightarrow 0.9$$
$$+ 0.37 \longrightarrow + 0.4$$
$$\text{about} \ \ \ 1.3$$

$$4.7 \longrightarrow 4.7$$
$$- 0.18 \longrightarrow - 0.2$$
$$\text{about} \ \ \ 4.5$$

$$8.8 \longrightarrow 9$$
$$+ 5.1 \longrightarrow + 5$$
$$\text{about} \ \ \ 14$$

Estimate the sum or the difference. Watch the signs.

1. 5.9 + 3.2	**2.** 9.7 − 4.6	**3.** 8.75 − 1.17	**4.** 9.38 + 6.04	**5.** 4.91 + 6.73
6. 42.3 − 6.7	**7.** 38.5 + 5.8	**8.** 56.2 − 4.84	**9.** 27.8 + 6.65	**10.** 85.43 − 1.7
11. 0.85 + 0.63	**12.** 10.3 − 0.81	**13.** 62.77 + 9.84	**14.** 48.5 − 0.69	**15.** 26.21 + 0.59
16. 74.36 + 18	**17.** 62 − 7.8	**18.** 49.95 − 5.2	**19.** 405.5 − 5.76	**20.** 380.4 + 2.35

21. 4.5 + 39.03   **22.** 17.03 − 1.5   **23.** 47 − 6.62

Using Front-End Estimation

You can use front-end estimation to estimate decimal sums and differences.

To make a front-end estimate with decimals:

- Add or subtract the nonzero front digits.
- Write zeros for the other digits.

$$
\begin{array}{r} 83.41 \\ +\ 71.3 \\ \hline \end{array}
$$
about   150.00

$$
\begin{array}{r} 9.3 \\ -4.76 \\ \hline \end{array}
$$
about   5.00

$$
\begin{array}{r} 0.65 \\ +0.5 \\ \hline \end{array}
$$
about   1.10

Estimate the sum or the difference. Use front-end estimation.

24. $\begin{array}{r} 30.98 \\ +56.44 \\ \hline \end{array}$ 25. $\begin{array}{r} 8.6 \\ +9.2 \\ \hline \end{array}$ 26. $\begin{array}{r} 43.21 \\ -12.04 \\ \hline \end{array}$ 27. $\begin{array}{r} 7.4 \\ -2.9 \\ \hline \end{array}$ 28. $\begin{array}{r} 58.4 \\ -21.62 \\ \hline \end{array}$

29. $\begin{array}{r} 0.94 \\ -0.55 \\ \hline \end{array}$ 30. $\begin{array}{r} 0.26 \\ +0.77 \\ \hline \end{array}$ 31. $\begin{array}{r} 23.2 \\ +96.09 \\ \hline \end{array}$ 32. $\begin{array}{r} 48.4 \\ -18.36 \\ \hline \end{array}$ 33. $\begin{array}{r} 74.6 \\ -21.09 \\ \hline \end{array}$

34. $\begin{array}{r} 8.09 \\ +8.9 \\ \hline \end{array}$ 35. $\begin{array}{r} 6.74 \\ -1.53 \\ \hline \end{array}$ 36. $\begin{array}{r} 81.2 \\ -27.35 \\ \hline \end{array}$ 37. $\begin{array}{r} 50.09 \\ +97.79 \\ \hline \end{array}$ 38. $\begin{array}{r} 59.5 \\ -24.07 \\ \hline \end{array}$

Solve. Use front-end estimation.

39. Maria jogged 97.5 miles. Audrey jogged 79.37 miles. About how many more miles did Maria jog than Audrey?

Skills to Remember

Find the quotient.

40. $2\overline{)\$37.32}$ 41. $4\overline{)\$10.40}$ 42. $9\overline{)\$2.79}$ 43. $3\overline{)\$9.36}$ 44. $8\overline{)\$64.16}$

45. $24\overline{)\$87.60}$ 46. $53\overline{)\$163.24}$ 47. $39\overline{)\$82.29}$ 48. $42\overline{)\$129.78}$

Dividing with Money

Martin designs greeting cards. They cost
$.50 each if you buy them separately,
or you can buy a box of 25 cards
for $12. Which is the better buy?

To find which is the better buy, find the cost
of one boxed card. Then compare the cost to $.50.

To find the cost of one boxed card,
divide: $12 ÷ 25 = ?

Before dividing, write a decimal point and two zeros in the dividend.	Divide as usual. Write the dollar sign and decimal point in the quotient.	Check.

$$25\overline{)\$12.00}$$

$$\begin{array}{r} \$\ \ .48 \\ 25\overline{)\$12.00} \\ -10\ 0\downarrow \\ \hline 2\ 00 \\ -2\ 00 \end{array}$$

$$\begin{array}{r} \$.48 \\ \times\ \ \ \ 25 \\ \hline 2\ 40 \\ 9\ 6 \\ \hline \$12.00 \end{array}$$

$.48 < $.50
So the better buy is a box of 25 cards for $12.

Study this example.

$$8\overline{)\$18} \longrightarrow \begin{array}{r} \$\ \ 2.25 \\ 8\overline{)\$18.00} \\ -16\ \downarrow\downarrow \\ \hline 2\ 0 \\ -1\ 6\downarrow \\ \hline 40 \\ -40 \end{array}$$

Find the quotient.

1. $27 ÷ 6   **2.** $41 ÷ 5   **3.** $54 ÷ 8   **4.** $38 ÷ 4

5. $19 ÷ 2   **6.** $90 ÷ 8   **7.** $45 ÷ 6   **8.** $78 ÷ 8

9. $6 ÷ 24   **10.** $48 ÷ 32   **11.** $60 ÷ 16   **12.** $72 ÷ 15

13. $8 ÷ 10   **14.** $21 ÷ 14   **15.** $32 ÷ 20   **16.** $9 ÷ 12

Divide. Then check.

17. $4\overline{)\$17}$ **18.** $5\overline{)\$2}$ **19.** $8\overline{)\$60}$ **20.** $6\overline{)\$39}$

21. $2\overline{)\$9}$ **22.** $8\overline{)\$10}$ **23.** $4\overline{)\$5}$ **24.** $6\overline{)\$15}$

25. $52\overline{)\$65}$ **26.** $25\overline{)\$8}$ **27.** $48\overline{)\$12}$ **28.** $46\overline{)\$23}$

29. $66\overline{)\$33}$ **30.** $72\overline{)\$54}$ **31.** $84\overline{)\$21}$ **32.** $75\overline{)\$45}$

Solve. Tell which is the better buy.

33. 8 erasers for $2.80
          or
10 erasers for $3

34. 5 notebooks for $10
          or
9 notebooks for $18.45

35. 6 bottles of shampoo for $21
          or
8 bottles of shampoo for $22

36. 12 pencils for $3
          or
10 pencils for $2

37. 20 plums for $14
          or
16 plums for $12

38. 10 melons for $12
          or
4 melons for $6

39. 8 juice cartons for $18
          or
12 juice cartons for $33

40. 6 boxes of detergent for $27
          or
4 boxes of detergent for $17

14-11 Problem Solving: Multi-Step Problem

Problem: Hector bought 3 jumbo magnets and 1 magnifying glass at the science sale. How much change did he get from $10?

Science Sale	
mini magnet	$ .45 each
jumbo magnet	$1.19 each
magnifying glass	$5.78 for 2

1 IMAGINE Put yourself in the problem.

2 NAME *Facts:* 3 jumbo magnets—$1.19 each
1 magnifying glass—2 for $5.78
paid $10

Question: How much change did Hector get?

3 THINK Plan the steps to follow.

Step 1: *Multiply* to find the cost of
3 jumbo magnets. 3 × $1.19 = _?_

Step 2: *Divide* to find the cost of
1 magnifying glass. $5.78 ÷ 2 = _?_

Step 3: *Add* to find the total cost.

Step 4: *Subtract* to find Hector's change from $10.

4 COMPUTE First estimate: cost of magnets 3 × $1 = $3
cost of magnifying glass $6 ÷ 2 = $3
$10 − $6 = $4 change

Then compute:

Step 1	Step 2	Step 3	Step 4

Step 1
$$\begin{array}{r} {\scriptstyle 2} \\ \$1.1\,9 \\ \times\ \ \ 3 \\ \hline \$3.5\,7 \end{array}$$

3 magnets
1 magnifying glass

Step 2
$$\begin{array}{r} \$2.8\,9 \\ 2\overline{)\$5.7\,8} \\ -4\ \ \ \ \\ \hline 1\,7\ \\ -1\,6\ \\ \hline 1\,8 \\ -1\,8 \end{array}$$

Step 3
$$\begin{array}{r} {\scriptstyle 1\ 1} \\ \$3.5\,7 \\ +2.8\,9 \\ \hline \$6.4\,6 \end{array}$$
total cost

Step 4
$$\begin{array}{r} {\scriptstyle 9\ 9} \\ {\scriptstyle 0\ \cancel{10}\ \cancel{10}\ 10} \\ \$\cancel{1}\,0.0\,0 \\ -\ \ 6.4\,6 \\ \hline \$\ \ \ 3.5\,4 \end{array}$$
Hector's change

5 CHECK The answer $3.54 is close to the estimate of $4.
The answer is reasonable.

Solve.

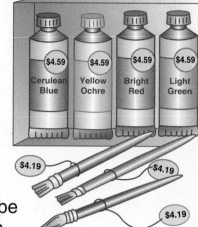

1. Mary wants 4 tubes of oil paint and 3 brushes. Tubes of paint are $4.59 each and brushes are $4.19 each. If she saved $30.75, how much more money does she need to buy the items?

IMAGINE   Create a mental picture.

NAME   *Facts:*   4 paint tubes at $4.59 a tube
                                  3 brushes at $4.19 a brush
                                    Mary saved $30.75.

                Question: How much more money does Mary need to buy the items?

THINK   Plan the steps to follow.

Step 1: Multiply to find the cost of 4 paint tubes.

Step 2: Multiply to find the cost of 3 brushes.

Step 3: Add to find the total cost.

Step 4: Subtract $30.75 from the total cost to find how much more money Mary needs.

         COMPUTE ⟶ **CHECK**

2. Mr. Ortiz collects 7.5 lb of honey. He gives 1.2 lb to a neighbor and 2.1 lb each to two office workers. How much honey is left?

3. A shelf is 104.5 cm long. An encyclopedia uses 64.6 cm of space and two books use 2.5 cm each. How much space is left?

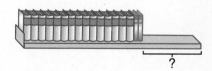

4. It takes Lyn 58.34 s to swim a lap doing the backstroke and 42.15 s to swim a lap doing the crawl. She does 2 laps using the backstroke and 1 using the crawl. How much less than 3 minutes does she swim?

14-12 Problem-Solving Applications

Solve.

1. On Monday, 2.4 cm of rain fell in the morning and another 1.8 cm fell in the afternoon. How much rain fell on Monday?

Use these steps:

2. The time between a bolt of lightning and the sound of thunder was 4.72 s. What is this time rounded to the nearest second?

3. A thunderstorm lasted 78.2 minutes. How much longer than an hour was the storm?

4. A meteorologist found that the diameter of a hail pellet measured 2.28 cm. What is this to the nearest tenth of a centimeter?

Imagine
Name

5. The meteorologist found hail pellets in the following widths: 2.28 dm, 1.09 dm, 1.9 dm, 0.98 dm, and 1.42 dm. Order the pellets from smallest to largest.

Think

6. The temperature during the hail storm started at 11.4°C and then dropped by 0.5 degree. What was the final temperature?

Compute

Check

7. Ms. Dell's car received 5 dents during the storm. She paid $85.50 to repair the damage. Each dent cost about the same amount to fix. About how much did it cost to repair each dent?

8. During a snowstorm, 12.3 dm of snow fell. There were already 45.9 dm of snow on the ground. How much snow was on the ground after the storm?

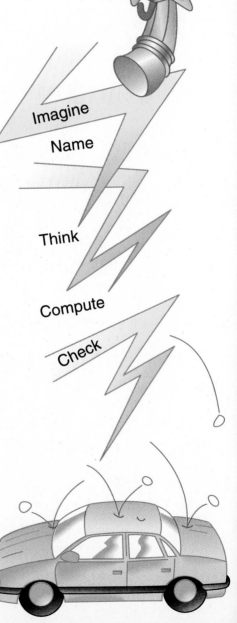

434

Solve.

9. At 6:00 A.M. the snow was 1.4 cm deep. It snowed 1.4 cm more every half hour. What time was it when the snow was 11.2 cm deep?

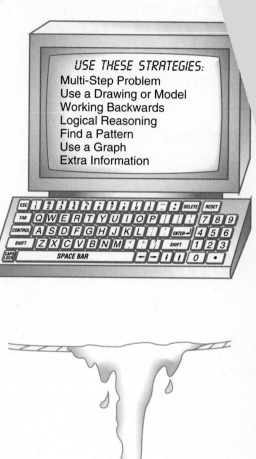

USE THESE STRATEGIES:
Multi-Step Problem
Use a Drawing or Model
Working Backwards
Logical Reasoning
Find a Pattern
Use a Graph
Extra Information

10. A gopher dug a tunnel in the snow. It began at the ground, rose 2.2 ft, fell 0.7 ft, and then rose 2.8 ft to a lair. How high off the ground was the lair?

11. A winter storm warning lasted 4.5 hours. It began at 2:30 P.M. The storm brought 4.3 in. of snow. When did the warning end?

12. Lina broke off 1.2 dm from a long icicle. It melted and lost another 0.8 dm. It was 3.5 dm long at the end of the day. How long was the original icicle?

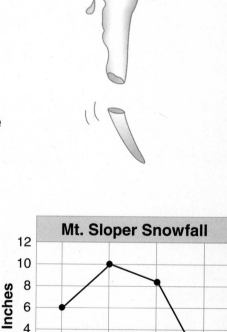

13. Hugh built a snow sculpture with three large snowballs. They weighed 45.2 lb, 32.7 lb, and 20.1 lb. Luke's snow sculpture used three 28.5 lb snowballs. Whose snow sculpture was heavier?

Use the line graph for problems 14 and 15.

14. Between which two months did the amount of snowfall change the most on Mt. Sloper?

15. Joan did not ski in March. She did ski during a month that received less than 7 in. of snow. During which month did Joan ski?

Mt. Sloper Snowfall

Inches: 12, 10, 8, 6, 4, 2, 0

Month: Dec. Jan. Feb. Mar.

...e of the underlined digit.

2. 2.4<u>2</u>   **3.** 0.9<u>6</u>   **4.** <u>1</u>.92

6. <u>8</u>.5   **7.** 2.2<u>3</u>   **8.** <u>1</u>5.49

...e as a decimal.

9. five tenths   **10.** thirty-two hundredths

11. three and four tenths   **12.** eight hundredths

Compare. Write <, =, or >.

13. 0.03 _?_ 0.7   **14.** 9.45 _?_ 12.8   **15.** 0.64 _?_ 0.05

16. 12.8 _?_ 12.80   **17.** 7.02 _?_ 7   **18.** 5.06 _?_ 5.6

Add or subtract.

19.   0.6
      + 0.2

20.   4.9
      − 2.73

21.   23.5
      + 13.95

22.   44
      − 6.8

Round each to the nearest one.
Then round each to the nearest tenth.

23. 12.17   **24.** 32.74   **25.** 0.88

Compute.

26. 3.8 + 5.17   **27.** 8)$\overline{\$2}$ **28.** $5 ÷ 25

Solve.

29. The weight of one bag of onions is 2.47 lb.
The weight of another is 0.73 lb.
Estimate the weight of the two bags of onions.

(See *Still More Practice*, p. 472.)

MAGIC SQUARES

In a **magic square** each row, column, and diagonal has the same sum, called the **magic sum**.

Copy and complete each magic square.

1.

6	7	?
?	5	9
?	3	?

2.

9	?	7
4	6	?
5	?	?

3.

?	3	?
7	10	?
?	17	5

4.

2.7	3.8	?
5.2	3.6	?
?	3.4	4.5

5.

3.5	7.5	8.5
11.5	?	?
4.5	5.5	?

6.

8.6	7	6.6
5.4	?	?
8.2	7.8	?

7.

?	63	68
?	67	?
?	71	64

8.

2.42	8	5.96
9	5.46	?
4.96	?	?

9. Use multiples of 3.

?	?	24
?	15	?
6	?	12

437

Check Your Mastery

Write the value of the underlined digit. See pp. 416–417

1. 4.<u>6</u>9
2. <u>4</u>7.33
3. <u>2</u>.26
4. 0.1<u>3</u>
5. 6.<u>6</u>1
6. 55.7<u>4</u>

Write as a decimal. See pp. 412–415

7. nine tenths
8. nine hundredths
9. four and six tenths
10. seven and seven hundredths

Compare. Write <, =, or >. See pp. 418–419

11. 0.8 _?_ 0.4
12. 0.7 _?_ 0.70
13. 0.46 _?_ 0.64
14. 2.43 _?_ 2.39

Write in order from least to greatest. See pp. 420–421

15. 13.4, 6.5, 13.3, 6.05
16. 2.15, 2.51, 2.05, 2.5

Compute. See pp. 424–427

17. 0.6 + 0.3 + 7.07
18. 1.40 − 0.4
19. 5.4 + 3.75
20. 4.07 − 2.1

Round to the nearest tenth. See pp. 422–423

21. 3.94
22. 17.25
23. 12.53

Solve. See pp. 430–431, 434–435

24. Last year Michele measured 153.8 cm. During the past year she grew 6.8 cm. How tall is she now?

25. Which is the better buy: 25 stickers for $3 or 20 stickers for $2?

26. What is the difference between 2.5 and 6?

Choose the best answer.

1. The distance around a figure is the:
   a. diameter   b. center   c. perimeter   d. area

2. A straight figure with one endpoint is a:
   a. ray   b. line segment   c. circle   d. line

3. Which is a factor of 27?
   a. 7   b. 9   c. 2   d. 18

4. What is the least common multiple (LCM) of 4 and 5?
   a. 9   b. 40   c. 20   d. 45

5. Name $\frac{14}{6}$ as a mixed number in simplest form.
   a. $2\frac{1}{2}$ b. $\frac{7}{3}$ c. $1\frac{1}{3}$ d. $2\frac{1}{3}$

6. $64{,}000 \div 80 = \underline{\ ?\ }$
   a. 8   b. 80   c. 800   d. 8000

7. $7846 \div 42$ is about:
   a. 2000   b. 200   c. 300   d. 3000

8. Which is the decimal for eight and three hundredths?
   a. 8.03   b. 8.3   c. 8.30   d. 80.03

Draw and label these figures.

9. right angle *BAC*

10. parallel lines $\overleftrightarrow{XW}$ and $\overleftrightarrow{YZ}$

Write whether each fraction is *closer to 0, closer to $\frac{1}{2}$*, or *closer to 1*.

11. $\frac{1}{6}$

12. five eighths

13. two sevenths

Compare. Write <, =, or >.

14. $\frac{7}{12}$ __?__ $\frac{5}{6}$

15. $1\frac{3}{5}$ __?__ $2\frac{1}{5}$

16. 0.35 __?__ 0.26

17. 0.45 __?__ 0.4

18. $.72 __?__ $.72

19. $7.09 __?__ $7.90

439

Add or subtract. Write the answers in lowest terms.

20. $\dfrac{3}{5}$
    $+\dfrac{1}{5}$

21. $\dfrac{7}{8}$
    $-\dfrac{2}{8}$

22. $\dfrac{1}{2}$
    $+\dfrac{3}{4}$

23. $7\dfrac{3}{7}$
    $+2\dfrac{2}{7}$

24. $\dfrac{5}{6}$
    $-\dfrac{2}{12}$

Compute.

25. $41\overline{)88}$

26. $34\overline{)272}$

27. $16\overline{)139}$

28. $25\overline{)\$48.75}$

29. $\quad 9.9$
    -3.6

30. $\quad 0.9$
    $+0.8$

31. $\quad 8.6$
    $+13.2$

32. $7.2 + 18.29 + 0.52$

Solve. Which is the better buy?

33. 5 pens for $4 or
    4 pens for $3

34. 4 cassettes for $25 or
    6 cassettes for $39

Find the perimeter and the area. Use formulas.

35.

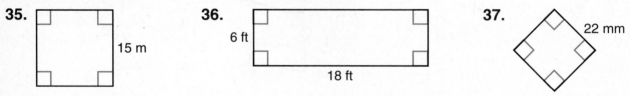

15 m

36.

6 ft

18 ft

37.

22 mm

Solve.

38. I have 1 face and a curved surface. Which space figure am I?

39. Of the 27 rose bushes planted, $\frac{1}{3}$ are yellow. How many are yellow?

40. The floor in Coretta's bedroom is 10 feet long and 12 feet wide. What is the area of a rug needed to cover the floor?

41. Mrs. Gallen made 432 prizes for the school fair. She packed them 12 in a bag. How many bags did she fill?

42. Greg ran 2.1 miles on Monday and 3.45 miles on Tuesday. How far did he run?

43. Luke jogged 86.5 miles and Mike jogged 78.27 miles. About how many more miles did Luke jog?

In this chapter you will:
Use variables to write
number sentences
Find missing numbers
and symbols
Use function tables
and number lines
Use parentheses and
order of operations
Use a variable
Solve problems by
more than one way

Do you remember?

The arrow is halfway between
0 and 500. It is pointing
to 250.

**Critical Thinking/
Finding Together**
Think of a number. Add 5.
Double the sum. Subtract 10.
Divide by your number.
What is the answer?

15-1 | Number Sentences

A scout troop is planning a trip to a cave. They rent a mini-bus for $17 per hour. The trip will take 5 hours. How much will the bus cost?

What do you know?	What do you need to know?	Which operation will you use?
• bus costs $17 per hour • trip takes 5 hours	• how much the bus will cost for 5 hours	• multiplication

Write a number sentence to help you solve the problem.

- Let n stand for the product.

- Write the number sentence. $5 \times \$17 = n$

- Solve for n. $\$85 = n$

The bus will cost $85.

Give the correct number sentence for each problem. Then solve.

1. The first cave chamber was 18 feet high. The second chamber was only 4 feet high. How much higher was the first chamber?

   a. $4 + 18 = n$ **b.** $4 \times 18 = n$ **c.** $18 - 4 = n$

2. The scouts discovered 225 bats in the first chamber and 172 in the second. How many bats did they discover in the two chambers?

   a. $225 + 172 = n$ **b.** $225 - 172 = n$ **c.** $172 \times 225 = n$

Write a number sentence. Then solve.

3. One chamber was 195 ft below sea level. Another chamber was 119 ft deeper. How many feet below sea level was the second chamber?

4. Each of 24 scouts brought 15 ft of rope. They tied their ropes together to form a long coil. How many feet of rope were in the long coil?

5. Zack found an arrowhead that was about 1500 years old. Chang found one that was twice as old. About how old was Chang's arrowhead?

6. Lucy's Lunches prepared 24 box lunches for the scouts. The total cost of the lunches was $94.80. What was the cost of each box lunch?

7. Each guide led a team of 5 scouts. There were 24 scouts in all. How many teams of 5 were there? How many guides were needed for all the scouts?

8. The lengths of five passages in the cave are 17.2 mi, 24.5 mi, 18.3 mi, 16.4 mi, and 23.6 mi. What is the total length of the five passages in the cave?

9. Carlsbad Caverns in New Mexico covers 46,755 acres. The Wind Cave in South Dakota covers 28,292 acres. How many more acres does Carlsbad Caverns cover?

10. Mammoth Cave in Kentucky has 144 miles of underground passages. If you could explore them 3 miles each day, how many days would it take to explore all the passages?

Skills to Remember

Find the missing number.

11. $7 + \underline{\ ?\ } = 15$

12. $\underline{\ ?\ } - 5 = 8$

13. $6 \times \underline{\ ?\ } = 36$

14. $40 \div \underline{\ ?\ } = 8$

15. $12 - \underline{\ ?\ } = 5$

16. $\underline{\ ?\ } \div 7 = 9$

17. $\underline{\ ?\ } \times 4 = 28$

18. $\underline{\ ?\ } \div 8 = 1$

19. $\underline{\ ?\ } + 5 = 5$

15-2 Finding Missing Numbers

▶ What number does *a* stand for?
    $8 + a = 7 + 6$

A letter can be used for an unknown number.

To solve:

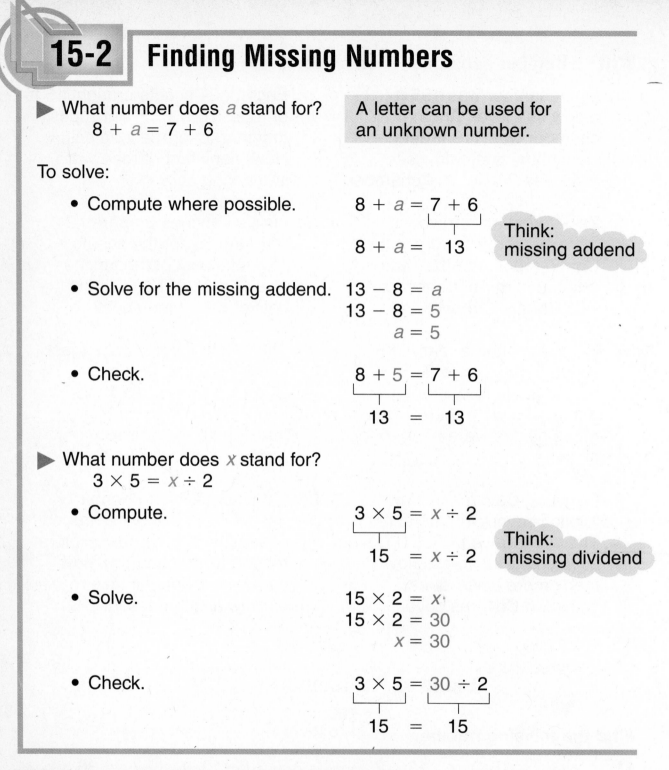

- Compute where possible.

    $8 + a = 7 + 6$
    $8 + a = 13$

    Think: missing addend

- Solve for the missing addend.
    $13 - 8 = a$
    $13 - 8 = 5$
    $a = 5$

- Check.
    $8 + 5 = 7 + 6$
    $13 = 13$

▶ What number does *x* stand for?
    $3 \times 5 = x \div 2$

- Compute.

    $3 \times 5 = x \div 2$
    $15 = x \div 2$

    Think: missing dividend

- Solve.
    $15 \times 2 = x$
    $15 \times 2 = 30$
    $x = 30$

- Check.
    $3 \times 5 = 30 \div 2$
    $15 = 15$

Write the number that *n* stands for in each number sentence.

1. $12 - 5 = n - 7$ **2.** $4 \times n = 8 \times 3$ **3.** $40 \div 8 = 30 \div n$

**Write the number that _y_ stands for
in each number sentence.**

4. $y \div 3 = 63 \div 7$ **5.** $9 + 7 = y + 8$ **6.** $2 \times 10 = y \times 5$

7. $9 + y = 3 \times 6$ **8.** $42 \div 7 = 16 - y$ **9.** $10 + 7 = y - 3$

10. $y \times 3 = 18 \div 3$ **11.** $y - 10 = 7 \times 2$ **12.** $25 - 15 = y \div 4$

13. $8 \times y = 26 - 26$ **14.** $9 \times 8 = y \times 72$ **15.** $100 + y = 9 \times 12$

16. $50 \times 3 = 200 - y$ **17.** $y \div 2 = 10 \times 25$ **18.** $12 \times 12 = 130 + y$

19. $y + 99 = 59 + 40$ **20.** $43 \times y = 0 \div 34$ **21.** $125 \times 2 = 400 - y$

22. $64 + y + 22 = 100 + 20 + 8$

23. $500 \div 50 \times 95 = y + 2 \times 450$

24. $8 \times 8 \times y = 2 \times 250 + 12$

Critical Thinking

**Write the number that _n_ stands for
in each number sentence.**

25. $n + n = 6$ **26.** $7 - n = 7$ **27.** $n \times n = 25$

What number
added to itself
equals 6?

28. $n \times 4 = n$ **29.** $n \div 5 = n$

30. $n + n = 30$ **31.** $64 \div n = n$

**Write the numbers that _x_ and _y_ stand for
in each pair of number sentences.**

32. $x + y = 9$ **33.** $x \times y = 24$ **34.** $x \times y = 8$
  $x + x = 8$ $y \times y = 9$ $y - x = 7$

15-3 Functions

▶ The table at the right is called a **function table**.

Rule: × 3	
Input	Output
2	6
4	12
5	15
8	24
12	?

For each number that you put into the table, there is only one output. You can find the output by following the rule.

The input is 12. What is the output?

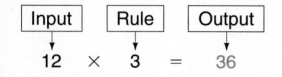

Input	Rule	Output
12	× 3	= 36

The output is 36.

▶ What is the rule for this function table?

Rule: ?	
Input	Output
40	10
32	8
28	7
20	5

Think how each input is related to its output.

$40 \div 4 = 10$ $32 \div 4 = 8$
$28 \div 4 = 7$ $20 \div 4 = 5$

The rule is ÷ 4.

Copy and complete.

1.

Rule: + 7	
Input	Output
4	11
8	?
25	?
42	?

2.

Rule: − 11	
Input	Output
12	?
20	?
45	?
63	?

3.

Rule: ÷ 2	
Input	Output
250	?
210	?
180	?
100	?

Copy and complete each table.

4.

Rule: × 9	
Input	Output
5	?
8	?
10	?
25	?
51	?

5.

Rule: ÷ 20	
Input	Output
500	?
240	?
180	?
120	?
80	?

6.

Rule: × 43	
Input	Output
8	?
15	?
37	?
105	?
232	?

Write the rule for each table.

7.

Rule: ?	
Input	Output
5	40
8	64
12	96
20	160

8.

Rule: ?	
Input	Output
70	55
65	50
58	43
42	27

9.

Rule: ?	
Input	Output
15	40
22	47
36	61
44	69

10.

Rule: ?	
Input	Output
99	33
66	22
36	12
33	11
30	10

11.

Rule: ?	
Input	Output
4	48
6	72
8	96
11	132
15	180

12.

Rule: ?	
Input	Output
15	71
21	77
34	90
46	102
56	112

Challenge

Copy and complete.

13.

Rule: × 7	
Input	Output
?	63
?	77
?	98
?	112

14.

Rule: ÷ 9	
Input	Output
?	25
?	22
?	18
?	15

15.

Rule: × 15	
Input	Output
?	75
?	120
?	165
?	225

Missing Symbols

The symbol = means "is equal to."

$$8 = 8$$
$$4 + 5 = 9$$
$$15 = 3 \times 5$$
$$6 + 1 = 5 + 2$$

The symbol ≠ means "is *not* equal to."

$$7 \neq 9$$
$$13 - 4 \neq 12$$
$$6 \neq 20 \div 5$$
$$4 \times 3 \neq 3 \times 5$$

Which symbol completes this number sentence?

$$8 \times 6 \ \underline{\ ?\ } \ 25 + 25$$

To find the correct symbol:

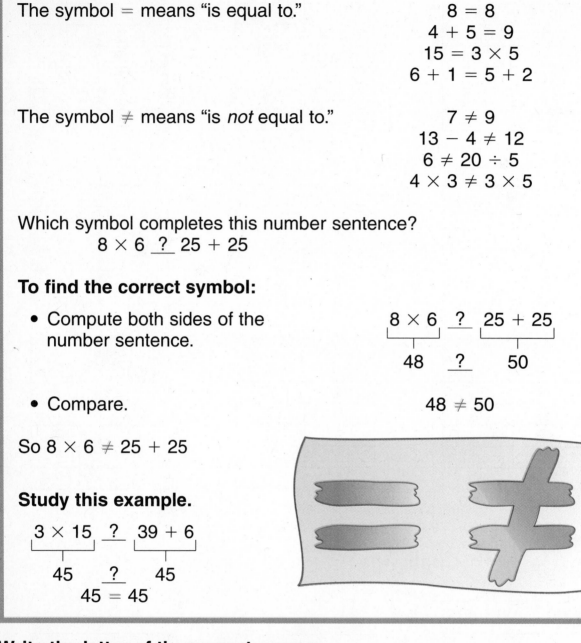

- Compute both sides of the number sentence.

$$8 \times 6 \quad ? \quad 25 + 25$$
$$48 \quad ? \quad 50$$

- Compare.

$$48 \neq 50$$

So $8 \times 6 \neq 25 + 25$

Study this example.

$$3 \times 15 \quad ? \quad 39 + 6$$
$$45 \quad ? \quad 45$$
$$45 = 45$$

Write the letter of the correct answer.

1. $6 + 4 \neq \underline{\ ?\ }$
  a. $13 - 3$
  b. $20 \div 2$
  c. 4×2

2. $7 \times 9 = \underline{\ ?\ }$
  a. $87 - 15$
  b. $39 + 24$
  c. $40 + 16$

3. $100 \div 2 \neq \underline{\ ?\ }$
  a. 2×25
  b. $30 + 30$
  c. $62 - 12$

4. $36 \div 6 = \underline{\ ?\ }$
  a. $30 \div 5$
  b. $36 - 6$
  c. 6×6

Compare. Write = or ≠ .

5. 10 + 8 _?_ 9 + 6   **6.** 13 − 5 _?_ 11 − 3   **7.** 5 × 8 _?_ 10 × 4

8. 54 ÷ 6 _?_ 56 ÷ 8   **9.** 4 + 5 _?_ 15 − 6   **10.** 2 × 3 _?_ 30 ÷ 6

11. 45 × 3 _?_ 125 + 10   **12.** 225 ÷ 25 _?_ 240 ÷ 30

13. 7250 + 100 _?_ 8450 − 200   **14.** 75 × 4 _?_ 900 ÷ 30

15. 586 − 139 _?_ 328 + 160   **16.** 396 ÷ 3 _?_ 12 × 11

17. 685 ÷ 5 _?_ 5 × 71   **18.** 8 × 525 _?_ 7 × 600

19. $4.50 + $1.15 _?_ 4 × $1.25   **20.** 6 × $5.95 _?_ 7 × $6.95

Compare. Write <, =, or >.

21. 500 ÷ 2 _?_ 200 ÷ 5   **22.** 50 × 600 _?_ 40 × 700

23. 2000 − 1500 _?_ 50 × 8   **24.** 850 − 125 _?_ 525 + 200

25. 2 × 550 _?_ 5 × 250   **26.** 400 ÷ 5 _?_ 500 ÷ 4

Solve.

27. Is the product of 8 and 45 equal to the difference of 500 and 140?

28. Is the sum of 534 and 166 equal to the product of 250 and 3?

Finding Together

Choose numbers from the box to complete each number sentence. Use each number only once.

1		5
	3	
7		9

29. 3 + 7 > 6 + _?_   **30.** 8 × _?_ ≠ 4 × 10

31. 80 ÷ 8 > _?_ + 4   **32.** 56 ÷ _?_ = 5 + _?_

15-5 | Number Line

A number line can help you find sums and differences.

▶ Let $n = 23$
What is $n + 32$?

To find a sum on a number line, count on from left to right.

Begin at 23.

Think: $32 = 30 + 2$ or 3 tens + 2
So count on 3 tens. Then count on 2.

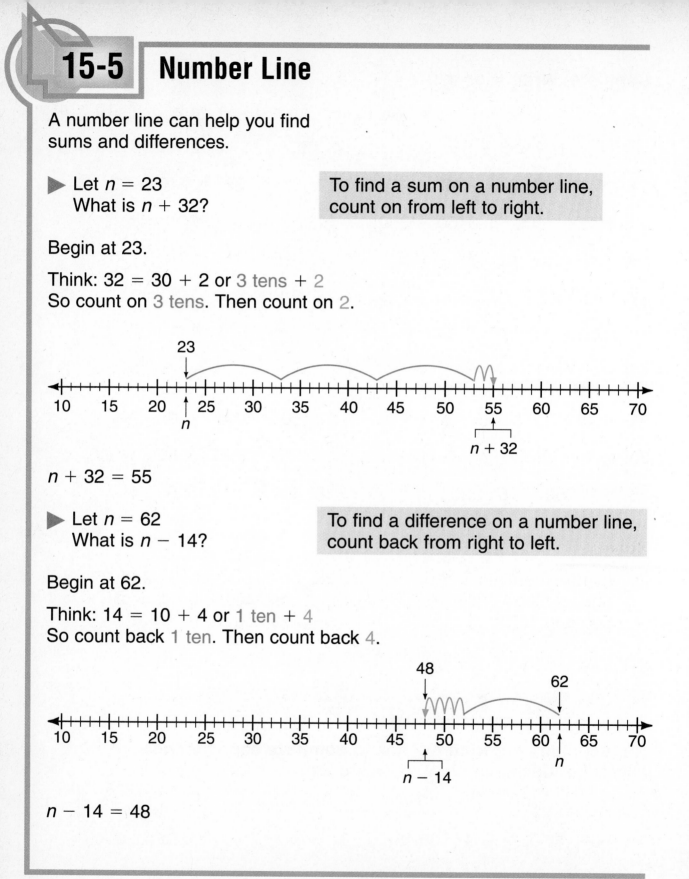

$n + 32 = 55$

▶ Let $n = 62$
What is $n - 14$?

To find a difference on a number line, count back from right to left.

Begin at 62.

Think: $14 = 10 + 4$ or 1 ten + 4
So count back 1 ten. Then count back 4.

$n - 14 = 48$

Copy and complete each table. You may use a number line.

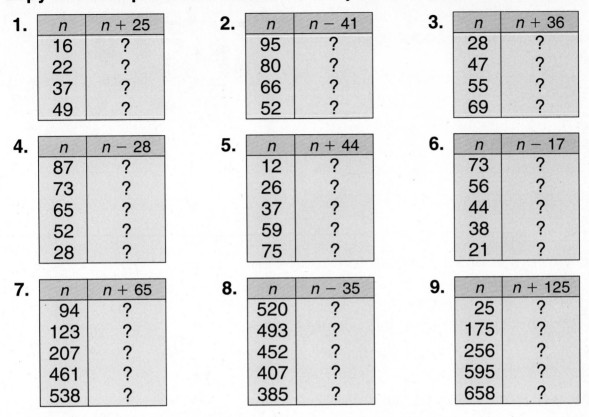

1.

n	n + 25
16	?
22	?
37	?
49	?

2.

n	n − 41
95	?
80	?
66	?
52	?

3.

n	n + 36
28	?
47	?
55	?
69	?

4.

n	n − 28
87	?
73	?
65	?
52	?
28	?

5.

n	n + 44
12	?
26	?
37	?
59	?
75	?

6.

n	n − 17
73	?
56	?
44	?
38	?
21	?

7.

n	n + 65
94	?
123	?
207	?
461	?
538	?

8.

n	n − 35
520	?
493	?
452	?
407	?
385	?

9.

n	n + 125
25	?
175	?
256	?
595	?
658	?

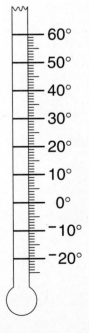

Challenge

Think of the thermometer as a number line.
Write temperatures below zero with a minus sign.
⁻12° "twelve degrees below zero"

Use the thermometer to copy and complete each table.

10.

n	n + 10°
65°	75°
12°	?
0°	?
⁻5°	5°
⁻8°	?
⁻25°	?

11.

n	n − 15°
75°	60°
50°	?
0°	?
⁻5°	⁻20°
⁻7°	?
⁻10°	?

451

15-6 | Using Parentheses

How would you go about solving this problem?

$$40 - 3 \times 5 + (10 \div 2) = \underline{\ ?\ }$$

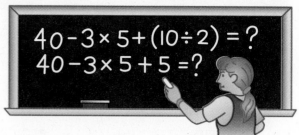

To solve:

- Always do the operations in parentheses first.

$$40 - 3 \times 5 + \underbrace{(10 \div 2)} = \underline{\ ?\ }$$

- Multiply or divide. Work in order from left to right.

$$40 - \underbrace{3 \times 5} + \qquad 5 \qquad = \underline{\ ?\ }$$

- Add or subtract. Work in order from left to right.

$$40 - \qquad 15 \quad + \qquad 5 \qquad = \underline{\ ?\ }$$
$$25 \qquad + \qquad 5 \quad = 30$$

Study these examples.

$$2 \times \underbrace{(4 + 3)} - 10 + \underbrace{(4 \times 4)} = \underline{\ ?\ }$$
$$2 \times \qquad 7 \quad - 10 + \qquad 16 \quad = \underline{\ ?\ }$$
$$14 \qquad - 10 + \quad 16 \quad = \underline{\ ?\ }$$
$$4 \qquad + \quad 16 \quad = 20$$

$$\underbrace{(4 \times 2)} + \underbrace{(9 \div 3)} - 10 + 1 = \underline{\ ?\ }$$
$$8 \quad + \qquad 3 \quad - 10 + 1 = \underline{\ ?\ }$$
$$11 \qquad - 10 + 1 = \underline{\ ?\ }$$
$$1 \qquad + 1 = 2$$

Solve.

1. $18 - 6 + 4$

2. $7 + 7 - 5$

3. $6 \times 8 \div 4$

4. $24 \div 6 + 10$

5. $38 - 2 \times 9$

6. $10 \times 10 \div 5$

7. $45 \div (3 \times 3)$

8. $(10 + 10) \times 8$

9. $25 + (5 \times 5) + 50$

10. $(3 + 5) + (10 + 2)$

11. $100 - (100 \div 10)$

12. $(500 \div 2) + 25$

Use the order of operations to solve.

13. $(6 - 2) + (6 \times 2)$ **14.** $(8 \div 4) \times (9 - 5)$

15. $(56 \div 8) \times (10 + 7)$ **16.** $(4 \times 12) - (20 - 15)$

17. $9.7 + (6.1 - 5.1)$ **18.** $20 - (10 - 5.5)$

19. $(8.1 - 8.1) \times (5 + 4)$ **20.** $(3.2 + 4.6) - (2 \times 2)$

21. $(6 \times 2) + (9.3 - 7.5)$ **22.** $(45 \div 5) + (10.75 - 2.25)$

23. $\frac{2}{5} + \left(\frac{4}{5} - \frac{2}{5}\right)$ **24.** $\left(\frac{7}{10} - \frac{4}{10}\right) + \frac{6}{10}$

25. $\frac{1}{2} + \left(\frac{1}{2} - \frac{1}{4}\right)$ **26.** $\frac{3}{4} + \left(\frac{1}{2} + \frac{1}{4}\right)$

27. $\left(\frac{1}{4} + \frac{1}{4}\right) + \left(\frac{1}{8} + \frac{1}{8}\right)$ **28.** $\left(\frac{2}{6} + \frac{3}{6}\right) - \left(\frac{1}{3} + \frac{1}{3}\right)$

29. $\left(\frac{7}{8} - \frac{1}{4}\right) - \left(\frac{2}{8} + \frac{1}{8}\right)$ **30.** $\left(\frac{5}{6} + \frac{1}{6}\right) \times \left(\frac{1}{2} + \frac{1}{2}\right)$

31. $\left(\frac{6}{8} - \frac{3}{4}\right) + \left(\frac{2}{4} + \frac{2}{4}\right)$ **32.** $\left(\frac{4}{9} + \frac{4}{9}\right) \times \left(\frac{2}{5} + \frac{3}{5}\right)$

Calculator Activity

Use a calculator to solve.

33. $6.5 + 7.2 \times 3.1$ **34.** $4.4 - 4.5 \div 1.5$

35. $6.2 \times (8.2 - 5.1)$ **36.** $10.5 \div 1.05 \times 5$

37. $5 + 5.5 + 5.5 - (9.2 - 3)$ **38.** $(8.4 \times 10) - 10 + 1$

39. $(7.25 \times 4) - (7.25 \div 5)$ **40.** $(5.2 \times 4) + (4.8 \div 2)$

15-7 Problem Solving: More Than One Way

Problem: Kim is making a rectangular sign 3 ft wide. She uses 14 ft of edging to go around the sign. How long is the sign?

1 IMAGINE Create a mental picture.

2 NAME *Facts:* width = 3 ft
perimeter = 14 ft

Question: How long is the sign?

3 THINK There is more than one way to find a solution. Here are 2 ways.

Method 1	*Method 2*
Draw a picture.	Use a formula.
	$P = 2 \times \ell + 2 \times w$
Guess and test to find the length.	Guess and test to find the length.

4 COMPUTE

Method 1	*Method 2*
First Guess ⟶ 3 ft	Let ℓ = length
3 ft + 3 ft + 3 ft + 3 ft = 12 ft not large enough	$P = 2 \times \ \ell \ + 2 \times w$ $14 = 2 \times \ \ell \ + (2 \times 3 \text{ ft})$ $14 = 2 \times \ \ell \ + 6 \text{ ft}$
Second Guess ⟶ 4 ft	$14 = 2 \times \underline{\ ?\ } \text{ ft} + 6 \text{ ft}$ $14 = 2 \times \ 4 \text{ ft} \ + 6 \text{ ft}$
3 ft + 3 ft + 4 ft + 4 ft = 14 ft correct sum	
The sign is 4 ft long.	The sign is 4 ft long.

5 CHECK

Use the formula to check your answer.	Draw a picture to check your answer.

454

Solve.

1. The temperature at Beal Beach was 32.4°C at dawn. It rose 4.7°C by noon, and then fell 6.1°C by dusk. What was the temperature at dusk?

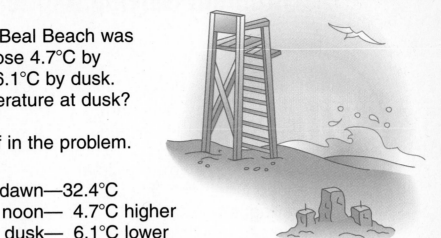

IMAGINE   Put yourself in the problem.

NAME   *Facts:*   dawn—32.4°C
                        noon— 4.7°C higher
                        dusk— 6.1°C lower

Question: What was the temperature at dusk?

THINK   What method will you use?

Method 1

Draw and label a number line.

Method 2

Write a number sentence.
$32.4 + 4.7 - 6.1 = \underline{\ ?\ }$

COMPUTE ⟶ **CHECK**

2. Karl has 25 wheels for wagons and scooters. How many of each toy can he make if the wagons have 4 wheels and scooters have 3 wheels?

3. The digits of a two-digit number have a sum of 7 and a difference of 5. The number is less than 70 and greater than 20. What is the number?

4. The Hoopsters scored 35 points in the first half of the game and 18 more than that in the second half. The other team scored 90 points in the game. Did the Hoopsters win?

15-8 Problem-Solving Applications

Solve.

Use these steps:

1. Carmen answers this riddle: "I am a number. If you add me to 28, the sum is 100." What is the number?

2. Mel's riddle states: "I am a decimal. If I am added together 5 times, the answer equals 43." What is the decimal?

3. Rob's riddle is: "I am a decimal equal to the sum of 2.8, 3.2 and 7.4." What is the decimal?

4. What number should Mel add to complete this sentence?
$8\frac{1}{4} + 2\frac{1}{4} + n = 11\frac{1}{2}$

5. Should Rob use $=$ or $\neq$ to complete this number sentence?
$3 \times 4 - 2 \underline{} 18 \div 2 + 4$

6. Which of Carmen's number sentences equals 25?
$5 + 10 \times 4 \div 2 = n$ or $35 - 10 \div 5 + 5 = n$

7. Carmen is asked to find the number halfway between 40 and 70. What is it?

8. Rob is asked to find the greatest number less than 65 that is divisible by 3. What is it?

9. On *Math Facts,* players scored 4 points for each correct answer. How many correct answers did the winner give? the contestant in 3rd place? (Use the bar graph.)

1 Imagine

2 Name

3 Think

4 Compute

5 Check

Contest Results

Number of Points: 72, 64, 56, 48, 40, 32, 24, 16, 8, 0

Place: 1st   2nd   3rd

Solve.

10. The winner may choose from 2 prizes: a dime a day for a year or a dollar a day during March. Which amount is greater?

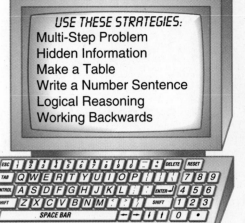

USE THESE STRATEGIES:
Multi-Step Problem
Hidden Information
Make a Table
Write a Number Sentence
Logical Reasoning
Working Backwards

11. There were three players on *Math Facts.* Mel did not win, but he scored more points than Rob. Did Carmen win?

12. The program began at 6:30 P.M. and ended at 7:00 P.M. There were two $4\frac{1}{4}$ minute commercial breaks. How long was the show itself?

13. The winner received a T-shirt that said "I'm Number $5 - 2 \times 2$." What does this mean? Create a shirt for the second-place winner.

14. Arrange the numbers in the box so their sum, product, difference, and quotient are equal.

$$\underline{} + \underline{} = \underline{} - \underline{} = \underline{} \div \underline{} = \underline{} \times \underline{}$$

15. *Math Facts* auditioned students. In the first round, $\frac{1}{2}$ were eliminated. In the second round, 30 more were eliminated. There were 10 students in the third round. How many students came to the audition?

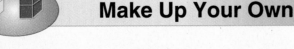

Make Up Your Own

16. Write a problem modeled on problem 10. Have a classmate solve it.

More Practice

Write the number *n* stands for in each number sentence.

1. $28 - n = 4 \times 6$

2. $11 \times 12 = 100 + n$

3. $n \div 4 = 12 \times 2$

4. $32 + 20 + n = 52 \times 4$

Copy and complete each table.

5.

Rule: ×3	
Input	Output
5	?
9	?
33	?
46	?

6.

Rule: ?	
Input	Output
24	4
36	6
48	8
60	10

7.

n	*n* + 39
15	?
67	?
85	?
92	?
98	?

Compare. Write = or ≠.

8. 36×3 _?_ $24 + 24$

9. $25 - 5$ _?_ $60 - 40$

10. $76 + 2$ _?_ $92 - 31$

Use the order of operations to solve.

11. $15 + 8 - 2 \times 9$

12. $9 \times 10 \div 5 + 6$

13. $30 + 4 \times 4 + 20$

14. $49 - 3 \times 7$

15. $(54 \div 6) \times (2 + 10)$

16. $\frac{1}{5} + \frac{3}{5} - \frac{2}{5}$

Write a number sentence. Then solve.

17. Mrs. Lam bought 720 yards of material to make curtains. If 8 yards of material are needed for each pair of curtains, how many windows can she decorate?

18. The school auditorium has 25 rows of seats. Each row has 15 seats. How many seats are in the auditorium?

(See *Still More Practice*, p. 472.)

NEGATIVE NUMBERS

Numbers that are written with a minus sign, such as ⁻6, ⁻25, and ⁻247, are called **negative numbers**.

You already know how to use negative numbers to write temperatures below zero.
⁻15°F   ⁻3°C

You can also use negative numbers to show distances below sea level.

⁻5 ft means "5 feet below sea level."

The scale at the right shows the location of different sites in Crystal Caverns.

Solve. Use the scale of Crystal Caverns.

1. Which site is located at ⁻90 ft?

2. About how many feet below sea level is Stalagmite Garden?

3. Which site is farthest below sea level? About how many feet below sea level is it?

4. How many feet difference is there between Bottomless Pool and Stalactite Chamber?

5. Which site is halfway between sea level and Pirate's Rest? How many feet below sea level is it?

6. Suppose there was a site at ⁻150 ft. How much lower than sea level would it be than Bottomless Pool?

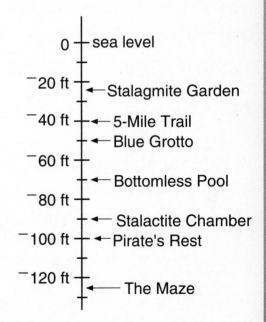

```
0  ─┬─ sea level
    │
⁻20 ft ─┼─← Stalagmite Garden
    │
⁻40 ft ─┼─← 5-Mile Trail
    ├─← Blue Grotto
⁻60 ft ─┼─
    │
    ├─← Bottomless Pool
⁻80 ft ─┼─
    │
    ├─← Stalactite Chamber
⁻100 ft ─┼─← Pirate's Rest
    │
⁻120 ft ─┼─
    ├─── The Maze
    │
```

Check Your Mastery

Write the number *n* stands for in each number sentence.

See pp. 444–445

1. $6 + 8 = n - 5$

2. $27 \times n = 112 - 4$

3. $n \div 20 = 17 - 12$

4. $700 - 7 + 20 = n + 100 - 5$

Copy and complete each table.

See pp. 446–447, 450–451

5.

Rule: ?	
Input	Output
5	40
8	64
10	80
12	96

6.

Rule: ÷3	
Input	Output
9	?
27	?
36	?
45	?

7.

n	n × 8
7	?
14	?
21	?
28	?
35	?

Compare. Write = or ≠.

See pp. 448–449

8. $65 \div 5 \ \underline{?} \ 8 + 5$

9. $7 \times 8 \ \underline{?} \ 66 - 9$

10. $3 \times 36 \ \underline{?} \ 6 \times 18$

Use the order of operations to solve.

See pp. 452–453

11. $16 \div 4 + 8$

12. $100 - 90 \div 10$

13. $9 + 8 - 7 + 5$

14. $250 \div (5 \times 2) + 100$

15. $8 \times (25 + 6) - 7$

16. $(2 + 6) \times (14 - 8)$

Write a number sentence. Then solve.

See pp. 441–442, 456–457

17. Brian has 87 rare stamps in his collection. Susan has 127 stamps, and Judy has 95 stamps. How many stamps do they have altogether?

18. Betty has 135 flowers. Each arrangement requires 15 flowers. How many arrangements can she make?

Practice 1-1

1a. $8 + 7$ **b.** $2 + 9$ **c.** $6 + 6$

2a. $4 - 1$ **b.** $7 - 2$ **c.** $8 - 8$

3a. 3×7 **b.** 6×8 **c.** 9×4

4a. $5 + 2$ **b.** $5 - 2$ **c.** 5×2

Write a family of facts for each set of numbers.

5a. 1, 2, 3   **b.** 3, 7, 10   **c.** 5, 8, 13

6a. 3, 9, 27   **b.** 2, 8, 16   **c.** 5, 6, 30

Copy and complete.

7a. $7 \times \underline{?} = 21$ **b.** $9 \times \underline{?} = 45$
$\ 3 \times \underline{?} = 21$ $\underline{?} \times 9 = 45$
$\ 21 \div \underline{?} = 3$ $45 \div 9 = \underline{?}$
$\ 21 \div 7 = \underline{?}$ $45 \div \underline{?} = 9$

8. One addend is 8. The sum is 15. What is the other addend?

9. Two numbers have a sum of 7 and a difference of 3. What are the two numbers?

10. One factor is 6. The product is 42. What is the other factor?

11. What is the product of 4 and 8?

12. The dividend is 64. The divisor is 8. What is the quotient?

13. Anya buys 8 packs of pens. There are 8 pens in each pack. How many pens does Anya buy?

14. There are 24 children in a class. They divide into 4 equal teams. How many children are on each team?

Practice 2-1

Chapter 2

Write the number in standard form.

1a. 8 thousands
2 tens   **b.** twenty-two thousand

2a. four hundred seventy-three   **b.** $400,000 + 10,000 + 700 + 200 + 1$

Write the word name for each number.

3a. 1,020,140   **b.** $80,000 + 4000 + 500$

Write each number in expanded form.

4a. 668   **b.** 8502   **c.** 5,884,901

Write the place and value of the underlined digit.

5a. 3<u>5</u>40   **b.** <u>6</u>08,721   **c.** 2,3<u>0</u>0,400

Compare. Write $<$, $=$, or $>$.

6a. 983 $\underline{?}$ 892   **b.** 1201 $\underline{?}$ 1021

7. Write the numbers 45, 54, 48, and 46 in order from greatest to least.

8. Write the numbers 5403, 3405, 4340, 3450, and 5430 in order from least to greatest.

9. Write LXIV in standard form.

10. Tell which has the greater value: CX or XC.

11. What number is 100 more than 4,506,722?

12. What number is 1000 less than 439,800?

13. What is the greatest even four-digit number?

14. The Beekman Library has 23,450 books. The Conrad Library has 24,355 books and the Doral Library has 25,320 books. Put the libraries in order from least books to most books.

Practice 2-2

Write each amount.

1a. 2 dollars,
2 quarters,
1 dime, 3 nickels

b. 5 quarters, 4 dimes,
8 nickels, 3 pennies

Write the fewest coins and bills you would
receive as change. Then write the value of
the change.

2a. Cost: $4.20
Amount given:
$5.00

b. Cost: $8.39
Amount given:
$10.00

Round to the nearest hundred or dollar.

3a. 2390   **b.** 821   **c.** 56,472

4a. $3.29   **b.** $12.90   **c.** $35.85

Round to the nearest thousand.

5a. 54,320   **b.** 8199   **c.** 65,328

About what number is each arrow pointing
toward?

6.
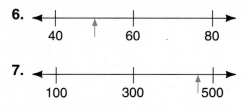

7.

8. What is 4809 rounded to the nearest ten?

9. What is $328.59 rounded to the nearest
ten dollars?

10. Suzy has $32.28. Can she buy a fig tree
that costs $23.82?

11. Yinka bought a bookbag for $15.95. He
gave the clerk a twenty-dollar bill. How
much change did he receive?

12. What number is halfway between 1000
and 2000?

Practice 3-1

Chapter 3

1a. 1 + 0   **b.** 4 + 4   **c.** 0 + 7

2a. 3 + 5 + 4   **b.** 6 + 1 + 6 + 1

3a. 3 − 1   **b.** 8 − 0   **c.** 7 − 7

4a. 17¢ − 8¢   **b.** 11¢ − 6¢   **c.** 2¢ − 2¢

Find the missing number.

5a. 9 + _?_ = 14   **b.** 9 = 7 + _?_

6a. 7 − _?_ = 1   **b.** 5 = _?_ − 8

Estimate the sum or difference.

7a. 28 + 22   **b.** 589 + 612   **c.** 825 − 592

8a. $1.28
    + $1.15

b. $309
    + $194

c. $8.89
    − $7.20

Find the sum or difference.

9a. 38 + 41   **b.** 211 + 544   **c.** $17 + $32

10a. 85 − 40   **b.** 54 − 43   **c.** $68 − $55

11. A quilt has 12 blue squares and 24
green squares. How many squares does
it have?

12. Max has 48 comic books. He sells 23 of
them. How many does he have left?

13. Jan scored 8 points in a basketball game.
Ina scored 19 points. How many more
points did Ina score than Jan?

14. There are 18 turtles in a pond. There are
7 adult turtles. How many are not adults?

15. Alma needs $14 to buy a compact disk.
She has $11. How much more money
does she need?

Chapter 4

Practice 4-1

1a. $\begin{array}{r} 32 \\ +\ 67 \\ \hline \end{array}$ **b.** $\begin{array}{r} 19 \\ +894 \\ \hline \end{array}$ **c.** $\begin{array}{r} 695 \\ +8126 \\ \hline \end{array}$

2a. $\begin{array}{r} 94{,}320 \\ +84{,}002 \\ \hline \end{array}$ **b.** $\begin{array}{r} 190{,}029 \\ +870{,}993 \\ \hline \end{array}$ **c.** $\begin{array}{r} \$18.26 \\ +\ \ 4.59 \\ \hline \end{array}$

3a. $\begin{array}{r} 2 \\ 97 \\ +73 \\ \hline \end{array}$ **b.** $\begin{array}{r} 79 \\ 500 \\ 639 \\ +322 \\ \hline \end{array}$ **c.** $\begin{array}{r} \$\ 919 \\ 610 \\ 8120 \\ +\ 1293 \\ \hline \end{array}$

4a. $25 + 75 + 50$ **b.** $\$45.99 + \$68.20$

5a. $8550 + 10{,}203$ **b.** $194{,}344 + 940{,}277$

Make a rough estimate. Then adjust.

6a. $\begin{array}{r} 920 \\ +735 \\ \hline \end{array}$ **b.** $\begin{array}{r} 2402 \\ +5111 \\ \hline \end{array}$ **c.** $\begin{array}{r} \$79.45 \\ +\ 60.99 \\ \hline \end{array}$

7a. $\begin{array}{r} 382 \\ 989 \\ +105 \\ \hline \end{array}$ **b.** $\begin{array}{r} 277 \\ 184 \\ +457 \\ \hline \end{array}$ **c.** $\begin{array}{r} \$18.95 \\ 27.72 \\ +\ 11.08 \\ \hline \end{array}$

8. A bulletin board has 19 notes in English and 12 in Spanish. How many notes are on the board?

9. Find the total number of pencils in a box of 24 red, 12 blue, 30 green, and 23 yellow pencils.

10. Mr. Kanin has 1940 postcards from the United States and 2430 from other countries. How many postcards are in his collection?

11. Add 19,200 to the sum of 394 and 377.

12. Mitch uses tiles to cover a floor. He uses 287 black tiles, 78 white tiles, and 118 blue tiles. How many tiles does he use?

13. The sum is 54,000. One addend is 28,250. What is the other addend?

14. A necklace has 26 glass beads, 48 metal beads, and 82 tiny wooden beads. How many beads are in the necklace?

Practice 4-2

1a. $\begin{array}{r} 89 \\ -19 \\ \hline \end{array}$ **b.** $\begin{array}{r} 300 \\ -\ 28 \\ \hline \end{array}$ **c.** $\begin{array}{r} 738 \\ -592 \\ \hline \end{array}$

2a. $\begin{array}{r} 5493 \\ -2500 \\ \hline \end{array}$ **b.** $\begin{array}{r} 7000 \\ -\ 429 \\ \hline \end{array}$ **c.** $\begin{array}{r} 69{,}504 \\ -18{,}366 \\ \hline \end{array}$

3a. $\begin{array}{r} \$9.29 \\ -\ 1.63 \\ \hline \end{array}$ **b.** $\begin{array}{r} \$43.50 \\ -\ 25.70 \\ \hline \end{array}$ **c.** $\begin{array}{r} \$50.22 \\ -\ 8.99 \\ \hline \end{array}$

4a. $280 - 223$ **b.** $29{,}302 - 10{,}233$

5a. $\$35.98 - \$7.23$ **b.** $\$600.75 - \$240.80$

Estimate the difference. Use front-end estimation.

6a. $\begin{array}{r} 849 \\ -290 \\ \hline \end{array}$ **b.** $\begin{array}{r} 8394 \\ -2011 \\ \hline \end{array}$ **c.** $\begin{array}{r} 73{,}382 \\ -14{,}006 \\ \hline \end{array}$

7a. $\begin{array}{r} \$51.20 \\ -\ 10.75 \\ \hline \end{array}$ **b.** $\begin{array}{r} \$757 \\ -\ 522 \\ \hline \end{array}$ **c.** $\begin{array}{r} \$98.35 \\ -\ 52.20 \\ \hline \end{array}$

8. How much greater than 427 is 549?

9. Ms. Brownell has 1327 salt shakers. There are 272 plastic shakers; the rest are ceramic. How many ceramic shakers does she have?

10. Ruth is reading a 178-page book. She is on page 67. How many pages does she still have to read?

11. Angie sells seed packs. She starts with a carton of 250 packs. She has 117 packs left. How many has she sold?

12. An adult's T-shirt costs $8.99 and a child's T-shirt costs $5.50. How much more expensive is the adult's T-shirt?

13. Subtract 3405 from the sum of 2847 and 5032.

Practice 5-1

1a. 3×0 **b.** 1×5 **c.** 0×8

2a. 7×6 **b.** 6×7 **c.** 9×1

3a. 3×21 **b.** 5×18 **c.** 6×94

4a. 7×100 **b.** 4×805 **c.** 2×4500

5a. $8 \times \$1.05$ **b.** $9 \times \$31.59$ **c.** $3 \times \$82.80$

Estimate each product. Use front-end estimation.

6a. 2×148 **b.** 5×822 **c.** 9×704

Find the missing numbers.

7a. $2 \times \underline{\ ?\ } = 18$ **b.** $21 = 7 \times \underline{\ ?\ }$

8a. $45 = 5 \times \underline{\ ?\ }$ **b.** $27 \times \underline{\ ?\ } = 27$

9. What is the product of 78 and 7?

10. What is 459 multiplied by 5?

11. The product is 81. One factor is 9. What is the other factor?

12. Which is greater: 7×1 or 0×7?

13. What is the product of 472 and zero?

14. Joel bought 3 boxes of peaches. There were 6 peaches in each box. How many peaches did he buy?

15. There are 8 shelves of books. Each shelf holds 45 books. How many books are there?

16. What is the product of $19.95 and one?

17. Meg bought 6 cassettes. Each cassette cost $9.98. How much did she spend?

Practice 5-2

1a. 10×34 **b.** 10×58 **c.** 10×985

2a. 20×12 **b.** 40×42 **c.** 50×50

3a. $\begin{array}{r} 24 \\ \times 18 \end{array}$ **b.** $\begin{array}{r} 57 \\ \times 21 \end{array}$ **c.** $\begin{array}{r} 61 \\ \times 63 \end{array}$

4a. 96×17 **b.** 27×793 **c.** 63×403

5a. $12 \times \$1.02$ **b.** $41 \times \$3.40$ **c.** $35 \times \$6.50$

Estimate by rounding. Then multiply.

6a. 32×41 **b.** 29×491 **c.** 47×307

7a. $12 \times \$1.25$ **b.** $22 \times \$4.59$ **c.** $84 \times \$8.82$

8. What is the product of 748 and 10?

9. A theater has 24 rows of seats. There are 18 seats in each row. How many seats are there?

10. A compact disc is on sale for $7.99. How much would it cost to buy 11 of the discs?

11. Zenia earns $4.15 an hour. She works 20 hours a week. How much does she earn in one week?

12. Each volume of an encyclopedia has 568 pages. There are 24 volumes. How many pages are in the entire encyclopedia?

13. What is the product of 409 and 89?

14. A pillowcase costs $4.25. How much would cases for 15 pillows cost?

15. A toy store has 52 bags of marbles. There are 35 marbles in each bag. How many marbles does the store have?

16. There are 115 windows on each floor of an office building. The building has 48 floors. How many windows does the building have?

Practice 6-1

Chapter 6

1a. $9\overline{)0}$ **b.** $1\overline{)8}$ **c.** $7\overline{)7}$

2a. $5 \div 5$ **b.** $0 \div 4$ **c.** $2 \div 1$

Estimate the quotient.

3a. $8\overline{)82}$ **b.** $4\overline{)51}$ **c.** $3\overline{)621}$

4a. $2\overline{)6905}$ **b.** $5\overline{)\$5.25}$ **c.** $7\overline{)\$34.89}$

Divide.

5a. $7\overline{)49}$ **b.** $5\overline{)48}$ **c.** $3\overline{)29}$

6a. $4\overline{)84}$ **b.** $9\overline{)90}$ **c.** $6\overline{)73}$

7a. $2\overline{)868}$ **b.** $8\overline{)969}$ **c.** $7\overline{)865}$

8. Is 3892 divisible by 2?

9. Is 193 divisible by 5?

10. Is 711 divisible by 3?

11. Is 25,570 divisible by 10?

12. A grove has 91 pear trees. They are in 7 equal rows. How many trees are in each row?

13. Elena has 98 inches of ribbon. How many 6-inch pieces can she cut? Will there be any ribbon left over? how much ribbon?

14. If 3634 is divided by 7, what is the quotient and the remainder?

15. What is the next number in this pattern: 3645, 1215, 405, 135, . . . ?

16. Each full page holds 8 pictures. The album holds 164 photos. How many pages are full? How many pages are partly filled?

17. What numbers between 107 and 125 are divisible by 2?

Practice 6-2

1a. $5\overline{)325}$ **b.** $7\overline{)421}$ **c.** $6\overline{)598}$

2a. $9\overline{)819}$ **b.** $4\overline{)110}$ **c.** $8\overline{)209}$

3a. $3\overline{)621}$ **b.** $6\overline{)650}$ **c.** $2\overline{)811}$

4a. $5\overline{)515}$ **b.** $7\overline{)745}$ **c.** $4\overline{)839}$

5a. $8\overline{)8968}$ **b.** $5\overline{)1005}$ **c.** $7\overline{)7325}$

6a. $3\overline{)\$.21}$ **b.** $2\overline{)\$24.40}$ **c.** $6\overline{)\$7.20}$

7a. $4\overline{)\$31.20}$ **b.** $9\overline{)\$9.36}$ **c.** $8\overline{)\$7.52}$

Use the order of operations to solve.

8a. $9 - 2 \times 3$ **b.** $15 \div 2 + 3$

9a. $5 \times 10 \div 2$ **b.** $360 \div 4 \times 2$

10a. $15 - 5 \times 2 + 1$ **b.** $21 \div 7 + 9 \times 3$

11. There are 3727 flyers. What is the greatest number of flyers there could be in each of 8 equal stacks?

12. Michael bought 8 oak saplings for $48.40. How much did each sapling cost?

13. Leila makes 850 muffins for a bake sale. She places them in bags of 8. How many bags can she fill? How many muffins are left over?

14. Zack spent $200.35 during a 5-day vacation. How much did he spend each day if he spent an equal amount daily?

15. What is the average of 104, 205, 47, and 36?

16. In their games this season, the Hoops scored 64, 68, 42, 70, 92, and 54 points. What is their average score per game?

17. A train travels 600 miles in 9 hours. About how many miles per hour does the train travel?

Chapter 7

Practice 7-1

Write *in., ft, mi, c, gal,* or *lb* for the unit you would use to measure each.

1a. the length of a finger

b. the weight of a bowling ball

2a. the capacity of a juice glass

b. the distance from San Diego to Las Vegas

3a. the height of a door

b. the capacity of an oil barrel

Add.

4a.   8 ft 3 in.
      + 4 ft 7 in.

b.   6 ft 8 in.
      + 3 ft 5 in.

Complete.

5a. 36 in. = _?_ ft

b. 4 gal = _?_ qt

6a. 3 lb = _?_ oz

b. 32 c = _?_ pt

7. Is a shoelace for a pair of sneakers about 3 in., 3 ft, 3 yd, or 3 mi long?

8. Would you need 2 fl oz, 2 c, 2 pt, or 2 gal of water to fill a large bucket?

9. Does a wild rabbit probably weigh 3 oz, 3 lb, or 33 lb?

10. A recipe calls for 3 c of milk. Janet has 1 qt of milk. Does she have enough for the recipe?

11. There are 5 apples in a bag. Each apple weighs 5 oz. Does the bag weigh more than 2 lb?

12. Does a soup ladle probably hold 4 fl oz, 40 fl oz, 4 c, or 4 pt?

13. How many inches are there in 12 ft?

14. Is a 5-lb box heavier than a 90-oz box?

Practice 7-2

Write *cm, m, km, mL, L,* or *g* for the unit you would use to measure each.

1a. the mass of a goldfish

b. the thickness of a book

2a. the distance from Rome to Madrid

b. the capacity of a fish tank

3a. the capacity of a teaspoon

b. the length of a large rug

Complete.

4a. 200 cm = _?_ m

b. 7 L = _?_ mL

5a. 6000 g = _?_ kg

b. 4 km = _?_ m

Write how much time has passed.

6. from 12:30 A.M. to 4:00 A.M.

7. from 10:20 P.M. to 11:15 P.M.

8. Is a room comfortable when it is 68°F or 68°C?

9. Will ice melt at 2°F or 2°C?

10. What time is it when it is 12 minutes before noon?

11. Does a postcard have a mass of 1 g or 1 kg?

12. Is a pencil about 15 mm, 15 cm, or 15 m long?

Use the map to solve.

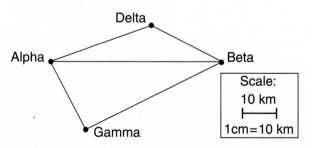

13. How far is it from Alpha to Beta in kilometers?

14. Is Beta closer to Alpha or Delta?

Chapter 8

Practice 8-1

Use the list to solve.

Favorite Numbers of Mr. Porter's Class
7, 5, 7, 19, 11, 2, 3, 13, 5, 7, 19, 11, 2, 8, 8, 7, 7, 5

1. Make a tally chart and a table from the data in the list.

2. Which was the most popular number?

3. Which numbers were equally popular?

Use the line graph to solve.

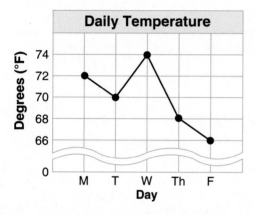

4. Which day was the warmest?

5. On which day was the temperature 70°C?

Use the chart to solve.

Type of Boat	Number
Motor Boat	45
Sail Boat	80
Canoe	60
Row Boat	35

6. Make a pictograph from the data in the chart.

7. What type of boat was second most popular?

Use the bar graph to solve.

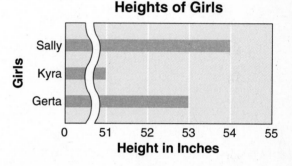

8. Which girl is 2 in. taller than Kyra?

9. How much taller is Sally than Gerta?

Practice 8-2

Use the circle graph to solve.

1. Does the shop have more *thank you* or *get well* cards?

2. How many cards in all does the shop have?

3. Molly has 3 blue shirts, 4 red shirts, and 1 white shirt. She picks one without looking. What is the probability that she will pick the white shirt?

4. A computer picks a random number between 1 and 100. Is it more or less likely to pick a number above 20?

5. Is the computer more likely, less likely, or equally likely to pick an odd number?

6. Andrew tosses a coin. What is the probability that it will land heads up?

7. Irene tosses a nickel. It lands tails up. What is the probability that it will land tails up on her next toss?

Write the fraction for the shaded part. Then write the fraction for the part that is not shaded.

1a.  **b.**

Write *more than half* or *less than half*. Then tell about what fraction of the region is shaded.

2.

Write the equivalent fraction.

3a. $\frac{1}{2} = \frac{?}{12}$ **b.** $\frac{3}{4} = \frac{?}{8}$

4a. $\frac{2}{3} = \frac{?}{9}$ **b.** $\frac{8}{10} = \frac{16}{?}$

5. A carnival wheel is divided into 10 equal parts. Three of the parts are red. Write a fraction to show what part is red.

6. An orange has 9 equal sections. Rose ate 6 sections. Write a fraction to tell what part was eaten.

7. Eight out of 32 students are honor students. What fraction shows how many are honor students?

8. Write two sevenths as a fraction.

9. How do you write $\frac{9}{12}$ in words?

10. Is $\frac{5}{8}$ closer to 0, $\frac{1}{2}$, or 1?

11. How many sixths are equal to one half?

Practice 9-2

Find the missing factor.

1a. $5 \times \underline{\ ?\ } = 10$ **b.** $16 = \underline{\ ?\ } \times 8$

List all the common factors of each set of numbers. Then circle the GCF.

2a. 8 and 10 **b.** 20 and 30 **c.** 6, 12, and 42

Write each fraction in lowest terms.

3a. $\frac{5}{25}$ **b.** $\frac{3}{9}$ **c.** $\frac{6}{18}$

4a. $\frac{20}{100}$ **b.** $\frac{2}{14}$ **c.** $\frac{8}{12}$

Compare. Write <, =, or >.

5a. $\frac{1}{2} \ \underline{\ ?\ } \ \frac{3}{4}$ **b.** $\frac{1}{10} \ \underline{\ ?\ } \ \frac{2}{20}$

6a. $\frac{1}{6} \ \underline{\ ?\ } \ \frac{1}{12}$ **b.** $\frac{5}{8} \ \underline{\ ?\ } \ \frac{1}{8}$

7a. $\frac{4}{5} \ \underline{\ ?\ } \ \frac{4}{6}$ **b.** $\frac{7}{8} \ \underline{\ ?\ } \ \frac{6}{12}$

8. What is the greatest common factor of 8, 12, 20, and 40?

9. How can you express twelve twentieths in simplest form?

10. Is $\frac{3}{11}$ written in simplest form?

11. A flag shows 15 equal sections, 5 of which are blue. What fraction tells the part of the flag that is blue? Write the fraction in lowest terms.

12. A group of 90 children visit Canada. Nine of the children were born there. What fraction tells how many of the children were born in Canada? Write the fraction in lowest terms.

13. Write nine and two ninths as a mixed number.

14. What whole number is equivalent to $\frac{16}{1}$?

15. What whole number is equivalent to $\frac{22}{22}$?

Practice 10-1

Chapter 10

Solve. Write the answer in lowest terms.

1a. $\frac{6}{8} + \frac{1}{8}$ **b.** $\frac{4}{10} - \frac{2}{10}$

2a. $\frac{4}{5} + \frac{1}{5}$ **b.** $\frac{7}{8} - \frac{3}{8}$

3a. $\frac{2}{3} + \frac{4}{6}$ **b.** $\frac{8}{10} + \frac{3}{5}$

4a. $\frac{1}{2} - \frac{1}{4}$ **b.** $\frac{2}{5} + \frac{3}{10}$

Write the first ten common multiples for each set of numbers. Then write the least common multiple.

5a. 4, 10   **b.** 2, 6   **c.** 3, 6, and 9

Write as a mixed number in simplest form.

6a. $\frac{12}{10}$ **b.** $\frac{16}{5}$ **c.** $\frac{22}{4}$

7. Len eats $\frac{1}{8}$ of a pizza and Mia eats $\frac{3}{8}$ of the pizza. What part of the pizza did they eat?

8. A recipe calls for $\frac{3}{4}$ cup of milk. Rachel has $\frac{1}{8}$ cup of milk. How much more does she need?

9. There are 6 red marbles and 3 blue marbles in a bag. Lou picks one without looking. What is the probability that Lou picks a red marble?

10. What is one fourth of 40?

11. What is $\frac{2}{5}$ of 25?

12. Alan makes 20 brownies. He sells $\frac{3}{4}$ of them at a bake sale. How many does he sell?

13. There are 35 horses. One fifth of them are brown. How many of the horses are brown?

Practice 11-1

Chapter 11

Name each figure.

1a. T   **b.** S R   **c.** M N

2a. A B C   **b.** D E F   **c.** M N O

3. Which lines are parallel?

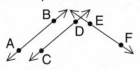

4. Which are *not* perpendicular?

a.   **b.**   **c.**

5. What shape is formed when two rays share a common endpoint?

6. How many sides does a triangle have? a pentagon? a hexagon?

7. How many vertices does a quadrilateral have? an octagon?

8. Name this figure.

9. Name the diameter and two radii.

10. Is this a simple closed curve?

11. How is a square different from a rectangle?

12. A sign has 4 straight sides and 4 vertices. None of the sides are the same length. What shape is the sign?

13. Is a circle a closed curve? Explain.

Practice 11-2

Write *triangle, right triangle,* or *equilateral triangle* to describe each figure.

1a. 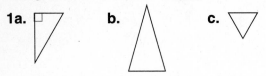 **b.** **c.**

How is the pattern made? Write *slide* or *flip.*

2.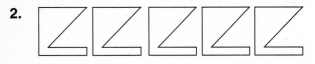

3.

4. Are these figures congruent?

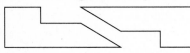

5. Are these figures similar?

6. Which figure is symmetrical?

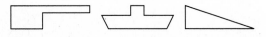

7. Which figure has half-turn symmetry?

Use the grid to answer each question.

8. What point is located at (1, 3)?

9. What ordered pair gives the location of point *X*?

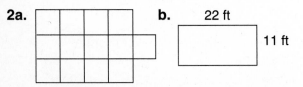

Practice 12-1

Chapter 12

Find the perimeter of each figure.

1a.
6 m
2 m
5 m

b.
3 in.
2 in.
4 in.
2 in.
5 in.

Find the area of each figure.

2a.

b.
22 ft
11 ft

3. A tabletop is 4 feet long and 5 feet wide. What is the perimeter of the tabletop?

4. One side of an equilateral triangle is 11 cm. What is the perimeter of the triangle?

5. A space figure has no faces and a curved surface. What is it?

6. How many faces, edges, and vertices does a cube have?

7. Name the shape of the figure made by the cut.

Find the volume of each figure.

8a. 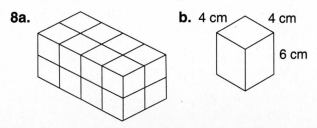 **b.** 4 cm 4 cm 6 cm

470

Chapter 13

Practice 13-1

1a. $8 \div 1$ **b.** $70 \div 10$ **c.** $400 \div 10$

2a. $420 \div 70$ **b.** $500 \div 50$ **c.** $210 \div 30$

3a. $20\overline{)4000}$ **b.** $80\overline{)640}$ **c.** $90\overline{)54{,}000}$

Estimate the quotient.

4a. $56 \div 11$ **b.** $249 \div 32$ **c.** $109 \div 48$

5a. $62\overline{)142}$ **b.** $74\overline{)657}$ **c.** $52\overline{)\$4.80}$

Divide.

6a. $21\overline{)88}$ **b.** $31\overline{)94}$ **c.** $33\overline{)\$.99}$

7a. $35\overline{)73}$ **b.** $72\overline{)360}$ **c.** $91\overline{)\$5.46}$

8. How many dozens are there in 48?

9. A factory can make 21 toy trains in one hour. How long will it take to make 147 trains?

10. Roger worked 30 hours a week at summer camp. He worked a total of 240 hours. How many weeks did he work?

11. A box can hold 52 cans. How many boxes are needed to hold 260 cans?

12. There are 682 baseball cards and 31 children. If each child takes the same number of cards, what is the greatest number each child will get?

13. Avi buys 11 marbles for $.99. How much does each marble cost?

14. The dividend is 549. The divisor is 61. What is the quotient?

15. Amy earns $44 in 11 hours. How much does she earn in 1 hour?

16. A ship travels 29 miles an hour. How long will it take the ship to travel 87 miles?

Practice 13-2

1a. $28\overline{)100}$ **b.** $12\overline{)90}$ **c.** $14\overline{)234}$

2a. $79\overline{)229}$ **b.** $98\overline{)877}$ **c.** $38\overline{)279}$

3a. $65\overline{)541}$ **b.** $72\overline{)630}$ **c.** $63\overline{)371}$

4a. $86\overline{)\$20.64}$ **b.** $92\overline{)5060}$ **c.** $54\overline{)2920}$

5a. $62\overline{)3000}$ **b.** $47\overline{)\$9.40}$ **c.** $24\overline{)2360}$

6a. $8\overline{)832}$ **b.** $16\overline{)\$32.16}$ **c.** $25\overline{)\$50.75}$

7. A carton can hold 24 cans of soup. A diner uses 627 cans in a month. How many full cartons does the diner use?

8. The diner has 576 drinking glasses stored on shelves. Each shelf holds 48 glasses. How many shelves are there?

9. Rita buys 25 postcards for $8.75. How much does each postcard cost?

10. A paper company donates 774 packs of paper to 18 schools. If the packs were shared equally, how many did each school receive? How many were left over?

11. The dividend is 4646. The divisor is 23. What is the quotient?

12. A train travels 68 miles per hour. How long will it take the train to travel 748 miles?

13. Trudy buys a newspaper everyday for 14 days. She spends $4.90. How much does each newspaper cost?

14. Glen's dog eats 14 oz of dry food every day. Will a 400-oz bag of dog food last four weeks?

15. Ruth buys 18 yards of ribbon for $18.90. How much does one yard of ribbon cost?

16. What is the remainder when 8244 is divided by 42?

Chapter 14

Practice 14-1

Write as a decimal.

1a.

b.

2a. eight hundredths **b.** $30 + 6 + 0.4 + 0.02$

3a. $\frac{72}{100}$ **b.** $3\frac{5}{10}$

Compare. Write $<$, $=$, or $>$.

4a. 5.54 ? 5.45   **b.** 7.12 ? 7.1

5a. 21.98 ? 22   **b.** 0.80 ? 0.8

Solve.

6a. $2.4 + 4.5$ **b.** $3.6 + 5.89 + 4$

7a.   7.2   **b.**   5   **c.**   0.57
      -2.7 4.2   0.75
                 $+6.81$ $+0.22$

8. Write 25.89 in expanded form.

9. What is 3.28 rounded to the nearest tenth?

10. What is 45.92 rounded to the nearest one?

11. Write 0.1, 1.1, 1.11, 1, and 0.11 in order from least to greatest.

12. An icicle is 34.8 cm long in the morning. 5.45 cm melt during the day. How long is the icicle at the end of the day?

13. Ben's cat is 28.8 cm tall. Gil's cat is 32 cm tall. How much taller is Gil's cat?

14. Which is a better buy: 18 crayons for $6.12 or 25 crayons for $8?

15. A bean plant is 46.3 cm tall at the end of May. It grows 10.45 cm in June. How tall is it at the end of June?

16. Write 6.5, 50.6, 65.5, 65.6, and 60.5 in order from greatest to least.

Chapter 15

Practice 15-1

Find each value for n.

1a. $32 + n = 50$ **b.** $100 - n = 19$

2a. $21 \times n = 105$ **b.** $693 \div n = 63$

Copy and complete.

3.

10	8	17	25	64	3	92
60	48	102	?	?	?	?

Rule: Multiply by 6.

Compare. Write $=$ or $\neq$.

4a. 14×5 ? $60 + 20$
  b. $210 \div 15$? $16 - 2$

5a. $2.2 + 1.7$? 39
  b. 7×7 ? $55 - 2 \times 3$

6. There are 8 boxes of books. Each box holds 16 books. Which number sentence will help you find how many books in all: $16 \times 8 = n$ or $16 \div 8 = n$?

7. Which is greater: $100 \div (2 + 3)$ or $100 \div 2 + 3$?

8. Which is equal to zero: $10 - 2 \times 5$ or $(10 - 2) \times 5$?

Use the number line to solve.

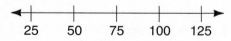

9. How far is it from 50 to 125?

10. What number is halfway between 25 and 125?

Test 1

Compare. Write <, =, or >.
1. $8 + 4 \underline{\ ?\ } 18 - 9$ 2. $16 - 8 \underline{\ ?\ } 7 + 6$

Compute.
3. $(3 \times 7) + 1 = \underline{\ ?\ }$ 4. $(5 \times 8) - 7 = \underline{\ ?\ }$
5a. $63 \div 7 = \underline{\ ?\ }$ b. $8\overline{)48}$

Give the place and the value of the underlined digits.
6. 5<u>2</u>8,<u>3</u>47,1<u>0</u>6

Give 4 related facts for:
7a. 9, 8, 17   b. 5, 7, 35

Write the number.
8. eighty thousand, forty-nine
9. Stickers cost $.06 each. How much will I pay for 9 stickers?

10. Joan has 356 stickers in her collection. Diane has 365. Which girl has more stickers?
11. Round the sum of $350 + 23 + 126$ to the nearest hundred.
12. At $.96 a yard, what is the cost of 8 yards of material?
13. A bookcase has 8 shelves. There are 6 books on each shelf. How many books are in the bookcase?
14. Forty strawberries were divided equally among 5 children. How many did each child receive?
15. How much greater is the product of 6 and 7 than the product of 5 and 8?

Test 2

Order from least to greatest.
1. 304, 340, 356, 324

Round to the place of the underlined digit.
2a. <u>9</u>2   b. <u>3</u>87

Write the standard numeral.
3a. one hundred four thousand, three hundred seventy
 b. $100,000 + 20,000 + 300 + 4$

Compute.
4a. $\underline{\ ?\ } - 8 = 5$ b. $15 = 6 + \underline{\ ?\ }$

5. $\begin{array}{r} 23 \\ + 34 \\ \hline \end{array}$
6. $\begin{array}{r} 651 \\ + 728 \\ \hline \end{array}$
7. $\begin{array}{r} 59 \\ - 24 \\ \hline \end{array}$
8. $\begin{array}{r} 738 \\ - 216 \\ \hline \end{array}$

9. $\$21.50 + \$7.25$ 10. $\$33.95 - \$1.84$

11. Helen buys a toothbrush for $.96 and soap for $.45. How much change will she receive from $2.00?
12. What four coins have the same value as one quarter?
13. How many odd numbers are there between 132 and 180? Name them.
14. Write $200 - 78 = 122$ in Roman numerals.
15. Jack gave the clerk $1.00 to pay for a $.32 item. The clerk then gave him 2 quarters, 1 dime, 1 nickel, and 2 pennies. Did he receive the correct change? Explain.

Test 3

Compute.
1. $3 + 6 + 4 + 5 = \underline{\ ?\ }$
2. Double 8 and add 3.

Estimate.
3. $\begin{array}{r} 46 \\ + 22 \\ \hline \end{array}$
4. $\begin{array}{r} 371 \\ + 119 \\ \hline \end{array}$
5. $\begin{array}{r} 68 \\ - 37 \\ \hline \end{array}$
6. $\begin{array}{r} 482 \\ - 245 \\ \hline \end{array}$

Compute.
7. $\begin{array}{r} 16 \\ + 25 \\ \hline \end{array}$
8. $\begin{array}{r} 572 \\ + 388 \\ \hline \end{array}$
9. $\begin{array}{r} 42 \\ - 19 \\ \hline \end{array}$
10. $\begin{array}{r} 610 \\ - 436 \\ \hline \end{array}$

11. Compute mentally.
 $75 + 60 + 50 + 40 + 25 = \underline{\ ?\ }$

12. Jan, Sue-ling, and Tanya scored 86, 80, and 100 on the math test. Jan's score was the lowest. Sue-ling had hoped to do better. Give each child's score.
13. Julio bought a sweater for $15.40 and shoes for $22.90. How much change will he receive from $40?
14. Find the total number of days in June, February, December, and July.
15. Mr. Doyle is traveling 682 km from Pensacola to St. Augustine. If he has already traveled 495 km, how much farther must he travel?

Compute.

1.
```
   3475
     63
 +8468
```

2.
```
 $ 6.95
  15.47
+ 38.56
```

3.
```
 4000
 −  96
```

4.
```
 3060
 − 987
```

5.
```
 4060
 ×    8
```

6.
```
 143
 ×   7
```

7.
```
 809
 × 76
```

8.
```
 $2.56
 ×   10
```

Estimate.

9. 4 × 18

10. 22 × 631

11. Patrick is 18 years old and is 6 ft tall. Bud is 23 years old. How much older is Bud?

12. How long will it take Traci to read a book of 168 pages if she reads 8 pages each day?

13. If a jet travels 300 miles an hour, how far will it go in 13 hours?

14. Each of the 36 students in the graduating class will be inviting 4 guests to the ceremonies. How many guests will be invited in all?

15. If Phillipe earns $4.50 an hour, how much will he earn if he works 120 hours?

Estimate. Then multiply.

1. 403 × 7

2. 3 × 242

Discover the pattern and complete.

3. 6, 8, 10, 7, 9, 11, 8, 10, __?__, __?__ .

Complete.

4. 6 × 7 = 42 is to 42 ÷ 6 = 7 as 4 × 9 = 36 is to __?__ .

Estimate.

5. 5)38

6. 7)$48.75

Compute.

7. 6)90

8. 4)86

Divisible by 3?

9. 75

10. 82

11. The Kane family drove 1800 miles in five days. How many miles did they average each day?

12. Patsy gave 8 stickers to her sister, and double that amount to each of her 4 friends. She still has 14 stickers left. With how many stickers did Patsy start?

13. Estimate the cost of 7 CDs if each one costs $8.98.

14. A notepad costs $.89 and a pen costs $.59. What is the total cost of six notepads and six pens?

15. If 466 apples are to be put equally into 9 baskets, how many apples will there be in each basket? How many apples will be left over?

Complete.

1. 30 in. = __?__ ft

2. 6 yd = __?__ ft

Compute.

3.
```
  2 ft 8 in.
 +3 ft 9 in.
```

4.
```
  4 yd 2 ft
 −3 yd 1 ft
```

Compare. Write <, =, or >.

5. 6 qt __?__ 2 gal

6. 3 pt __?__ 6 c

Complete.

7. 24 oz = __?__ lb __?__ oz

8. 6500 lb = __?__ T __?__ lb

Choose the better answer.

9. length of a paper clip: 30 cm or 30 mm?

10. capacity of a swimming pool: 2000 L or 2000 mL?

11. Which is the longer distance: 1800 m or 2 km?

12. There were 936 library books. If an equal number were placed on each of 9 shelves, how many books were on each shelf?

13. Find the average of Rashon's 4 math test scores: 86, 80, 93, 96.

14. Dad needs 95 nails to make a doghouse. If they come packaged 10 nails to a bag, how many bags will Dad need to buy?

15. If the temperature starts at 0°C and drops 4°, what is the temperature? If it then rises 6°, what will the temperature be? If it rises another 3°, what will the temperature be then?

Complete.

1. 3 h = _?_ min   **2.** 96 h = _?_ days

Compute.

3.   365   **4.**   965   **5.**   384   **6.** $3\overline{)106}$
    $+\,279$ $-\,298$ $\times\ \ 52$

Use the graph to answer questions 7 and 8.

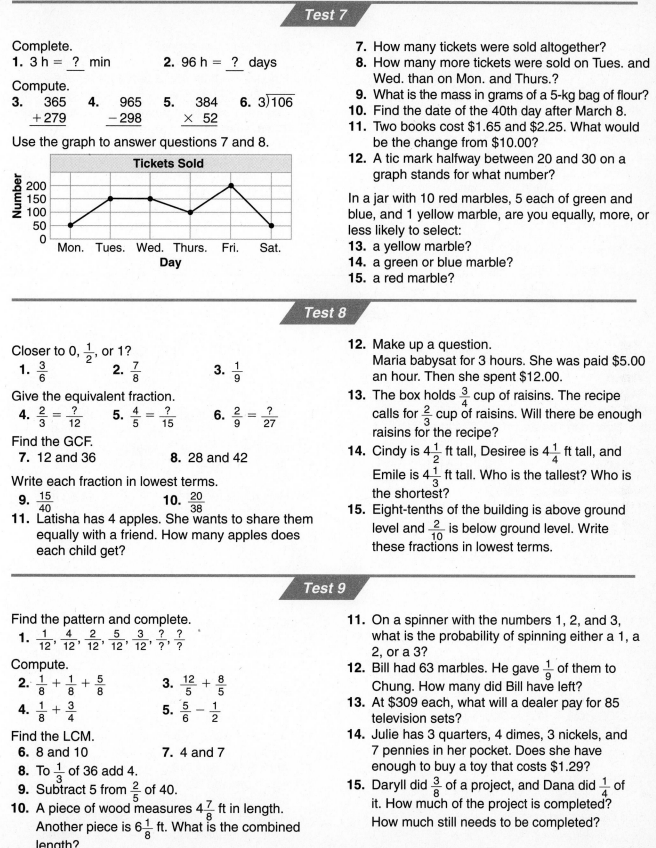

Tickets Sold

(Number vs. Day: Mon., Tues., Wed., Thurs., Fri., Sat.)

7. How many tickets were sold altogether?

8. How many more tickets were sold on Tues. and Wed. than on Mon. and Thurs.?

9. What is the mass in grams of a 5-kg bag of flour?

10. Find the date of the 40th day after March 8.

11. Two books cost $1.65 and $2.25. What would be the change from $10.00?

12. A tic mark halfway between 20 and 30 on a graph stands for what number?

In a jar with 10 red marbles, 5 each of green and blue, and 1 yellow marble, are you equally, more, or less likely to select:

13. a yellow marble?

14. a green or blue marble?

15. a red marble?

Closer to 0, $\frac{1}{2}$, or 1?

1. $\frac{3}{6}$ **2.** $\frac{7}{8}$ **3.** $\frac{1}{9}$

Give the equivalent fraction.

4. $\frac{2}{3} = \frac{?}{12}$ **5.** $\frac{4}{5} = \frac{?}{15}$ **6.** $\frac{2}{9} = \frac{?}{27}$

Find the GCF.

7. 12 and 36   **8.** 28 and 42

Write each fraction in lowest terms.

9. $\frac{15}{40}$ **10.** $\frac{20}{38}$

11. Latisha has 4 apples. She wants to share them equally with a friend. How many apples does each child get?

12. Make up a question.
Maria babysat for 3 hours. She was paid $5.00 an hour. Then she spent $12.00.

13. The box holds $\frac{3}{4}$ cup of raisins. The recipe calls for $\frac{2}{3}$ cup of raisins. Will there be enough raisins for the recipe?

14. Cindy is $4\frac{1}{2}$ ft tall, Desiree is $4\frac{1}{4}$ ft tall, and Emile is $4\frac{1}{3}$ ft tall. Who is the tallest? Who is the shortest?

15. Eight-tenths of the building is above ground level and $\frac{2}{10}$ is below ground level. Write these fractions in lowest terms.

Find the pattern and complete.

1. $\frac{1}{12}, \frac{4}{12}, \frac{2}{12}, \frac{5}{12}, \frac{3}{12}, \frac{?}{?}, \frac{?}{?}$

Compute.

2. $\frac{1}{8} + \frac{1}{8} + \frac{5}{8}$ **3.** $\frac{12}{5} + \frac{8}{5}$

4. $\frac{1}{8} + \frac{3}{4}$ **5.** $\frac{5}{6} - \frac{1}{2}$

Find the LCM.

6. 8 and 10   **7.** 4 and 7

8. To $\frac{1}{3}$ of 36 add 4.

9. Subtract 5 from $\frac{2}{5}$ of 40.

10. A piece of wood measures $4\frac{7}{8}$ ft in length. Another piece is $6\frac{1}{8}$ ft. What is the combined length?

11. On a spinner with the numbers 1, 2, and 3, what is the probability of spinning either a 1, a 2, or a 3?

12. Bill had 63 marbles. He gave $\frac{1}{9}$ of them to Chung. How many did Bill have left?

13. At $309 each, what will a dealer pay for 85 television sets?

14. Julie has 3 quarters, 4 dimes, 3 nickels, and 7 pennies in her pocket. Does she have enough to buy a toy that costs $1.29?

15. Daryll did $\frac{3}{8}$ of a project, and Dana did $\frac{1}{4}$ of it. How much of the project is completed? How much still needs to be completed?

Identify each.

1. $\overleftrightarrow{A \quad B}$ **2.** •C **3.** $\overset{\bullet\quad\quad\bullet}{D \quad\quad E}$

Draw 3 angles:

4a. a right angle **b.** less than 90° **c.** more than 90°

5. The rungs of a ladder form ? lines.

6. Trace a penny. Then draw a diameter and a radius. Label these line segments.

7. Draw a hexagon. How many angles are there?

8. Draw 2 special quadrilaterals. Label them.

9. Is the figure a flip or a slide? **a.** **b.**

10. Write congruent or similar figures. **a.** **b.**

11. How many rectangles?

12. Find the perimeter of a pentagon whose sides measure: $1\frac{1}{8}$ in., 2 in., $1\frac{5}{8}$ in., 2 in., and $2\frac{1}{8}$ in.

13. The baseball field measures 125 yd long and 75 yd wide. Find the area.

14. Which space figure has 8 edges and 5 faces?

15. A box measures 2 m long, 1 m wide, and 2 m high. Find the volume of the box. Then decide whether you can fit a television that measures 150 cm long, 75 cm wide, and 120 cm high into the box.

1a. 83 + 74 + 36 **b.** 80 + 24 + 65
2a. 651 − 289 **b.** 708 − 498
3a. 7)749 **b.** 20)180
4a. 30)241 **b.** 23)74
5a. 52)676 **b.** 13)117
6. How many 8s are in: 26; 37; 43; 57?

Estimate the quotient.

7a. 36)82 **b.** 41)211

Write the number.

8. seven + 2 tenths + 9 hundredths

9. $2.59
.09
+ 3.84

10. $23.50
− 7.65

11. Vince puts a border around his room. It measures 8 ft by 11 ft. How many feet of border does he need?

12. Mrs. Taylor spent $86.40 to buy 27 pairs of scissors. How much did each pair cost?

13. There are 1902 people in line for the roller coaster. Each ride holds 28 people. How many times will the roller coaster need to run?

14. Tom's ski run was 61.458 s. Carol's time was 61.464 s. Whose time was faster?

15. How many feet are in a spool of cotton that contains 30 yards?

Round to the nearest one; then to the nearest tenth.
1a. 36.18 **b.** 12.96 **c.** 44.50

Write +, −, ×, or ÷ to make each sentence true.
2a. 48 ? 3 = 9 ? 7 **b.** 6 ? 8 = 59 ? 11

Solve.
3. 0.7 + 0.6 − (0.2 × 0.3) ÷ (0.9 − 0.8) = ?

Order from least to greatest.
4. 1.3, 1.36, 0.3, 1.63 **5.** 2.4, 2.43, 2.423

Estimate.
6. 8.6 + 2.9 **7.** 15.3 − 10.4

Find the missing number.
8. ? × 15 = 25 × 3 **9.** ? ÷ 4 = 120 ÷ 6

Compute. Use a number line.
10. 1 + 7 − 2 + 3 + 4 − ? = 5

11. Mrs. Riso bought 1 dozen donuts at $.30 each and $\frac{1}{2}$ dozen muffins at $.65 each. How much change will she receive from $10?

12. Complete the pattern.
0.1, 0.5, 0.7, 0.2, 0.6, 0.8, ? , ?

13. If a ship travels 409 miles in one day, how far will it travel in six days?

14. After Greg paid $40.00 for shoes and $3.50 for socks, he had $20.50 left. How much money did Greg have at first?

15. Maggie had 2 dozen eggs. She used $\frac{2}{3}$ of them for baking. How many eggs were left?

1

DRILL

1.
$$\begin{array}{cccccc} 3 & 2 & 5 & 3 & 4 & 7 \\ +7 & +9 & +2 & +6 & +8 & +7 \end{array}$$

2.
$$\begin{array}{cccccc} 7 & 10 & 9 & 16 & 14 & 8 \\ -3 & -2 & -4 & -8 & -9 & -3 \end{array}$$

3. Give related facts. 8 + 2, 6 + 5, 7 + 4, 5 + 3, 6 + 7, 9 + 7, 1 + 9

4.
$$\begin{array}{cccc} 2 \times 3 & 2 \times 5 & 3 \times 6 & 3 \times 8 \\ 2 \times 9 & 3 \times 8 & 2 \times 7 & 3 \times 4 \end{array}$$

5.
$$\begin{array}{cccc} 4 \times 2 & 4 \times 6 & 5 \times 9 & 5 \times 6 \\ 4 \times 8 & 5 \times 2 & 4 \times 7 & 5 \times 7 \end{array}$$

MENTAL

1. Don is 9 years old. How old will he be 6 years from now?
2. A farmer had 11 cows. He sold 8 of them. How many cows did he have left?
3. Crackers are 9¢ each. How much will Joey pay for 3 crackers?
4. How many nickels are worth 50 cents?
5. Anna picked 9 flowers. Laura picked 3. How many flowers did they pick in all?

2

DRILL

1.
$$\begin{array}{cccccc} 9 & 8 & 7 & 5 & 6 & 7 \\ +9 & +6 & +9 & +8 & +9 & +8 \end{array}$$

2.
$$\begin{array}{cccccc} 16 & 17 & 15 & 18 & 14 & 13 \\ -7 & -9 & -6 & -9 & -7 & -7 \end{array}$$

3.
$$\begin{array}{cccc} 7 \times 3 & 6 \times 4 & 7 \times 7 & 6 \times 9 \\ 7 \times 5 & 7 \times 6 & 6 \times 8 & 6 \times 6 \end{array}$$

4.
$$\begin{array}{cccc} 8 \times 4 & 8 \times 8 & 9 \times 4 & 9 \times 7 \\ 8 \times 6 & 9 \times 8 & 8 \times 5 & 9 \times 3 \end{array}$$

5.
$$\begin{array}{cccc} 8 \div 2 & 10 \div 2 & 12 \div 3 & 18 \div 3 \\ 15 \div 3 & 4 \div 2 & 21 \div 3 & 14 \div 2 \end{array}$$

MENTAL

1. Josh has 8¢. Therese has twice as much. How much money does she have?
2. At 9¢ each, what will 7 pencils cost?
3. Thirty-five cents is divided equally among 5 students. How much will each receive?
4. Tom paid 24¢ for 3 balloons. How much did each balloon cost?
5. The dividend is 42. The divisor is 7. What is the quotient?

3

DRILL

1. Give related facts. 6 ÷ 2, 9 ÷ 3, 10 ÷ 2, 3 ÷ 3, 8 ÷ 4, 6 ÷ 3
2. Subtract 3 from: 21, 18, 15, 12, 9, 6, 3, 24, 27, 30
3. 28 ÷ 7   24 ÷ 4   30 ÷ 5   48 ÷ 6
   49 ÷ 7   32 ÷ 4   40 ÷ 5   36 ÷ 6
4. 10 more than: 58, 14, 82, 95, 103, 191
5. Give value: 5̲63; 721̲; 34̲5; 2̲97; 65̲8; 8̲26; 908̲

MENTAL

1. When 67 is divided by 9, what is the quotient? the remainder?
2. What is 78 as a Roman numeral?
3. What is 5000 + 100 + 60 in standard form?
4. What number is ten thousand less than 56,201?
5. There are 3189 adults and 3819 children at the fair. Are there more adults or children?

DRILL

1. Order from least to greatest: 35, 53, 32; 501, 550, 515; 261, 162, 216; 8778, 8887, 7887
2. Round to the nearest ten: 57, 111, 363, 288, 435, 519, 604, 792
3. Divide by 4: 24, 16, 36, 28, 32, 8, 12
4. Multiply by 7, by 8, by 9: 3, 5, 6, 4, 8, 2, 9, 0, 1, 7
5. Round to the nearest hundred: 649, 752, 3150, 2310, 4281, 5399, 5046

MENTAL

1. What is XXXVI in standard form?
2. What is 4,000,000 + 500,000 + 30,000 + 2000 + 10 + 8?
3. There are 18 caps. Six are red. How many caps are not red?
4. What number comes between 13,725 and 13,727?
5. One half-dozen cookies costs 72¢. If I give the clerk $1.00, how much change will I get?

DRILL

1. Round to the nearest dollar: $2.75, $36.10, $42.89, $18.25, $7.60, $1.37
2. Name the period: 74,118; 25,308,433; 8,065,243; 117,589; 608,145
3. Add 7 to: 8, 18, 28, 38, 58, 78, 48, 68
4. Subtract 8 from: 15, 25, 45, 65, 85, 35
5. Count back by 10 from: 200–150, 390–210, 510–380, 220–90, 165–15, 605–505, 412–342, 1110–890

MENTAL

1. How much money: 1 ten-dollar bill, 2 quarters, 3 dimes, 1 nickel
2. Which is less? by how much? 3575 or 3775
3. What is the value of 3 in 630,241?
4. Tony scored 5 points in the 1st quarter, 6 in the 2nd, and 4 each in the 3rd and 4th quarters. How many points did he score?
5. What must be added to 9 to make a sum of 17?

6

DRILL

1. $8 + 0 + 4$ $7 + 2 + 3$ $6 + 4 + 1$
   $5 + 6 + 0$ $8 + 9 + 2$ $1 + 9 + 5$
2. Double each and add 2: 4, 2, 6, 5, 7, 3, 8, 1, 9
3. $\underline{\ ?\ } + 8 = 11$ $4 + \underline{\ ?\ } = 13$
   $12 - \underline{\ ?\ } = 7$ $9 = 16 - \underline{\ ?\ }$
   $\underline{\ ?\ } - 3 = 9$ $12 = 6 + \underline{\ ?\ }$
4. Add 9 to: 5, 15, 45, 35, 55, 75, 37, 87, 17, 57, 43, 63, 73, 23
5. Estimate. $46 + 21$ $52 + 38$
   $12 + 17$ $29 + 33$ $13 + 76$
   $42 - 22$ $38 - 11$ $59 - 18$
   $15 - 11$ $67 - 45$

MENTAL

1. Is the sum reasonable? Check by estimation. 524 + 46 = 984
2. Complete the pattern.
   9, 18, 27, _?_ , _?_ , 54, _?_ , 72
3. Nora had 68¢ and spent 35¢. How much money did she have left?
4. Grace is 23 years old. Mary is 11 years older than Grace. How old is Mary?
5. Ned needs $17. He has $8. How much more money does he need?

7 DRILL

1. Add 110 to: 34, 134, 244, 354, 424, 564, 634, 714, 844
2. Add 8 to: 7, 17, 57, 37, 47, 27, 67, 77
3. Subtract 9 from: 13, 43, 73, 25, 55, 85, 14, 74, 34, 12, 92, 62, 82, 52
4. Estimate. 123 + 164   185 + 216   351 + 435   694 − 375   716 − 297
5. 4000 + 1200   2300 + 6000   6100 + 3400   5300 + 2400   7500 + 1300

MENTAL

1. Bob's coat cost $67. Ted's coat cost $8 more than Bob's. How much did Ted's coat cost?
2. Gina is 47 in. tall. Don is 5 in. shorter. How tall is Don?
3. Add 138 + 22 + 19.
4. Ramon has $17.30 and Joe has $8.70. How much do the boys have altogether?
5. Rosa had 24 cookies. She gave 7 to Jane. How many cookies did Rosa have left?

8 DRILL

1. Subtract 5 from: 13, 43, 73, 33, 53
2. $10.00 − $4.00 $12.00 − $6.00 $25.00 − $20.00 $36.00 − $24.00
3. Multiply by 3, then add 4: 4, 8, 0, 9, 1, 5, 3, 6, 2, 7
4. Estimate. 584 − 126   431 − 279   1842 − 1256   3421 − 1538   7186 − 4515
5. Multiply by 7: 2, 4, 5, 7, 9, 1, 0, 3, 6, 8

MENTAL

1. How much greater than 15 is 22?
2. Frank is 7 years old. His sister is 5 years older than Frank. How old is Frank's sister?
3. What is 4 more than the product of 9 times 7?
4. Add 2300 + 3200 + 132.
5. Pedro is 42 in. tall. Dave is 9 in. taller. How tall is Dave?

9 DRILL

1. 1 × 6   4 × 6   7 × 6   9 × 6
   6 × 1   6 × 4   6 × 7   6 × 9
2. 3 × 0   5 × 1   4 × 0   6 × 0
   1 × 7   8 × 0   9 × 1   2 × 0
3. 8 × ? = 24   5 × ? = 45
   ? × 2 = 12   ? × 6 = 48
   7 × ? = 35   ? × 4 = 36
4. Multiply by 2: 10, 20, 30, 40, 50, 70, 90, 60, 80
5. 3 × (2 + 5)   (1 + 4) × 4
   2 × (1 + 3)   6 × (2 + 2)
   (3 + 2) × 5   (3 + 3) × 1

MENTAL

1. Myra pulled out fourteen white socks from the laundry basket. How many pairs of socks can she make?
2. Which is the greater product? 3 times 40   or   4 times 20
3. Paul is 20 years old. Jack is 3 times as old as Paul. How old is Jack?
4. About how much will 5 toys cost if each toy costs $.98?
5. There are 24 stickers on a sheet. How many stickers are on 2 sheets?

DRILL

1. Multiply by 6, then add 2: 0, 8, 6, 2, 4, 10, 1, 3, 5, 9, 7
2. Multiply by 8, then add 5: 2, 4, 0, 3, 7, 1, 9, 10, 5, 8, 6
3. Estimate. $3 \times \$.48$ $2 \times \$.12$ $4 \times \$.23$ $5 \times \$.36$ $6 \times \$.38$
4. Estimate. 28×21 39×12 13×17 43×36 51×22 14×67
5. 20×100 30×100 20×300 40×200 30×300 20×200

MENTAL

1. Mr. Lass sold 52 tickets on each of the 4 days before the dance. How many tickets did he sell?
2. Tanya bought 2 kites that cost $18 each. How much did she pay for the kites?
3. Velvet costs $8 a yard. How much do 4 yards cost?
4. Complete the pattern. 0, 4, 3, 7, 6, _?_ , _?_
5. How much greater is the product of 7 and 6 than the product of 0 and 6?

DRILL

1. 30×60 90×20 30×31 10×210 10×880 40×31
2. $8\overline{)8}$ $1\overline{)7}$ $6\overline{)0}$ $5\overline{)5}$ $1\overline{)4}$ $3\overline{)0}$ $9\overline{)0}$ $4\overline{)4}$
3. $2\overline{)14}$ $5\overline{)30}$ $7\overline{)28}$ $6\overline{)36}$ $8\overline{)64}$ $9\overline{)72}$ $4\overline{)36}$ $8\overline{)40}$
4. Divide by 4: 25, 17, 37, 29, 33, 9, 13, 21, 26, 18, 38, 30, 34, 10, 22
5. $\underline{?} \times 4 = 32$ $6 \times \underline{?} = 24$ $\underline{?} \times 2 = 18$ $\underline{?} \times 7 = 21$ $8 \times \underline{?} = 56$ $\underline{?} \times 8 = 72$

MENTAL

1. The factors are 23 and 68. Estimate the product?
2. The product is 42. One factor is 6. What is the other factor?
3. What is the remainder when 20 is divided by 9?
4. It took Sam 6 hours to pack 325 cartons. About how many cartons did he pack each hour?
5. Five ties cost $60. Each tie costs the same. How much does 1 tie cost?

DRILL

1. Divide by 9: 29, 11, 46, 20, 38, 40, 31, 15, 48, 33, 14, 49, 19, 42, 44
2. Which are divisible by 2? by 5? by 10? 12, 25, 42, 90, 63, 75, 110, 68, 130
3. $2\overline{)222}$ $5\overline{)555}$ $3\overline{)363}$ $4\overline{)484}$ $4\overline{)888}$ $2\overline{)462}$ $3\overline{)393}$ $2\overline{)846}$
4. Divide by 8: 73, 74, 78, 79, 69, 71, 65, 12, 19, 21, 30, 31, 35, 38, 37, 59, 61, 57, 63, 49, 52, 55, 53
5. $12 + 4 - 3$ $16 - 9 + 5$ $8 + 7 - 4$ $12 \div 4 \times 5$ $5 \times 6 \div 2$ $40 \div 5 \div 2$

MENTAL

1. Sue has 72¢ to share equally with Meg. How much money will each girl receive?
2. Jim spent $1.40 for 2 feet of wire. How much did each foot cost?
3. A farmer plants 800 corn plants in 4 equal rows. How many plants are in each row?
4. Which is greater? by how much? 2626 or 2662
5. What number comes next after 124,169?

DRILL

1. Rename as feet: 12 in. 36 in. 24 in. 48 in. 72 in. 60 in. 84 in.
2. Name the time a half hour later. 8:15, 10:30, 12:00, 3:45, 5:20, 6:10, 4:05, 7:15, 9:25
3. Compare. Use <, =, >. 3 c ◯ 2 pt 3 pt ◯ 6 c 1 gal ◯ 6 qt 8 pt ◯ 4 qt
4. Name the date 1 week later. Jan. 8, Mar. 12, Aug. 23, Oct. 2, Nov. 18, Dec. 20
5. Divide by 9: 27, 29, 81, 84, 72, 75, 9, 13, 45, 49, 53, 63, 64, 69

MENTAL

1. Mr. Jones spends $25 every work week on tolls. He works 5 days a week. How much does he spend each work day on tolls?
2. Which is longer, 1 meter or 98 centimeters?
3. Pete's pet weighs 30 oz. How many more ounces does it need to gain to weigh 2 lb?
4. How much longer is 5 feet than 1 yard?
5. Which distance is longer, 10 kilometers or 1000 meters?

14

DRILL

1. Multiply by 4: 6, 7, 8, 0, 1, 2, 5, 4, 3
2. Count by 1000: 1400–6400; 2300–7300; 5900–10,900; 9700–18,700
3. Divide by 7: 61, 62, 58, 57, 60, 59, 31, 36, 38, 37, 40, 41, 29, 34
4. Subtract 99 from: 109, 239, 479, 658, 918, 338, 525, 865, 785
5. Give the fraction for the shaded part of each region.

MENTAL

1. Lori needs 1 L of water. She has 600 mL. How much more does she need?
2. What is XLIX in standard form?
3. Would you go ice skating at 35°C?
4. Can Jan go skiing at 20°F?
5. Randy worked from 11:30 A.M. to 1:00 P.M. on his bike. How long did Randy work?

15

DRILL

1. What part of a dollar is: 10¢, 50¢, 25¢, 5¢, 1¢, 75¢, 30¢, 70¢, 20¢
2. $\frac{1}{3} = \frac{?}{6}$ $\frac{1}{4} = \frac{?}{16}$ $\frac{1}{2} = \frac{?}{10}$
   $\frac{2}{5} = \frac{?}{15}$ $\frac{2}{3} = \frac{?}{12}$ $\frac{3}{4} = \frac{?}{20}$
3. $\frac{1 \times 2}{8 \times 2} = \frac{?}{}$ $\frac{3 \times 3}{7 \times 3} = \frac{?}{}$
   $\frac{1 \times 4}{3 \times 4} = \frac{?}{}$ $\frac{4 \times 3}{5 \times 3} = \frac{?}{}$
4. Closer to 0 or to 1? $\frac{1}{8}$, $\frac{6}{7}$, $\frac{2}{6}$, $\frac{1}{9}$, $\frac{8}{10}$, $\frac{4}{5}$, $\frac{2}{3}$, $\frac{1}{4}$, $\frac{11}{12}$
5. Name the GCF of: 6 and 12; 3 and 15; 8 and 24; 10 and 12; 9 and 12

MENTAL

1. Would you use centimeters or meters to measure the length of a pencil?
2. One paper clip weighs 1 g. How many paper clips do you need to equal 1 kg?
3. Key: each ▽ = 10 cones How many cones does ▽ ▽ ▽ ꟷ equal?
4. A ? graph is used to show change over a period of time.
5. If 1 mi equals 5280 ft, how many feet are there in 2 mi?

16

DRILL

1. Express in lowest terms: $\frac{3}{6}$, $\frac{6}{8}$, $\frac{5}{10}$, $\frac{2}{4}$, $\frac{7}{21}$, $\frac{4}{12}$, $\frac{6}{18}$, $\frac{5}{20}$, $\frac{9}{18}$, $\frac{2}{10}$

2. Fraction or mixed number? $\frac{5}{6}$, $1\frac{2}{3}$, $2\frac{4}{5}$, $\frac{5}{8}$, $3\frac{1}{9}$, $\frac{6}{7}$, $4\frac{7}{8}$, $\frac{9}{10}$

3. Order from least to greatest: $\frac{2}{3}$, $\frac{1}{3}$, $\frac{3}{3}$, $\frac{2}{5}$, $\frac{4}{5}$, $\frac{1}{5}$, $\frac{3}{6}$, $\frac{5}{6}$, $\frac{2}{6}$

4. Multiply by 6, then add 7: 10, 8, 6, 4, 2, 0, 1, 3, 5, 7, 9

5. Subtract a nickel from: 25¢, 18¢, 50¢, $1.35, $2.05, $1.16, $6.96

MENTAL

1. A jar has 10 red beans, 5 green beans, 5 blue beans, and 1 yellow bean. What is the probability of choosing: red? yellow? blue? green?

2. In a survey of 100 people, 30 people chose hot dogs. What part of the people chose hot dogs?

3. At 0°C, water __?__ .

4. Roy rolled a ball 6 yards. Was that more or less than 20 feet?

5. What is 3 more than the product of 9 times 5?

17

DRILL

1. $\frac{3}{5}+\frac{1}{5}$ $\frac{2}{7}+\frac{3}{7}$ $\frac{1}{6}+\frac{4}{6}$
$\frac{1}{3}+\frac{1}{3}$ $\frac{3}{9}+\frac{5}{9}$ $\frac{4}{10}+\frac{5}{10}$

2. $\frac{5}{8}-\frac{2}{8}$ $\frac{2}{3}-\frac{1}{3}$ $\frac{6}{7}-\frac{4}{7}$
$\frac{3}{5}-\frac{2}{5}$ $\frac{8}{9}-\frac{3}{9}$ $\frac{7}{8}-\frac{3}{8}$

3. Express as a mixed number.
$\frac{15}{2}$, $\frac{7}{4}$, $\frac{11}{3}$, $\frac{17}{5}$, $\frac{9}{2}$, $\frac{13}{6}$, $\frac{15}{4}$

4. $3+1\frac{1}{4}$ $2\frac{1}{2}+4$ $3+5\frac{2}{3}$
$1+3\frac{2}{5}$ $4+1\frac{3}{4}$ $2\frac{7}{8}+6$

5. Multiply by 3, then add 4: 4, 8, 0, 9, 5, 6, 7, 10, 2, 3, 1

MENTAL

1. Tom ate $\frac{1}{3}$ of the pizza. Sal ate $\frac{2}{3}$. Who ate more?

2. Six ninths minus four ninths is __?__ .

3. In a pet store $\frac{1}{5}$ of the pets are cats and $\frac{2}{5}$ are dogs. What part of the pets are cats and dogs?

4. Sasha bought $5\frac{3}{4}$ lb of chicken. She cooked $3\frac{1}{4}$ lb. How much is left?

5. Estimate the sum of $2\frac{1}{8}+3\frac{3}{4}+4\frac{1}{2}$.

18

DRILL

1. Subtract 2 from: $3\frac{1}{2}$, $4\frac{1}{5}$, $7\frac{1}{8}$, $8\frac{2}{3}$, $5\frac{2}{5}$, $2\frac{7}{8}$, $2\frac{1}{3}$

2. How many nickels are there in: 25¢, $.20, $.35, $.50, 45¢, 60¢, $.30, $.55, $.40

3. Find $\frac{1}{6}$ of: 6, 18, 42, 54, 24, 36, 12

4. Find half of: 14, 10, 8, 18, 20, 6, 4

5. Add 5 to: 9, 19, 59, 29, 38, 68, 28

MENTAL

1. If 47 is divided by 8, what is the quotient? the remainder?

2. Al did $\frac{1}{6}$ of his homework in school and $\frac{1}{2}$ before dinner. What part of his homework does he have left to do?

3. In a set of 10 pens, 3 are black. What fractional part of the set is black?

4. Of 20 fish, $\frac{3}{4}$ are striped. How many fish are striped?

5. Estimate. $6\frac{5}{10}-3\frac{1}{3}$

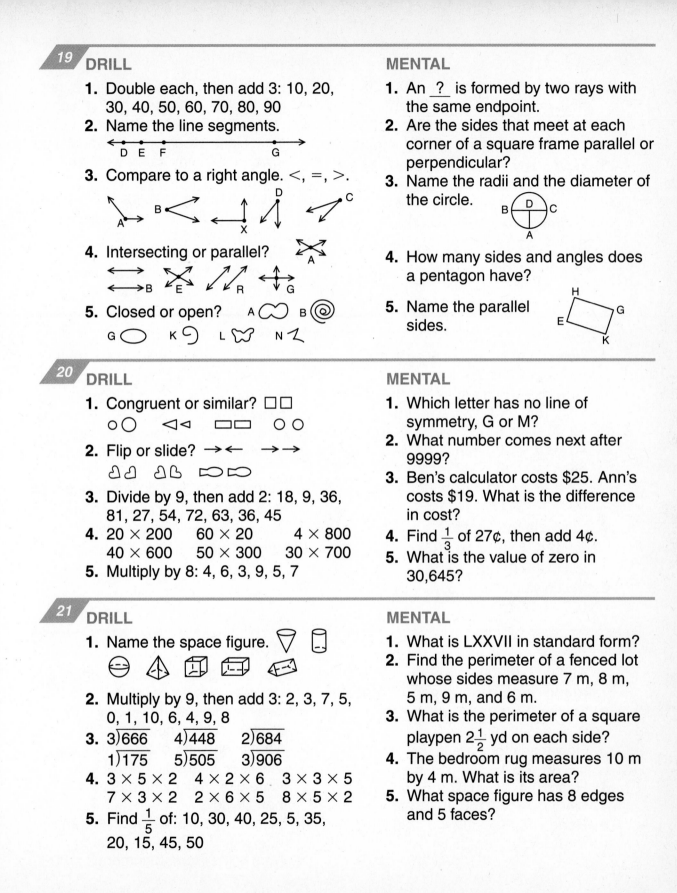

19

DRILL

1. Double each, then add 3: 10, 20, 30, 40, 50, 60, 70, 80, 90
2. Name the line segments.

   D E F   G

3. Compare to a right angle. $<$, $=$, $>$.

4. Intersecting or parallel?

5. Closed or open?

MENTAL

1. An ___?___ is formed by two rays with the same endpoint.
2. Are the sides that meet at each corner of a square frame parallel or perpendicular?
3. Name the radii and the diameter of the circle.
4. How many sides and angles does a pentagon have?
5. Name the parallel sides.

20

DRILL

1. Congruent or similar?
2. Flip or slide?
3. Divide by 9, then add 2: 18, 9, 36, 81, 27, 54, 72, 63, 36, 45
4. 20×200 60×20 4×800
   40×600 50×300 30×700
5. Multiply by 8: 4, 6, 3, 9, 5, 7

MENTAL

1. Which letter has no line of symmetry, G or M?
2. What number comes next after 9999?
3. Ben's calculator costs $25. Ann's costs $19. What is the difference in cost?
4. Find $\frac{1}{3}$ of 27¢, then add 4¢.
5. What is the value of zero in 30,645?

21

DRILL

1. Name the space figure.
2. Multiply by 9, then add 3: 2, 3, 7, 5, 0, 1, 10, 6, 4, 9, 8
3. $3\overline{)666}$ $4\overline{)448}$ $2\overline{)684}$
   $1\overline{)175}$ $5\overline{)505}$ $3\overline{)906}$
4. $3 \times 5 \times 2$ $4 \times 2 \times 6$ $3 \times 3 \times 5$
   $7 \times 3 \times 2$ $2 \times 6 \times 5$ $8 \times 5 \times 2$
5. Find $\frac{1}{5}$ of: 10, 30, 40, 25, 5, 35, 20, 15, 45, 50

MENTAL

1. What is LXXVII in standard form?
2. Find the perimeter of a fenced lot whose sides measure 7 m, 8 m, 5 m, 9 m, and 6 m.
3. What is the perimeter of a square playpen $2\frac{1}{2}$ yd on each side?
4. The bedroom rug measures 10 m by 4 m. What is its area?
5. What space figure has 8 edges and 5 faces?

483

DRILL

1. How many tens are in: 370, 420, 550, 600, 780, 190, 830, 240, 960
2. $2\overline{)140}$ $3\overline{)210}$ $4\overline{)160}$ $7\overline{)350}$
   $20\overline{)180}$ $30\overline{)150}$ $40\overline{)200}$ $50\overline{)450}$
3. How many 20s are in: 49, 67, 84, 182, 121, 165, 108, 114, 143
4. How many 7s are in: 45, 66
5. Estimate the quotient. $24\overline{)42}$, $31\overline{)89}$, $47\overline{)99}$, $43\overline{)82}$, $20\overline{)85}$, $34\overline{)69}$, $27\overline{)88}$

MENTAL

1. Find the volume of a dollhouse that is 3 ft long, 2 ft wide, and 2 ft high.
2. Dan put 480 soccer cards on the floor. He put them into 20 equal rows. How many cards were in each row?
3. Bus fare to the zoo was $18. About how much did the driver collect from 19 children?
4. Express 6 feet as yards.
5. Each box holds 8 crayons. How many crayons are in 4 boxes?

DRILL

1. How many 9s are in: 56, 19, 12, 39, 46, 68, 76, 29, 84, 65
2. How many 30s are in: 95, 62, 159, 277, 158, 243, 126, 214, 181
3. $16 = \underline{?} \times 8$ $56 = \underline{?} \times 8$
   $40 = \underline{?} \times 8$ $24 = \underline{?} \times 8$
   $64 = \underline{?} \times 8$ $48 = \underline{?} \times 8$
   $32 = \underline{?} \times 8$ $72 = \underline{?} \times 8$
   $80 = \underline{?} \times 8$
4. Estimate the quotient. $32\overline{)124}$, $51\overline{)98}$, $16\overline{)135}$, $23\overline{)144}$, $49\overline{)152}$, $62\overline{)188}$
5. Multiply by 6: 1, 2, 5, 8, 9, 6, 0, 7, 4, 3, 10

MENTAL

1. A box of cupcakes costs $2.40. If there are 24 cupcakes in a box, how much does each cupcake cost?
2. How many dimes are in $4.00?
3. What is the difference in cents between 1 quarter and 3 nickels?
4. Ramon earns $63 dollars a week. He saves $\frac{1}{7}$ of this amount. How much does he save weekly?
5. What is the sum of 9, 17, and 11?

DRILL

1. $4\overline{)200}$ $5\overline{)300}$ $6\overline{)300}$ $7\overline{)700}$
   $8\overline{)400}$ $2\overline{)100}$ $3\overline{)900}$ $9\overline{)900}$
2. Multiply by 7, then add 4: 6, 3, 4, 1, 9, 2, 0, 5, 7, 8
3. How many tens are in: 85, 62, 77, 43, 38, 22, 15, 94, 51
4. Read. 0.4, 0.9, 0.07, 0.5, 0.03, 0.46, 0.72, 0.01, 0.35, 0.11
5. Read. 1.6, 3.7, 8.6, 4.9, 12.5, 5.03, 8.07, 26.3, 6.18, 35.01

MENTAL

1. A parking garage holds a total of 480 cars with an equal number of cars on 4 levels. How many cars does each level hold?
2. What is one fifth of 20 cents?
3. Dan is 36 years old. David is 9 years old. How much older is Dan than David?
4. Name a decimal between 0.1 and 0.3.
5. What is the Roman numeral for 80?

25 DRILL

1. Give the value. 0.4$\underline{2}$, 6.2$\underline{3}$, 14.$\underline{3}$, 0.0$\underline{5}$, 3$\underline{6}$.1, 8.0$\underline{7}$, 1.$\underline{4}$8
2. Compare. <, =, >. 0.7 ◯ 0.3
   0.16 ◯ 0.19   2.36 ◯ 2.63
   6.35 ◯ 6.3   1.7 ◯ 1.72
3. Order least to greatest: 0.3, 0.1, 0.6; 0.13, 0.25, 0.20; 3, 0.3, 0.03
4. Complete the pattern. 0.1, 0.4, 0.7, $\underline{?}$; 0.05, 0.15, 0.25, $\underline{?}$; 1.1, 2.1, 3.1, $\underline{?}$; 3.4, 3.6, 3.8 $\underline{?}$; 5.9, 5.6, 5.3, $\underline{?}$
5. 0.5 + 0.2   0.6 + 0.2   1.3 + 1.4
   2.1 + 1.6   0.8 + 0.1   1.7 + 1.2

MENTAL

1. Name two decimals between 3 and 4.
2. Jesse ran 3.25 m and Thanh ran 3.55 m. Who ran farther? by how many meters?
3. Round $2.87 to the nearest dollar.
4. Missy spent 2.3 min on the first problem and 3.5 min on the next. How long did she spend on both problems?
5. What is the rule for this pattern? 0.3, 0.1, 0.5, 0.3, 0.7, 0.5, 0.9

26 DRILL

1. Add 0.2 to: 1.2, 0.3, 2.7, 1.4, 3.9, 2.1, 0.6, 1.5
2. Add 5 cents to the sum of:
   $.04 + $.06 $.25 + $.50
   $.02 + $.03 $.18 + $.02
3. Round to the nearest one: 8.6, 4.9, 6.2, 7.8, 2.3, 3.4, 5.5, 0.7
4. Round to the nearest tenth: 4.18, 5.61, 3.22, 2.73, 7.45, 1.55
5. $\underline{?}$ + 2 = 7 − 1
   $\underline{?}$ ÷ 4 = 3 × 3
   6 × $\underline{?}$ = 9 + 9
   24 ÷ $\underline{?}$ = 10 − 2

MENTAL

1. The finishing times for the race were 59.1 s for 1st place and 59.6 s for 2nd place. What is the difference in the times?
2. Milk costs $2.89 and bread costs $1.64. About how much money do both items cost in all?
3. Pam bought 2 six-packs of soda. She spent $6.00. What did each can cost?
4. What is LXVIII in standard form?
5. How much greater than 0.2 is 0.48?

27 DRILL

1. Subtract 0.1 from: 9.6, 0.4, 6.3, 1.8, 0.6, 5.4, 3.3, 2.7
2. 3 + 4 − 2 = $\underline{?}$
   10 − 7 + 2 = $\underline{?}$
   7 + 8 − 9 = $\underline{?}$
   9 + 9 − 10 = $\underline{?}$
3. Divide by 5, then subtract 2: 35, 20, 45, 15, 25, 40, 30, 10, 50
4. (3 + 3) ÷ 9   10 × (4 − 4)
   (6 − 2) ÷ 1   (4 + 4) × 2
5. 2)$\overline{$1.80}$ 3)$\overline{$2.70}$ 4)$\overline{$4.00}$
   5)$\overline{$4.50}$ 6)$\overline{$4.80}$ 7)$\overline{$4.20}$

MENTAL

1. Tom had $1.40. He spent $.50. Then he found $1.00. How much money does he have now?
2. Multiply 6 and 4, add 2, subtract 5.
3. 1 quarter, 2 dimes, 3 pennies = $\underline{?}$ ¢
4. Three friends share $1.86 equally. How much does each friend receive?
5. There are 25 cookies in each of 3 bags. Tony eats 2 from each bag. How many cookies are left?

A

addend   A number that is added to another number or numbers.

$$3 + 4 = 7$$
addends

A.M.   Letters that indicate time from midnight to noon.

angle   The figure formed by two rays that meet at a common endpoint.

area   The number of square units needed to cover a flat surface.

associative (grouping) property   Changing the grouping of the addends (or factors) does not change the sum (or product).

average   A quotient derived by dividing a sum by the number of its addends.

axis   The horizontal or the vertical number line of a graph.

B

balance   The tool used to measure mass.

bar graph   A graph that uses bars to represent data. The bars may be of different lengths.

benchmark   An object of known measure that can be used to estimate the measure of other objects.

C

capacity   The amount, usually of liquid, that a container can hold.

circle   A simple closed curve; all the points on the circle are the same distance from the center point.

circle ⟶ (·)

circle graph   A graph that uses sections of a circle to represent data.

common factor   A number that is a factor of two or more products.

common multiple   A number that is a multiple of two or more numbers.

commutative (order) property   Changing the order of the addends (or factors) does not change the sum (or product).

compatible numbers   Two numbers, one of which divides the other evenly.

composite number   A whole number other than 1 that has more than two factors.

cone   A space or solid figure that has one circular base.

cone ⟶

congruent figures   Figures that have the same size and the same shape; congruent line segments have the same length.

cube   A space or solid figure with six congruent square faces.

cube ⟶

customary system   The measurement system that uses inch, foot, yard, and mile; cup, pint, quart, and gallon; and ounce and pound.

cylinder   A space or solid figure that has two congruent circular bases.

cylinder → ⬭

D

data   Facts or information.

decimal A number in base ten that is written with a decimal point.

2.04 ← decimal
└───── decimal point

degree (°) A unit used to measure angles.

degree Celsius (°C) A unit for measuring temperature. The freezing point of water is 0°C.

degree Fahrenheit (°F) A unit for measuring temperature. The freezing point of water is 32°F.

denominator The numeral below the bar in a fraction; it names the total number of equal parts.

$\frac{1}{2}$ ← denominator

diameter A line segment that passes through the center of a circle and has both endpoints on the circle.

difference The answer in subtraction.

digit Any one of the numerals 0, 1, 2, 3, 4, 5, 6, 7, 8, or 9.

distributive property The product of a number and the sum of two addends is the same as the sum of the two products.

dividend The number to be divided.

24 ÷ 4   4)24
└──── dividend ────┘

divisible One number is divisible by another if it can be divided by that number and yield no remainder.

divisor The number by which the dividend is divided.

36 ÷ 9   9)36
└──── divisor ────┘

E

edge The line segment where two faces of a space figure meet.

 edge

endpoint The point at the end of a line segment or ray.

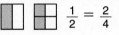
endpoints

equation (see **number sentence**)

equilateral triangle A triangle whose three sides are congruent.

equilateral triangle ⟶ △

equivalent decimals Decimals that name the same amount.

0.4 = 0.40

equivalent fractions Different fractions that name the same amount.

$\frac{1}{2} = \frac{2}{4}$

estimate An approximate answer; to find an answer that is close to an exact answer.

even number Any whole number that has 0, 2, 4, 6, or 8 in the ones place.

event A set of one or more outcomes.

expanded form A way to write a number that shows the place value of each of its digits.

400 + 20 + 8 = 428

F

face A flat side of a space figure.

 face

factors Two or more numbers that are multiplied to give a product.

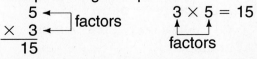

$3 \times 5 = 15$
factors

487

family of facts A set of related addition and subtraction facts or multiplication and division facts that use the same digits.

flip The movement of a figure over a line so that the figure faces in the opposite direction.

fluid ounce (fl oz) A customary unit of capacity. 8 fluid ounces = 1 cup

formula A rule that is expressed by using symbols.

fraction A number that names part of a whole or part of a set.

front-end estimation A way of estimating by using the front, or greatest, digits to find an approximate answer.

function A quantity whose value depends on another quantity.

G

graph A pictorial representation of data.

greatest common factor (GCF) The greatest number that is a factor of two or more products.

H

half-turn symmetry A figure that matches its image when it is turned halfway around has half-turn symmetry.

hexagon A polygon with six sides.

hexagon ⟶ ⬡

I

identity property (property of one) The product of one and a number is that number.

improper fraction A fraction whose numerator is greater than or equal to its denominator.

intersecting lines Lines in the same plane that meet or cross.

K

key A symbol that identifies the meaning of each picture in a pictograph.

L

least common denominator (LCD) The least common multiple of two or more denominators.

least common multiple (LCM) The least number that is a multiple of two or more numbers.

line A straight set of points that goes on forever in both directions.

⟵⟶

line graph A graph that uses points on a grid connected by line segments to represent data.

line plot A graph of data on a number line.

line segment A part of a line that has two endpoints.

•———————•

lowest terms A fraction is in lowest terms when its numerator and denominator have no common factor other than 1.

M

mass The measure of the amount of matter an object contains.

metric system The measurement system that uses centimeter, decimeter, meter, and kilometer; milliliter and liter; and gram and kilogram.

millimeter (mm) A metric unit of length.
10 millimeters = 1 centimeter

minuend A number from which another number is subtracted.

missing addend (or factor) An unknown addend (or factor) in addition (or multiplication).

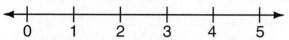

mixed number A number that is made up of a whole number and a fraction.
$1\frac{1}{2}$ ← mixed number

mode The number that appears most frequently in a set of numbers.

multiple The product of a given number and any whole number.

N

net The shape made by opening a solid figure and laying it flat.

number line A line that is used to show the order of numbers.

0 1 2 3 4 5

number sentence An equation or inequality.
16 = 9 + 7   28 < 52

numerator The numeral above the bar in a fraction; it names the number of parts being considered.
$\frac{3}{4}$ ← numerator

O

octagon A polygon with eight sides.
octagon →

odd number Any whole number that has 1, 3, 5, 7, or 9 in the ones place.

order of operations The order in which operations must be computed when more than one operation is involved.

ordered pair A pair of numbers that is used to locate a point on a grid or coordinate graph.

outcome The result of a probability experiment.

P

parallel lines Lines in the same plane that are always the same distance apart.

parallelogram A quadrilateral whose opposite sides are parallel and congruent.
parallelogram →

pentagon A polygon with five sides.
pentagon →

percent (%) The ratio or comparison of a number to 100.

perimeter The distance around a figure.

period A group of three digits set off by commas in a whole number.

perpendicular lines Lines in the same plane that intersect at right angles.

pictograph A graph that uses pictures or symbols to represent data.

place value The value of a digit, depending on its position in a number.

plane   A flat surface that never ends.

P.M.   Letters that indicate time from noon to midnight.

point   An exact location.

polygon   A simple closed flat figure made up of three or more line segments.

prime factorization   The expression of a composite number as the product of prime numbers.

prime number   A whole number other than 1 that has exactly two factors, itself and 1.

probability   The chance or likelihood of an event occurring.

product   The answer in multiplication.

protractor   The tool used to measure angles.

pyramid   A space or solid figure that has a polygon for a base and has triangular faces that meet at a point. A square pyramid has a square base.

pyramid ⟶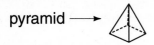

Q

quadrilateral   Any four-sided polygon.

quotient   The answer in division.

R

radius   A line segment with endpoints at the center of a circle and on the circle.

range   The difference between the greatest and least numbers in a set of data.

ratio   The comparison of two numbers, often expressed as a fraction.

ray   A part of a line that has one endpoint and goes on forever in one direction.   •⟶

rectangle   A parallelogram with four right angles.

rectangle ⟶

rectangular prism   A space or solid figure with six rectangular faces.

rectangular prism ⟶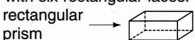

regrouping   Trading one from a place for ten from the next lower place, or ten from a place for one from the next higher place.

remainder   The number left over after dividing.

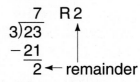

right angle   An angle that measures 90°. It forms a square corner.

right angle ⟶

right triangle   A triangle that has one right angle.

right triangle ⟶

Roman numerals   Symbols for numbers used by the Romans.

rounding   Writing a number to the nearest ten or ten cents, hundred or dollar, and so on.

S

scale   The tool used to measure weight.

set   A collection or group of numbers or objects.

side   A line segment that forms part of a polygon.

similar figures   Figures that have the same shape. They may or may not be the same size.

simple closed curve A path that begins and ends at the same point and does not cross itself.

simplest form (see **lowest terms**)

skip counting Counting by a whole number other than 0 or 1.

slide The movement of a figure along a line.

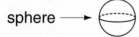

space (or solid) figure A figure that is not flat but that has volume.

sphere A space or solid figure that is shaped like a ball.

sphere

square A parallelogram that has four right angles and four congruent sides.

square

square number The product of a number multiplied by itself. It can be represented by a square array.

standard form The usual way of using digits to write a number.

subtrahend A number that is subtracted from another number.

sum The answer in addition.

T

tally A count made by using tally marks.

ton (T) A customary unit of weight. 2000 pounds = 1 ton

triangle A polygon with three sides.

triangle

triangular prism A space or solid figure with two parallel triangular faces.

triangular prism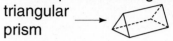

turn The movement of a figure around a point.

V

variable A letter or other symbol that replaces a number in an expression, equation, or inequality.

vertex A common endpoint of two rays or line segments. In a space figure, the point at which three or more edges meet.

volume The number of cubic units needed to fill a space figure.

W

weight The heaviness of an object.

whole number Any of the numbers 0, 1, 2, 3, 4, . . .

Z

zero (identity) property of addition The sum of zero and a number is that number.

zero property of multiplication The product of zero and a number is zero.

Mathematical Symbols

=	is equal to	.	decimal point	$\overleftrightarrow{AB}$	line *AB*
≠	is not equal to	°	degree	$\overline{AB}$	line segment *AB*
<	is less than	+	plus	$\overrightarrow{AB}$	ray *AB*
>	is greater than	−	minus	∠*ABC*	angle *ABC*
$	dollars	×	times	‖	is parallel to
¢	cents	÷	divided by	⊥	is perpendicular to
				(3, 4)	ordered pair

Table of Measures

Time

60 seconds (s)	= 1 minute (min)
60 minutes	= 1 hour (h)
24 hours	= 1 day (d)
7 days	= 1 week (wk)
12 months (mo)	= 1 year (yr)
52 weeks	= 1 year
365 days	= 1 year
366 days	= 1 leap year

Money

1 nickel	=	5¢ or $.05
1 dime	=	10¢ or $.10
1 quarter	=	25¢ or $.25
1 half dollar	=	50¢ or $.50
1 dollar	=	100¢ or $1.00
2 nickels	= 1 dime	
10 dimes	= 1 dollar	
4 quarters	= 1 dollar	
2 half dollars	= 1 dollar	

Metric Units

Length

10 millimeters (mm)	= 1 centimeter (cm)
100 centimeters	= 1 meter (m)
10 centimeters	= 1 decimeter (dm)
10 decimeters	= 1 meter
1000 meters	= 1 kilometer (km)

Capacity

1000 milliliters (mL)	= 1 liter (L)

Mass

1000 grams (g)	= 1 kilogram (kg)

Customary Units

Length

12 inches (in.)	= 1 foot (ft)
3 feet	= 1 yard (yd)
36 inches	= 1 yard
5280 feet	= 1 mile (mi)
1760 yards	= 1 mile

Capacity

8 fluid ounces (fl oz)	= 1 cup (c)
2 cups	= 1 pint (pt)
2 pints	= 1 quart (qt)
4 quarts	= 1 gallon (gal)

Weight

16 ounces (oz)	= 1 pound (lb)
2000 pounds	= 1 ton (T)